THEORY AND METHODOLOGY OF TRAINING

The Key to Athletic Performanc
Third Edition

Tudor O. Bompa, Ph.D.

Department of Physical Education
York University
Toronto, Ontario Canada

Edited by
Orietta Calcina

KENDALL/HUNT PUBLISHING COMPANY
4050 Westmark Drive P.O. Box 1840 Dubuque, Iowa 52004-1840

8785578

To Romana

CONTENTS

CHAPTER ONE

The Scope, Objectives, and System of Training

WHAT IS TRAINING

Over the past few years athletic performance has displayed dramatic progress. Levels of performance which just a few years ago were hard to imagine are now commonplace and the number of athletes capable of outstanding results is increasing continuously.

One legitimately may ask "What are the reasons behind such dramatic improvements?" Obviously there is not a simple answer to this question; however, among others one may consider the fact that athletics is a very challenging field, and that high levels of motivation have encouraged long hard hours of work. Similarly, coaching has become more sophisticated, partially as a result of the assistance received from sport specialists and scientists. There is now a much broader base of knowledge regarding these special human beings called athletes, and this is directly reflected in the methodology of training. New methods are surfacing which are often found to be useful in daily training. It seems that on the whole, sport sciences have progressed from a descriptive nature into a distinct science.

Most sources of knowledge (i.e. experience, research), regardless of the science from which they come, are directed at improving and understanding the effects of an exercise on the body. Thus, exercise is the focal point of the sports sciences endeavors. By the same token, research from several sciences serves as a feeding system, enriching the theory and methodology of training, which has become a science of its own (figure 1). The theory and methodology, as the science of training, has its own subject of applied research, which is the athlete. The athlete represents a vast source of information for both the coach and sport scientist.

During training the athlete experiences reactions to various stimuli, some of which may be predicted with more certainty than others. The information collected from the training process includes physiological, biochemical, psychological, social and also methodological information. Although this information is diverse it comes from the

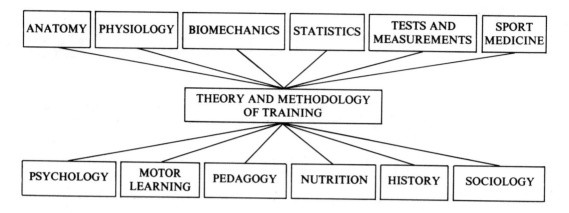

Figure 1.   The auxiliary sciences which enrich the field of knowledge of the theory and metodology of training.

same source, namely the athlete, and is produced by the same process, the training process. The coach who is the builder of the process, may not always be in a position to evaluate the training process. Coaches must evaluate all information feedback from the training process in order to understand the athlete's reactivity to the quality of training so that future programs will be properly planned. In light of the above, it becomes clear that the coach requires scientific assistance in order to ensure that his/her program will be based on objective evaluations.

The theory and methodology of training is a vast area. A close observation of the information available from each science will make the coach more proficient in his/her training endeavours. The principles of training represent the foundations of this complex process, while the acquaintance with training factors will enable the coach to understand the role played in training by each factor in accordance with the characteristics and specifics of a sport/event.

A training program must be designed in consideration of the age of the participants. Since success depends in part on the quality and abilities of the individual athlete involved, consideration must be given to the selection of athletes. Not all athletes have the physiological capabilities to become world class champions.

The chapter referring to the methodology of developing biomotor abilities (strength, speed, endurance, flexibility, and co-ordination) will assist the coach in selecting the optimal method of training. The knowledge acquired from the planning section will provide the coach with the ability to train his/her athletes in such a way that maximum performance will be achieved at the desired time. A training program needs to also include periods of regeneration and recovery between training lessons, which is a necessary factor to ensure continuous improvement in the athlete's performance.

Scope of Training

Training is not a novelty or a recent discovery. It existed in both ancient Egypt and later in Greece where people systematically trained for both military and olympic endeavors.

Today through training, as in ancient times, the athlete prepares himself/herself for a definite goal. In physiological terms, the goal is to improve the body's systems and functions in order to optimize athletic performance. In order to elevate athletic performance, the main scope of training centers around increasing the athlete's working capacity and skill capabilities, as well as developing strong psychological traits. Training is led, organized and planned by a coach, whose role among many others, is that of an educator, whose task is very complex since he/she deals with many physiological, psychological and sociological variables. Training, above everything, is a systematic athletic activity of long duration, progressively and individually graded, aiming at modeling the human's physiological and psychological functions to meet demanding tasks.

The aspiration of achieving high results in competitions should be closely linked with physical excellence. This coupling should be emphasized within the individual, who strives toward combining harmoniously spiritual refinement, with moral purity and physical perfection. Physical perfection signifies a multilateral and harmonious development, the acquisition of fine and varied skills, the cultivation of high volitional (psychological) qualities, and extremely good health. It means the ability to cope with highly stressful and demanding stimuli in both training and especially in competitions. Furthermore, physical excellence should evolve from an organized and well-planned training program based on a high volume of practical experience.

Paramount to training endeavors, a novice or a professional athlete is to have an achievable goal, which needs to be planned in accordance with the individual's abilities, psychological traits, and social environment. Some athlete's objective is to win a competition or improve previous performance, while others may consider the acquisition of a technical skill or the further development of a biomotor ability, as a goal. Whatever the objective, communication between the athlete(s) and coach is necessary.

Each goal needs to be as precise and as measurable as possible. In any plan, be it short or long term, goals need to be set and procedures in achieving the goals need to be determined before actual training begins. The deadline for the final goal to be achieved is the date that represents a major competition.

THE OBJECTIVES OF TRAINING

In order to achieve the main goal of training, namely the improvement of the athlete's level of skills and performance, the athlete, led by the coach, needs to meet the general objectives of training. These objectives, presented below, are general but will be useful in comprehending the concepts throughout the book.

Objectives

1. Multilateral Physical Development

A multilateral physical development is required as a base for training the athlete. This is similar to having an overall general physical fitness. The purpose of this area is to: increase the level of general endurance; increase general strength, further the development of speed; improve general flexibility required to perform most movements; obtain a high level of co-ordination and thus achieve a harmoniously developed body.

2. Sport Specific Physical Development

The objective of this area is to develop and improve: absolute and relative strength, muscle mass and elasticity; specific strength (power or muscular endurance) in accordance with the sport's requirements; movement and reaction time, and co-ordination and suppleness. The result of this training should be the ability to perform all movements, especially those required by the sport or event, without strain but instead with ease and smoothness.

3. Technical Factors

Sport specific techniques are developed and refined. The technical aspect involves: developing the capacity to perform all technical actions correctly; perfecting the required technique based on a rational and economical performance, yet with the highest possible velocity, high amplitude, and a demonstration of force; performing specific techniques under both normal and unusual circumstances (i.e. weather); improve the technique of performing related sports; and finally, ensure the ability to perform all the movements in the area of general and special exercises correctly.

4. Tactical Factors

Learning and improving the strategies of the sport and games by: learning the tactics of future opponents; expanding on the optimal tactics and variations within the athlete's capabilities; perfecting and varying selected strategies; developing a strategy into a model with consideration of future opponents.

5. Psychological Aspects

Psychological preparation is also necessary in order to ensure enhanced physical performance. Psychological training also improves: discipline, perseverance, willpower, confidence and courage.

6. Team Capability

In some sports (team sports, relays, rowing, cycling, etc.), an adequate preparation of a team is one of the main objectives of a coach. The fulfillment of such may be secured by the establishment of harmony between the team members' level of physical, technical, and strategical preparation. Similarly, such a concordance needs to be established for psychological preparation, implying a necessity for sound relationships, friendships, and common goals among team members. Consolidation of the team and the feeling of belonging to the same team will be enhanced by training competitions and social gatherings. The whole team must be encouraged to act as a unit rather than as individuals composing a team. Specific plans and roles should be established of each individual athlete according to the needs of the team.

7. Health Factors

Strengthening each individual athlete's state of health is important. Proper health is accomplished by: periodical medical examinations; a proper correlation of the intensity of training with individual effort capacity; the alternation of hard work with an appropriate regeneration phase; following illness or injuries training must commence when the athlete is completely recovered, and an adequate progression must be ensured.

8. Injury Prevention

Injury prevention occurs by taking all the safety precautions but by also: increasing flexibility above the level required to perform necessary movements; strengthening muscles, tendons and ligaments, especially during the initiation phase of any beginner; developing muscle strength and elasticity to such a degree that when unaccustomed movements are performed accidents will be less likely.

9. Theoretical Knowledge

Training also involves increasing athletes' knowledge regarding: the physiological and psychological basis of training, planning, nutrition and regeneration. The athlete-coach, athlete-opponent and team-mate relationships should be discussed in the hopes that such comprehensions will assist the athletes in working together in reaching the set goals.

The above is a summary of some of the general training objectives that a coach may consider in developing a training program. Specific characteristics of most sports, and of individuals performing them may require the coach to be more selective, or to establish other training objectives in addition to the above suggested ones. However, the objectives of training ought to be pursued in a successive manner. The earlier part of the program should develop the functional basis of training, and then move toward achieving sport specific goals. For instance, Ozolin (1971) suggests that at first one should develop general endurance followed by specific, or anaerobic endurance. Another example is the Romanian gymnasts who commence each annual training program with a phase (approximately one month) of strength development prior to starting their work on technique. The sequential approach is also extensively used in long term training programs.

THE CLASSIFICATION OF SKILLS AND SPORTS

The Classification of Skills

In the past there have been several attempts to classify physical exercises. One of the criterion used was based on the anatomical idea where if a person "looked good" then a person was thought to be healthy and strong. This criteria was specific to the Swedish gymnasts whose initiator was I. Ling (Torngren, 1924). The founder of German gymnastics, Friederich Jahn, employed as a criteria the equipment used by the athletes (Eiselen, 1854), while Leshaft (1910) based his exercises on the progression method. Leshaft divided all exercises into three groups. Group one was formed out of simple exercises (i.e. calisthenics); the second group incorporated more complex exercises and exercises with progressive loading (i.e. jumping, wrestling); while the third group was composed of exercises of a complex nature (games, skating, fencing).

Aside from classifying athletes into individual sports (i.e. track and field, gymnastics, boxing) and team sports (basketball, volleyball, rugby), a widely accepted classification uses the biomotor abilities as a criteria. The biomotor abilities include: strength, speed, endurance and co-ordination (Grantin, 1940). Of high practical importance for coaches is the classification of exercises according to the characteristics of a motor performance requirement (Farfel, 1960). Skills performed in sports may be distinguished into three groups of exercises: cyclic, acyclic and acyclic combined.

The CYCLIC group includes sports such as walking, running, cross-country skiing, speed skating, swimming, rowing, cycling and kayak-canoeing. The main characteristic of these sports is that the motor act involves repetitive movements (i.e. cyclic). As soon as a cycle of the motor act is learned then it can be duplicated continuously for longer periods of time. However, each cycle is composed of distinct phases which are always identical and repeated in the same succession. For example, the rowing stroke incorporates four phases: the catch, drive through the water, finish, and recovery. These four phases are part of a whole and are performed in the same succession during the cyclic motion of rowing. All cycles performed by an athlete are linked together: the present one is preceded and will be followed by another one.

The ACYCLIC group is comprised of sports such as shot putting, discus throw, most gymnastics and team sport skills, wrestling, boxing and fencing. These skills are composed of integral functions performed in one action. For instance, the skill of discus throw incorporates the preliminary swing, transition, the turn, delivery and reverse step, but all of them are performed in one action.

The ACYCLIC COMBINED skills are the result of the combination of a cyclic movement followed by an acyclic movement. This group includes all jumping events in track and field, figure skating, tumbling lines and vaulting in gymnastics, and diving. Although all actions of the above skills are linked together, distinguishes can easily be made between the acyclic movement of a high jumper or vaulter and the preceded cyclic pattern approach of running.

The coach's comprehension of the above classification and characteristics of each skill plays an important role in selecting the appropriate teaching method to be employed. Apparently, for cyclic sports the "whole" method (i.e. entire skill) of teaching seems to be the most efficient, since for one to break-down the respective skills of running, speed skating, or cross-country skiing would be a difficult task. As for the acyclic skills the "parts" method resulted in quicker retention. The "parts" method refers to breaking down a skill and teaching the components separately. Thus, for learning purposes, the hitch kick technique in long jump can be divided in its components (i.e. steps) until each part is acquired properly and than learned together as a whole.

The Classification of Sports

Athletes' voluntary motor acts are the result of a complex ensemble of muscle contractions which may be performed under dynamic or static conditions, involving a certain degree of force, speed, endurance, co-ordination and amplitude. The assemblage of sports in a certain category is based on physiological and skill similarities which are necessary in order to attain and ensure an adequate performance as well as a consideration of training objectives. With this in mind, Gandelsman and Smirnov (1970) divided all sports into seven groups:

1. Perfecting the co-ordination and form of skills.
2. Attaining a superior speed in cyclic skills.
3. Perfecting the strength and speed of a skill.
4. Perfecting the skill performed in a contest with opponents.
5. Perfecting the conduct of different means of travel.
6. Perfecting the activity of the central nervous system under stress and low physical involvement.
7. Combined sports.

A concise presentation of the particularities of each of the above groups is provided below.

1. Perfecting the co-ordination and form of skills

The first group of sports embodies gymnastics, modern rhythmic gymnastics, figure skating, and diving. The performance in the competition very often depends on the perfection of co-ordination, technical complexity of a skill, and its artistical presentation, where the competitors' act is expressed in points based on a subjective judgment. Most of the skills employed by the athletes are of an acyclic nature, although some of them are cyclic, as is the case of the approach in tumbling and vaulting in gymnastics, and the jumps in figure skating. The acyclic structure of the majority of skills are diverse, defining a high variety of types and intensities of work utilized in training, which leads to numerous alterations and adjustments in body functions.

2. Attaining a superior speed in cyclic skills

The second group incorporates sports like running, walking, speed skating, rowing, cycling, canoeing, cross-country skiing and swimming, where the main goal and objectives of training are to develop a superior velocity. Another common attribute possessed by the above sports is the cyclic manner in which the skill is performed. The speed developed for the competition distance for each of these sports depends on the perfection of the cyclic movements as well as the athletes' ability to overcome fatigue. Fatigue appears to become more difficult for longer distances, mainly because of the stress placed on the cardio-respiratory system.

3. Perfecting the strength and speed of a skill

Sports incorporated in the third classification are related to improvement in performance by the development of maximum force. Force may be developed either through 1) increasing the mass used during an exercise and maintaining the rate of constant acceleration (i.e. weight lifting) or, 2) increasing the rate of acceleration with which an exercise is performed while maintaining constant mass (throwing and jumping events in athletics). The first case, refers to the development of strength, and in the second the development of power.

4. Perfecting the skill performed in a contest with opponents

The group incorporates all team sports but also individual sports performed against opponents (boxing, wrestling, judo, and fencing). Perfecting the functions of sensory organs and the capacity to perceive and act quickly under the continuous changes of the contest circumstances are specific qualities required of athletes involved in these sports. In addition, the athletes' decisions in a complex game situation depend on his/her capacity to perceive external stimuli. The athletes' quickness and precision of interpretation serves to prevent the opponent from performing a successful tactical maneuver, or to assist his/her own team to a successful action.

5. Perfecting the conduct of different means of travel

The fifth group of sports incorporates activities such as horse riding, sailing, motorcycling, and water skiing. This group is not researched as most others, although some of the skills developed are beneficial for daily life. In some of these sports (sailing, motorcycling, etc.) the quality of equipment plays a determinantal role in the outcome of the competition. However, the perfection of the skills required to handle the equipment plays a paramount role. These skills are very complex and their development requires many long hours of training. Processing the information received by the Central Nervous System (CNS) through proprioceptors must be extremely fast since the athlete has to make quick decisions during a race. Good physical preparation, with specific strength development in accordance with the needs of the sport, is considered to be an important attribute of the athletes' success. Aside from strength and reaction time, balance and general endurance seem to be among the dominant biomotor abilities required by an athlete competing in this group of sports.

Table 1. The characteristics of the classification of sports group.

Group #	Training Goal	Example of Sports	Skill's Structure	Dominant Intensity	Dominant Bimotor Ability	Functional Demand
1	Perfect the co-ordination and the form of a skill	Gymnastics, Figure Skating	Acyclic	Alternative	Complex blending of co-ordination, strength, and speed	CNS, Neuro-muscular
2	Attain a superior speed in cyclic sports	Running, Rowing, Swimming	Cyclic	All intensities from maximum to low. Alternative	Speed, Endurance	CNS, Neuro-muscular and cardio-respiratory
3	Perfect the strength and speed of a skill	Weight lifting, Throwing, Jumping	Acyclic and acyclic combined	Alternative	Strength, Speed	Neuro-muscular, CNS
4	Perfect the skill performed in a contest with opponents	Team sports, some individual sports	Acyclic	Alternative	Co-ordination, Speed, Strength, Endurance	CNS, locomotor, cardio-respiratory
5	Perfect the conduct of different means of travel	Sailing, Horse-riding, Motorcycling	Acyclic and acyclic combined	Alternative	Co-ordination, Speed	CNS
6	Perfect the activity of CNS under stress and low physical involvement	Shooting, Chess	Acyclic	Low	Co-ordination, Endurance	CNS
7	Combined sports	Decathlon, Biathlon	All	Specific to each event	Complex blending of most abilities	CNS, locomotor and cardio-respiratory

6. Perfecting the activity of the CNS under stress and low physical involvement

Although the activities included in this group (shooting, archery, chess) are well recognized sports, they are not physical exercises since the motor component is very low. However, as Gandelsman and Smirnov (1970) have suggested, the above sports reflect the main tendency of modern training, that is, the CNS's increased role of guiding the activity. During training and competition, the CNS is under a great deal of stress. Though a competitor is not really exposed to a high physical involvement, both chess players and shooters are involved in a well-planned physical exertion. Both these sports require excellent endurance so that they can focus their concentration, patience, and psychological self-control during a prolonged competition. Greater strength of the upper limbs also appears to be beneficial for shooting to the extent that one may hold the weapon still, without any deviation from the target.

7. Combined sports

The last group is composed of the combined sports which incorporates many events (i.e. decathlon) or different sports such as modern pentathlon (horse riding, fencing, swimming and cross-country running). In addition, woman's heptathlon in athletics and biathlon (cross-country skiing and shooting) are also included in this group.

Both physiological and psychological interpretations have to be made in accordance with the specifics of each event composing the combined sport since most of them include different activities from various sports groups and zones of intensities. The variety of events/sports that dictates the type of training to be used is complex, thus producing "all round athletes".

Although the classification of sports proposed by Gandelsman and Smirnov (1970) is schematic, since a sport incorporated in a group may have some features characteristic of another group, it is believed to be beneficial for the coach to have a better understanding of the attributes of all sports activities. The understanding of the features and related characteristics of a sport may be beneficial for the coach's training endeavors. The outcome may be a more effective, more varied training program.

Table 1 is a summary of the sport classification.

System of Training

Webster's Third New International Dictionary (1971) defines a system as an organized or methodically arranged set of ideas, theories, or speculations. A system should encompass, in an organized whole, the experience accumulated over the years as well as pure and applied research findings. A system should not be imported, although in order to develop one, it may be of great benefit to first study those of other countries. Furthermore, the creation or the development of a better system has to take into consideration a country's social and cultural background.

As far as a sports system is concerned, it should make reference to: 1) physical education and sports organization of a nation, in which school programs, recreation and sports clubs, and the organizational structure of sports governing bodies may be considered, and 2) the systems of athletic training.

The organization of a nation's system should first define its goals and based on that should create its structure so that all the echelons and units are linked together in a solid and sequential setup (Figure 2). The system suggested above has a pyramidal structure, with its base being formed by the mass of youngsters taking part in physical education, and with the peak encompassing the high performance unit, which incorporates the nation's athletic ambassadors.

A national sports system should consider its values and traditions, climatic conditions and the emphasis of those sports, especially for the young participants. Young people must develop the basic skills and abilities required to benefit from general physical instruction as well as to perform appropriately in most sports. The latter refers to the emphasis placed on track and field for the merits of developing the basic skill required in most sports (running, jumping and throwing); swimming for both lifeguard and an appropriate development of the cardio-respiratory functions, and gymnastics for the virtue

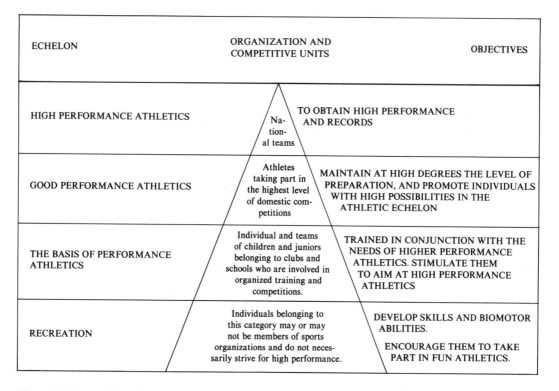

ECHELON	ORGANIZATION AND COMPETITIVE UNITS	OBJECTIVES
HIGH PERFORMANCE ATHLETICS	National teams	TO OBTAIN HIGH PERFORMANCE AND RECORDS
GOOD PERFORMANCE ATHLETICS	Athletes taking part in the highest level of domestic competitions	MAINTAIN AT HIGH DEGREES THE LEVEL OF PREPARATION, AND PROMOTE INDIVIDUALS WITH HIGH POSSIBILITIES IN THE ATHLETIC ECHELON
THE BASIS OF PERFORMANCE ATHLETICS	Individual and teams of children and juniors belonging to clubs and schools who are involved in organized training and competitions.	TRAINED IN CONJUNCTION WITH THE NEEDS OF HIGHER PERFORMANCE ATHLETICS. STIMULATE THEM TO AIM AT HIGH PERFORMANCE ATHLETICS
RECREATION	Individuals belonging to this category may or may not be members of sports organizations and do not necessarily strive for high performance.	DEVELOP SKILLS AND BIOMOTOR ABILITIES. ENCOURAGE THEM TO TAKE PART IN FUN ATHLETICS.

Figure 2. A potential national sports system.

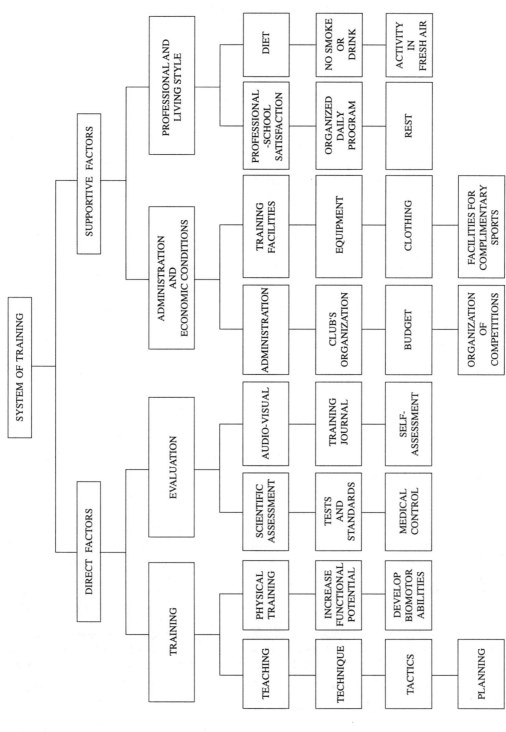

Figure 3. The components of a system of training.

of evolving balance and co-ordination. These three sports are part of the children's general instruction in most of the European countries, especially in Russia, Germany and Romania.

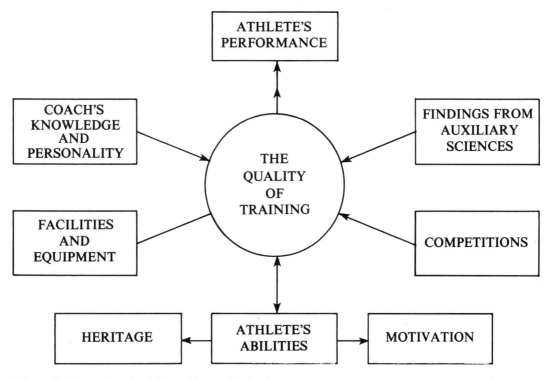

Figure 4. The quality of training and factors involved.

The creation of a training system for a sport may stem from the general knowledge in the theory and methodology of training, scientific findings, the experience of the nations' best coaches, and the approach utilized in other countries. The highlights of the development of a training system should be the creation of a model of training, for both a short and long term approach. The model then should be applied by all coaches. Such an approach does not exclude the possibility of expression of each individual coach. Within the system each individual has his/her own place, and a coach, through his/her talent, may attempt to enrich the system. Furthermore, a coach, through his/her abilities and skills should apply the system according to the club's specifics, the social and natural environment, and athletes' individual characteristics.

An important place in the creation and especially evolution of a training system is occupied by the sports specialists and scientists. Through their research, with special emphasis on applied research, they could enrich training know-how, improve methods of athlete evaluation, selection, and peaking; improve methods of recovery and regeneration following training, and increase knowledge of how to cope with stress.

The quality of a training system, as suggested in Figure 3, depends on direct and supportive factors. Although each link of the system has its important role, the utmost importance lies with the two branches of the direct factors; namely, training and the evaluation of training.

The direct result of a high quality training system and program should be a high level of performance. The quality of training does not depend on one single factor, the coach, but instead on many factors which quite often are not commanded by the coach, and which by any means could affect the athlete's performance (Figure 4). Hence, all factors affecting the quality of training should be effectively utilized (i.e. information from auxiliary sciences) and constantly improved, such as facilities and abilities of the athletes involved in training.

TRAINING ADAPTATION AND DETRAINING

Training Adaptation

A high level of performance is the result of many years of well planned, methodical and hard training. During all this time the athlete tries to adapt his/her organs and functions to the specific requirements of the chosen sport. The level of adaptation is reflected by performance capabilities. The greater the degree of adaptation, the better the performance.

Adaptation to training is the sum of transformations brought about by the systematic repetition of exercise. These structural and physiological changes are the result of a specific demand placed upon the body by the specific activity pursued, and are dependent on the volume, intensity and frequency of training. Physical training is beneficial only as long as it forces the body to adapt to the stress of a physical effort. If the stress is not sufficient to challenge the body, then no adaptation occurs. If a stress is so great that it cannot be tolerated, injury or over training may result. Therefore, the "highly trained athletes have a faster response time in which to adapt" (Powers et al, 1985).

The time required for a high degree of adaptation depends on the skill complexity and the physiological and psychological difficulty of the event/sport. The more complex and difficult the sport, the longer the training time required for neuro-muscular and functional adaptation.

Following a systematic and organized program there are several alterations induced by training. Although the greatest number of organic and functional changes have been observed in endurance athletes (Astrand and Rodhal, 1970; Matthews and Fox, 1976), almost all athletes are subject to neuro-muscular cardio-respiratory and bio-chemical modifications. There are also psychological improvements which result from a physical exercise.

Research in the area of anatomical adaptation has shown that there is a decrease in material (bone composition) strength with high intensity exercise, and that the mechanical properties of bones are not strictly dependent on chronological age but rather on the mechanical demands on the athlete. Therefore, low intensity training, at an early age, may stimulate long bone length and circumference increases. High intensity, on the other hand, may inhibit bone growth (Matsuda, 1986).

Bone adaptation to exercise is also believed to be a function of age. Immature bones are more sensitive to cycle load changes than are more mature bones. For example, at a young age, strength training accelerates the maturation process causing permanent suppression of the bone growth (Matsuda, 1986). Therefore, the purpose of training is to stress the body so that the response results in adaptation and not aggravation.

Strength and power training performed at near or maximal voluntary contraction increases the cross-sectional area of muscle fibers (hypertrophy). The growth of a muscle and its weight is largely due to hypertrophy, occasionally muscle fiber splitting (hyperplasia), and the increase of protein content.

High performance in power or speed dominated events are often linked with genetics and the dominant muscle fiber type. However, Simoneau (1985) suggests that fiber type composition is not solely determined genetically. Conflicting results have been observed within transfer from fast twitch to slow twitch muscle fiber type. Activation of the whole muscle by electrical stimulation favours shifts from fast to slow twitch muscles (Pette, 1984). There has been results verifying that when the stimulus is appropriate, the potential for conversion of one fiber type to another does exist. Therefore, adaptation to fiber type areas could depend on the nature and duration of the training program as well as on the pre-training status of the athlete. Thus, it is not solely a genetic factor (Simoneau, 1985).

Enhancements of explosive power performance and the corresponding biological adaptation of a specific training stimulus are not fully understood. Gravity normally provides the major portion of mechanical stimulus responsible for the development of muscles structure during every day life and during training. Therefore it is reasonable to assume that high gravity conditions could influence the muscle mechanics of even well-trained athletes. Improvements as a result of the fast adaptation to the simulated high gravity field are reported. It is suggested that adaptation has occurred both in neuro-muscular functions and in metabolic processes (Bosco et al, 1984).

The specificity of changes to the training velocities are attributable to neural adaptation, which coupled with the observed enhancements of the muscle mitochondria (a subcellular structure), plus capillary density, underlies the increased ability to maintain power production (Rosler, 1986).

Performance improvements are also due to changes in the neuro-muscular system. During sustained maximal or submaximal activities the average firing rate of a motor unit increases over time. This neuro-muscular strategy can increase the time over which the contraction is held. During submaximal prolonged activity, as contractile failure develops in active motor units, force output is maintained by new units. However, units with the highest initial frequencies during sustained maximal voluntary contraction showed the most rapid rate of decrease.

High speed and short duration activity are responsible for small adaptive changes in enzymes (a protein product which induces chemical reactions) and increases creatine phosphate (CP). The more intensive an activity, the higher its enzyme activity as with oxidative glycolytic metabolism. The greater the hypertrophy the higher the oxidative enzyme activities. It is known that aerobic exercise is ineffective in inducing changes in glycolytic processes. Therefore, the longer an athlete participates in training, the more hypertrophied are his/her slow twitch muscle fibers (Boros, et al, 1986).

Endurance training at a prolonged and moderate intensity improves aerobic capacity mainly through levels of myoglobin (an oxygen binding pigment which stores and diffuses oxygen), mitochondrial enzymes (both in size and number), glycogen stores and a greater oxidative capacity. A very prominent adaptation to prolonged activity is the enhancement of respiratory capacity, respiratory rates, increase of oxygen transport, augmentation of cardiac output and forming structural changes of the volume density of muscle mitochondria. Thus the increase in maximum oxygen consumption demonstrates enhancement in aerobic capacity to prolonged exercises and increases enzyme activity in working muscles. A major benefit of increased levels of enzymes is the oxidation of fatty acids, which thus improves the organisms ability to use fat as an energy source. It is believed that the increases in muscle mitochondria and myoglobin account for approximately 50% of the increase in maximal oxygen consumption, the other 50% is probably accounted for by better oxygen transport through the cardiovascular system (de Vries, 1980). The dominant aerobic training also increases the anaerobic capacity by a considerable margin (Gollnick et al, 1973).

Adaptation, Improvement, and the Overcompensation Cycle

The human organism adapts and improves in direct relationship to the type of stimuli to which it is exposed. The work performed in training is considered to be the cause, while the organism adaptation is the effect—the optimal training effect. In order to achieve an optimal training effect, one has to plan training programs which are specific to the sport and which are prescribed in an appropriate dose. The quantity of work to be performed in a training lesson must be set in accordance with individual abilities, the phase of training, and a correct ratio between the volume and intensity of training. Therefore, if the training dosage is properly administrated, a correct athletic development will result leading to performance improvement.

In training there are two forms of dosage: external and internal (Harre, 1982). The EXTERNAL dosage of the amount of work planned for an athlete, is a function of the volume and intensity of training. In order to construct a correct training program, the intimate characteristics of the external rating which has the following components needs to be correctly assessed: volume, intensity, density, and frequency of stimuli. Since all these components are easy to measure they can easily be rated. The external dosage usually elicits a physical and psychological reaction from the athlete. The physical and psychological reaction which the organism displays is known as the INTERNAL dosage, and it expresses the degree and magnitude of fatigue which the athlete experiences in training. The size and intensity of the internal reaction is affected by each component of the external dosage.

When planning the external dosage one must take into consideration that applying the same dosage all the time not always produces similar internal reactions. Since the internal dosage is a function of each individual athletic potential, its reaction can be estimated in general terms only. However, an adequate training diary and periodic testing may facilitate a reading of the internal reaction. The external dosage may be affected by circumstances such as the athlete's degree of training, the opponent's athletic caliber, equipment, facilities, meteorological conditions, and social factors.

The application and correct dosage of training results in several anatomical, physiological and psychological alternations in an athlete. The positive changes which occur following a systematic training are regarded as the organism's improved adaptation.

The adaptability processes occur only when the stimuli reach an intensity proportional to the individual's threshold capacity (Harre, 1982). A high volume of work without a minimal intensity (for example, below 30% of one's maximum) does not facilitate adaptation since a higher level of intensity is required to initiate such adaptation. It is possible, however, to exceed the "optimal" level of stimulation by demanding too much work from the athlete or by miscalculating the volume–intensity ratio in which case the process of adaptation lessens, leading to a decline in performance or even regression.

The process of an adequate adaptation to training and competitions facilitates the increase of the athlete's degree of training, correct peaking, and improvement in the athlete's physical and psychological capacities. The effects of a standard dosage and stimulus diminishes after a while, resulting in modest performance. Therefore, the external dosage should be increased periodically (as suggested by the principle of progressive increase of the load in training). If the stimulus is reduced, the training effect is diminished resulting in an involution phase. The benefits of training may also be reduced if the interruption of training is too long. For instance, if the transition phase is too long, or if it is comprised totally of passive as opposed to active rest, in either case, all the improvements realized from the preparatory and competitive phases disappear, requiring the athlete to start training for the next preparatory phase at a very low level.

The adaptation process is the result of a constant alteration between stimulation and compensation, between work and regeneration. This constant alternation is illustrated by the overcompensation, or super compensation cycle.

OVERCOMPENSATION (or Supercompensation) refers mostly to the relationship between work and regeneration as a biological bases for physical and psychological arousal before a main competition. All individuals have a specific level of biological functioning that predominates during normal daily activities. When an individual is involved in training he/she is exposed to a series of stimuli which disturbs the normal biological state by burning supplementary food stuff. The outcome of this burning of food stuff is overall fatigue and high lactic acid concentration in blood and at cell level. At the end of a training lesson an athlete acquires a certain level of fatigue which temporarily reduces the organism's functional capacity. The abrupt drop of the homeostasis curve (figure 5) illustrates the rapid acquisition of fatigue, which assumes a simultaneous reduction of functional capacity. Following training, and between two training sessions, there is a phase of compensation during which the biochemical sources of energy are replenished. The return of the curve towards normal biological state is performed slowly and progressively, suggesting that the organism's replenishment of the loss of energy is a slower process which requires several hours. If the time between two training sessions of high intensity is longer, the energy sources (especially glycogen) are fully replaced. This is achieved by acquiring some reserves, facilitating the organism to rebound thus be in a state of overcompensation. The overcompensation should be considered as the foundation of a functional increase of athletic efficiency as a result of organism adaptation to the training stimulus, and the replenishment of the glycogen stores in the muscle. If the resulting phase, or the time between two stimuli is too long, the overcompensation will fade away, leading to a process of the involution or phase of little if any improvement in performance capacity.

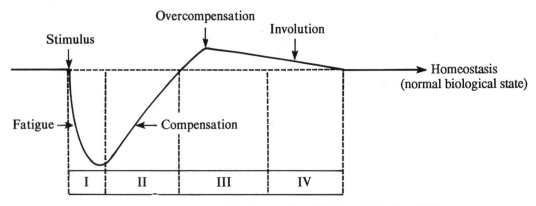

Figure 5. The overcompensation cycle of a training lesson. (modified from Yakovlev, 1967)

THE OVER COMPENSATION CYCLE (Figure 5). Following the application of exercises in training, the organism experiences fatigue (phase I). During the rest period (phase II) biochemical stores are not only replenished but exceed normal levels. The organism compensates fully, followed by a rebounding or overcompensation phase (phase III), when a higher adaptation occurs, duplicated by a functional increase of athletic efficiency. If another stimulus is not applied at the optimal time (during overcompensation phase) then involution occurs (phase IV)—a decrease with a loss of the benefits obtained during the overcompensation phase.

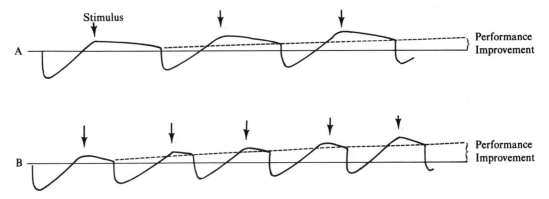

Figure 6. An illustration of the sum of training effect (from Harre, 1982).

Following the optimal training stimuli of a training lesson the recovery period, including the overcompensation phase, is approximately 24 hours (Herberger, 1977). But variations regarding the occurrence of overcompensation depends on the type and intensity of training. For instance following a training lesson where development of aerobic endurance is attempted, overcompensation may occur after approximately six hours. On the other hand high intensity activity, which places a high demand on the CNS, may need even more than 24 hours and sometimes as much as 36 hours for the overcompensation to occur. However, since elite class athletes follow a training program that often does not allow 24 hours between training lessons, they are exposed to a second workout before involution can occur. In fact, as suggested by figure 6, the rate of improvement is higher when athletes are exposed to more frequent training sessions, provided of course, that the frequency is not so great as to prevent the overcompensation phase all together. Because the overcompensation is subject to a progressive involution, long intervals between training stimuli (figure 6A) results in smaller overall improvement than in the case of short intervals (figure 6B).

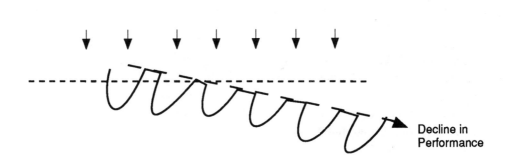

Figure 7. The decline in performance as a result of exposure to prolonged maximal intensity stimuli.

The strength of various stimuli has a direct effect on the organism's reaction to training. Consequently, as illustrated by figure 7, a phase in which maximal intensity stimuli are overemphasized may lead to a state of general exhaustion and a decrease in performance. This is the typical approach of some overzealous coaches who intend to project an image of being "tough" and "hard working", and who, believe that in each workout they have to reach the state of exhaustion. Under such circumstances there is never time to compensate since the depth of the curve of fatigue sinks deeper, a reality which requires not another "hard" workout, but rather time to regenerate. Regeneration will allow compensation and ultimately overcompensation as well.

It is certainly true that in order to constantly increase performance the coach has to regularly challenge the potential reached by an athlete in order to elevate the ceil ing of adaptation. In practical terms this means that high intensity stimuli have to be planed alternatively, so that days of high intensity training are substituted with low intensity days. This will enhance compensation and lead to the desired state of over compensation (figure 8).

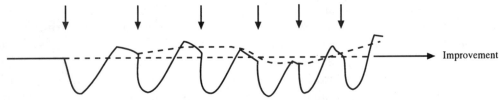

Figure 8. The alteration of maximal and low intensity stimuli prodeces a wave-like curve of improvement.

DETRAINING. Provided that all physiological and psychological alterations occur as a result of prolonged training, the maintenance of the achieved level or any further improvement requires intensive training stimuli. When such a stimuli is ceased, an athlete is exposed to functional and even psychic disturbances, which Israel (1972) calls the syndrome of decreasing the training status or "detraining'h Basically, there are two main reasons for ceasing training: due to illness, accidents, or training inter ruptions during the transition (off season) phase or due to retirement.

In the first case, training benefits are lost within a relatively short period of time if training has stopped. In such a case the speed of detraining varies, from several weeks to several months. A sizable decrease (6-7%) has been noted in maximum volume of oxygen, physical working capacity, total hemoglobin and blood volume, following just one week of complete rest (Friman, 1979). Fitness benefits are com pletely lost after 4-8 weeks of detraining (Fox et al, 1988), therefore, the duration of the transition phase (of~:season) should be carefully monitored and re-evaluated, es pecially in professional team sports.

In the case of retirement, within a few days following the interruption of training, functional disturbances occur. Israel (1972) indicated that headache, insomnia, the feeling of exhaustion, lack of appetile and psychological depression are among the usual symptoms. Although such symptoms are not pathological, if the cessation of training persists, they may be displayed for a long time, even years, indicating the inability of the human body to adjust quickly to a state of inactivity.

Obviously, in such circumstances the best therapy is physical activity. For athletes who experience an injury or illness, the coach should co-operate with the physician in prescribing adequate, if any, physical training. Although during most illnesses physical activity is not advisable, the injured athletes may be in a position to endure limited exertion, which still may maintain a certain level of physical preparation and may lessen the detraining syndrome. During the recuperation, especially following illness, training must be progressive with the body's re- adaptation to previous stimuli as the main objective. The duration of training may be increased from 10–15 minutes to 60 minutes and later to 90 minutes, with a load of up to 50% of the load utilized prior to the illness. In such circumstances, according to Israel (1972), the heart rate may reach levels of between 140–170 beats per minute.

Of special concern to each coach should be those athletes who retire from train-ing. Throughout each athlete's career he/she ought to learn that after retirement the cessation of training has to be reduced progressively. Detraining has to be organized over many months and even years, so that the athlete's body may be progressively brought down to a low level of activity. There are so many examples of Olympic class athletes who have had an organized detraining program. Some of the German athletic stars like swimmers Cornelia Ender, Roland Mathes and the rowing team from Dresden, Germany, were given a detraining program organized over four years.

As far as the content, volume and intensity of training is concerned, it may be planned according to each individual's free time and sporting facilities. Among the first training parameters to be reduced progressively are the number of training les-sons and the intensity. The number of lessons may be reduced to 3–5 sessions per week, with a progressively lower intensity. As time progresses, the volume of train-ing, especially its duration, ought to be lessened as well. The content of physical activity should be diverse. In fact, in most cases, exercise from other sports may be considered since the athletes may be saturated by those from their own specialty, which were performed for several years. Running, swimming and cycling may be considered by most athletes, since they can be performed individually and serve to maintain an adequate level of fitness.

Although the above are just general suggestions, detraining is of concern to all athletes. All athletes, following their retirement, should remain physically active for their own general physical and mental well-being.

Sources of Energy

Energy should be viewed as the capacity of an athlete to perform work. And work is nothing else but the application of force; the contraction of muscles to apply force against a resistance.

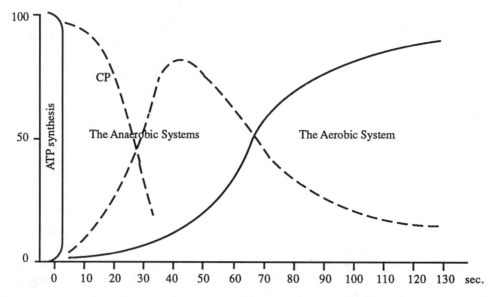

Figure 9. The participation of main sources of energy in sports activity. (Modified from Dal Monte et al., 1985).

Energy is a necessary prerequisite for the performance of physical work during training and competitions. Ultimately, energy is derived from the conversion of food stuffs at the muscle cell level into a high energy compound known as adenosine triphosphate (ATP) which is stored in the muscle cell. ATP, as its name suggests, is composed of one molecule of adenosine and three molecules of phosphate.

Energy required for muscular contraction is released by the conversion of high energy ATP into ADP + P (adenosine diphosphate + phosphate). As one phosphate bond is broken ADP + P is formed from ATP and energy is released. There is a limited amount of ATP stored in the muscle cells thus ATP supplies must be continually replenished to facilitate continued physical activity.

ATP supplies may be replenished by any of three energy systems, depending on the type of physical activity being undertaken. They are as follows: 1) the ATP—CP system, 2) the lactic acid system and 3) the oxygen (O_2) system. The first two systems replenish ATP stores in the absence of O_2 and is therefore known as the anaerobic system. The third is known as an aerobic system due to the presence of O_2.

The Anaerobic Systems

The ATP-CP system (anaerobic alactic or phosphagen system)

Since only a very small amount of ATP can be stored in the muscle, energy depletion occurs very rapidly when strenuous activity begins. In response to this, creatine phosphate (CP) or phosphocreatine, which is also stored in the muscle cell, is broken down into creatine (C) and phosphate (P). The process releases energy which is used to resynthesize ADP + P into ATP. This can then be transformed once more to ADP + P causing the release of energy required for muscular contraction. The transformation of CP into C + P does not release energy that can be used directly for muscular contraction. Rather, this energy must be used to resynthesize ADP + P into ATP.

Since CP is stored in limited amounts in the muscle cell, energy can be supplied by this system for about 8–10 seconds. This system is the chief source of energy for extremely quick and explosive activities such as 100m dash, diving, weight lifting, jumping, and throwing events in track and field, vaulting in gymnastics and ski jumping.

ENERGY PATHWAY	ANAEROBIC PATHWAY		AEROBIC PATHWAY			
	ALACTIC	LACTIC				
PRIMARY ENERGY SOURCE	ATP PRODUCED WITHOUT THE PRESENCE OF O_2		ATP PRODUCED IN THE PRESENCE OF O_2			
FUEL	Phosphate System. ATP/ CP Stored in Muscle	Lactic Acid (LA) System Glycogen → LA Byproduct	Glycogen Completely Burned in the Presence of O_2		Fats	Pro-tein
DURATION	0 Sec. 10 Sec.	40 Sec. 70 Sec.	2 Min. 6 Min. 25 Min.	1^h 2^h 3^h		
SPORTS EVENTS	-Sprinting 100 Dash\n\n-Throws\n\n-Jumps\n\n-Weight Lifting\n\n-Ski Jumping\n\n-Diving\n\n-Vaulting in Gymnastics	-200-400M\n\n-500 Speed Skating\n\n-Most Gym Events\n\n-Cycling Track\n\n-50M Swimming	-100M Swimming\n\n-800 M Track\n\n-500M Canoeing\n\n-1000M Speed Skating\n\n-Floor Exercise Gymnastics\n\n-Alpine Skiing\n\n-Cycling Track: 1000M and Pursuit	-Middle Distance Track, Swimming, Speed Skating\n\n-1000M Canoeing\n\n-Boxing\n\n-Wrestling\n\n-Martial Arts\n\n-Figure Skating\n\n-Synchronized Swimming\n\n-Cycling - Pursuit	-Long Distance: Track, Swimming, Speed Skating, Canoeing\n\n-Cross Country Skiing\n\n-Rowing\n\n-Cycling, Road Racing	
	Most Team Sports / Racquet Sports / Sailing					
SKILLS	Mostly Acyclic	Acyclic amd Cyclic			Cyclic	

Figure 10. Energy sources for competitive sport.

Restoration of Phosphagen

Through restoration, the body attempts to recover and replenish the energy stores to the pre-exercise conditions. The body, with its biochemical means, attempts to return to the state of a physiological balance (homeostasis), when it has the highest efficiency.

Phosphagen restoration occurs quite rapidly (Fox et al, 1989):

- in the first 30 seconds it reaches 70%, and
- in 3–5 minutes it is fully restored (100%).

The lactic acid system (anaerobic lactic or anaerobic glycolysis)

For events of slightly longer duration, up to approximately 40 seconds, which are still very intensive in nature (200m, 400m in sprinting, 500m speed skating, some gymnastic events), energy is provided at first by the ATP-CP system and continued after 8–10 seconds by the lactic acid system. The latter system breaks down glycogen which is stored in the muscle cells and the liver, releasing energy to resynthesize ATP from ADP + P. Due to the absence of O_2 during the breakdown of glycogen, a by-product called lactic acid (LA) is formed. When high intensity work is continued for a prolonged period of time, large quantities of lactic acid accumulate in the muscle causing fatigue, which eventually leads to a cessation of physical activity.

Restoration of Glycogen

Full restoration of glycogen requires longer time, even days, depending on the type of training and diet.

For intermittent activity, typical of strength or interval training (say 40 seconds work, three minutes rest) restoration takes:

- 2 hours to restore 40%
- 5 hours to restore 55%, and
- 24 hours for full restoration (100%)

If the activity is continuous, typical of endurance related activities, but of higher intensity, restoration of glycogen takes much longer:

- 10 hours to restore 60%
- 48 hours to achieve full restoration (100%)

From the above information (Fox et al, 1989) it can be observed that continuous activity needs twice the amount of time necessary for the restoration of glycogen following intermittent activity. The difference between the two can be explained by the fact that intermittent work consumes less glycogen, and as such, shorter time is required for the resynthesis of glycogen.

Following a demanding training session, liver glycogen decreases considerably. For a normal, or carbohydrate-rich diet, it takes approximately 12–24 hours to replenish the liver glycogen. During training there could be a LA accumulation in the blood, which has a fatiguing effect on the athlete. Before returning to a balanced resting state, LA has to be removed from the systems. However, it takes some time before this will be achieved (Fox et al, 1989):

- 10 minutes to remove 25%
- 25 minutes to eliminate 50%, and
- 1 hour and 15 minutes to remove 95%.

The normal biological process of LA removal can be facilitated by 15–20 minutes of light aerobic exertion, such as jogging or using a rowing machine. The benefit of such an activity is that sweating continues, and the elimination of LA and other metabolic residues is maintained.

Fitness level is also another element which facilitates recovery. The better the fitness level the faster the recovery.

The Aerobic System

The aerobic system requires approximately 60–80 seconds to commence producing energy for the resynthesis of ATP from ADP + P (figure 9). The heart rate and respiratory rate must be increased sufficiently to transport the required amount of O_2 to the muscle cells in order that glycogen may be broken down in the presence of oxygen. Although glycogen is the source of energy used to resynthesize ATP in both the lactic acid and aerobic systems, the latter breaks down glycogen in the presence of O_2 and thus produces little or no lactic acid, enabling the athlete to continue the exercise for a longer period of time.

The aerobic system is the primary source of energy for events of duration between 2 minutes and 2–3 hours (all track events from 800m on, cross-country skiing, long distance speed skating etc.). Prolonged work in excess of 2–3 hours may result in the breakdown of fats and proteins to replenish ATP stores as the body's glycogen stores near depletion. In any of these cases, the break down of glycogen, fats or protein produces the by-products carbon dioxide (CO_2) and water (H_2O), both of which are eliminated from the body through respiration and perspiration.

The rate at which ATP can be replenished by an athlete is limited by his/her aerobic capacity, or the maximum rate at which one can consume oxygen (Mathews and Fox, 1971).

Overlap of the Two Energy Systems

During exercise, energy sources are used or depleted according to the intensity and duration of the activity. Except for very short activities, most sports employ both energy systems to varying degrees. Therefore, it is safe to claim that in most sports there is an overlap between the anaerobic and aerobic systems.

A good indicator of which energy system contributes the most in a given exercise is the level of lactic acid in the blood. Blood samples may be taken and lactic acid levels measured. The threshold of 4 millimoles of lactic acid indicates that the anaerobic and aerobic systems contributed equally to the resynthesis of ATP. Higher levels of lactic acid indicates that the anaerobic or lactic acid system dominates, while lower levels indicate that the aerobic system dominates. The equivalent threshold heart rate is said to be 168–170 beats per minute, although individual variation exists. Higher heart rates indicate that the anaerobic system is predominant, while lower rates indicate that the aerobic system is predominant (Howald, 1977). Such testings are paramount if intention is to monitor and especially to design training programs in accordance with the predominate energy systems in a given sport, (i.e. anaerobic and aerobic).

The fact that O_2 requires some two minutes to reach the muscle cell led many authors and coaches to believe that around that time energy was derived equally from the anaerobic and aerobic systems. Consequently, sports with a duration of two minutes were considered to gain energy equally from both systems which was incredibly emphasized in many sports (including hockey). Interval training employing short repetitions were, and still are dominating many training programs. Such training concepts leads to a good performance at the beginning of the race or game only; Canadian middle distance runners and Canada—USSR hockey series are typical examples.

Other research (Keul et al, 1969) suggests that the splitting, or the 50%—50% contribution level of the two energy systems occurs at approximately 60–70 seconds after the start of exercise. Mader and Hollman (1977) discovered that even by the end of the first minute of an intensive event the contribution of the aerobic system is 47%. The dominant role in training the aerobic system for most sports has been emphasized for a long time (Bompa, 1968), and as suggested by MacDougall (1974) a well-trained aerobic system "increases the total energy available even though the event is largely anaerobic". Similarly, a high aerobic capacity is also beneficial to a performer involved in anaerobic work. During the recovery phase following anaerobic training an athlete with a well-trained aerobic system recovers faster than someone who lacks it. Therefore, in order to improve training methodology as well as the physiological working capacity, an increase in the total volume of work with emphasis on the aerobic system is vital.

Table 2 attempts to provide information regarding the delivery systems of performance of many sports. This information represents the state of the art: some are based on thorough scientific investigation, others employ the guidelines proposed by Mathews and Fox (1976) and Dal Monte (1983), and other authors. The latter information though, seems to be slightly biased on the contribution of the anaerobic systems. Often such analysis seem to consider a rally, in the case of racquet sports, or a tactical segment of the game (i.e. basketball, ice hockey) and thus emphasizing the contribution of the alactic and lactic systems. Therefore, before taking for granted some of the information provided by table 2, one should try to answer if the rest interval between two rallies in volleyball (average 9 seconds) is long enough to remove the lactic acid from the system, resynthesize ATP from ADP + P, and thus resupply the body with the fuel produced under the anaerobic system.

For other team sports, such as football, soccer and rugby, the energy requirements and thus the training, should consider the position played in the team. In soccer, for instance, discrimination should be made between a sweeper, where the energy is provided mostly by the anaerobic systems, and the midfielder, which often covers 12–16 km per game. The aerobic requirements for the latter are more than obvious. Take into account that an elite ice hockey player skates at a very high velocity, over 5 km per game, and a wide receiver in football often runs maximum velocity 25–40 segments of 25–50 meters and the duration of games often lasts for 2–3 hours. Therefore, the re-evaluation of the contribution, and especially of the needs or aerobic training is long overdue.

Table 2. The energy delivery systems (ergogenesis in percentage) for sports.

Sports/Events		ATP/CP	LA	O$_2$	Source
Archery		0	0	100.00	Mathews and Fox, 1976
Athletics:	100 m	49.50	49.50	1.00	Mader, 1985
	200 m	38.27	56.69	5.05	" "
	400 m	26.70	55.30	18.00	" "
	800 m	18.00	31.40	50.60	" "
	1500 m	20	55	25	Mathews and Fox, 1976
	3000 m.s.c.	20	40	40	" "
	5000 m	10	20	70	" "
	10,000	5	15	80	" "
	Marathon	0	5	95	" "
	Jumps	100	0	0	" "
	Throws	100	0	0	" "
Baseball		95	5	0	" "
Basketball		80	20	0	Dal Monte, 1983
Biathlon		0	5	95	" "
Canoeing:	c1 1000 m	25	35	40	" "
	c2 1000 m	20	55	25	" "
	c1, 2, 10,000 m	5	10	85	" "
Cycling	200 m Track	98	2	0	" "
	4,000 Pursuit	20	50	30	" "
	Road Racing	0	5	95	" "
Diving		100	0	0	" "
Driving (motor sports, luge, etc.)		0	0–15	85–100	" "
Equestrian		20–30	20–50	20–50	" "
Fencing		90	10	0	" "
Figure Skaating		60–80	10–30	20	" "
Gymnastics (except floor)		90	10	0	" "
Handball		80	10	10	" "
Ice Hockey		80–90	10–20	0	" "
Judo		90	10	0	" "

Table 2. *Continued.*

Sports/Events		ATP/CP	LA	O$_2$	Source
Kayaking:	K1 500 m	25	60	15	Dal Monte, 1983
	K2,4. 500 m	30	60	10	" "
	K1, 1000 m	20	50	30	" "
	K2,4. 1,000 m	20	55	25	" "
	K1,2,4. 10,000 m	5	10	85	" "
Rowing		2	15	83	Howald, 1977
Rugby		30–40	10–20	30–50	Dal Monte, 1983
Sailing		0	15	85–100	" "
Shooting		0	0	100	Dal Monte, 1983
Skiing					
Alpine:					
Slalom	45"–50"	40	50	10	Alpine Canada: 32, 1990
Giant Slalom	70"–90"	30	50	20	" "
Super Giant	80"–120"	15	45	40	" "
Downhill	90"–150"	10	45	45	" "
Nordic		0	5	95	Dal Monte, 1983
Soccer		60–80	20	0–10	" "
Speed Skating					
	500 m	95	5	0	" "
	1,500 m	30	60	10	" "
	5,000 m	10	40	50	" "
	10,000 m	5	15	80	" "
Swimming:	100 m	23.95	51.10	24.95	Mader, 1985
	200 m	10.70	19.30	70.00	" "
	400 m	20	40	40	Mathews and Fox, 1976
	800 m	10	30	60	" "
	1,500 m	10	20	70	" "
Tennis		70	20	10	Dal Monte, 1983
Volleyball		40	10	50	Gionet, 1980
Waterpolo		30	40	30	Dal Monte, 1983
Wrestling		90	10	0	" "

CHAPTER TWO

Principles of Training

The theory and methodology of training, as a distinct unit of physical education and sports, has its own specific principles based on the biological, psychological and pedagogical sciences. These guidelines and regulations which systematically direct the whole process of training are known as the principles of training.

Derived from the need to fulfill important goals of training, namely to increase the level of skill and performance, these principles are specific and reflective of the particularities of this process. All principles of training are part of a whole concept and should not be viewed as isolated units, although for the purpose of a more understandable presentation they are described separately. Correct utilization of these training principles by each coach will result in superior organization and more functional content, means, methods, factors and components of training.

THE PRINCIPLE OF ACTIVE PARTICIPATION IN TRAINING

A clear and precise comprehension of three factors, namely, the scope and objectives of training, the athlete's independent and creative role, and his/her duties during long phases of the preparation is vital in consideration of these principles. The coach, through his/her leadership and expertise, should promote an independent but conscientious development of his/her athletes. They must perceive the coach's conduct as further improving their skill, biomotor abilities, and psychological traits in order that they may overcome difficulties experienced in training.

Conscientious and active participation in training will be maximized if the coach periodically, but consistently, discusses his/her athlete's progress with him/her. Knowing this, the athlete should relate the objective information received from the coach with the subjective assessment of his/her performance. By comparing his/her performance abilities with his/her subjective feelings of speed, smoothness and ease of performing a skill, the perceptions of being strong, relaxed, and the like are developed. The athlete will be able to understand the positive and negative aspects of his/her performance, what he/she has to improve and how he/she may go about improving his/her results. Training involves active listening and participation from both the coach and the athlete. The athlete should take care of his/her well being and since personal problems may have an impact on performance, he /she should share them with the coach so that through a common effort the problems will be dealt with.

Active participation should not be limited to the training session only. An athlete should take responsibility for his/her actions when not under the supervision and care of the coach. There is strong evidence that alcohol and smoking do affect an athlete's performance; consequently, the athlete should vigorously and actively resist such temptations. During free time, the athlete may engage in social activities which provide satisfaction and relaxation, but he/she must be sure to get adequate rest. This will ensure that physical and psychological regeneration will occur prior to the next training lesson. If the athlete does not faithfully observe all the requirements of non-supervised training, he/she should not expect to perform at his/her maximum level. The coach, regardless of his/her capabilities and knowledge, cannot perform miracles. Ritter (1981) suggests that the following rules can be derived from this principle:

1. The coach should elaborate training objectives together with his/her athletes. They should take an active role in establishing objectives in accordance with their abilities.

2. The athlete should actively participate in planning long and short term training programs, as well as in analyzing them. The athlete should have an adequate self-assessment capacity so that he/she will have a positive role in these matters. One should expect that experienced athletes may be more involved compared to those who are just beginning in the sport. Elite class athletes may sometimes be encouraged to develop their own programs. The coach should then modify them in accordance with their quality and the athletes' objectives.

Of important assistance in designing a program are the notes and comments made by the athlete in his/her training journal. A critical evaluation of the previous plan may also be of assistance. Other rules that might be followed are:

3. The athlete should periodically establish and pass tests and standards. In doing so, there will be a clearer picture of the level of performance and degree of improvement in a given period of time. He/she may then draw the appropriate conclusions based on objective information. Future programs should be based on this important analysis.

4. The athlete must undertake individual assignments (homework) and/or individual training sessions without the coach's supervision. Quite often some athletes, especially prospective athletes, and their coaches, cannot afford more than one organized training lesson per day. Still, they may have set high objectives for themselves, knowing that they will not easily be achieved. Furthermore, such athletes may have to compete against individuals who may be more fortunate as far as training time is concerned. In order to overcome this problem, one of the most efficient ways may be for the individual to supplement his/her training with additional activity at home, in the morning before going to school or work. Supplementary training lessons reflect positively on performance. The athlete's rate of development of general endurance, and abilities such as flexibility and strength are increased, due to this self-motivated training. Such an approach is an additional and effective way to make the athlete

more aware of his/her role. The athlete will participate more conscientiously in achieving his/her objectives.

A conscience attitude toward training should also be reflected through setting precise and achievable objectives for the athlete. This will elevate the athlete's interest in training, and the desire and enthusiasm to participate successfully in competitions. It will enhance the development of psychological traits such as willpower, and perseverance to overcome training difficulties. Objectives should be set in such a way that they are difficult enough to be challenging yet realistic enough to be achievable (McClements and Botterill, 1979). The coach should plan both long and short term goals for each athlete, where the latter represents an effective way to stimulate athlete's training interests.

PRINCIPLE OF MULTILATERAL DEVELOPMENT

The necessity of a multilateral development appears to be an accepted requirement in most fields of education and human endeavors. Regardless of how specialized the instruction may become, initially there should be exposure to a multilateral development in order to acquire necessary fundamentals.

It is not uncommon to observe extremely rapid development in some young athletes. In such cases it is of paramount importance that the coach resist the temptation to develop a training program leading to narrow specialization. A broad, multilateral base of physical development, especially general physical preparation, is one of the basic requirements necessary to reach a highly specialized level of physical preparation and technical mastery. Such an approach to training should be considered as a prerequisite for specialization in a sport or event. Figure 11 illustrates the sequential approach to training which is common in the East European countries.

The base of the pyramid, which through analogy may be considered to be the foundations of any training program, consists of multilateral development. When this development reaches an acceptable level, especially in dealing with the physical

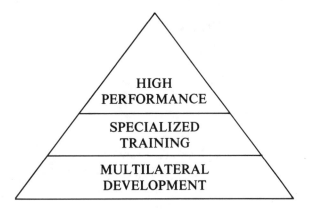

Figure 11.   The main phases of athletic training.

development, the athlete enters his/her second phases of development. This leads to the highlights of an athletic career, namely training for high performance.

The principle of multilateral development evolves from the interdependence between all human organs and systems, and between physiological and psychological processes. The numerous changes which occur following training are always interdependent. An exercise, regardless of its nature and motor requirements, always requires the harmonious input of several systems, along with various biomotor abilities, and psychological traits. Consequently, at the early stages of an athlete's training, the coach should consider an approach directed towards proper functional development of the body.

Muscle groups, joint flexibility, stability and the activation of all the limbs corresponding to the future requirements of the selected sport should be the focus of attention. In other words, development to a superior level of all morphological and functional abilities which will be required to perform efficiently at a higher level of technical and tactical skills is necessary.

The road to specialization and athletic mastery is functionally based on multilateral development. In any sport the chance to obtain high performance lies with the individual who, during the early stages of athletic training, is exposed to a plural morphological and functional development, a systematic training during which he/she performs, besides the skills of a chosen sport, other skills and motor actions. Such an athlete should be fast, almost like a sprinter, strong like a weight lifter, resistant like a distance runner and coordinated like a juggler. Although the above may sound more than ideal, one may recall the abilities shown by decathlete Bruce Jenner, winner of the Montreal Olympic Games, Nadia Comaneci and many other top athletes who have developed amazing abilities over the years.

The multilateral principle should be employed mostly when training children and juniors. However, multilateral development does not imply that an athlete will spend all of his/her training time for such a program only. On the contrary, as illustrated by figure 12, as an athlete matures and elevates his/her level of athletic mastery, his/her training should be of a more specialized nature. Coaches involved in all sports may contemplate the merits and importance of this principle. However, the advantage of a multilateral development in a training program brings a high variety of exercises and fun through playing games, and this decreases the likelihood of boredom.

PRINCIPLE OF SPECIALIZATION

Whether training on a field, in a pool or in a gymnasium, from the beginning of an athletic career, the intent and motives are to specialize in a sport or event. Specialization represents the main element required to obtain success in a sport.

Specialization, or for that matter, exercises specific to a sport or event, lead to anatomical and physiological changes related to the necessities of that sport. Researchers, captivated by the uniqueness of athletes' physiological traits, demonstrated

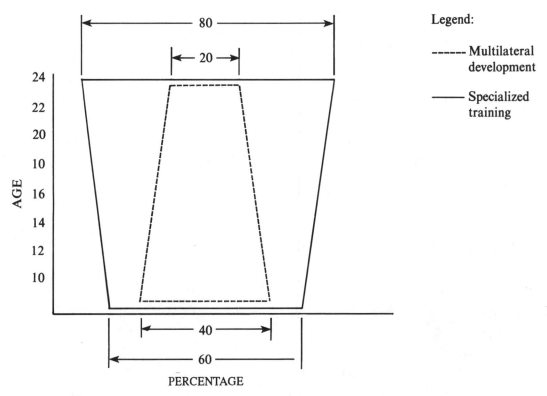

Figure 12.   The ratio between multilateral development and specialized training for different ages.

that the human body adapts to the activity that an individual is exposed to (Astrand and Rodahl, 1970, Matthews and Fox, 1976). Such an adaptation does not refer to physiological changes only, since specialization applies to technical, tactical and psychological features as well.

Specialization is not a unilateral process but rather a complex one which is based on a solid groundwork of multilateral development. From the first training lesson of a beginner to the mastery of a mature athlete, the total volume of training, and the portion of special exercises are progressively and constantly increased.

As far as specialization is concerned, Ozolin (1971) suggests that the means of training or, more specifically, specialized motor acts used to obtain a training effect, should be of two natures: 1) exercises from the specialized sport, and 2) exercises utilized to develop biomotor abilities. The former refers to exercises that "parallel" or "mimic" the movement requirements of the particular sport in which the athlete is specializing. The latter refers to exercises which develop strength, speed and endurance. The ratio between these two groups of exercises is different for each sport depending on its characteristics. Thus, in some sports such as long distance running, almost 100% of the entire volume of training is comprised of exercises from the first group, while in others, like high jumping, these exercises represent

Table 3.   The age of starting, specializing and reaching high performance in different sports.

Sport	Begin to Practice a Sport	Age of Specialization	Age to Reach High Performance
Athletics (track and field)	10–12	13–14	18–23
Basketball	7–8	10–12	20–23
Boxing	13–14	15–16	20–25
Cycling	14–15	16–17	21–24
Diving	6–7	8–10	18–22
Fencing	7–8	10–12	20–25
Figure Skating	5–6	8–10	16–20
Gymnastics (women)	6–7	10–11	14–18
Gymnastics (men)	6–7	12–14	18–24
Rowing	12–14	16–18	22–24
Skiing	6–7	10–11	20–24
Soccer	10–12	11–13	18–24
Swimming	3–7	10–12	16–18
Tennis	6–8	12–14	22–25
Volleyball	11–12	14–15	20–25
Weight lifting	11–13	15–16	21–28
Wrestling	13–14	15–16	24–28

only 40%. The remaining percentage is made up of exercises aimed at developing leg strength and jumping power, for example, bounding, and weight training (Dyachikov, 1960). Similarly, as opposed to most Western world coaches, the east European team sport coaches dedicated only 60–80% of the total training time to exercise from the specialized sport. The remaining percentage is dedicated to the development of specific biomotor abilities. An almost identical approach is utilized in boxing, wrestling, fencing and gymnastics. As for the seasonal sports like rowing and canoeing, the ration between the two groups of exercises is almost equal.

The principle of specialization should be properly understood and applied in childrens' and juniors' training where multilateral development should be the basis from which specialization develops. However, the ratio between multilateral and specialized training has to be carefully planned, considering the fact that in contemporary sports there is an obvious tendency to lower the age of athletic maturation; the age at which high performance could be achieved (i.e., gymnastics, swimming and even figure skating). No one is surprised anymore to see children two or three years of age in the swimming pool or on the ice rink, or six year olds in the gym. The same trend appears in other sports as well: ski jumpers and basketball players start training at the age of eight. The general age that a person begins to train for a sport, the time when specialization may start, and the age when high performance is reached are presented in table 3.

Since the early 1960's, the age of introduction to a sport as well as the age of achieving high performance dropped dramatically (i.e., woman's gymnastics and swimming); early age initiation to a sport is not a novelty. However, youngsters' high efficiency in athletics seem to be based on the fact that what really counts in athletics is not chronological but rather biological age. Functional potential, the ability to adapt to a certain stimulus, is more important than age. The rate of developing skills and athletic abilities seems to be higher for young athletes than for mature ones.

Practicing the same sport regularly over several years, with an adequate intensity suited to one's potential, leads to special adjustments in a youngster's organism according to the specifics and needs of the sport. This creates the physiological premises for specialized training at a later age. In sports requiring mastery of skills, coordination, or speed (i.e. gymnastics), high results may be achieved at a very early age. Nadia Comaneci was alraedy one of the best in the world at the age of 12. In sports where cardio-respiratory and muscular endurance are the dominant abilities (i.e. cross-country skiing, running, rowing, speed skating, cycling), attempts to lower the age of athlete maturation will result in negative consequences— "quick burnout". This burnout leads to shortening the duration of producing top athletes, which occurred in a dreadful experience according to a Russian study (Ozolin 1971). The demands of endurance and its components require an athlete to reach his/her limits in training and especially in competition. Therefore, a well developed and adjusted body is essential. Sometimes the coach disregards such realities, and in his/her desire to reach high levels of performance prematurely, requires his/her athletes to perform difficult training tasks, worst of all high intensity training, thus exceeding his/her athlete's adaptability potential. Under these circumstances, an inadequate physiological recovery process is experienced, leading to a state of exhaustion. This type of program may also affect a person's natural growth, sometimes even personal health as well.

PRINCIPLES OF INDIVIDUALIZATION

Individualization in training is one of the main requirements of contemporary training and it refers to the idea of each athlete, regardless of level of performance, being treated individually according to his/her abilities, potential, learning characteristics and specificity of the sport. The whole training concept should be modelled in accordance with the athlete's physiological and psychological characteristics so that training objectives may be naturally enhanced.

Individualization should not be perceived only as a method used in individual technical corrections or the specialization of an individual in an event or position played in a team, but rather as a means through which an athlete is objectively assessed and subjectively observed. The coach may then realize the athlete's training needs and maximize his/her abilities.

Quite often coaches apply a completely unscientific approach in training by literally following training programs of successful athletes, completely disregarding his/her athlete's personality, experience and abilities. What is even worse, such programs are sometimes implemented into juniors' training schedules. These athletes are both physiologically and psychologically unfit to follow such advanced programs, especially the intensity component. In Ritter's (1982) option, coaches' effectiveness in training may be maximized if due regard to certain rules are paid:

1. A comprehensive analysis of the athlete's work capacity and personality development is necessary to determine his/her highest limits of effort tolerance. The coach should plan the loads in training accordingly. Each individual's effort capacity depends on the following factors:

a) Biological and chronological age, especially for children and juniors whose bodies have not reached maturity yet. Their training, as compared to adult athletes, should be of more broad nature, multilateral and of moderate intensity. Juniors may more readily tolerate a high volume of training rather than high intensity or heavy loads. Both high intensity and heavy loads over-tax their anatomical structures, especially the bones (which are not ossified yet), ligaments, tendons and muscles.

b) Experience, or the starting age of participation in sports. The work demand on the part of the athlete should be proportional to his/her experience. Although the rate of improvement of some athletes is different, the coach still has to be cautious with regard to the load which is undertaken. Similarly, when athletes of different backgrounds and experiences are assigned to train in the same group, the coach should not under-estimate their individual characteristics and potential.

c) Individual capacity for work and performance. Not all athletes who are capable of the same performance have the same work capacity. There are several biological and psychological factors which are determinant to work abilities. Counsilman (1971) provided interesting behind the scene examples regarding the work capacity and pain tolerance of swimmers Mark Spitz and John Kinsella. As opposed to Spitz, Kinsella really liked to push himself, and yet no other athlete matched Spitz's performances.

d) Training and health status. Training status dictates the content, load and rating in training. Athletes with the same level of performance have different levels of strength, speed, endurance development, and skill. Such dissimilarities justify the needs of individualization in training. Further, individualization is strongly recommended for athletes who experience illness or accidents. Thus, health status also determines the limits of the training capacity. Such limits and limitations should be known by the coach and only a close co-operation between the coach and a physiologist or physician may resolve the problem.

e) Training load and the athlete's rate of recovery. When planning and rating the work in training, there are other consideration factors outside of training which may place a high demand on the athlete. Heavy involvement in school, work or family, and distance to travel to school of training, can affect the rate of recovery between training lessons. By the same token, lifestyle and emotional involvement should also be know by the coach. These factors must be properly regarded in planning the content and stress in training.

f) Athlete's body build and nervous system type. This could play an important role in both training load and performance capacity. Individual characteristics could be established through adequate testing, for which the coach may solicit the assistance of appropriate specialists. Similarly, the coach may also study and observe the athlete's behavior in training, competition or even during participation in social events. Behavior in school or work place, or with family and friends may also provide important information for the coach. However, in this regard a coach should ask for scientific assistance from both a physiologist and psychologist.

2. Work adaptation is a function of individual capacity. Although precise standards regarding training demands are scarcely found, as far as childrens' and juniors' training are concerned, they tend to adapt easier to a higher volume of training with moderate intensity, rather than to a lower volume but very demanding stimuli. Ritter (1982) also suggests that adolescents appear to adjust to daily training provided that they do not burn all their energetic reserves and that sufficient time to play is also allowed.

Children, as opposed to adult athletes, have relatively unstable nervous systems, thus their emotional state is sometimes altered very quickly. This phenomenon requires a harmony between their training and other involvements, especially their school work. Furthermore, training of prospective athletes must have much variety, so that their interest and concentration may be kept up more consistently. Also, in order to enhance a good rate of recovery from injuries, a correct alternation between training stimuli and rest should persist. This is so especially for intense exercise, where cautions should be placed on the method of doing work in training.

3. Sexual differences also plays an important role as far as performance and individual capacity in training is concerned, especially during puberty. A coach should also be aware of the fact that the individual motor performance is related to individual chronological and biological age.

Anatomical structure and biological differences should be appropriately regarded in training. Women tend to be able to withstand strength training that has a rigorous continuity without long interruptions. But because of the specifics of hip shape and size and the lumbar (lower back) region, abdominal muscles must be properly strengthened. As far as endurance training is concerned, the main difference between men and women is mostly the degree of intensity that can be tolerated. The volume or quantity of training is also fairly equivalent between men and women. Variations in women's training and performance needs to take into consideration the menstrual cycle and thus the consequent hormonal activity. The hormonal changes relate to physical and psychological efficiency and capacity. More consideration needs to be taken with younger female athletes rather than the older, more mature female. As with most young athletes, training should start off with adaptation to moderate exercises before moving onto more intense or heavier training. The amount of work should be determined on an individual basis. In many cases, during the post-menstrual phase, training efficiency was found to be higher (Ritter, 1982).

Following delivery of a baby, female athletes may start training only after the genital organs resume normal activity. Regular but careful training may start in the fourth post-natal month, but training for competition may commence only after the tenth post-delivery month (Ritter, 1982).

Individualization in training also refers to the fact that a coach should make individual training plans for each athlete based on, and reflecting each athlete's abilities. It is required that such plans are also necessary for each training lesson. Although the preparation for and conclusion of a training lesson may be organized and performed in a group, for the main part of the lesson the coach must direct attention to individual or small group needs provided that the small groups have similar physical and technical abilities.

THE PRINCIPLE OF VARIETY

Contemporary training is a very demanding activity requiring many hours of work from the athlete. The volume and intensity of training are continuously increasing and exercises are repeated numerous times. In order to reach high performance, the volume of training must surpass the threshold of 1,000 hours per year. The following are some examples to give an idea of the amount of work required for an athlete. A world class weight lifter should commit him or herself to 1200–1600 hours of heavy work per year, a rower covers 40–60 kilometers (km) in 2–3 training lessons per day, while it is a fact of life that a world class gymnast must train 4–6 non-stop hours per day during which time he/she may repeat 30–40 full routines. Such a high volume of training demonstrates that certain exercises or technical elements be repeated many times. This, unfortunately, may lead to monotony and boredom. This repetitiveness is prominent in sports where endurance is a dominant factor and the technical elements repertoire is minimal (running, swimming, rowing, canoeing, cross-country skiing).

In order to overcome monotony and boredom in training, a coach needs to be creative by having a knowledge and a large resource of exercises to allow for periodic alteration. Skills and exercises may be enriched by adopting movements of similar technical pattern, or those which may develop biomotor abilities required by the sport. For a volleyball player, or high jumper who intends to improve leg power, or for that matter, every sport requiring a powerful take-off, it is not necessary to spike or jump every day. A high variety of exercises are available (half squats, leg press, jumping squats, step ups, jumping or stair bounding exercises, exercises with benches and depth jumps) allowing the coach to alternate periodically from one to the other, thus eliminating boredom but maintaining the same training effect.

The coach's capacity to create, to be inventive and to work with imagination represents an important advantage for successful variety in training. Furthermore, a coach should plan his/her program in such a way that in both the training lesson and micro-cycle (weekly program) a high variety of exercises will be utilized. When a coach makes his/her training program, he/she should consider all skills and movements which are necessary to fulfill his/her goals, and then plan them alternatively for each day. As far as the training lesson is concerned, by concluding with elements that the athletes may enjoy, the coach will maintain interest and avoid monotony. Weight lifters, following a heavy workout, may conclude their training by playing 20 minutes of basketball or volleyball, which, besides bringing fun into their training, may also develop general endurance and co-ordination. Similarly, during the preparatory phase of training, certain biomotor abilities may be developed by using other means of training or by performing sports which may be of high benefit for the athlete. Boxers, wrestlers, rowers, canoers and other athletes could develop their general endurance through cycling, swimming, and cross-country skiing. The above suggestions, could easily enrich the content of a training program, bringing into it greater variety which in the end will reflect positively upon mental and psychological well being of the athletes. Athletes always need variety in training and the coach should ensure it.

THE PRINCIPLE OF MODELING THE TRAINING PROCESS

Model training, although not always well organized and often employing a random approach, has existed since the 1960's. Although the East European sports specialists for some time have managed to acquire knowledge and experience in this area of training, it has only been since the 1970's that a strong desire to link athletes' training process through modeling, has existed.

In general terms a model is an imitation, a simulation of a reality, made out of specific elements of the phenomenon which is observed or investigated. It is also an isomorphous (similar form with the competition) type of image, which is obtained through abstraction; a mental process of making generalizations from concrete examples. During the creation of a model, setting a hypothesis is of high importance for both its evolution and results analysis.

A model is required to be single, so that it eliminates variables of secondary importance, and reliable, meaning that it is somewhat similar and consistent with a previously existing one. In order to meet these two requirements, a model should incorporate only those means of training which are identical to the nature of competition. The goal of a model is to achieve an ideal, and although the abstract notion of ideal is above the concrete reality, it also represents something which one strives to reach; an event which should be achievable. Thus, an established model is an abstract representation of the actions which someone is interested in, at a given time.

Through model training the coach attempts to direct and organize his/her training lessons in such a way that the objectives, methods and content are similar to those of a competition. Under these circumstances the competition does not represent just a reference point for training, but rather a strong component for training. The coach's acquaintance with the specifics of competition represents a necessary prerequisite of successfully modeling the training process. Specifics of the work structure, such as volume, intensity, complexity, and number of games or periods, must be fully understood. Similarly, of extreme importance, the coach needs to know his/her sport's/ event's ergogensis (generations of work, from the Greek word ergon which means to work, and genesis, which means generation, production). Familiarity with the contribution ratio of the aerobic and anaerobic systems for a sport/event is of capital importance in understanding the needs and aspects which should be emphasized in training.

The development of a model is not a short process. On the contrary, a future model should rely on previous examples but eliminating the previous errors. Such a process may require a few years. The more effort and time contributed to improving the model the better it will be. As far as the introduction of new elements is concerned, they should reflect the coaches' gains in knowledge in technique, tactics or methods of developing biomotor abilities. Figure 13 suggests an approach in developing a model.

The creation of a model commences with the contemplation phase, during which the coach observes and analyzes the actual state of training. Following this is the inference stage when the coach, based on the conclusions of his/her observations decides which elements of the training concept should be retained and which ones are in need of improvement. In the next step the coach introduces new (1) qualitative elements, which refer to the intensity of training, technical, strategical and psychological aspects, and (2) quantitative components, concerning the volume of training, duration and number of repetitions required to automize the new qualitative elements. Based on the new additions, the coach elaborates and attempts to improve both the qualitative and quantitative models. The new model is then tested in training and afterwards in a competition of secondary importance or an exhibition game. Following this, the coach draws conclusions regarding the validity of the new model and eventual slight alterations to be performed. This phase leads to the ultimate model, which is assumed to be complete and ready to be applied to training for an important competition.

A model has to be specific for an individual or team. A coach or athlete should resist the common temptation to copy the training model of a successful athlete or

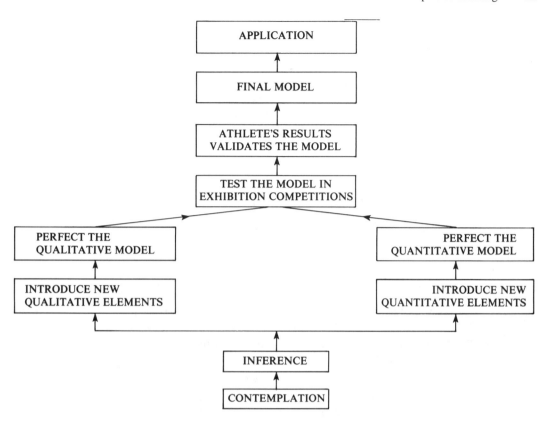

Figure 13. The sequence of developing a model of training.

team. A model of training should consider, among many other factors, the athletes' psychological and physiological potential, facilities, and social environment. Each sport or event should have an accepted technical model which has to be applied to all athletes, but with slight alterations to accommodate each athlete's anatomical, physiological and psychological characteristics. Audio-visual aids would be of great assistance in both the study of the accepted technical model and acquisition of it by the athletes.

As already mentioned, a training model should simulate the specifics of competitions. It should incorporate training parameters of high magnitude such as volume and intensity, and utilize exercises of high efficiency. Each training lesson should be similar, especially during the competitive phase, to the specifics of a game or race. For instance, based on the rowing races fatigue co-efficient (Popescu, 1957; Bompa, 1964; Bielz, 1970), illustrated in Figure 14, and the specifics of the sport, a training lesson model for the competitive phase was developed (Bompa, 1975). From this model, individualized training plans for each of the athletes may be derived.

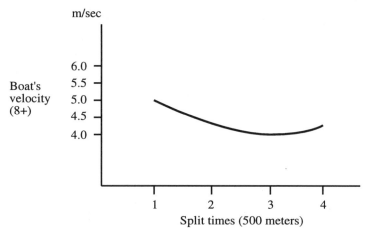

Figure 14.   The curve of the co-efficient in rowing races.
("8+1" signifies the number of rowers)

The velocity of the boat reaches the highest values in the first part of the race right after the start, and at the end, when the finish takes place. During the beginning of the race, energy is provided anaerobically, thus creating an oxygen debt in the athlete. In the main part of the race, the aerobic energy system is dominant. Resulting from these observations, a training lesson model was developed to reflect these conditions of the race. Hence, the beginning of the training lesson always uses high intensity exercises performed under anaerobic conditions. The main part of the lesson stresses a high volume of work involving the aerobic system followed by other types of training, characterized by high velocity, paralleling the final portion of a race. Such an approach, besides duplicating the model of a race, also develops the psychological traits of "will" and "fighting power" since towards the end of training the athletes have to perform repetitions of high intensity when already experiencing a high level of fatigue. A similar model may be utilized in other individual sports resembling the above characteristics (i.e. swimming, running events, canoeing and speed skating).

As far as the team sports are concerned, there are models intended for training lessons and others to be applied in games (Teodorescu, 1975). These two models are strongly related to one another since most training lessons should be performed under circumstances similar to the specifics of the game. In preparation for the game, the coach elaborates an entire model, which should be considered as a system containing simple models for each of the subsystems: technical and tactical, physical and environmental.

The technical and tactical model consists of each individual player's game plan and actions which should be integrated with the teammates' model. Similarly, the physical preparation model refers to players' reactions, and adaptation to the game's intensity and stress. The environmental model, refers to: 1) the circumstances under which the game is played, such as: equipment, time of the game, quality of officiating, and whether a workout would be performed on the court prior to the official game, and 2) the socio-psychological climate predicting how hostile spectators may affect team performance. Often, an unfavorable environment could develop high tension disturbing psychological processes such as: concentration, self-control, combativity, perception, lucidity, quick reaction and decision-making. A friendly audience could stimulate all the above traits resulting in a better performance.

The methodology of developing an integral model calls for a sequential approach involving four phases (Teodorescu, 1975):

1. devise the technical and tactical model for each individual player, for both offence and defence.
2. elaborate the model of tactical combinations, for both offence and defence, having in mind future opponents.
3. establish exercises and drills to learn and perfect the individual's and team's models.
4. relate individual's and team's model to the physical preparation model. Select complex drills which refer to both technical and tactical, as well as physical factors. All these should then be incorporated in the general training plan.

The environment model should be introduced progressively to the players a few weeks after the beginning of training. Elements such as a hostile or noisy audience, if necessary, could be reproduced in certain parts of training so that the athletes can develop resistance to the negative effects on performance.

Acquiring the integral model requires a long period of time. It has to be divided into subsystems to allow for progressive assimilation, especially during the preparation phase. During the end of this phase, prior to the exhibition games, simple models should be incorporated into the integral model and tested against opponents of various abilities. During the pre-competitive phase the coach may plan on which competitions to enter with special regards to tournaments. High results in a tournament should not be expected unless the coach trains his/her team for it. During such a rehearsal, the coach should consider the time of the games, their frequency and time difference between them, as well as means used to recover prior to each game.

The concept of modeling is also applicable in planning long term training programs, including the annual plan (see the planning chapter). Modeling usually occurs during the transition phase so that the coach can make a comprehensive and critical retrospective analysis of the previous year's model, re-evaluating whether the objectives, tests and standards, training content, peaking and other training parameters were accomplished and set adequately. Similarly, an analysis regarding how the athletes coped with training and competition stress and ways to improve this in the future, should be conducted. The coach should then proceed to an objective selection of the methods and means of training which will materialize in the new model, eliminating those which proved to be ineffective.

PRINCIPLE OF PROGRESSIVE INCREASE OF LOAD IN TRAINING

Improvement in performance is a direct result of the amount and quality of work achieved in training. From the initiation stage up to the stage of elite class athletes, workload in training has to be increased gradually, in accordance with each individual's physiological and psychological abilities.

The physiological basis of this principle, as a result of training the body's functional efficiency, and thus capacity to do work, gradually increases over a long period of time. Any drastic increase in performance requires a long period of training and adaptation. The athlete reacts anatomically, physiologically and psychologically to the demand of the increase in training load. Improving the development of the nervous system's functions and reactions, neuro-muscular co-ordination and the psychological capacity to cope with the stress resulting from heavy training loads, evolves gradually, requiring time and competent leadership.

The principle of gradual load increase forms a basis for planning athletic training, from a micro-cycle to Olympic cycle, and should be followed by all athletes regardless of their level of performance. The rate of improvement in performance depends directly on the rate and manner in which the load is increased in training. Standard load leads to a diminishing of training effect, and in the long run will be reflected through a physical and psychological deterioration, diminishing performance capacity. As illustrated in figure 15, the consequence of a standard stimulus is evolution, followed by a plateau, and ultimately involution, or a decrease in performance.

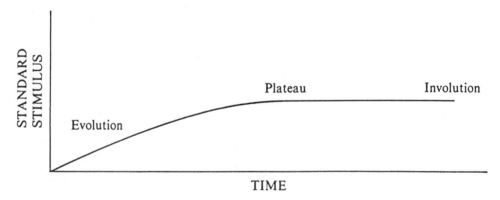

Figure 15.   The three phases of the curve resulting from a standard stimulus.

In the past, several studies have been done which investigated methods of increasing the work in training. The overloading or the linear and continuous methods were found to be less efficient than the step or undulatory approach (Harre, 1982; Ozolin, 1971). As opposed to the overload approach, the step type method ensures the physiological and psychological requirement that a training load increase must be followed by a phase of unloading, during which the athlete adapts and regenerates, thus preparing for a new increase. The frequency of the increase in training load must be determined in accordance with each individual's needs, rate of adaptation and the calendar of competition. A very abrupt training load increase surpasses the ability to adapt, affecting physiological and especially psychological balance. Such an approach may result in overtraining symptoms and even injuries. Excessive training demands may be discouraging, depressing and downwarding in an athlete's confidence in his/her potential, bringing the athlete almost to the state of abandoning the sport.

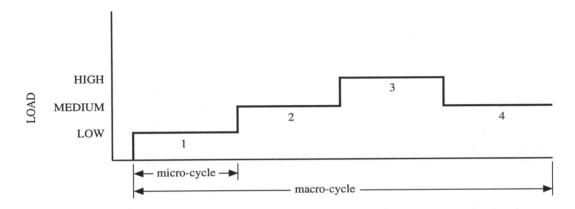

Figure 16.   The increase of training load in steps.

The step type approach (figure 16) of elevating the training load should not be understood as a steady increase in each training lesson through an arithmetical addition of equal quantities of work. One training lesson is insufficient to provoke visible physical or mental changes in the athlete which may lead to an adequate adaptation. In order to accomplish an adaptation, it is necessary to repeat the same type of training lessons or training stimulus several times. Often, training lessons of the same characteristics may be planned for an entire micro-cycle, followed then by another increase in the training load. Figure 16 is an illustration of how the training load is increased in a macro-cycle, which is a phase of training of 2–6 (usually 4) weeks. Each vertical line represents a change in training load while the horizontal line represents the phase of adaptation required by the new demand. The load is increased gradually in the first three micro-cycles followed by a preparatory decrease or unloading phase, allowing the athlete to regenerate. The purpose of regeneration is to allow the athlete to accumulate physiological and psychological reserves in anticipation of further increases in load. Improvement in the degree of training usually occurs following a regeneration phase. The unloading phase, or the fourth cycle in this example represents the new lowest step for another macro-cycle. However, since the athlete has already adjusted to the previous loads, the new low step is not of the same magnitude as the previous low, but rather equal to the medium one. An in crease in training load produces a slight physiological and psychological imbalance followed by an adaptation phase during which the athlete adjusts to the training demand, concluding with an improvement in degree of training and performance.

There is a direct relationship between the length and height of the step. The longer the length, or adaptation, the higher an increase in either or both the volume and intensity of training. A high amount of work needs to be accumulated before per-formance improves.

As mentioned before, training load increase from one step to another has to be performed carefully and gradually. For endurance sports, especially the cyclic ones where the main training objective is to increase physiological potential, the increase in training load should not be high. Ozolin (1971) suggests that an increase in load should be around 3-6% of one's maximum speed, otherwise the volume of training has to be decreased, resulting in a reduction of the number of repetitions. In such a case, the individual's working capacity does not increase according to the needs of the racing distance but rather with the needs of a much shorter race.

For sports with high technical complexity, or acyclic sports such as team sports, gymnastics, and wrestling, where technical and tactical mastery is one of the major training objectives, the increase in load may be based on higher demands being placed on motor co-ordination. Changing the rhythm of technical movement, com-bination of different technical and tactical elements, the introduction of new skills, and the al teration of external conditions (performed against increased resistance like heavier ball, wrist weights, ankle or waist belt, reproduction of noisy audience) may be considered.

Although the increase of load in training does progress in steps, in a training plan of longer duration the curve of rating the load appears to have an undulatory shape, which is enhanced by the continuous changes of increase and decrease of the com ponents of training (Figure 17).

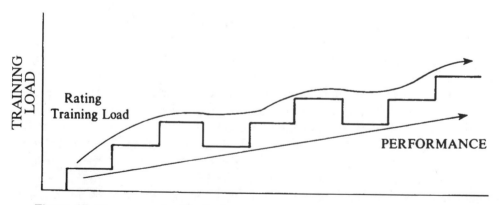

Figure 17. The curve of rating load appears to be unadultary while the performance improves linearity (the arrow).

During the training process, various exercises, biomotor abilities and bodily functions have a different rate or tempo of development. Improvements in flexibility could be achieved in a much shorter time, 2–3 months, while improvement in cardio-respiratory endurance requires a much longer time, probably up to 12 months. As far as biomotor development is concerned, Ozolin (1971) suggests the following ratio: flexibility improves from day to day, strength from week to week, speed from month to month, and endurance from year to year. The time required from step to step for the above abilities also differs quite drastically: for flexibility perhaps 2–3 days will be required, for strength development a micro-cycle, and for the development of the functional basis of endurance, a macro-cycle.

The ratio of the amount of increase in training load (height of the step) to the adaptation phase (length of the step) is much lower for strength development than for flexibility. As for endurance, the ratio will be the lowest (see figure 18). Although the step may be higher for strength training or endurance training than it would be for training for complex sports, the adaptation phase is much longer resulting in the overall rate of improvement in being lower. As a general guideline, the more complex and difficult the training task is, the lower the increase in training load (height of the step) should be. The increase in training load should also be governed by the rate of improvement of performance in a sport. The quicker the rate of performance improvement, the heavier the required training loads. Otherwise, the athlete will be unable to catch up with contemporary performance.

COMPLEX   FLEXIBILITY   STRENGTH   ENDURANCE
SPORTS

Figure 18.   The relative ratio between increase in training load and adaptation.

The magnitude of the training load should be elevated not only for smaller training cycles, but also from year to year. Both the volume and intensity of training has to be increased every year, otherwise a stagnation in performance occurs. On the basis of a systematic investigation involving top Soviet athletes, Matveev (1965) suggests that each year the volume of training has to be increased by 20–40% depending on the characteristics of the sport. However, in most cases, the elevation of the volume of training is determined not by the athlete's ability to cope with it, but rather by the lack of time, implying that quite often time is a limiting factor in training. In any case, since there appears to be a high correlation between the rhythm of increasing an athlete's performance and the index of increasing his/her yearly training loads, careful organization and allocation of an adequate portion of time to training is necessary. Whatever method is used, as illustrated by Table 4, coaches and athletes must increase the yearly volume of training in order to achieve results.

The dramatic increase over the short period of time reflected in Table 4 should be considered as a direct result of the growth of the number of training lessons per day. If in the 1960's, 4–6 training lessons per week for an elite athlete were considered adequate, nowadays it is insufficient. The increase of especially the volume of training per year is the outcome of the necessary rise in number of training lessons per day. Athlete's training for a top international competition ought to plan two, and in some cases, even three training lessons per day. Such an increase will enlarge the number of lessons per week and obviously per year, resulting in an elevation of physical and psychological potential, which certainly will affect performance. However, the increase in the number of training lessons has to allow for individual capacity, adaptability, training time, level of performance and the needs to alternate continuously different training intensities.

Table 4. Volume of training 1965–80

Sport	Elements/Distance	1965	1975	1980
Women's Gymnastics	Elements/Week	2300	3450	6000
	Routines/Week	52	86	180
Rowing (Women)	Kilometers/year	2300	4500	6800
Fencing	Training hours/year	600	980	1150
Canoeing	km/year	3200	4000	5175
	Training hours/year	960	1210	1552
Swimming (100 m back stroke)	Training hours/year	600	980	1070
Boxing	Training hours/year	946	1100	1280

CHAPTER THREE

The Training Factors

The fundamental factors of training, namely physical, technical, tactical, psychological and theoretical preparation should be incorporated in all athletic programs. The training factors are an essential part of any training program regardless of the athlete's age, individual potential, level of preparation or phase of training. However, the relative emphasis placed on each varies in accordance with the above features as well as the characteristics of the selected sport/event

Although training factors are strongly interrelated, there is a manner in which each is developed. As suggested by figure 19, physical and technical preparation represent the basis on which performance is built. As the athlete acquires a better technique, tactical preparation is emphasized. And when tactical preparation is acquired, psychological preparation is emphasized.

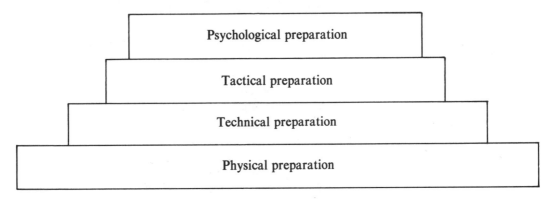

Figure 19. The training factors' pyramid.

PHYSICAL PREPARATION

Physical preparation has to be considered as one of the most, and in some cases, the most important ingredient in training required to achieve high performance. The main objectives are to increase the athlete's physiological potential and to develop biomotor abilities to the highest standards. In an organized training program physical preparation is developed in the following sequence: 1) a general physical preparation (G.P.P.), 2) a phase of specific physical preparation (S.P.P.), 3) a high level of biomotor abilities. The first two phases are developed during the preparatory phase when a solid foundation is built. The third phase is specific to the competitive period, when the objective is to maintain what was previously gained and perfect the abilities required by the sport/event (figure 20).

TRAINING PHASES	PREPARATORY PHASE		COMPETITIVE PHASE
PHASE OF DEVELOPMENT	1	2	3
OBJECTIVE	General Physical Preparation	Specific Physical Preparation	Perfect Specific Biomotor Abilities

Figure 20.   The sequential approach to developing physical preparation in an annual plan.

The longer the duration of the first phase the better the performance is in the next one. In the first phase a high volume of training with moderate intensity should prevail. As the training program progresses, intensity is increased in accordance with the needs of the sport. In some cases the dynamic characteristics of the sport requires that the intensity be emphasized right from the first phase. The duration of the above phases depends on the needs of the sport and the competition schedule.

This three phase or three step approach may also be considered for long term planning, especially for young athletes. Throughout the first few years of training (2–4) development is concerned with the foundations of training, that is, a solid G.P.P. This phase may be followed by a shorter one (1 year) when a special foundation for training is built (S.P.P.). The whole program concludes with the third phase (6–8 months) when the specific biomotor abilities are perfected.

General Physical Preparation (G.P.P.)

The main objective of G.P.P., regardless of the specifics of the sport, is to improve the athlete's working capacity. The higher the working potential, the more easily the body will adapt to the continuous increase in both the physical and psychological demands of training. Similarly, the broader and stronger the G.P.P. the higher the level of biomotor abilities that may be reached. Of significant importance is that through G.P.P, emphasis must be placed on the physical potential. For young, prospective athletes, G.P.P. is approximately the same regardless of sport specialization. For advanced athletes it has to be linked with the specifics and needs of the sport as well as individual characteristics.

Specific Physical Preparation (S.P.P.)

The S.P.P. is built on the foundation created by the G.P.P. The main objective of the S.P.P. is to further the athlete's physical development in regards to the physiological and methodical characteristics of the sport. The performance level reached by all athletes is so high that a very high level of physiological specialization is predominant to successful competitions. Such adjustments in the athlete's potential facilitates a greater amount of work in training and ultimately in competitions. In addition, a very high physiological capacity enhances rapid recovery between training lessons. Yakovlev (1967) claims that an organism which was previously fortified and strengthened would develop to high physiological levels more readily. Consequently, the improvement of specific endurance may be enhanced if training programs to achieve such capacity are preceded by the development of general endurance.

The general endurance developed in cross-country running is inaccurately considered to improve specific endurance for all sports. Although such an assumption is valid for middle and long distance running, for other sports, cross-country running should be regarded just as a means of training for G.P.P. Therefore in order to obtain specific physiological development, stress should be obtained through training which is directly linked to the sports' technical, tactical and psychological sophistications. For cyclic sports the accomplishment of such a goal is quite simple. However, for sports with complex actions (team sports, gymnastics, throwing and jumping events) the above task is not easily achieved. In any case, a multiple repetition of parts or full routines, or phases of the game, may lead to the achievement of the same objective. Therefore, it appears that the selection of appropriate means of training is paramount to the final success. On the contrary, non-specific elements may lead to an erroneous specialization of the athlete's body development and consequently to an inadequate performance. If it is not directly linked to training it may hamper performance.

The accomplishment of S.P.P. requires a very high volume of training, which is possible only by lowering the intensity. By emphasizing the intensity without previous strengthening of the athlete's organs and systems, the CNS and entire body might be overstressed thus resulting in exhaustion, fatigue and injuries.

In such circumstances, the nerve cells, and for that matter the whole body, might reach a state of exhaustion thus decreasing the athlete's working capacity. Ozolin (1971) claims that athletes exposed to a medium intensity program were very successful in activities of long duration, displaying high physiological potential. Working potential may not be elevated unless both the volume and intensity of training are increased accordingly. However, since most athletes are involved in daily training lessons, the increase in training load should be influenced by the athlete's rate of recovery between lessons.

The performance of the skill under conditions similar to those of competitions also serves to increase S.P.P. However, the athletes may, especially in the late preparatory phase, participate in unofficial competitions without a special preparation for them.

The duration of S.P.P. may be between 2–4 months, depending on the characteristics of the sport and the competition schedule. As for long term planning, it could be organized for six months or even up to 1–2 years.

Perfection of Specific Biomotor Abilities

Although this phase prevails during the competitive period, the development of specific biomotor abilities may commence at the end of the preparatory phase. The general objective is to improve and perfect specific biomotor abilities and the athlete's potential to meet the specific needs of the chosen sport. The main means of training are derived from the sport performed and may be executed under increased load or decreased load conditions. In the first case, the strength or power is developed, while the latter enhances speed. The intensity of an exercise could be equal to the competition's requirement, slightly lower for the decreased load conditions, or slightly higher for exercises performed under increased load conditions.

The duration of this last phase of physical preparation varies according to the competition schedule. It is shorter for sports with a long competitive phase (soccer, hockey, and basketball) where time is a limiting factor, and longer for sports with a short competitive phase (cross-country skiing, figure skating). In the first case, the perfection of biomotor abilities is planned parallel with the basic training (at the end of the training lesson), while for the second it is realized at the end of the preparatory and beginning of the competitive phase.

Exercise as the Main Means of Physical Preparation

In the general framework of training, exercise is a motor act repeated systematically. Exercise represents the main means of training in order to increase the athlete's performance.

In both physical education and training there is a large number of exercises, varying from a narrow to a very complex effect. For example, simple two-foot take-off vertical jump with 180° rotation may be performed with the goal of developing leg power, but it will also enhance balance and space orientation. From the high number of exercises available, a coach should carefully choose those which will best fit the goals and maximize the highest rate of improvement.

Performing an exercise provides physical development and it also develops aesthetic and psychological traits (Bucher, 1972). Based on forms and structure, exercises can be classified into three categories: 1) exercises for general physical development; 2) specific exercises to develop biomotor abilities, and 3) exercises from the selected sport.

1. EXERCISES FOR GENERAL PHYSICAL DEVELOPMENT, also referred to as exercises with INDIRECT ACTION. These exercises contribute to the level of

physical preparation and are further divided into two groups based on their orientation and effects.

a) Exercises performed without implements (calisthenics) or with objects other than those used during competitions (stall bars, benches, skipping ropes, medicine balls). Such exercises should be performed by all athletes, especially those who lack a good general physical development. These exercises should be performed during the preparatory phase, and can also be included in the set of exercises performed during the competitive phase.

Longitudinal studies conducted in Germany (Harre, 1982) concluded that, although athletes who stressed special exercises only improved more quickly and at a younger age, the expected high level of performance was rarely accomplished. On the other hand, it was found that those athletes who, during their initiation phase used exercises designed to develop the general physical component, obtained their best results slightly later, but their highest performances were superior to those of the other group. Of great significance is the fact that those athletes from the latter group were also more consistent in their performance.

It also seems that individuals lacking the solid foundations of training based on general physical development exercises were prone to accidents more often and when they reached athletic maturation they infrequently continued to improve their performance. Using general physical development exercises also assists in improving coordination, and enhancing learning abilities. A multilateral technical instruction is relevant in sports that require complex motor coordination (gymnastics, diving, team sports, figure skating), where the acquired skills may have a positive transfer upon the new skill to be learned.

As far as the development of young athletes is concerned, a heavy amount of exercises may lead to injuries due to bones and ligaments not yet having matured. Therefore, exercises aiming at a general development appear to be most desirable. Such exercises are not only less demanding for the athlete's anatomical structure but following a normal progression they will also assist the athletes to strengthen their muscle and bones systems so that by the time they reach athletic maturity injuries will be less likely to occur. Exercises for general development are very beneficial to those sports which, because of climatic conditions (skiing, football, speed skating, rowing and rugby), can not be performed year round. Such exercises assist the athletes to develop a high level of physical preparation for the coming season of competitions.

b) Exercises derived from related sports, have to be chosen in accordance with the characteristics and needs of the sport in which the athlete has chosen to specialize. Quite frequently wrestlers play mini-soccer and basketball in order to develop general endurance, and speed and also for fun. Similarly, throwers playing volleyball and basketball, are involved in intensive weight training, and perform various bounding exercises. Their preparation is varied yet meets the needs of their events. Some athletes also partake in cross-country skiing and running. Running should be practiced by most athletes, since endurance is a fundamental ability from which all athletes may benefit. Some of the team sports (i.e. basketball) and certain gymnastic elements develop co-ordination which is much needed by each athlete, while exercises performed against resistance enhance strength. Other activities (swimming and diving) and sports/games (basketball, volleyball) are also encouraged in order to provide fun relaxation and active rest from the more intense and routine sport/event.

2. SPECIFIC EXERCISES TO DEVELOP BIOMOTOR ABILITIES, or exercises with DIRECT ACTION, serve to directly improve specific physical preparation. In addition to this, such exercises also enhance technical skills since they are similar to the technical pattern of a skill. During most of the training phases specific exercises ought to dominate since an exercise has a training effect proportional to the period of time used, and in accordance with its frequency of use.

Specific exercises should be directed toward the involvement of prime movers, which are "muscles that act directly to bring about a desired movement" (*Dorland's Dictionary,* 1974). However, a training program which incorporates specific exercises only fails to properly develop the synergistic muscles, or those which co-operate with prime movers to perform a motor act. Often in certain training programs the back and abdominal muscles are neglected, although they have an important contribution in many movements. In this case, a training program should introduce exercises for general development which have a compensatory effect.

Specific exercises ought to be selected to have a technical pattern and kinematic (motion) structure that is similar to movements that are essential to the performance of the selected sport. Both the specific and imitative exercises are of great benefit to the athlete's technical and to a lesser extent, physical improvement. This is explained through the idea that a strict repetition of a skill, for example spiking in volleyball, does not develop the physical abilities (i.e. leg power) to the extent which may be expected. The number of repetitions per training lesson can not reach the load required to develop higher degrees of power. Similarly, some of the best high jumpers in the world do not high jump more than 500–800 times per year (Dyachikov, 1960). Such a number of jumps would be insufficient to adequately develop leg power. Therefore, in order to overcome a slow rate of improvement, high jumpers perform tens of thousands of specific exercises aimed at developing leg power (i.e. leg press, bounding exercises, jumping over, on, and off benches, and depth jumping). The number of specific exercises per set preformed by elite class athletes might be extremely reduced (10–20) but each would be repeated a great number of times per year (50–60 thousands repetitions or even more).

Specific exercises are a very valuable means of training and play an important role in sports with high physical demands (speed, strength, power). They should be performed during the preparatory, but mostly during the competitive phase. Quite often some athletes tend to perform them during the preparatory phase only, excluding them from their set of exercises during the competitive phase. Research performed in Germany (Harre, 1982) concluded that this latter part is the reason why some athletes reach a good level of performance early in the competitive season but are unable to maintain that level until the main competition.

The complexity of special exercises can vary widely. The simpler and more elementary, as far as co-ordination and number of biomotor abilities involved are concerned, the more efficient and localized will be the action a specific exercise will have. For instance, a knee flexion could be used to develop joint flexibility, strength, speed and movement time.

Specific exercises may be used for the development of certain biomotor abilities, but also for the sake of skill acquisition. In the latter case the first priority will be on learning; by performing the same movement against a resistance, the resulting fatigue will positively affect learning (Singer et al 1972).

An effective method used to acquire a motor act or to improve a biomotor ability is the ideomotor (from the Greek idea and the Latin motor), or mental imagery method (Cratty, 1967). Research in this area goes back as far as 1853 when Faraday observed that a mental representation of a movement is followed by an involuntary, difficult to observe, muscular contraction. Later studies (Krestovnikov, 1938) confirmed that a mental representation of a known motor act or movement is paralleled by delicate physiological changes such as the elevation of nervous excitability, increase of the cardiorespiratory systems, and the intensification of the metabolic processes.

Ozolin (1971) suggests that a mental representation of an exercise, or portion of it, could be used as a method to improve an athlete's degree of training. In fact, during learning, performing an exercise does not occur without a mental representation of it. However, of much importance is the repetition of a skill prior to competition. This enables the athlete to repeat a dynamic stereotype (a well acquired movement is called a dynamic stereotype) such as the technique of performing the event, tactical maneuvers, a routine, or racing strategy, thus facilitating a better performance in the competition. Ozolin (1971) also claims that the ideomotor method may enhance the development of a biomotor ability-mental representation of a movement performed with high speed may assist the development of maximum speed. The ideomotor method may also be useful for the athlete to overcome certain mental barriers, to risk certain actions and to have courage, confidence, and willpower. It appears that ideomotor exertion, although still underutilized, may have some strong merits in training.

3. EXERCISES FROM THE SELECTED SPORT. This category includes all the elements and variants of movements specific to that sport, performed at various speeds, amplitudes and loads. These exercises may also be performed under unofficial competitive conditions, especially during the preparatory and pre-competitive phases, as the main means to improve the degree of training and to adapt the athlete to the specifics of a competition. If during training the coach could reproduce an environment similar to that of a competition (i.e. refereed games, or routines in gymnastics and figure skating), then such a method could create the link between the components of

training and could accelerate the athlete's physical, technical, tactical and psychological adjustment to the specifics of a competition. This method may be applied towards the end of the preparatory phase when the rhythm of increasing training stimuli will result in performance improvements. Similarly, this type of competition rehearsal may represent a valuable method to test the efficiency of different technical and tactical skills. Since such "house competitions" are unofficial, the difficulty of performing the skills could be increased or decreased (i.e. play on a smaller court to stress the speed of performing a skill or increase the reaction time; running on inclined fields, jumping with a heavy belt, swim or row against an artificial resistance, etc.).

TECHNICAL PREPARATION

One of the entities which discriminates between various kinds of sports is their specific motor structure. In fact, technique encompasses all the technical structures and elements incorporated in a precise and efficient movement through which the athlete attempts to perform an athletic task.

Technique may be considered as the specific manner of performing a physical exercise. It is the ensemble of procedures which, through their form and content, ensures and facilitates the performance of a bodily movement. In order to obtain a good result in sports, an athlete needs to have a perfect technique, namely the most efficient and rational performance of an exercise. The more perfect the technique the less the required energy to achieve a given result. Therefore, the following equation seems to express an athletic reality:

$$\text{Good technique} = \text{High efficiency}$$

Often the technique is regarded only as the form of a physical moment. But, the form always has to be innately linked with its content. Thus, every exercise has to be viewed from two angles: its form and its content. The content of an exercise is characterized through its scope, the activity of the CNS, volitional effort, muscle contraction or relaxation, its force and inertia.

Technique and Style

In every sport there must be a generally accepted standard of a perfect technique. This will be considered as a model which every coach/athlete should follow. In order that a model be widely accepted it has to be biomechanically sound and physiologically efficient. The technique of a champion rarely should be regarded as a model, since it does not always meet the above two conditions. Therefore, copying the technique of a winner is not advisable. The model should not be considered a rigid structure but rather a flexible one since recent findings should be consistently incorporated into it. However perfect a model may be, it is not always performed identically. Almost every individual imparts their own characteristics (styles) to the basic technique. The model to follow is called technique and the individual pattern of performing a skill represents the style. Thus the style is the distinction of one's individual pattern of performing a technical model. The main structure of the model is not changed. But instead the personality, character, anatomical and physiological traits of the athlete/coach is added.

The style should also be regarded as the result of an individual's imagination in solving a technical problem or manner of performing a motor act. For instance, in the early 1950's Perry O'Brien revolutionized the technique of shot putting by the backward-facing position and his original action across the circle. Initially this was considered as O'Brien's style, but later on when it was acclaimed and followed by all the athletes his style became a technique.

In team sports, a certain style of approaching and playing the game is also considered the attributes of a specific team. Therefore, the term 'style' has tactical implications as well as being suitable for utilization in both technical and tactical preparation.

The term 'technique' also incorporates two other expressions: technical elements and technical procedures. Technical elements refer to the fundamental parts which constitute the whole technique of a sport. On the other hand, technical procedures refer to various ways of performing a technical element. For instance, shooting in basketball represents a technical element. One hand, two hands, or hook shots are considered to be the technical procedures of that technical element.

Technique and Individualization

The model of a contemporary technique is not always accessible to every athlete beginning a sport. A novice involved in a certain sport or event should sometimes be introduced to a simplified technique. However simplified it may be, it always has to incorporate the basic elements of the most logical technique. Such basic, plain techniques must ultimately lead to the acquisition of the whole and correct technique. For instance, in a hammer throw a beginner is initially exposed to one turn only, and progressively as his/her ability improves, the coach may introduce an additional turn until the whole technique is learned. Therefore, youngsters' technique may, at least in some sports, be different from that of elite athletes.

Variations in performing a technique depend strictly on its complexity. The simpler the technique, the less the individual differences. Cyclic sports offer less individual differences than do acyclic or acyclic combined sports. The coach should always adapt a certain technique in accordance with each athlete's characteristics and abilities. The technique of a particular sport/event does not have to be automatically adopted as the only available variant.

When teaching a technical element or the whole technique, the coach should always take into consideration the athlete's level of physical preparation, since an inadequate physical preparation is a limiting factor in acquiring a skill. Variations in teaching a technique should be based on individual physical and psychological distinctions. As far as the role of physical preparation is concerned, Ozolin (1971) claims that as long as physical preparation is not improved, learning and especially the perfection of a skill, is limited. Such a reality must be considered especially in gymnastics, where coaches often attempt to teach their athletes difficult elements but fail to first develop the necessary strength. Therefore, figure 19 shows the reality that physical preparation is the foundation of all training factors.

It often happens that an athlete, for whatever reason (illness, accidents), is forced to interrupt his/her training. The discontinuation of training affects mostly the level of physical preparation. When training is resumed the athlete may happen to observe that his/her technique is slightly altered, or that he/she can not perform certain technical elements (i.e. sit spin in figure skating). Technical deterioration is usually found along with decline in physical preparation. When physical preparation reaches previous levels, technique should be re-established, thus technique is a function of physical preparation. Technical deterioration is also the result of fatigue, especially for athletes with a low physical preparation level.

Learning and Skill Formation

Learning is defined as the changes in one's behavior brought about through practice, or the changes in an individual's skill level as a result of repeated trials. Ability to learn depends on many factors: motor experience, or the initial learning level seems to affect learning (Cratty, 1967), as well as, the complexity of a skill (Lachman, 1965).

During learning concern should be placed with both of the following aspects of technique: 1. the external technique; the kinematic structure, or the form of the skill; and   2. the internal; the dynamic structure, or the physiological basis of performing a skill. Ozolin (1971) suggests that technique acquisition occurs in two phases: 1) the learning phase, where the task is to feature the technique, the correct structure of movements and to perform a skill without useless movement and effort. The duration of this phase is about 2 years, depending on the athlete's abilities and talent as well as the complexity of the skill involved (i.e. the technique of distance running can be acquired in 2-6 months); 2) the perfection phase, whose goal is to improve and master the technique at the highest possible level. The duration of this phase does not have a limit, since as long as an athlete is involved in training, one major objective will be the perfection of technique.

The acquisition of a skill does not occur at once, but rather through three phases (Krestovnikov, 1951):

1. During the first phase, on the basis of a poor neuro-muscular co-ordination, useless movements occur. A nervous irradiation, or the dispersion of nervous impulses beyond the normal path of conduction stimulates supplementary muscles. The coach should not misjudge the lack of neuro-muscular co-ordination as insufficient talent potential, but rather as a physiological reality;

2. The phase of tensed movements; and
3. The phase of establishing a motor skill through an adequate co-ordination of the nervous processes. Thus, the skill or the dynamic stereotype is formed.

In addition to the above three phases, a fourth one may be considered: the phase of mastery, characterized by performing fine movements with high efficiency, as well as the ability to adapt the performance of a skill to eventual environmental changes.

The acquisition of a skill is based on thousands of repetitions, which Thordike (1935) calls the law of exercise. Without an immense number of repetitions, the skill can not become automatized or reach a high level of technical stability.

The Evolutional Character of Technique

As a result of a coach's/athlete's continuous investigation of new moves, technique is in continuous evolution. What seems to be advanced today may be outdated tomorrow. The content and techniques of technical preparation never remain the same. Whether from the coach's imagination, a prominent source of technical novelties, or research in biomechanics of sports, all technical novelties ought to meet the concrete requirements of athletic competition. Therefore any technique has to become a "competitional technique," which implies that the technique must permanently be modeled to the specifics of competition. Since the competition's characteristics, rhythm and intensity, vary in accordance with the opponent's level of preparedness and with the environment, the athlete's technical model, the competitional technique, has to be adjusted accordingly. Thus technique should not be geared to what may be normal or ideal conditions only. The nature of technique ought to be developed in such a way that the athlete has the capability to adjust his/her performance to cope with the complex situations occurring in a competition. The improvement and perfection of technique also has to be dynamically linked to physical and psychological traits, since improvement in speed or, say, perseverance, may lead to slight technical modifications.

TACTICAL PREPARATION

Both of the terms 'tactics' and 'strategy' are important components of the coaches' and athletes' vocabulary. Although they are meant to refer to the same thing, namely the art of performing a skill in a competition with direct or indirect opponent(s), they signify a slightly different concept. Both terms are borrowed from the military dictionary and have a Greek origin. "Strategos" in Greek means general, or the art of the general, while "taktika" refers to the matters of arrangement. In the theory of warfare, strategy and tactics are separately categorized. Both terms have been given unique dimensions. Strategy focuses on wide spaces, long periods of time, and also large movements of forces. On the other hand, tactics refers to something on a smaller scale of space, time and force. Strategy basically precedes war planning, while tactics refers to the action of the battlefield itself.

In the field of training strategy refers to the general concept of organizing the play or competition of a team or athlete. It represents a characteristic, a specific philosophy or way of approaching athletic competitions. Such a fundamental concept is used for a long period of time, often longer than a competitive phase. On the other hand, the term tactics, refers to the plan used for a game or competition and it is an essential part of the general framework of a strategy. In daily language both terms are widely used, although a preference exists based on geographical locations. In North America strategy is preferred to tactics while in Eastern Europe the reverse is true. In any case, through strategy reference is made to the general art of projecting and directing the plans for a team or athlete for a whole season or even longer, while tactics is the attribute of organizing the plans of a team or athlete for a game or competition only.

Tactical preparation refers to the means through which the athletes absorb methods and possible ways of preparing and organizing offensive and defensive actions in order to fulfill an athletic objective (i.e. to score, achieve a certain performance, or obtain a victory). Tactical preparation may follow generally accepted theories but it is specific for each sport. All offensive and defensive actions taken by the athlete/team in a competition are to be performed according to tactical plans established prior to a competition. Such tactical actions ought to be part of the general framework of the athlete's strategy. During competition an athlete applies all his/her biomotor abilities and skills in accordance with the real, practical conditions met in a confrontation with an opponent(s). The basis of a successful tactical plan from any sport is a high level of technique. Thus, it may be correctly said that technique is a limiting factor for tactical maneuvers; or that tactics is a function of an athlete's technique.

The value and importance of tactical preparation is not the same for every sport. A mastery of tactics is one of the determinant factors of success in team sports, wrestling, boxing and fencing. The same may not be said about other sports such as gymnastics, figure skating, shooting, weight lifting, and ski jumping, where the athlete's psychological profile assumes a greater importance than tactical preparation.

The Tasks and Specificity of Tactical Preparation

In several sports, elite athletes have achieved almost equal technical and physical preparation. Often, when all other variables are equal, the victors are those who employ more mature and rational tactics. Although tactical preparation relies heavily on physical preparation and is also a function of technique, there is also an important link between psychological and tactical preparation.

Tactical mastery is founded also on deep theoretical knowledge and on the capacity to apply the tactics depending on the specifics of the competition. Tactical preparation may include the following tasks:

1. Study the general principles of the sport's strategy;
2. Study competition rules and regulations in the chosen sport/event;
3. Investigate and be aware of the tactical abilities of the best athlete(s) in the chosen sport;
4. Research the strategy of future opponents as well as their physical and psychological potential;
5. Study the specifics of the facilities and environment of the future competition;
6. Develop individual tactics for the up-coming competition, based on personal strengths and weaknesses, in light of No. 4 and 5 above;
7. Analyze past performances in view of future opponents;
8. Develop an individual tactical model with variations;
9. Learn and repeat this model in training until it becomes a dynamic stereotype.

The acquisition of a tactical maneuver follows the same principles as does the learning of a skill and based on a theoretical plan, multiple repetitions would lead to its acquirement. Since tactical preparation is a function of a good technique and physical preparation, a new tactical maneuver should be preceded by adequate physical and technical improvement. However, there is also the possibility that the above three training factors, supplemented with psychological preparation, may be developed simultaneously.

Tactical preparation, as a general principle, follows concepts and rules which are sometimes generalized to several sports. Based on the similarity of their tactical characteristics, sports can be classified into five groups:

Group 1 consists of those sports in which the athletes compete separately, with no direct contact. They follow a certain order which is drawn prior to the competition as is the case for alpine skiing, figure skating, gymnastics, diving, throwing and jumping events in track and field and, weight lifting.

Group 2 is identifiable through the fact that the athletes start the competition at the same time; be they all together or in smaller groups. Some co-operation with team mates is possible. The following sports are included in this group: running events in track and field, cross-country skiing (including relays), cycling, and swimming,

Group 3 is characterized by a direct contact with the opponent. The result of this bilateral contest is the determinant means of classifying the athletes. Sports incorporated in this group are tennis, boxing, wrestling and fencing.

Group 4 is composed of sports where the opponents are organized into teams, and the athletes have direct contact during the games: basketball, soccer, hockey, football, and rugby.

Group 5 is characterized through athletic participation in combined sports. The tactics in combined events are in fact composed of the tactics of each sport incorporated as well as the general plan of participation in competition. The following sports are members of group 5: heptathlon and decathlon in track and field, biathlon (shooting and cross-country skiing), and modern pentathlon.

The above classification facilitates a better and more comprehensive examination of sport tactics. It also simplifies the understanding of the subject matter by capitalizing on the fact that certain sports have similarities in their tactical approach. In many cases a strategy is designed to achieve one of, or a combination of the several objectives presented below:

1. The perfection of equal distribution of energy through a steady pace.

This may be achieved by applying the following methods: a) set specific training tasks leading to a uniform distribution of the athlete's potential. During such tasks, the athlete should defeat restricting (fatigue) or opposing factors. The capacity to maintain a steady velocity or rhythm is essential for a successful performance in some sports (especially for those of the second group of the sports classification), therefore it has to be part of tactical preparation for competition. The sense of speed, or the ability to feel the velocity which covers a certain distance, may be developed in training by using at first the stop watch, and then just the time called by the coach. b) Practice the finish, or the final part of a game/competition. Very often, especially in close races, games, or competitions, success depends strictly on the capacity to give everything, to mobilize all the forces for the final moment. This may be accomplished either by stressing the end of each repetition, or by having the coach announce the time left for performance. The coach's call may represent a stimulus for the athlete to intensify the rhythm or speed for the duration of the performance. c) Prolonging the duration of performance, either by informing the athletes prior to the commencement of the training lesson, or by a sudden decision made during training. d) Employ several rested, sparring partners during training which would force the athlete/team to constantly perform at a high level.

Method "a" is more suitable for sports from the 2nd and 4th group; method "b" for the first four groups; method "c" for the 2nd and 3rd group; and method "d" for groups 2-5.

2. The perfection of a variety of technical means to solve precise tactical tasks.

Often athletes have to perform under adverse, or unusual environmental conditions (wet field, strong wind, cold water, noisy spectators). Such special circumstances may be adapted by: a) performing skills and tactical maneuvers correctly and effectively under unusual circumstances. b) Organizing exhibition games/competitions with partners who follow the same tactics as the future opponents. c) Creating unique situations demanding tactical resolution for each athlete to solve independently using his/her creative potential. Athlete's tactical discipline is a very important requirement of training. However, often an athlete is exposed to tactical problems which were not foreseen by the coach. The athlete has to solve the tactical problem instantly, based strictly on his/her background, imagination and creativity. Therefore, during training and exhibition competitions the coach should expose the athlete to various situations so that each individual can enhance his/her creativity.

It is advisable that method "a" and "c" be generally considered for all five groups while method "b" is appropriate for the 3rd and 4th groups only.

3. Maximization of co-operation with teammates. Along with some of the above-mentioned methods, the coach may achieve a better co-operation among teammates by: a) Limiting external conditions (i.e. decreasing the available time and playing space). When a fatigue factor is added the athletes are exposed to more awkward circumstances which represent a superior challenge and stimulation; b) Performing various tactical maneuvers against a conventional opponent, who attempts to counteract the play. The opposing team or, during training the spare players, may facilitate such a situation. In either case, the opponents should behave as if they were not familiar with the applied tactical maneuvers. c) Periodically involving spare players in game tactics. Often the first string players co-ordinate their tactics successfully since they are accustomed to playing together. When some athletes are replaced by spare players because of illness, or fatigue, the game harmony suffers. Therefore, the coach should frequently involve and familiarize spare players with the team's tactical concepts. d) Developing new tactical combinations which improve and upgrade the team's competitive capabilities.

The above methods are suggested for sports from group 2 and 4.

4. The perfection of the team's ability to switch effectively from one system of play to another. This refers to either changing the play from defence to offence or vice-versa, or switching among various tactical maneuvers when playing offence or defence. It is expected that such tactical variation will surprise the opponents; therefore, the switch must occur quickly and smoothly. Variations to be considered include the following: a) Substitute different tactical maneuvers at a signal made by the coach or a designated player (game co-ordinator or captain). b) Substitute players who bring to the team new and unexpected game changes. c) Expose the team to exhibition games against teams who use various styles of play. This would prepare the athletes for similar tactical changes implemented by future opponents.

The first method is suitable for groups 2–5 while the last two methods are suitable for all five groups.

The Game Plan and Tactical Thinking

Tactical thinking is a fundamental component in any athlete's tactical preparation. It is limited by the athlete's tactical knowledge and multiple tactical skill repertoire. Tactical thinking encompasses the following abilities:

1. to realistically and correctly evaluate the opponent, as well as himself/herself;
2. to instantly recall tactical skills and combinations to be used under specific game situations;
3. to anticipate the opponent's tactics, and to counteract them;
4. to disguise or conceal tactics which should prevent the opponents from sensing and counteracting the plan of attack;
5. to co-ordinate perfectly individual actions with team tactics.

On the basis of all the details regarding future competition, the coach, together with the athlete(s), make the competition's game plan. Such a plan, which is part of the general tactical preparation, may be performed progressively over the last 2–3 micro-cycles. A good detailed plan, in which everything is foreseen, promotes optimism and a good psychological preparation for competition. The plan is the result of anticipation and mental preparation, based on previous information and predictions. The game/competition plan may serve the following purposes:

1. inform the athlete with regard to place, and specific facilities and conditions under which the contest will be organized;
2. know and analyze future opponent(s). The analysis should consider the strong and weak points for each training factor;
3. use the athlete's past performance as a reference to build up confidence. Without disregarding the athlete's weaknesses, stress the strong points on which a realistic optimism could be built;
4. utilizing all the above as a reference, set realistic objectives for the competitions.

As far as the game plan and tactical thoughts are concerned, they occur in the following three phases:

Preliminary planning of the game plan

This moment precedes the game and assumes a critical and reasonable analysis regarding the tactical difficulties which the team is likely to encounter. A selection of the appropriate means to solve all imagined problems depends on the team's tactical knowledge and skills. On the basis of a comprehensive analysis of both the opponent's and his/her own team's abilities, the coach should suggest the tactical plan and the appropriate tactical objectives. According to his/her team's general plan, the coach designates to each individual player his/her objectives in accordance with their abilities.

Of next essential importance is to select the proper system of play and to advise the athletes how to assess their energy effectively.

However accurate the plan may be during the game, many unperceived technical and tactical occurrences may take place. Therefore, the plan has to be flexible to allow the athletes to act with their abilities and imagination as the phase of the game requires.

During the last few days prior to the competition, if possible, changing the athlete's habits should be avoided so that he/she will not feel an adverse environment. Two to three days prior to the start of competition, details of the game plan should be reinforced. During all these days, attractive training lessons should be organized. A good performance of a skill/tactical maneuver should be handled by the coach in order to build the athlete's confidence, to motivate and to build up the desire to start the competition under optimal conditions. It is also important that relaxation training be employed following each training session in order to enhance a complete physical and mental regeneration prior to the competition's commencement. If possible, every single training lesson should follow the model of competition.

Hours prior to the start, remind the athletes of just the major point of the plan, in order to reinforce previously explained and trained details of the plan. Too many instructions may block the athletes' input (Vanek, 1971).

Before the start, the athletes are quiet and in a state of "operational silence" (Uhtomski, 1950; Bompa, 1970). At this point in time, the coach should not offer any additional advice since athletes are too excited to listen or pay attention to the comments. Even if they seem to listen to the coach, their attention is oriented towards the competition soon to start, and therefore, they are not receptive to additional advice.

The application of the game plan and its tactical objectives in the game situation

The second phase refers to the implementation of the general plan in a game situation. The beginning of the game (a match in boxing or wrestling) often commences with a short phase where the contenders test the main elements of the tactical plan. This indeed requires some experience in order to successfully unveil the opponents plan and to hide that of the home team. In addition, qualities such as initiative, shrewdness, and the ability to anticipate tactical thinking, are of great importance. During the game or match, the athletes have to solve a link from the chain of tactical elements which a team or individual employs. Puni (1974) inferred that an athlete's tactical objectives refer mostly to the knowledge of acting in each moment of the athletic dispute. The athlete has to:

1. comprehend the game's concrete circumstance, and
2. decide which tactical action to take in order to solve a problem. The comprehension of the game's concrete, specific circumstances means that the athlete, based on his/her tactical knowledge, attempts to anticipate the opponent's and teammate's tactical thoughts and intentions. Likewise, the athlete has to estimate other players' favorable and unfavorable positions in a given phase of the game, foresee how a certain phase of the game may evolve, and foresee its eventual repercussions. As a result of correct game comprehension, instinctively solving a given tactical circumstance is avoided, and selection of the most favorable tactical skill to solve a problem occurs. Players' tactical thought demonstrates many mental operations such as: analysis, synthesis (the combination of separate parts into a whole), comparison and generalization. During the game tactical thoughts are manifested through quick, simple, but significant gestures, or meaningful words.

The application and decision making process for the game plan is the result of a collaboration between an individual athlete and the rest of the team. Such co-ordination should lead to a rational, original, rapid, economical, and efficient solution to a difficult tactical problem.

The analysis of the game plan application

The third phase of the game plan is the analysis of its application which is done by the coach with the athletes' constructive contribution. The most appropriate time for this depends on the game outcome. If the result was favourable, the discussion may be planned for the beginning of the first training lesson. On the other hand, the analysis of an unsuccessful effort should occur 2-3 days later in order to reflect more realistically and critically upon the past performance, as well as allowing time to heal psychological wounds.

The analysis should dissect how the plan was made; how correctly the coach evaluated his/her own team's and the opponent's strengths and weaknesses; the individual roles in the whole tactical plan; and causes of the lack of success. The deeper the analysis, the more valuable the conclusions. However, at the end of the meeting the coach must come forth clear and reasonable but with a note of optimism, proposing a few tactical elements to be stressed in training in preparation of future opponents.

Perfecting Technique and Tactical Preparation: Some General Considerations

The mastery of both technique and strategy is a sport phenomenon in continual evolution. Methods discovered through experience and through researching new spheres represent a substantial contribution regarding the advancement of technical and tactical knowledge. The outcome of such explorations lead to an obvious elevation of athletic effectiveness in training and especially in competitions.

For sports in which very complex motor skills play an important role in performance (first and fourth groups) the following factors may be considered:

1. Create and establish an adequate model to match the efficient technique and strategy;
2. Disclose the directions and most effective ways of perfecting the mastery in both the technique and strategy;
3. Employ the most rational approach for the process of perfecting the technique and strategy, in order to produce the best model of achieving mastery in the field.

According to Teodorescu and Florescu (1971), the achievement of technical and strategical mastery should be based on establishing and employing the optimal relationship between the following three conflicting couples presented below:

1. INTEGRATION-DIFFERENTIATION. The process of learning or perfecting a skill as well as training an ability is a multistructural system. Through this system fulfillment of technical and strategical mastery is possible. Within this system is

unfolded an integration and differentiation process. Integration refers to combining in a whole the components or parts of a skill or tactical maneuver while differentiation concerns the analytical processing of each component of a skill or tactical element.

The classical approach in learning always emphasizes the progression method, whereby progression occurs from simple to complex technical or tactical elements. However, in the perfecting or mastery concept of a skill or tactical maneuver, the process is reversed. It starts from studying the complex components and their functions, leading to the tracing out and processing of the components and their connections which prevent the function of the whole system. In other words, if the multistructural process (the whole skill or tactical maneuver) does not work out properly, the skill or maneuver must be dissected into substructures (parts or functional subsystems). Each substructure should be examined and analyzed separately to discover the fault. If each subsystem works adequately, this means that the fault may be found in the connections of the subsystem (i.e. connective parts or two elements in a gymnastic routine or other sports skill). If after an analysis of these connections the fault remains unresolved, it may be necessary to further divide the subsystems until the underlying elements and the imperfection is reached. The methods of improvement should aim at the fault or weakest link.

The integration-differentiation processes may be applied to either perfecting a technical or tactical model, or to changing the model. Figure 21 illustrates the perfection of a skill through automation of the component parts (differentiation process)

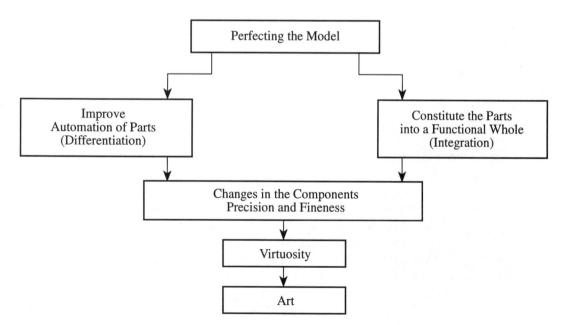

Figure 21. The perfecting model (modified from Teodorescu and Florescu, 1971).

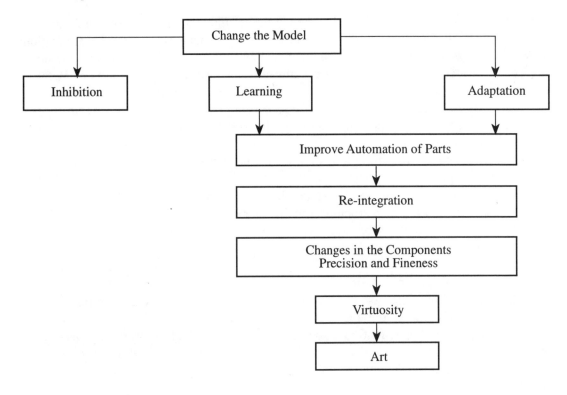

Figure 22. Changing an inefficient model (modified from Teodorescu and Florescu, 1971).

and resynthesis of the parts into a functional whole (integration process). The outcome of these two procedures will be materialized through changes in the accuracy and fineness of the components, which then would lead to virtuosity and to an art of skill performance.

When a technical skill or tactical maneuver is found to be insufficient the previously used model should be altered. Given this circumstance the coach should attempt to trace out why the mistake occurred (i.e. spiking outside of the court) and change useless components (figure 22). As explained above, the process of detecting a mistake is performed backward. The coach figures out that the ball was spiked outside of the court. Next he/she looks at the way the player hit and covered the ball. If this technical element is correctly performed, then the coach observes the airborne body position and the take-off place in respect to the net, to find out whether the athlete is under the ball. The coach decides that the player has a take-off fault. The player customarily took off from a place too close to the net, therefore he/she always was under the ball, restricting a proper cover of the ball, which, as a result, was sent outside of the court.

When changing the model, in order to assure that the coach does not restrict the acquisition of the new technical element it is necessary to inhibit the technical element which now appears to be useless. The inhibition of an incorrect distance for a take-off may be achieved by placing a tape on the floor which should be considered as a sign for an improved take-off. Consequently, as illustrated by figure 22, when changing a model the useless technical element is inhibited so the athlete can start to learn and adapt to the newly created condition. Then through training, the parts of the skill will become automatized (differentiation), re-integrated into a whole, which will result in a precise and fine skill, virtuosity and then art.

2. STABILITY-VARIABILITY. In sports there is an immense number of different types of movements, technical elements, and tactical schemes. Many of these movements and skills have to be employed in training in order to enhance variety, eliminate boredom and keep the athlete's interest up. The employment of a great variety of exercises, according to the needs of the selected sport, represents a solid background for the creation of new elements or tactical maneuvers. Variability, when used in training for either adaptation of the athlete to an exercise or skill, or compensation of an athlete's needs, stabilizes general skill and performance level. Furthermore, variability plays the role of blocking the factors which disturb this stability.

3. STANDARDIZATION-INDIVIDUALIZATION. The conflict between the standardization of a skill and the athlete's individual traits and characteristics is another conflict which has to be solved in training. Thus, the coach has to properly correlate the structure of a technical skill with each individual's psychological and biological particularities.

4. PHASES OF PERFECTING TECHNICAL AND TACTICAL PREPARATION. The process of perfecting the technique and tactics rests not only on the coach's knowledge and teaching abilities, but mostly on the athlete's abilities to acquire new elements. As far as the athlete's learning potential is concerned, the capacity to process new information is based on previous models and on individual biomotor abilities. The coach's explanation, the use of preparatory and progressive drills as well as audio-visual facilities should be considered as being effective tools in perfecting the athlete's skills.

The improvement of technical and tactical skills is achieved in three phases (Teodorescu and Florescu, 1971) as suggested by figure 23.

1. During the first phase the main objective is to perfect the components, parts and technical elements of a skill (differentiation). As each component becomes more refined, they should be progressively integrated into a whole system. Parallel with the perfection process, the dominant or the supporting biomotor abilities have to be perfected as well since technique is a function of physical preparation.

Since the main objective of the first phase is to perfect the skills, participation in competitions is unadvisable. This phase is suitable for the preparatory phase of the annual plan.

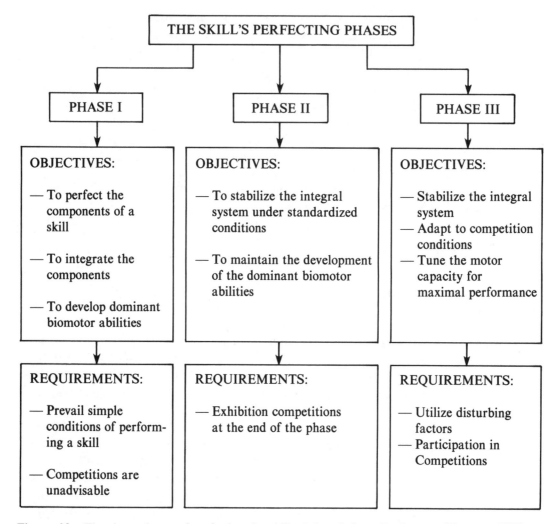

Figure 23. The three phases of perfecting the skills (adapted from Teodorescu, Florescu, 1971).

2. The main objective of the second phase is to perfect the integral system (whole skill) under relatively standardized conditions which are similar to a competition. Therefore, by the end of this phase participation may take place in exhibition competitions. The dominant biomotor abilities have to at least be maintained at the previously achieved level. The second phase of perfecting a skill may be planned for the end of the preparatory phase.

3. During the last phase aim should be at stabilizing the system and adapting it to the specifics of competition. Consequently, among other methods, the coach may expose the athletes/team to disturbing factors (noise, fatigue) to adjust them to actual competition circumstances.

The Correction of Technical and Tactical Errors

Very often an athlete's technical improvement or his/her mastery of a skill is delayed because of improper or incorrect learning. The elimination of a technical or tactical fault is every coach's goal. The quicker the athlete can correct a mistake, the faster the improvement. A fault which interferes with improvement could have several causes. Any mistake is the effect of a cause, and as far as technical or tactical faults are concerned, causes can be divided into three areas:

1. THE ATHLETE may be the cause of misperforming a skill. An athlete's learning limitations may result from the following causes:

a. Psychological limitation. The athlete sets low achievement goals, thus being satisfied with the level of skill acquisition.

b. An insufficient physical preparation or the lack of a good correlation between the level of biomotor abilities and the skill complexity and difficulty level. Since technique is a function of physical preparation, the acquisition of a skill may be slowed down, delayed or limited by an insufficient development of an ability. Co-ordination is a limiting factor in the acquisition of a skill as is strength in certain sports. For instance, a technical element in gymnastics may not be learned without an appropriate level of strength, therefore, technique may be restored as a result of physical improvement.

c. A misunderstanding or misrepresentation of the technical pattern of a skill as well as the correlation between movement, form, and muscular sensation (Teodorescu, 1975).

d. The interference of new skill acquisition with skills already acquired.

e. Fatigue, which may be caused by a poor physical preparation, or inadequate rest, may also limit learning abilities.

f. Incorrect handling or grasping of an implement, object, or apparatus.

g. And finally, there may also be morale or mental causes such as: lack of self-confidence, desire and fear of accidents or injuries.

2. THE COACH'S methodical approach, also may cause technical faults by:

a. Using inappropriate methods of teaching: the demonstration or explanation of a skill is inadequate, incomplete, or may even be incorrect.

b. The lack of appropriate individualization in teaching a skill by misunderstanding an athlete's level of biomotor abilities, individual learning capacities, or applying unsuitable teaching methods.

c. Using a random approach in developing a team's strategy, or including technical elements in a tactical maneuver.

d. The personality, behavior, coaching style, and his/her character (lack of patience with athletes, or pushing for quick skill acquisition).

3. ORGANIZATION, EQUIPMENT OR ENVIRONMENTAL CAUSES:

a. The use of poor quality equipment, apparatus, or surface of a field/court affects the quality and rate of skill improvement.

b. Improper training lesson organization, or planning does not represent an adequate learning arrangement.

c. A lack of individual training lesson plans for slow learners or athletes with incorrect technical or tactical skills will have a detrimental end effect on learning.

d. The adverse environment or climate may lead to impaired skill acquisition: unfriendly or cynical teammates, cold, windy weather, and waves (for rowing and canoeing).

METHODICAL RECOMMENDATIONS: Prior to this section, various means of perfecting the technique and strategy were discussed. However, additional methodical recommendations intended specifically for the correction of mistakes ought to be presented. Prior to exposing any methodical recommendations, it must be made known that the coach, through his/her teaching methods, should always be concerned with the idea of preventing a mistake which would eliminate the need for further efforts to correct it. If, for whatever reason this fails, then correcting a mistake should start as soon as possible. From the planning point of view, the ideal time to be concerned with an athlete's technical or tactical corrections is during the preparatory phase of the annual plan. Since the stress of competitions is absent, both the coach and athlete can dedicate some time in a quiet environment to correct certain faults.

Among the first measures to be taken for technical remedy is the isolation of the fault from the other technical elements of a skill. As soon as the athlete is no longer exposed to an inhibitory element such as a technical fault, the coach should begin to teach the athlete the element which will replace it. When the new part of the skill is acquired it should be integrated with the system or the whole skill. Concurrent with this, the biomotor ability which is needed as a physical support for the new element must be developed as well.

The correction of a mistake always should be performed immediately after the warm-up when the athlete is still fresh and thus in a position to concentrate on technical accumulation. Since fatigue may affect learning, the coach should avoid any such objectives towards the end of a lesson. If learning takes place in the body of the lesson, then the coach ought to allow a longer time for rest and regeneration between skill repetitions.

Mental practice, or rehearsal of the new element, may assist the athlete in his/her endeavors to correct a mistake. Also, as is the case in any other learning activity, audio-visual aids are of significant benefit in the process of technical corrections. And finally the repetition of a new element with a highly skilled athlete (i.e. in team sports) is another factor which allows for technical progress.

THEORETICAL PREPARATION

The concept that an athlete has to be trained not only practically but also theoretically is not yet widely agreed to, let alone used. Although they are rarely found today, there are still coaches who believe that they should think for their athlete. The athlete is there just to train and compete, the coach does the rest of it. Obviously, such a concept is not only ancient, but may also affect the athlete's rate of skill and performance improvement.

The acquisition and application of current theoretical knowledge in practice is not only an important means to accelerate the development of the athlete's skills and abilities, but also an important incentive for his/her motivation in training. Therefore, concurrent with skill and abilities development, a young athlete must be introduced progressively into the theory of training; to be exposed to everything that the coach knows about the selected sport. Certainly, the coach must be a knowledgeable individual who is concerned with his/her own education in the science of sports, and thus be one step ahead of his/her athletes.

All the scientific gains made by the coach should not represent a taboo or prohibited area for the athlete. On the contrary, the athlete should have access to the coach's expertise since the coach is the closest resource person for the athlete. This implies that the coach's responsibility is not restricted to training only, but extends to the athlete's general and sport specific education. Sharing knowledge with the athlete from the following areas may represent an adequate guideline for a coach:

1. Rules and regulations governing the selected sport.
2. The scientific basis for understanding and analyzing the technique of the sport involved. Biomechanics should be viewed as the science with the highest implications in both technical comprehension of a skill as well as in skill analysis. Sports such as gymnastics, throwing and jumping events in athletics, diving, and skiing have the most to gain from such knowledge. In addition, a correct understanding of the biomechanical bases of skill performance may aid in the elimination of injuries.
3. The scientific and methodical basis of the biomotor abilities development.
4. The planning concept in training. Reference should be made in the area of periodization of training, preparation for competition, and peaking.
5. Anatomical and physiological adaptation following training.
6. Causes, prevention and cure of injuries.
7. Sociology of sport (inter-group conflicts)
8. Sport psychology with emphasis on communication skills, behavior modification, stressors and how to cope with them, and relaxation techniques.
9. Nutrition and athletics—how it affects performance and the diet to follow in accordance with the phase and type of training, as well as pre-, during and post competition diets.

Among the means to be considered for the athlete's theoretical preparation are the following: discussions between the coach and athletes, film analysis, discussions with other athletes and coaches, clinics, relevant periodicals and other pertinent publications. However, of great importance in an athlete's theoretical preparation is the coach's explanation, and knowledge sharing process during each training session, pre and post-training discussions, and conversations while traveling or during camps.

Throughout his/her activities and involvements, the coach should strive to develop correct moral behavior, respect for other athletes, referees and the audience, as well as build a strong patriotic sentiment.

CHAPTER FOUR

The Components of Training

Any physical activity performed by an athlete leads to anatomical, physiological, biochemical, and psychological changes. The efficiency of a physical activity is a result of its: duration, distance, and number of repetitions (volume); load, and velocity (intensity); and the frequency of performance (density). When a coach plans the dynamics of training, he/she must consider the above aspects, which will be referred to as the components of training. All these components should be modeled in accordance with the functional and psychological characteristics of a competition. Throughout the training phases preceding a competition, the coach has to concretely define which of these components should be emphasized in order to achieve the planned performance objective. As a general rule, for sports requiring speed and power intensity is emphasized, while for endurance sports volume is emphasized. Finally, for those sports requiring intricate skills, the complexity of training is of prime importance.

All components of training ought to be increased in proportion with the athlete's overall improvement. The dynamics of such a balanced increase has to be carefully monitored not only throughout all phases of the annual plan but also during a players entire athletic career.

THE VOLUME OF TRAINING

As a prime component of training, volume is the quantitative prerequisite needed for high technical, tactical and especially physical achievements. The volume of training, which sometimes is inaccurately called the duration of training, incorporates the following integral parts:

1. the time or the duration of training;
2. distance covered or weight lifted per unit time ;
3. the number of repetitions of an exercise or technical element performed in a given time.

Thus, the notion of volume implies the total quantity of activity performed in training. Volume also refers to the sum of work performed during a training lesson or phase of training. When reference is made to the volume of a specific phase of training, the number of training lessons and the number of hours and days of work should be specified.

As an athlete becomes capable of high levels of performance, the overall volume of training becomes more important. As far as training for elite class athletes is concerned, there are no shortcuts regarding the high quantity of work which must be performed. A continuous increase in the volume of training is probably one of the highest priorities of contemporary training. A high volume of training has a clear physiological justification to the extent that physiological adaptation may not be achieved without it. An increased volume of work is paramount to the training for any sport/event which possesses any aerobic component. Similarly, the same increase is also necessary for any sports requiring the perfection of technical or tactical skills. Only a high number of repetitions may ensure the quantitative accumulation of skills necessary for quantitative improvements in performance.

An athlete's performance improves as a result of increasing the number of training lessons and increasing the amount of work accomplished during each lesson. This is true for all categories of sports. The recovery process is also accelerated as a result of the athlete's adjustment to an elevated quantity of work. It is obvious that the amount by which the volume of work is increased is a function of individual characteristics and specifics of the selected sport. For an elite class athlete to perform adequately, at least 8–12 training lessons per micro-cycle is necessary. There is also a high correlation between the volume of hours of training per year and the desired performance. Thus, an athlete expecting to place in the top twenty in the world has to perform over 1000 hours of training per year. Athletes to be entered in international meets ought to consider 800 hours, while national calibre athletes, require at least 600 hours of training. And finally, 400 hours of work may be planned if an adequate performance is designed in regional or state championships. However, too great an increase in the volume of work per training lesson can be harmful to the athlete. Harre (1982) suggests that such an unwise increase leads to fatigue, low efficiency in training, uneconomical muscular work, and an increased danger of injuries. Consequently, provided that the volume per training lesson is already sufficient, it is wiser to increase the number of training lessons per micro-cycle than the volume of work per lesson.

In order to accurately evaluate the volume of training, it is necessary to select a unit of measurement. For some sports (running, canoeing, cross-country skiing, and rowing) the appropriate unit seems to be space or distance covered during training. On the other hand, the load in kilograms (kg) seems to be appropriate for weight lifting, or weight training for strength improvement. However, time, which regulates other sports (boxing, wrestling, judo, gymnastics, team sports), seems to be a common denominator for most sports, although a coach has to often use two measuring units, time and distance, in order to express the volume more correctly (i.e. to run 12 km in 60 minutes).

In training two types of volumes may be calculated: 1. RELATIVE VOLUME refers to the total amount of time dedicated to training by a group of athletes/team during a specific training lesson or phase of training. The relative volume seldom has any value for an individual athlete, meaning that while the coach knows the total duration of training, he/she does not have any information regarding each individual athlete's volume of work per unit of time. 2. ABSOLUTE VOLUME is a measure of the amount of work performed by an individual athlete per unit of time, usually expressed in minutes.

The dynamics of the volume of training throughout the training phases varies according to the characteristics of the sport and its ergogenesis, the training objectives, the needs of the athlete and the calendar of competitions. Details on the dynamics of the volume of training are presented in Chapter Nine.

THE INTENSITY OF TRAINING

The intensity, along with the volume and density, is one of the most important components of training. It refers to the qualitative component of work performed in a given period of time. Thus, the more work performed per unit time, the higher the intensity. Intensity is a function of the strength of the nervous impulses employed in training; the strength of a stimulus depends on the load, speed of performing a movement, and the variation of intervals, or rest between repetitions. The last, but not least, important element of intensity is the psychological strain which accompanies an exercise. The intensity is determined not only by the muscular work but also by the CNS involvement during a performance in training or competition. It is very important to acknowledge the psychological element of an exercise, thus admitting that even sports requiring a low level of physical exertion (shooting, archery, chess) possess a component of intensity.

The degree of intensity can be measured in accordance with the type of exercise. Exercises involving speed are measured in meters/second (m/s), or the rate/minute of performing a movement. The intensity of activities performed against resistance can be measured in kg or kgm (a kg lifted 1 m against the force of gravity), while for team sports the rhythm of the game determines the intensity.

The intensity of an exercise varies in accordance with the specifics of the sport. Since the level of intensity varies in almost every sport/event, it is advisable to establish and use varying degrees of intensity in training. There are several methods available to measure the strength of the stimuli and, thus, the intensity. For example, for exercises performed against resistance, or exercises developing high velocity, a percentage of the maximum intensity is employed, where 100% represents best performance. But, for example, in a 100 m dash, best performance signifies the mean velocity developed over that distance (i.e. 10 m/s). The same athlete though, over a shorter distance, may generate a higher velocity (i.e. 10.2 m/s). Therefore, this velocity should be regarded as 105% of maximum and is included in the table of intensities (table 5). As for exercises performed against resistance, 105% represents a load that the athlete cannot move through the whole range of movement but that may be attained isometrically. According to this classification of intensities, a distance runner (i.e. 5,000 or 10,000 m) may even train at 125% or more of the maximum since his/ her maximum is considered to be his/her race pace.

Table 5. The scale of intensities proposed for speed and strength exercises (with additions, from Harre, 1982).

Intensity Number	Percentage of the Maximum Performance	Intensity
1	30–50%	Low
2	50–70%	Intermediate
3	70–80%	Medium
4	80–90%	Submaximum
5	90–100%	Maximum
6	100–105%	Supermaximum

An alternative method of evaluating intensity is based on the energy system used to fuel the activity. This classification (Farfel, 1960, Astrand and Saltin, 1961, Margaria et al., 1963 and Matthews and Fox, 1971) is most appropriate for cyclic sports (table 6).

Table 6. The five zones of intensities for cyclic sports.

Zone No.	Duration of Work	Level of Intensity	System producing the energy for work	Ergogenesis %	
				Anaerobic	Aerobic
1	1–15 sec	Up to maximum limits	ATP-CP	100–95	0–5
2	15–60 sec	Maximum	ATP-CP and LA	90–80	10–20
3	1–6 min	Sub-maximum	LA +aerobic	70-(40-30)	30-(60-70)
4	6–30 min	Medium	Aerobic	(40-30)-10	(60-70)-90
5	over 30 min	Low	Aerobic	5	95

ZONE ONE of intensity places a strong demand on the athlete to reach higher limits. It is comprised of activities of short duration, up to 15 seconds. These activities are extremely intense, as demonstrated by a very high frequency of movement and a high mobility of the information reaching the CNS. The short duration of activity does not allow the autonomic nervous system (ANS) to adapt, thus the cardio-vascular systems do not have enough time to adjust to meet the physical challenge. The physical demand for the sports specific to this zone (i.e. 100 m dash) requires a high flow of O_2 which cannot be provided by the human body. According to Gandelsman and Smirnov (1970), during a 100 m dash the O_2 demand is 66–80 litres/minute, and since the O_2 stored in the tissue does not meet the athlete's needs, he/she may encounter an O_2 debt up to 80–90% of the O_2 necessary for a fast race. This O_2 debt is "repaid" by extra utilization of O_2 after the activity has been concluded in order to allow replenishment of ATP-CP stores that were used during the race. The continuation of such a demanding activity may be limited by the O_2 supply within the athlete and the amount of ATP-CP that is stored within the muscle cells as well as the ability to withstand a high O_2 debt.

ZONE TWO or the maximum zone of intensity includes activities performed between 15–60 seconds (i.e. 200 and 400 m run, 100 m swim). The velocity and intensity is maximum, placing an enormous strain upon the CNS and locomotor systems, which diminishes the ability to maintain a high velocity longer than 60 seconds. The energetic exchanges within the muscle cells reach extremely high levels, yet the cardio-respiratory system does not have sufficient time to react to the stimulus and is, therefore, still operating at quite a low level. This characteristic causes the athlete to encounter an O_2 debt of up to 60–70% of the actual energy requirements of the race. Energy is derived predominantly from the ATP-CP system with a low lactic acid (LA) component. The O_2 system does not contribute significantly to the energy requirement since it is employed primarily during exercises of 60 second duration or more. It is also significant to mention that energy demands for one of the events included in this zone, the 400 m run, is among the highest.

ZONE THREE, also called the submaximum zone, incorporates those activities which last between 1–6 minutes, where both speed and endurance play dominant roles in athletic success (i.e., 400 m swim, canoeing, rowing, 1500 m run, and 100–3000 m speed skating.) The extremely complex activity of these sports, with drastic physiological changes (i.e., a heart rate of up to 200 bpm and a maximum blood pressure of around 100 mm Hg), hardly may be prolonged more than 6 minutes. Following a race of such a duration and intensity the athlete may compile an O_2 debt of 20 litre/minute and the LA may be up to 250 mg (Gandelsman and Smirnov, 1970). Under such circumstances, the athlete reaches a state of acidosis where it accumulates much more LA than the normal balance (pH7).

The athlete adjusts to the rhythm of the race very quickly, especially for the well-trained athletes. Following the first minute of the race, the O_2 system assists in producing energy while it dominates during the second part of the race. At the end of a race, the athlete accelerates the pace. This extra strain placed upon the athletes uses the circulatory and respiratory compensating mechanisms to physiological limits. This acceleration also demands maximum energy production from anaerobic glycolysis as well as the aerobic system, resulting in the athlete encountering high O_2 debt. Both the LA and aerobic systems are called upon to produce the required energy for the performer, with the percentages of each depending (within the bounds defined) on the event/sport it falls into.

ZONE FOUR, or the medium intensity zone, represents a high challenge for the athletes body since it is exposed to activity for up to 30 minutes. Sports/ events such as 800 and 1500 m swim, 5,000 and 10,000 m run, cross country skiing, walking and longer distance events in speed skating are among those incorporated in this zone. The circulatory system is considerably accelerated and the cardiac muscle is exposed to stress over a prolonged period of time. During the race the blood O_2 saturation is in deficit (hypoxia), or 10-16% below the resting level (Gandelsman and Smirnov, 1970). The aerobic energy system is dominant (up to 90%) although at the beginning and finish of the race athletes use the anaerobic system as well. Pacing and therefore even energy distribution throughout the race is an important requirement for athletes involved in races of such a duration.

ZONE FIVE includes activities where the intensity is low but the volume of energy expenditures is great, as in marathon running, 50 km cross-country skiing, 20 and 50 km walking, and road racing in cycling. This zone represents a difficult test for the athlete. The extension of work leads to the depletion of glucides (hypoglycemia) in the blood stream which is a burden for the CNS. The circulatory system is in high demand and heart hypertrophy (a functional enlargement of the heart) is a common characteristic and a functional necessity for athletes competing in the above sports/ events. Likewise, these athletes have a high ability to adapt to hypoxia and following a race they experience a blood O_2 saturation which often is between 10-14% below resting level (Gandelsman and Smirnov, 1970). Because of the high and prolonged demand on the athlete's functions, the recovery is very slow, sometimes taking up to 2-3 weeks which is one of the reasons why these athletes do not take part in many races (3-5) per year.

For the second and even for the third zone of intensity, the perfection of aerobic endurance, uniform distribution of energy, and the sense of self assessment of the abilities throughout the entire race appear to be among the determining factors of success. The physiological nature of self assessment depends on the perfection of the function of sensory organs (specialized part of the nervous system which controls the organism's reaction to the external environment) and therefore the development of so called time, water, track, ball or implement sense. Time sense is derived from rhythmical impulses coming from the proprioceptors of the muscles and tendons, which are repeated at different time intervals. Experienced athletes (i.e. boxers, runners, swimmers) develop, based on the muscle's sensors, a sense of the time remaining in a round, split times or the time performed in a race. All these senses, together with the sense of fatigue, represent information for the athlete regarding his/her body's state, thus assisting in the adaptation to the training/race session and external environment.

During training, athletes are exposed to various levels of intensity. The body adapts to the level of intensity by increasing physiological functions to meet the training demand. Based on these physiological changes, especially heart rate (HR) the coach may detect and monitor the intensity of a training program. A final classification of intensities, on the basis of HR, is suggested in table7 (Nikiforov,1974).

Table 7. The four zones of intensity based on HR reactions to training load (Nikiforov, 1974).

Zone	Type of Intensity	Heart Rate/Min
1	Low	120–150
2	Medium	150–170
3	High	170–185
4	Maximum	>185

In order to develop certain biomotor abilities, the intensity of a stimulus has to reach or exceed a threshold level beyond which significant training gains take place. Hettinger (1966) revealed that, for strength training, intensities below 30% of one's maximum do not provide a training effect. Similarly, for sports where endurance is a dominant factor (cross-country skiing, running, rowing, swimming), the threshold HR beyond which the cardio-respiratory system will experience a training effect is suspected to be 130 bpm (Harre, 1982). This threshold is subject to a certain amount of variation from athlete to athlete due to individual differences, thus Karvonen et al (1957) proposed that it should be determined by the sum of the resting heart rate plus 60% of the difference between maximum and resting heart rates.

$$HR_{threshhold} = HR_{rest} + .60(HR_{max} - HR_{rest})$$

Thus, the threshold HR is dependent upon the resting and the maximum HR. Furthermore, Teodorescu (1975) advocates that an athlete should employ stimuli in excess of 60% of his/her maximum capacity in order to achieve a training effect.

The employment in training of lower level loads or exercises leads to a relatively slow rate of development, but ensures sufficient adaptation and thus consistency of performance. On the other hand, high intensity exercises results in quick progress but also leads to less stable adaptations and therefore, a lower degree of consistency. This should lead to the conclusion that the use of highly intensive exercises only is not the most effective way to train. Thus, the alternation of volume and intensity of training is necessary. The high volume of relatively low intensity training experienced during the preparatory phase provides a foundation for high intensity training and serves to enhance performance consistency as well.

In the area of the theory of training, there are two types of intensities: 1) the absolute intensity, which is a measure of the percentage of one's maximum necessary to perform the exercise; and 2) relative intensity, which measures the intensity of a training lesson or micro-cycle, given the absolute intensity and the total volume of work performed in that period. The higher the absolute intensity the lower the volume of work for any given training lesson. In other words, exercises of high absolute intensity (>85% of maximum) may not be repeated extensively in a training lesson. Similarly, such training lessons should comprise not more than 40% of the total lessons per microcycle with the remaining lessons employing a lower absolute intensity.

The Relationship between Volume and Intensity

When an athlete performs an exercise, it usually involves both the components of quantity, and quality, therefore it is quite difficult to differentiate between them in training. For instance, when a swimmer performs a sprint, the distance and time duration of the event represent measures of the volume component, while the velocity of performance is an indicator of the intensity. Placing different relative emphasis on these components in training yields different effects upon the body's adaptation and training status. The higher the intensity and the longer it is maintained, the higher the energy requirements, and the higher the stress placed upon the CNS and athlete's psychological sphere.

Running long distances may be possible provided that the intensity is low, but may not maintain maximum velocity for a distance in excess of the competition distance. Decreasing a sprinter's intensity of training by 40% may allow the volume of work to be increased by about 400–500%; thus it appears that the efficiency with which work of a reduced intensity can be performed may facilitate a very substantial elevation of the volume of work (i.e. number of repetitions). Of course, such a drastic increase in the volume capacity would not prevail for an endurance athlete (long distance runner, skier, swimmer) when the intensity is decreased from his/her maximum because his/her maximum intensity scores low on the absolute scale to begin with. Rather, this 40% decrease in intensity must be measured from the highest supermaximum load the athlete can handle in order to facilitate an equivalent (400–500%) increase in the volume.

Ozolin (1971) exemplifies accurately the relationship between the volume and intensity of training over a period of one year, for sports with varied intensity requirements. Thus, high jumpers spend approximately 2 hours on jumps with a full approach; pole vaulters 3 hours, triple jumpers 10–12 minutes, gymnasts (high bar combinations) 6 hours, and long distance runners 70–100 hours (for repetitions close to the competition's speed). The remaining time is dedicated to other exercises leading to the development of the abilities required by that particular event. A completely different approach may be used for team sports, boxing, wrestling and martial arts, where a standard duration of competition determines the relationships between volume and intensity.

The determination of the optimal combination of volume and intensity is a very complex task and usually depends on the specifics of the sport. This operation is relatively simplified in sports where there are objective methods of assessment. For instance, in canoeing the volume is based on the distance covered in training while the intensity expressed by the velocity at which a given distance is performed. When reference is made to other kinds of sports such as team sports, gymnastics and fencing, the total number of actions, elements, repetitions, their distance and the speed with which they are performed, are just some elements to be considered in defining the accurate proportions between the components of training. However, very often the duration of a training lesson or the number of repetitions of certain skills, is the basic tool used to calculate the volume of training. Although not accessible to most coaches, the computation of the energy expenditure may be a more accurate method of assessing the weight placed upon either the volume or intensity.

Very often, as has already been specified, the HR may be used as an indicator of the level of work. However, while this method may suffice the needs of beginners, the elite category of athletes may not benefit as much from it since training involves all body functions and changes in the HR is just one of the many body reactions to work. Therefore, the use of HR as the only method may restrict some athletes from employing the optimum training stimuli, and, as a consequence, may affect the rate of improvement. However, the HR used as a method of assessing the rate of recover between training lessons may be of more assistance in estimating the work and the athlete's reaction to it.

The Dynamics of Increasing the Volume and Intensity

The amount of work performed presently by international class athletes was not conceivable a decade ago. Eight to twelve or even more training lessons per week of 2–4 hours each is considered to be normal. As far as the additional amount of work is concerned, most coaches are concerned with means and ways of maximizing the athlete's free time for training purposes. As was suggested in the chapter referring to the principles of training, the addition of the components of training has to be made progressively and on an individual basis. Training sessions are to be elevated in steps. A session which was optimal in a given cycle of training may be inadequate in the following one since its level of intensity may not reach the threshold and this may not provoke the required training effects. An optimal session produces an optimal body adaptation. Thus, an optimal session has to be related to the index of effort capacity, otherwise the session may be either too weak or too powerful. The index of effort capacity is accumulated, in qualitative steps as a result of quantitative accumulations of work done and the athlete's adaptation to it. Therefore, during training, the athlete's adaptation and the index of work capacity are increased periodically in steps, and not in a continuous straight line. On the basis of such a reality, it seems that one of the coach's attributes has to be a great deal of patience, to wait for the expected improvement to result from his/her training program.

The intensity of training may be increased in a number of ways:

1. increasing the velocity of covering a given distance, or elevating the load;
2. increasing the ratio between absolute and relative intensity, so that absolute intensity may prevail;
3. decreasing the rest intervals between repetitions or sets;
4. increasing the density of training; and
5. increasing the number of competitions.

On the other hand, the volume could be increased by:

1. prolonging the duration of a training lesson;
2. increasing the number of lessons per training cycle;
3. extending the number of repetitions of a given distance; and
4. by increasing the distance covered in each repetition of training.

The dynamics of intensity employed in training depends on the three factors presented below:

1. THE CHARACTERISTICS OF THE SELECTED SPORT dictate the intensity level of training. For sports where the athlete's performance is determined by maximum efforts (weight lifting, throwing, jumping events, and sprinting), the intensity level during the competition phase is usually very high for between 70-100% of the total amount of work in training. For sports where the performance is defined by mastery of skills (figure skating, diving, synchronized swimming) high intensity is rarely employed. According to Ozolin (1971), the average intensity used in such sports is of a medium level. On the other hand, the intensity of training in team sports is very complex since the rhythm of the game is very fast while the intensity alters continually between low and maximum. Therefore in order to meet such requirements, a training program should include some high but also a continuous variety of intensities.

2. THE TRAINING ENVIRONMENT is demanding on the athlete, and therefore affects the intensity. Consequently, a wet snow in cross-country skiing, running on sand or uphill, or dragging an object which slows down a swimmer's or rower's velocity are just a few examples of how the intensity of training can be increased. Rivalry between athletes, or the presence of spectators may elevate the intensity as well.

3. PREPARATION AND THE ATHLETE'S LEVEL OF PERFORMANCE. The same content of training used for athletes of various levels of preparation or performance capabilities may represent a different level of intensity for each. What may be

Table 8.   The HR value of 10 of the exercises used in a boxer's training.

No	Exercise	HR/Min
1	Jogging and calisthenics	110
2	Specific warm-up exercises	120
3	Shadow boxing with moderate intensity	120
4	Shadow boxing	140
5	Repetitions of technical elements	120
6	Rope jumping	170
7	Exercises at boxing bag	170
8	30 sec. repetitions at the boxing bag	190
9	Simple tumbling and flexibility	140
10	Cooling down exercises	80

medium intensity for an elite class athlete, may represent maximum intensity for a prospective athlete. Although athletes of various levels of preparation may train together, the coach's training program must be different in order to meet each athlete's needs.

The elevation of intensity in training may be achieved by either increasing the intensity during a lesson or phase of training, or by increasing the density of a training lesson. Obviously the first mode should be highlighted since it increases the individual's potential in accordance with the specifics of the selected sport or event. The second method should be employed mainly when the coach seeks to increase the total means of training, aiming at developing intensity, general physical preparation, or cultivating specific endurance.

As suggested above, the HR method may often be of assistance in calculating the intensity of training. A coach, by employing the HR method as an objective measure of the athlete's reaction to a stimulus, may be able to compute the overall intensity (OI) in training as an expression of the total demand to which an individual is exposed during a lesson. The OI may be calculated by using the following equation proposed by Iliuta and Dumitrescu (1978):

$$OI = \frac{\Sigma(PI \cdot VE)}{\Sigma(VE)}$$

where PI stands for percentage of partial intensity and VE for the volume of exercises. However, since the percentage of partial intensity must be calculated first, the following equation may be employed:

$$PI = \frac{HR_p \cdot 100}{HR_{max}}$$

where HRp represents the heart rate resulting from the performance of the exercise of which partial intensity has to be calculated, and the HRmax stands for the maximum heart rate achieved by a given athlete in performing the sport (for boxing, which is shown below, it is considered to be 200 bpm).

The calculation of both the PI and OI is shown in the following example from boxing (Iliuta and Dumitrescu, 1978). At first, the heart rates of each exercise performed in training is calculated, which is presented in table 8.

Then the PI is calculated for each exercise separately by applying the above equation. Example for this first exercise:

$$PI = \frac{110 \cdot 100}{200} = 55\%$$

Thus the partial intensity for jogging and calisthenics is 55%. Below (table 9) are the PI's for each of the above 10 exercises which are then multiplied by the number of repetitions or volume of exercise (VE) performed in training for the particular exercise. The right-hand side column represents the product of the partial intensity times the volume of each exercise.

Therefore, substituting the above data into the OI equation will find that:

$$OI = \frac{4910}{77} = 63.8\%$$

Table 9.   Percentage of partial intensity for the 10 boxing exercises.

Exercise No.	PI	VE	PI . VE
1	55%	25	1375
2	60%	5	300
3	60%	5	300
4	70%	6	420
5	60%	5	300
6	85%	6	510
7	85%	2	170
8	95%	3	285
9	70%	15	1050
10	40%	5	200
		$\sum = 77$	$\sum = 4910$

This signifies that the hypothetical boxer performs at an overall level of intensity of 63.8% which, according to the above scale of intensities (table 4), is just an intermediate intensity.

The dynamics of volume and intensity is also a function of the dominant biomotor ability in a given sport. For sports where the dominant ability is either speed or strength, intensity must be emphasized to attain progress, especially during the competitive phase. On the other hand, for sports where endurance is the dominant biomotor ability, volume represents the main element of progression in a given phase, intensity plays a much lesser role. Thus, it appears that volume and intensity are inversely proportional. The intensity increases only as volume decreases.

As far as the content of training is concerned, a high, absolute intensity should prevail for those exercises with duration of less than two minutes. At the zone of two minutes the ratio between the anaerobic and aerobic energy systems is equal or 50:50 (Astrand and Rodahl, 1970). This means that for sports which last approximately two minutes, the volume and intensity should be equally stressed. However, the importance of the aerobic energy system is evident even in the first minute of a race (Mader and Hollman, 1977). Therefore, sports which have a duration of less than two minutes still require some emphasis on volume of training, especially during the preparatory, and early competitive phases. Over the two minute zone, aerobic power is evidently dominant; therefore, for sports which last longer than two minutes, volume of training should be emphasized. The volume and intensity of training are further discussed in the planning section (the annual plan).

Improvement of the Training State through Rating the Volume and Intensity

The human body adapts and improves in direct relationship to the type of stimuli to which it is exposed. The work performed in training is considered to be the cause, while the body adaptation is the effect. The optimal stimuli results in an optimal training effect. In order to achieve an optimal training effect, training programs which are specific to the sport and which are prescribed in an appropriate dose need to be planned. The quantity of work to be performed in a training lesson must be set in accordance with individual abilities, the phase of training, and a correct ratio between the volume and intensity of training. Therefore, if the training dosage is properly administered, a correct athletic development will result, leading to an adequate degree of training (the physical and psychological level in a given phase of training). In training there are two forms of dosage; external and internal (Harre, 1982).

The EXTERNAL dosage is a function of the volume and intensity training. In order to construct a correct training program, there is a need for a correct assessment of the intimate characteristics of the external rating which has the following components: volume, intensity, density, and frequency of stimuli. Since all these components are easy to measure they can easily be rated. The external dosage usually elicits a physical and psychological reaction from the athlete. The physical and psychological reaction which the individual displays is known as the INTERNAL dosage, and it expresses the degree and magnitude of fatigue which the athlete experiences in training. The size and intensity of the internal dosage is affected by each component of the external dosage.

When planning the external dosage, applying the same dosage does not always produce similar internal reactions. Furthermore, since the internal dosage is a function of the individual's athletic potential, its reaction can be estimated in general terms only. However, an adequate training diary and periodic testing may facilitate a reading of the internal reaction. The external dosage may be affected by circumstances such as the athlete's degree of training, the opponent's athletic calibre, equipment, facilities, environmental conditions and social factors.

The Relationship between Volume and Adaptation

The application and correct dosage of training sessions results in several anatomical, physiological and psychological changes in the athlete. The positive changes which occur following a systematic training are regarded as the individual's adaptation to various stimuli. There is a high correlation between the process of adaptation and the dosage in training.

The adaptability processes occur only when the stimuli reach an intensity proportional to the individual's threshold capacity (Harre, 1982). A high volume of work without a minimal intensity (for example below 30% of one's maximum) does not facilitate body adaptation since a higher level of intensity is required to initiate such adaptation. It is possible, however, to exceed the "optimal" level of stimulation by demanding too much work from the athlete or by miscalculating the volume—intensity ratio in which case the process of adaptation decreases, leading to performance stagnation or even regression. The adaptation process is the result of a correct alternation between stimulation and regeneration, between work and rest.

The process of an adequate adaptation to training and competitions facilitates the increase of the athlete's degree of training, correct peaking, and improvement in the athlete's physical and psychological capacities. The effects of a standard dosage and stimulus diminishes after a while, resulting in modest performance. Therefore, the external dosage should be increased periodically (as suggested by the principle of progressive increase of the load in training). Furthermore, if the stimulus is reduced, the training effect is diminished resulting in an involution phase. The benefits of training may also be reduced if the interruption of training is too long. For instance, if the transition phase is too long, or if it is comprised totally of passive as opposed to active rest, all the improvements obtained from the preparatory and competitive phases disappear, requiring the athlete to start training for the next preparatory phase at a very low level.

THE DENSITY OF TRAINING

The frequency at which an athlete is exposed to a series of stimuli per unit of time is called the density of training. The term, density, refers to the relation expressed in time between working and recovery phases of training. An adequate density insures the efficiency of training, thus preventing the athletes from reaching a state of critical fatigue or even exhaustion. A balanced density may also lead to the achievement of an optimal ratio between training sessions and recovery.

The rest interval planned between two training sessions depends directly on the intensity and duration of each session, although factors such as the athlete's training status, the phase of training and the specifics of the sport may also be considered. Sessions above the submaximum level of intensity require relatively long rest intervals in order to facilitate recovery prior to the following session. On the other hand, sessions of lower intensities require less time for recovery since the demand placed upon the athlete is lower.

An objective way which may be used to calculate the required rest intervals is the HR method. Harre (1982) and Herberger (1977) suggest that prior to applying a new session, the HR should slow down to 120–140 bpm. Harre (1982) on the other hand proposes an optimal density ratio between work and rest. For the development of endurance, the optimal density is between 2:1—1:1, where the first digit refers to the working time and the second to the rest interval. Thus, a ratio of 2:1 means that the rest interval endures for half as long as the work interval. Furthermore, for the development of endurance, when employing highly intensive stimuli, the density is 1:3—1:6. Thus, the rest interval may be between 3–6 times the duration of the work interval. For strength training, especially for programs dedicated to developing maximum strength or power, the rest interval is indicated to be between 2–5 minutes depending on the percentage of load and the rhythm of performance.

Density may also be computed by using other parameters. Thus relative density (RD), which refers to the percentage of the volume of work performed by an athlete as compared to the total volume per training lesson may be calculated by employing the equation:

$$RD = \frac{AV \cdot 100}{RV}$$

Where AV stands for absolute volume (please refer to the volume of training), or the volume of training performed by a individual, and RV refers to the relative volume or the duration of a training lesson. For example, let AV be 102 minutes and RV be 120, or two hours of training for the hypothetical boxer discussed earlier in this section. Substituting these two figures in the above equation will find that:

$$RD = \frac{102 \cdot 100}{120} = 85\%$$

The above percentage suggests that the athlete has an RD of 85% or that the athlete worked only 85% of the time he/she was supposed to. Although the RD has certain significance for both the coach and the athlete, of higher importance is the absolute density (AD) of an athlete's training. AD is considered to be the ratio between the effective work performed by an athlete and the AV. The effective work performed by an athlete is found by subtracting the volume of rest intervals (VRI) for the lesson from AV. The following simple equation would assist the coach to figure the AD:

$$AD = \frac{(AV - VRI)\,100}{AV}$$

Let VRI be 26 minutes, and AV 102 minutes, a figure which was already used above. By substituting these figures into the formula the results will be:

$$AD = \frac{(102 - 26)\,100}{102} = 74.5\%$$

Thus, our hypothetical athlete has an AD of 74.5%. Since density of training is considered to be a factor of intensity, the above index of absolute density is of medium intensity (please refer to the above scale of intensities). The reader may agree that the above approach can assist a coach in conducting effective training lessons, especially for some sports such as gymnastics where the density of training is often unsatisfactory.

THE COMPLEXITY OF TRAINING

Complexity refers to the degree of sophistication of an exercise employed in training. The complexity of a skill, its co-ordination demand, could be an important cause of increasing the intensity in training. A complex technical skill or element may cause learning problems and therefore extra muscular strain, especially during the phase when the neuro-muscular co-ordination is inferior. The exposure of a group of individuals to complex skills discriminates very quickly between well and poorly co-ordinated individuals (provided that none were previously exposed to the skills), and as Astrand and Rodahl (1970) advocated, the more complex an exercise, the greater will be individual differences and mechanical efficiencies.

Even previously acquired skills of high complexity may represent a source of volitional and nervous stress. Therefore, the complexity of a skill or tactical maneuver should also be associated with stress in the psychic sphere. Korcek (1974) claims that tactical complexity in team sports represents an important stressor and that the athletes are often affected by such circumstances. Players' reactions to complex tactics were signified through the elevation of the HR by 20–30 bpm. Therefore, in the planning process of training the coach must take into consideration the complexity of a task so that the athletes are not overworked. Similarly, the arrangement of game schedules should take into consideration highly demanding games not only from a physical point of view, but also from the complexity of the tactics involved. Under such circumstances, the coach should allow sufficient recovery time following the game, or plan demanding games at longer intervals.

The Index of the Overall Demand in Training

The volume, intensity and density are the main components which affect the demand encountered by athletes in training. Although these three components may complement each other, an increased emphasis on one may cause an increased demand on the athlete. For instance, if the coach intends to maintain the same demand in training but the needs of the sport require developing endurance, then the volume has to be increased. Under these new circumstances, the coach has to decide how the density will be affected and how much the intensity has to be decreased. On the other hand, if it is decided that the overall demand in training has to be evaluated by varying the intensity, then there is need to forecast how this new situation would affect the volume and/or density of training.

The planning and the general direction in training is a function of the three main components of training. The evolution of the curve of these components, especially the volume and intensity (refer to the planning section), has to be guided in direct relationship with the athlete's index of adaptation, phase of training and the competition schedule. Furthermore, the science of knitting the components of training may facilitate a correct peaking for the main competition.

The index of overall demand (IOD), which expresses the level of demand in training, may be calculated by employing the equation proposed by Iliuta and Dumitrescu (1978):

$$IOD = \frac{OI \cdot AD \cdot AV}{10,000}$$

From the earlier boxing example:

OI (Overall Intensity) was found to be: 63.8%
AD (Absolute Density) was: 74.5%, and
AV (Absolute Volume) was hypothesized to be: 102 min.

By substituting these figures in the above equation the following results:

$$IOD = \frac{63.8 \times 74.5 \times 102}{10,000} = 48.5\%$$

The above hypothetical figures led to an IOD of slightly below 50%, suggesting that the demand has to be qualified as low.

CHAPTER FIVE

Training States

PEAKING

The achievement of superior athletic performance is the direct outcome of an athlete's adaptation to various types and methods of training. Training is a very complex process which is organized and planned over various phases and implemented in a sequential manner. Throughout these phases of training, and especially during the competitive phase, an athlete reaches certain training states. Peaking for a competition, is very complex, it cannot be realized on short notice, but rather is attained in a sequential, cumulative manner. Prior to the state of peaking progress must be made through other training states.

Figure 24 displays the evolution of peaking during a mono-cyclic annual plan. A detailed explanation of each term will enhance a better understanding of the concept of training states.

DEGREE OF TRAINING (see figure 24) represents the foundation on which other training states are based. As a result of organized and systematic training, the athlete's

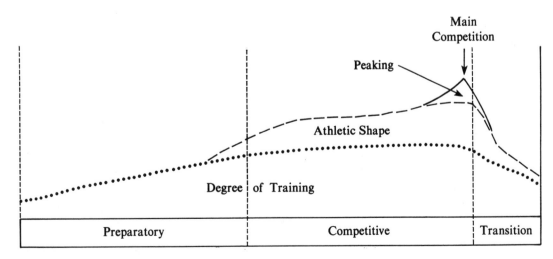

Figure 24. A conventional illustration of the accumulation and elevation of training states throughout phases of training in a mono-cycle.

working capacity, acquisition of skills and tactical maneuvers all reach high levels which, toward the end of the preparatory phase, is reflected through above average results and, thus, high standards in all tests. An athlete who is considered to have reached a high degree of training, therefore, is someone who has achieved a very high level of physical preparation, and who has perfected all the biomotor abilities required by the sport/event. The higher the degree of training, the higher the athlete's effectiveness. When the degree of training is poor, other training states are adversely affected, lowering the magnitude of athletic shape and, implicitly, peaking. The degree of training may be: 1. General, which signifies a high adaptation to different forms of training, and 2. Specific, meaning that adaptation to the specific training requirements of a sport has been achieved. On such a solid base, or degree of training, during the competitive phase, the state of athletic shape is attained.

ATHLETIC SHAPE. During the competitive phase athletes are often heard saying that they are in "good" or "bad" shape. The state of athletic shape is understood to be an extension of the degree of training, during which the athletes may perform and attain results close to their maximum capacity. This paramount training state, achieved as a result of employing very specialized training programs, may precede or incorporate the process of peaking for the main competition of the year. The state of athletic shape is generally understood to be the basis from which peaking is initiated.

PEAKING, as the highlight of athletic shape, results in the athlete's best performance of the year. It is considered to be a temporary state of training when physical and psychological efficiencies are maximized and where the levels of technical and tactical preparation are optimal. During this state of training, the individual's physiological and anatomical adaptation capacities are maximum as well, and the nuero-muscular co-ordination is perfect. Peaking is a superior, special biological state which is characterized by perfect health, optimal physiological state expressed through a quick adaptability to training stimuli, and a very good rate of recovery following training or competition. The athlete's body reflects a high state of functional synergism (acting together) in which organs and systems are channeled in the direction of achieving optimum efficiency and, thus, the highest possible performance. As far as the biological characteristics of peaking are concerned, they vary in accordance with the specifics of certain sports (table 10).

Table 10.   The characteristics of the state of peaking for various groups of sports.

Group of Sports	Characteristics
1. Dominant anaerobic	Capacity to involve all the athlete's abilities in a short period of time with a quick recovery
2. Dominant aerobic	High working capacity based on a very high physiological efficiency
3. Combined (aerobic and anaerobic)	Capacity to handle many repeating moments of maximum intensity on the bases of high physiological efficiency

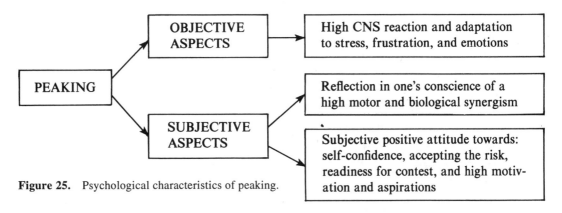

Figure 25. Psychological characteristics of peaking.

From the psychological point of view, peaking is perceived as a state of readiness for action, with an intense emotional arousal (Oxendine, 1968). It is also a state of objective and subjective analyzing all levels of integration-adaptation for the main competition (Serban, 1979). The objective aspects of peaking refer to the nervous system's capacity to adapt quickly and effectively to the stress and demand of competition while the subjective aspects refer to the athlete's self confidence, level of motivation and perception of motor and biological synergism. An important attribute of peaking seems to be the athlete's capacity to tolerate various degrees of frustration which occur pre, during and post competition. In order to facilitate this, many training lessons must be modeled so that psychological circumstances specific to the main competition are created. Similarly, taking part in various competitions during the pre competitive and competitive phases also enhances the athlete's capacity to cope with frustration. As suggested by figure 25, peaking is a special training state characterized by a high CNS adaptation, motor and biological harmony, high motivation, ability to cope with frustration, accepting the implicit risk of competing and high self-confidence.

FACTORS FACILITATING PEAKING

Peaking, as the result of many complex factors, is a rather intricate concept and an ultimate training task. Isolating singular aspect which would lead to its accomplishment is not possible. On the contrary, there are several factors which have to be considered by the coach. A correct manipulation of the factors explained below insures that an athlete is likely to peak adequately for the competition of major interest. It is important to specify that one factor can not be substituted for or compensated by another. All factors are essential for the optimization of the physical, technical, tactical and neuro-psychological qualities.

HIGH WORKING POTENTIAL AND QUICK RATE OF RECOVERY are two es-sential attributes of any athlete who reaches a high training status. An inability to cope with a high volume of work means that high performance expectations are groundless. Similarly, the athlete's capacity to recover quickly following training symbolizes an optimal adaptability to the specifics of the effort or stimuli employed in training and competition.

NEAR-PERFECT NEURO-MUSCULAR CO-ORDINATION, refers strictly to the capacity to perform skills and tactical maneuvers flawlessly, without errors which might impair the performance of a routine or skill. Technical imperfection signifies that a skill was not acquired, or automized properly. Consequently, the probability of a correct technical and/or tactical performance is low, thus degenerating overall performance.

OVERCOMPENSATION refers mainly to the effects of work and regeneration on the individual as a biological foundation for physical and psychological arousal for the main competition of the year. Further information can be found in Chapter One under training adaptation and detraining.

UNLOADING. A correct unloading phase prior to the main competition of the year represents one of the most important factors in facilitating peaking. The modality of manipulating the volume and intensity of training represents an important training concept which has to be carefully considered by the coach. For further information, please refer to the unloading section of the planning chapter.

Correct unloading is a significant factor for the achievement of overcompensation prior to the main competition (figure 26). Figure 26 illustrates the last five micro-cycles prior to the main competition. While, during the first three cycles, the load in training is still progressively and carefully increased, during the last two, the coach unloads the program to facilitate overcompensation.

RECOVERY and adequate body regeneration following training and competitions is perceived as an important factor which enhances peaking. If recovery techniques are not used consistently, the athletes acquire fatigue, which may evolve into physical and neuro-psychological exhaustion. Under such circumstances performance expecta-

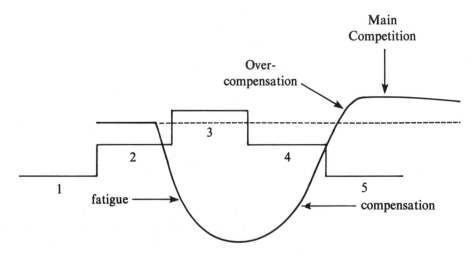

Figure 26.   A correct unloading prior to the main competition facilitates overcompensation.

tions should be drastically altered. Details regarding certain recovery techniques employed in training are presented in Chapter Six.

MOTIVATION, AROUSAL AND PSYCHOLOGICAL RELAXATION are instrumental factors for peaking as well. The reader is suggested to refer to topics related to specialized psychological information.

NERVOUS CELL WORKING CAPACITY. An athlete whose training factors are properly developed for competitions can not maximize his/her abilities unless the CNS is in an excellent state, and consequently possesses a high working capacity. Under optimal conditions the nervous cells' high working capacity can not be maintained for long. It may be considerably increased only during the last 7–10 days prior to the main competition (Ozolin, 1971) and may, in fact, be the normal outcome of recovery, relaxation, and the achievement of overcompensation. It is important to mention that athletes' activities, the performance of skills, are the outcome of muscular activities caused by nervous impulses. Thus, as Gandelsman and Smirnov (1970) put it, the force, speed, and maximum number of contractions depends on the nervous cell's working capacity. Such capacity depends not only on the athlete's training state, but also on the cell's level of excitability which alters and varies quite dramatically even in a 24 hour span (fig. 27).

A nervous cell's high working capacity can not be maintained for a prolonged period of time without being strained or fatigued. When training demands reach the nervous cell's limits, or when the athlete drives him or herself over such limits, the cell reacts to training or competition stimuli impairingly. Under such circumstances, the working capacity decreases quite abruptly as a result of the cell being fatigued. In

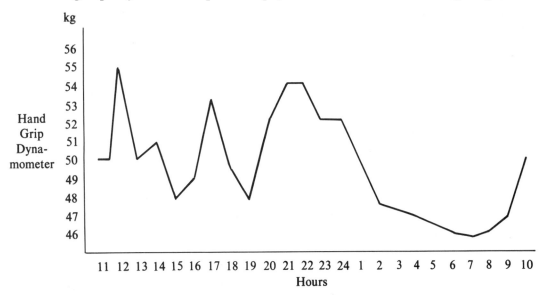

Figure 27. Variations of CNS excitability over a 24 hour span. Data based on hand grip dynamometer techniques (from Ozolin 1971).

order to protect itself from further stimuli, the nervous cell assumes a state of inhibition (Pavlov, 1927), restraining its processes. Certainly, the athlete, appealing to his/her willpower, may continue to train, but progressively he/she may be driven to the state of complete exhaustion. Under such circumstances performance is far below the normal levels. This is why regeneration micro-cycles and training lessons are so important.

The dynamics of nervous cell excitability alters according to the vicinity of the competition. It increases progressively during the days prior to the competition, reaches its maximum peak during the day(s) of contest and decreases following competition (figure 28). Although in most cases excitability levels decrease to the normal values, it may happen that excitability levels fall below normal, signifying a high level of exhaustion. Under such circumstances the training program should be light in order to enhance a full regeneration prior to commencing a normal load.

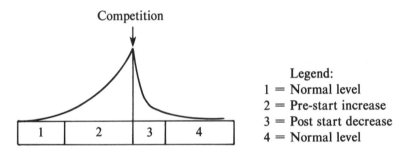

Figure 28.   The dynamics of CNS excitability level pre, during and post competition (modified from Ozolin, 1971).

However, athletic peaking, as well as the dynamics of excitability may be affected by the dynamics of loading the work in training and achievement of overcompensation. Figure 29(a) illustrates a situation in which an athlete peaked too early as a result of: 1. exaggerated intensive training, and; 2. a heavy competition schedule during the pre competitive, or even during the competitive phase. Under such circumstance the main competition of the year falls in the phase of post-start decrease. Figure 29(b) illustrates a case in which the best performance was achieved on a later date than the main competition. As is often the case, following an important competition, there are several days of relaxation and light training, which enhance overcompensation. Also, peaking was not achieved by the date of the main competition probably because the coach did not unload properly, consequently overcompensation did not occur.

COMPETITION SCHEDULE is an important factor for periodization and therefore also for peaking. Methods of selection and planning competitions are explained in chapter 11.

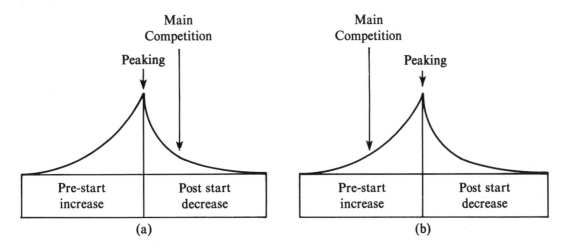

Figure 29.   Early peaking (a) and late peaking (b).

THE NUMBER OF PEAKS per competitive phase is also a determinant factor for peaking. The outcome of all factors facilitating or affecting peaking is not a steady horizontal line. Consequently, the curve of athletic shape, which is a plateau on which peaking is built, is an undulatory one. The ups and downs of such a curve depend on each factor separately. When the coach integrates all the above factors properly, peaking, or the peak performance of the year takes place. Throughout the competitive phase there may be 2–4 very important competitions, which are not spread out evenly, or in the order of importance. Therefore, the curve of peaking (figure 30) may be altered in accordance with such a schedule. However, from this figure it may be concluded

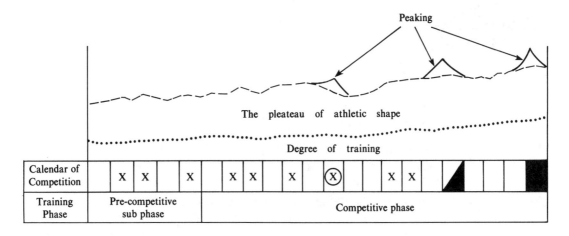

Figure 30.   A hypothetical calendar of competitions and the curves of athletic shape and peaking.

that peaking was facilitated only for three very important competitions; all others were considered to be of secondary importance. Although a short unloading phase was performed for the purpose of enhancing overcompensation, the integration of all factors facilitating peaking was performed only for these three top competitions. An attempt to peak for almost all competitions would be an impossibility from the nervous cell working capacity and excitability point of view. Such an approach may lead to exhaustion; Pavlov (1927) calls it inhibition of protection. Under such circumstances the cell protects itself from complete exhaustion. Thus, the cell will not react to external, or competition stimuli; consequently an expectation of outstanding performance towards the end of the competitive phase may be unrealistic.

Studies regarding means and techniques used for long term planning (Bompa, 1968; Ghibu, 1978) revealed some precise data with regards to peaking. It is believed that 7–10 competitions are sufficient to reach a high state of readiness for major or official competitions. Also, in an annual training plan (mono-cycle), most elite class athletes requires 32–36 micro-cycles in order to reach peak performance of the year. This estimation, though considered only as a general guideline, may be used when planning for the main competition of the year. Similarly, assuming that an athlete is involved in a program of daily training lessons, it is advocated that peaking may be reached after enduring 65–80% of the total days of training (Ghibu, 1978). Therefore, peaking may not be reached very quickly, but rather following a hard and prolonged effort. On the basis of the above claim, on the average, an athlete may require approximately 200 days of training before reaching an adequate physical and psychological capacity for peaking. The greater the number of important competitions or peaks per year the less the number of training days. However if 2–4 peaks per year are planned properly, this should not represent a hindrance since peaking may be achieved, and accumulated in a sequential manner.

In order to accomplish high performances every year, the degree of training has to be increased as well. This could be realized by elevating the physical aspect of training from year to year. On such a solid foundation a higher plateau of athletic shape may be realized from which higher peak performances will be attained. Ignoring such an approach leads to a plateau–off of an athlete's performances rather than continuous improvements.

METHODS OF IDENTIFYING PEAKING

The identification of peaking is both difficult and controversial. One of the most objective criteria seems to be the dynamics of the athlete's performances (Matveev et al, 1974). Athletes from sprinting and mid distance running were used as subjects (N=2300) for a longitudinal study regarding the establishment of zones of calculation for peaking. Considering the past year's personal best performance as a reference point (or 100%) the first zone or the zone of high results was considered to consist of performances not less than 2.0% below the reference point. Medium results were those within 2–3.5% deviation of best performance while low performances, 3.5–5% deviation were grouped in the third zone. Finally, the last or fourth zone was composed of poor results, or performances with a deviation of over 5% from the previous year's best. The authors then concluded that when an athlete can achieve performances within 2% (first zone) of best, then it may be concluded that he/she is in high athletic shape, close to a peak performance. From this point on, peaking can easily be facilitated and outstanding performances achieved.

When athletes achieve performances classified in the first zone, the adaptation to training is complete. The reaction to training stimuli is consistent, and as a result, the heart rate taken early in the morning reaches consistently low levels. In addition to this, other objective data may be considered so that a precise estimation regarding training states may be made. Ghibu et al (1978) suggests the following tests: urine biochemical test, tonometry (an indirect estimation of the intra-occular pressure from determination of the resistance of the eyeball to indentation by an applied force; *Dorland's Medical Dictionary,* 1974), hand grip dynamometer test, electrocardiography in resting conditions, aerobic or anaerobic power test, and the interval of the systolic tension. Obviously such specialized tests have to be performed by qualified personnel. Data from various phases of training, especially during the competitive phase, are collected and compared. When all scores are superior, the coach is advised that his/her athlete is in a very good state of training.

Peaking may also be identified by interpretation of subjective data, namely the athlete's subjective feelings such as: being alert, optimistic, good appetite, deep and resting sleep, high willingness in training and competitions, and ease in everything the athlete does.

Of great importance is that the coach must be in good shape as well. The coach's behavior, optimism, confidence, enthusiasm, encouragement, and cheerfulness also represents an important prerequisite for an athlete's peaking, especially when the relationship between them is very close. The coach's role is not only the training activity, but also he/she has the responsibility to bring the athlete to high psychological shape as well. A coach has to be psychologically well-balanced and calm, hiding his/her emotions prior to a competition. A well-controlled behavior has a tremendous impact upon the athlete. Similarly, the coach must strive to neutralize all the stressors (peers, family, job, intra-group conflicts,) which might affect an athlete's performance.

DURATION OF MAINTAINING PEAKING

Because precise research data scarcely exists regarding this paramount training aspect, among coaches and athletes there exists a high diversity of opinions. Often false-hoods such as "an athlete can peak only once a year" and for "one day only" still is imprinted in some people's minds. Since both the phase of athletic shape and peaking depend on many physiological, psychological and sociological factors, it is rather difficult to make precise statements with regard to their duration. Therefore, it is rather safe to say that the duration of peaking is very individualized. The individual training program followed by each athlete and the duration and type of training performed during the preparatory phase both have a substantial influence upon the duration of peaking. The longer and more solid the preparatory phase, the higher the probability of prolonging the athletic shape and consequently peaking.

When discussing this topic, it is rather difficult to separate peaking from the athletic shape. As already explained, athletic shape is a very high plateau during which the athlete has a very high working and psychological capacity. The highlight of this plateau is zone one, when an athlete's performances are within 2% of the previous peak performance. Assuming that the coach led and organized an adequate training program, the duration of zone one may be between 1–2.5 months (Matveev et al., 1974). Therefore, during this time, 2–3 peaks may be facilitated, when very high, or even record performances may be achieved. It is suggested that the duration of peaking may be up to 7–10 days since the nervous cell's optimal working capacity may be maintained that long (Ozolin, 1971). Following each peaking for a top competition, a short phase of regeneration is strongly desirable, followed by training. Failing to do so, the duration of zone one will likely be reduced. This approach is a reminder that there is a need to alternate stress with regeneration, an interplay of dramatic importance in training.

The duration of peaking, as well as zone one, may be affected by the number of starts, or competitions the athlete is exposed to. The longer the phase with weekly competitions, the lower the probability of duplicating high results. A high number of competitions does not necessarily lead to good and progressively higher performances. Often there is a contrary effect: results decrease towards the end of a competitive phase, when championship competitions are usually planned. From the 8th micro-cycle with competitions there often begins a critical phase. This does not necessarily mean that performance towards the end of the competitive phase might be compromised. On the contrary, it should draw the coach's attention to a better alternation of stressful exercises with regeneration activities. In addition, the above claim may also bring a coach's attention to the methods and means of selecting and planning the competitions during pre and competitive phases. This should be of significant importance for some college coaches, especially for team sports, where the competitions schedule is heavily loaded with many games even during the preparatory phase.

An important method to ensure adequate peaking is to prolong zone one and consequently the ability to peak. The peaking index (please refer to the planning chapter) can be employed in order to diminish the stress placed on athletes. By alternating very important competitions with those of secondary importance a coach enhances the undulatory shape of the peaking curve, substituting stress with regeneration. Similarly, a rational approach to planning competitions also refers to the fact that a competitive macro-cycle should usually end up with a very important competition, which ensures a progression in the arrangement of competitions. As far as planning the competitions is concerned, the grouping approach capacitates not only the alternation of phases of training with periods of competitions, but also facilitates the prolongation of athletic shape. More information can be found in Chapter Eleven.

Of determinant importance as far as peaking is concerned is also the duration, or time required to reach zone one. Although this might differ according to each individual athletes' abilities, the average time needed to elevate the capacity from a precompetitive level to the aptitude of zone one is about 4–6 micro-cycles. During the first 3–4 micro-cycles, dramatic increases may not be seen, since hard work, stressing mainly the intensity, results in a high level of fatigue which restricts the achievement of any good performances. However, following the last 1–2 micro-cycles, when the athlete has adapted to the training load and when a slight decrease in the stress of training allows the occurrence of overcompensation, higher performance is feasible. Although the duration of this transitory phase, from lower performances to zone one, varies according to many factors, it also varies according to the specifics of each sport, and the coach's approach to training. Thus, Ghibu et al (1978) suggests the following duration: gymnastics and water polo 6 micro-cycles, track and field, rowing, swimming and wrestling approximately 4 micro-cycles.

FACTORS WHICH MIGHT ADVERSELY AFFECT PEAKING

Peaking is the natural and highly desirable outcome of several months of hard work and a properly planned training program. As described above, training states may be facilitated by many factors; on the other hand, there are several factors which may adversely affect peaking, and it is the coach's responsibility to be aware of this and to be able to control them. By doing so the coach will be in a position to eliminate them and consequently enhance peaking.

1. Factors Related to the Organization of Competitions

Before taking part in a competition, both the athlete and the coach are expecting normal, standard conditions. In fact it may often happen that in an athlete's mind everything may be idealized and he/she may be expecting perfect circumstances. Consequently, every unforeseen change in the conditions actually experienced at the competition, may affect the athlete's peaking and performance. Natural factors such as strong wind or heavy rain may disturb athletes who are not familiarized with them. In sports such as cycling, canoeing, and rowing, strong winds could impede an athlete's performance. Big waves developed by the wind substantially affect rowers' and canoers' performances, especially for those with improper technique. On the other hand, heavy rain affects the performance of cyclists, walkers, and team sports exposed to play on a wet or muddy field, under such conditions ball control is impaired.

The snow's quality influences a skiers' final performance quite substantially. In cross-country skiing, a peak performance is directly dependent on the quality of snow and consequently the skills and experience of waxing the skis in accordance with terrain and the state of the snow. Similarly, all athletes are affected by extreme en-

Table 11.   Symptoms of fatigue following the application of varied intensity stimuli (adapted from Harre, 1982).

	Low Intensity Stimuli	Optimal Stimuli	Stimuli Up to One's Limits	Stimuli at or Slightly in Excess of One's Limits
Fatigue level	low	great	Exhaustion	Exhaustion
Skin colour	slightly flushed	flushed	very flushed	paleness for several days
Sweating	light to medium	heavy sweat in upper body	heavy sweat in the lower body	may sweat some
Quality of technical movements	controlled movements	loss of precision, inconsistency, some technical faults.	poor co-ordination, technical uncertainty, many technical faults.	motor inconsistency, lack of power (24 hours), precision/accuracy impaired.
Concentration	normal, athletes react quickly to coach's remarks, maximum attention	low ability to acquire technical elements, reduced span of attention	low concentration span, nervousness, inconsistency	mindlessness, unable to correct movements 24–28 hrs., unable to concentrate on intellectual activities
Training and health status	perform all training tasks	muscular weakness, lack of power, low working capacity	muscle and joint soreness, headache and stomach upset, vomiting sensation, and feeling of malaise.	sleeping difficulties, muscle soreness, physical discomfort, high heart rate for up to and even longer than 24 hrs.
Training willingness	eager to train	desire for longer rest and recovery phase, but still willing to train	desire to stop training, need for complete rest	abhorrence to train next day, carelessness, negative attitude to training requirments.

vironmental temperature, climate, and altitude. The answer to all the above problems is model training, to prepare and train the athletes under such conditions so that they may not drastically affect peaking. Of no lesser impact upon the athlete are changes in the initial draw, biased officiating and an adverse audience. Exposing the athletes to competitions which duplicate the social climate of the main competition is a necessary prerequisite to peak performance if that social climate differs significantly from what the athletes are accustomed to.

2. Factors Related to an Athlete's States

The coach can observe, and therefore have direct control over the athlete only during training hours. Although it is a coach's responsibility to positively influence the athlete's "unseen training," or the time when the athlete is on his/her own, it is often found that behaviors and lifestyles contradictory to athletic moral standards prevail. Negative behaviour does affect an individual's working capacity and therefore peaking as well. Unforeseen training and lifestyles such as inadequate sleep, use of alcohol, smoking, and poor diet, reduce an athlete's rate of recovery thus adversely affecting training states. Similarly, social dissatisfaction with family, coach, peers, and school/work, do reflect negatively in a persons attitude during training and competitions, resulting in inappropriate performances. In sports where some risk or strong initiative is required, a fear of competitions or accidents decreases self-control, leading to an inferiority complex. This may often play a restrictive roll in ones ability to perform. Therefore the coach should observe the athlete, collect information from persons close to the athlete and make all the possible attempts to correct such negative attitudes and behaviours.

3. Factors Related to Training and the Coach

Training programs planned improperly, with overly high intensity, quick increases of intensity, or too many scheduled competitions are not only very stressful and taxing, but also impair adequate peaking. The truth of such matters is even more obvious when the competitive phase is very long. Under such circumstances the maintenance of zone one, and a correct peaking for the main competition, (usually at the end of the phase), is almost impossible. Overlooking the needs of alternating work with regeneration may not only reduce the ability to peak but may even lead to injuries. Should the athlete be continually exposed to many such stressors the probability of reaching the state of overtraining will increase.

A coach's knowledge, and attitude and behaviour, as well as his/her ability or inability to disguise personal emotions and frustrations also affects an athlete's performance. A lack of confidence in the coach's abilities and knowledge, especially if present prior to the main competition, will adversely affect a player's performance, and therefore peaking for that contest. The remedy for such problems is relatively simple: further personal training knowledge, improve self-control, or be honest and advise the athlete to look for a superior coach.

Several Weeks (Beginning Stages)	2 Weeks	1–2 Weeks	1 Weeks	1 Week
Normal level of fatigue which does not inhibit over-compensation	Capacity to tolerate fatigue is increased. Adaptive responses are created	Acute level of fatigue. Rest intervals inadequate for compensation	Athletes appeal to motivation to defeat the strain of fatigue	Inhibition. Inadequate nerve activation to external stimuli. Performance starts to decrease

Figure 31. A hypothetical illustration of the steady progression of the stages of acquisition of fatigue and overtraining.

FATIGUE AND THE OVERTRAINING STATE

Fatigue

As the main restrictive element of human performance, fatigue has concerned sport scientists and professionals alike for a long time. By defining its sources, often there were attempts to annihilate it, to overcome its negative effects on performance. Irrespective of its definition, it is certain that fatigue is the consequence of physical work, which, as a result, reduces the capacity of the neuro-muscular and metabolic systems to continue physical activity. Although researchers have attempted to identify sites of fatigue, and performance failure, through a conventional simplification of a complex phenomenon with many unknown elements, the focus of this section will be on the two main sites: neuro-muscular, and metabolic.

1. NEURO-MUSCULAR FATIGUE. Increasing evidence suggests that the CNS may be involved in the limitation of performance to a greater extent than once was assumed. The CNS has two basic processes: excitation and inhibition. Excitation is a very favorable, stimulating process for physical activity, while inhibition is a restraining process.

Throughout training there is a constant alternation of the two processes. For any stimulation, the CNS sends a nerve impulse to the working muscle ordering it to contract and to perform work. The speed, power and frequency of the nerve impulse directly depends on the state of CNS. When (controlled) excitation prevails the nerve impulses are the most effective, evidenced by a good performance. Where the opposite is the case, namely that as a result of fatigue, the nerve cell is in a state of inhibition, then the muscle contraction is slower and weaker. Thus, the force of contraction is directly related to the electrical activation sent by the CNS and dependable for the number of motor units (muscle fibers) recruited. The nerve cell working capacity cannot be maintained for a very long time. Under the strain of training or competition demand, the working capacity decreases. However, if high intensity is maintained, as a

1 Week	2 Weeks	1 Week	2 Weeks (Ending /Later Stages)
Pressure to continue: from the coach, peers, family, and competition schedule.	Inhibition of protection. Nerve cell protects itself from further stimuli. Performance decreases. Prone to injuries.	Athletes appeal to last resort of willpower, and continue to train.	Overtraining. Athlete "out of shape". Emotional problems. Injuries.

Figure 31. *Continued*

result of fatigue, the nerve cell assumes a state of inhibition, protecting itself from external stimuli.

Should the coach disregard the needs of alternation of high with low intensity training days, the new intensive stimuli results in exhaustion, when the nerve cell is in a state of "inhibition of protection." In this state, it is not responding with the same activation, with performance being well below normal. Emotional disturbances are associated with such behavior of the nervous system. In the end, a continuation of training beyond this level results in overtraining, when the athlete is completely out of shape (figure 31).

Skeletal muscle produces force by progressively activating its motor units and regulating their firing frequency which is progressively increased in order to enhance force output. Fatigue, which inhibits muscular activity, could be neutralized to some degree by a modulating strategy, by responding to fatigue through the ability of the motor units to alter firing frequency. As a result, the muscle can maintain force more effectively under a certain state of fatigue. However, if the duration of sustained maximum contraction increases, the frequency of motor units firing decreases (Bigland-Ritchie, et al, 1983; Hennig and Lomo, 1987) signaling that inhibition will become more prominent.

Marsden et al (1971) demonstrated that, as compared to the start of a 30 second maximum voluntary contraction, the end firing frequency decreased by 80%. Similar findings were reported by Grimby et al (1992) who stated that as the duration of contraction increased, activation of large motor units decreased, lowering the firing rate below the threshold level. Any continuation of contraction beyond that level was possible through short bursts (physical firing), but not appropriate for a constant performance.

The above findings should send a strong message of caution to those who promote the theory (especially in football and body building) that strength can be improved only by performing each set to exhaustion. The fact that as a contraction progresses the firing frequency decreases, discredits this highly acclaimed method. As the con-

Table 12. Causes of fatigue of various sports.

	Neural Factors	ATP/CP Depletion	Lactic Acidosis	Glycogen Depletion	Blood Glucose Depletion	Hyperthermia
Archery	X					
Athletics (Track and Field):						
—100, 200 m	X	X				
—400 m		X	X			
—800, 1,500 m		X	X			
—5,000, 10,000 m			X	X		
—Marathon				X	X	X
—Jumps	X					
—Throws	X					
Badminton		X	X			
Baseball		X	X			
Basketball		X	X			
Boxing		X	X			
Cycling						
—sprint 200 m	X	X				
—4000 pursuit		X	X			
—Road racing				X	X	X
Diving	X					
Driving (Motor Sports)	X					
Equestrian	X					
Fencing	X	X				
Field hockey		X	X			
Figure skating		X	X			
Football	X	X	X			
Gymnastics	X	X	X			
Ice hockey		X	X			
Judo		X	X			
Lacrosse		X	X			
Kayak-canoeing						
—500, 1000 m		X	X			
—10,000 m			X	X		
Rowing		X	X			

Table 12. *Continued*

	Neural Factors	ATP/CP Depletion	Lactic Acidosis	Glycogen Depletion	Blood Glucose Depletion	Hyperthermia
Shooting	X					
Skiing						
—Alpine	X	X	X			
—Nordic			X	X		
Soccer		X	X			
Speed Skating						
—short/medium distances		X	X			
—long distances			X	X		
Squash/handball	X	X	X			
Swimming						
—50 m	X	X				
—100–200 m, 400 m		X	X			
—800–1500 m			X	X		
Synchronized swim.		X	X			
Team handball		X	X			
Tennis		X	X			
Triathlon				X	X	X
Volleyball		X	X			
Water polo		X	X	X		
Weight lifting	X					
Wrestling		X	X			
Yachting	X					X

traction progressed, fuel reserves depleted, resulting in longer motor units relaxation time, and the detected muscle contraction had a lower frequency. Since the cause of such neuro-muscular behavior was assumed to be fatigue, it should warn the practitioners that short rest intervals (the standard 2 minutes) between two sets of maximum contraction is not sufficient to relax and regenerate the neuro-muscular system in order to expect high activation in the subsequent set(s).

When analyzing the functional capacity of the CNS during fatigue, consideration must be taken into the athletes perceived fatigue and past physical capacity achieved in training. When the athlete's physical capacity was above the level of fatigue experienced in testing or competition, it enhances his/her motivation, and as a result, the capacity to overcome fatigue. Therefore, the level of motivation has to be related to past experience, and the state of conditioning.

2. METABOLIC SOURCES OF FATIGUE. Muscle fatigue may be associated with the mechanism of calcium flux in skeletal muscle, although the interrelationship between them still remains a mystery.

The complex cycle of muscle contraction is triggered by the nerve impulse which depolarizes the surface membrane of the muscle cell, and then is conducted into the muscle fibre. This is followed by a series of events where calcium is bound together with protein filaments (actin and myosin), resulting in contractile tension.

The functional site of fatigue is suggested to be the link between excitation-contraction, which results in either reducing the intensity of these two processes, or in decreasing the sensitivity to activation. Changes in flux of calcium ions affects the operation of excitation-contraction (Tesch, 1980).

The elevation of lactic acid level in blood and muscle was found to negatively affect performance of medium and longer duration, suggesting a cause-effect relationship between local muscle fatigue and lactate accumulation (Karlsson, 1971).

The biochemical exchanges during muscle contraction results in the liberation of hydrogen ions, which in turn produces acidosis, or the not clear yet "lactate fatigue", which seem to determine the point of exhaustion (Sahlin, 1986). The more active a muscle is the greater its hydrogen ion concentration, increasing blood acidosis, a state in which the hemoglobin will have less affinity for oxygen. However, in order to counteract the eventual low level of oxygen at the muscle cell level, during its transport through the capillaries, the hemoglobin will release even more oxygen (Brooks and Fahey, 1985).

An increased acidosis also inhibits the binding capacity of calcium through inactivation of troponin, a protein compound. Since troponin is an important contributor to the contraction of the muscle cell, its inactivation may explain the connection between fatigue and exercise. The depression of calcium also makes the cardiac muscle more sensitive then skeletal muscle, which probably explains why it has a more pronounced depression on contractibility during acidosis (Fabiato and Fabiato, 1978).

A high state of acidosis represents another factor for physical performance: it has an inhibitory effect on some enzymes, the result being a slow glycolysis, and as such a limitation of the energy derived from it. (Mainwood and Renaud, 1984). The discomfort produced by the sensation of acidosis could also be a limiting factor in psychological fatigue. (Brooks and Fahey, 1985).

From the energy systems point of view, fatigue occurs when the creatine phosphate is depleted in the working muscle, when muscle glycogen is consumed, or when the carbohydrate store is exhausted as well (Sahlin, 1986). The end result is obvious: the work performed by the muscle is decreased, the possible reason being that in a glycogen depleted muscle the ATP is produced at a lower rate than it is consumed. Several studies show that carbohydrate is essential to the ability of a muscle to maintain high force (Conlee, 1987), and that endurance capabilities during prolonged moderate to heavy physical activity is directly related to the amount of glycogen in the muscle prior to exercise. This indicates that fatigue occurs as a result of muscle glycogen depletion (Bergstrom et al, 1967).

For the activities of very high intensity but of a short duration, the immediate source of energy for muscular contraction are ATP and CP. Complete depletion of these stores in the muscle would certainly limit the ability of the muscle to contract (Karlsson and Sahlin, 1971).

With prolonged, submaximum work, the fuels called to provide energy are the free fatty acids and glucose, the latter being supplied in significant amounts by the liver. Inhibition of free fatty acids (by beta-receptor blockade) can increase the rate of glycogen degradation, affecting performance (Sahlin, 1986).

The power of oxidation is also dependent upon the availability of oxygen, which when in limited quantity, oxidizes carbohydrates instead of free fatty acids. Therefore, the maximum free fatty acids oxidation will be determined by the inflow of the fatty acids to the working muscle, and by the aerobic training status of the athlete since aerobic training increases both the availability of oxygen and the power of free fatty acids oxidation (Sahlin, 1986).

THE OVERTRAINING STATE

Peaking, is the normal, or positive outcome of a well-organized and methodically conducted training program. As long as training demand meets or slightly surpasses (occasionally only) the athlete's working capacity, improvements in various training factors are experienced. As a result of exposing the athlete to training fatigue is acquired, but under normal circumstances is recuperated within 12–24 hours.

Causes and Identification of Overtraining

Overtraining is a pathological state of training. It is the result of overlooking the work-recovery ratio, and exposing the athlete to high intensity training when he/she is in a state of fatigue. The recovery ratio is a function of the intensity of training. As opposed to submaximum or medium, high intensity training requires longer regeneration phases. When the coach does not pay close attention to the work-recovery ratio, the balance between the two is upset. As a consequence a fatigued athlete will not recover, overcompensation will not occur and he/she may reach a state of exhaustion. When a coach fails to take adequate measures even at this late time, on the basis of an acute residual fatigue and exhaustion, the overtraining state results.

An athlete is exposed to a high variety of stressors, and training is not always the most harmful. When all stressors to which the athlete is exposed (work, family, peers) along with heavy training loads surpass his/her capacities he/she then reaches the overtraining state. It is obvious that an athlete's body can not regenerate from

Table 13.   Activities which may cause or facilitate overtraining (from Harre, 1982).

Training Faults	Athlete's Lifestyle	Social Environment	Health
—overlooking recovery higher demand than athlete's capacity —abrupt increase of load in training following long pauses (rest, illness) —high volume of high intensity stimuli	—insufficient hours of sleep —unorganized daily program —smoking, alcohol, coffee —inadequate living facilities (space) —quarrel with peers —poor diet —over exciting and agitated life	—overwhelming familiar responsibilities —frustration (family, peers) —professional dissatisfaction —overstressful professional activities —excessive emotional activities (TV, noisy music) —quarrel with family re: sports involvement	—illness, high fever —nausea —stomach aches

overtraining as long as the causes prevail. Table 13 illustrates various causes of overtraining. Being familiar with these and taking adequate preventative measures, the coach can easily avoid the undesirable state of overtraining. The athlete him or herself presents an important factor in making a program a success or failure. It is the coach's responsibility to familiarize the athlete with the danger of overloading, the "unseen training," namely an individual's personal lifestyle. This indeed may upset the intended work-regeneration ratio, which in turn could lead to overtraining.

The outcome of overtraining is the decrease in working capacity and performance. However, such symptoms are usually preceded by insomnia, poor appetite, heavy sweat and even night sweat. The coach can identify the symptoms of overtraining by checking daily the remarks made by the athletes in their training journal. Identification of the overtraining state is facilitated by consulting its symptoms as shown in table 14.

Treatment and Prevention of Overtraining

When the overtraining state is identified, training has to be reduced or stopped immediately, irrespective of the causes. If the state of overtraining is very severe, in addition to a complete training abstinence, the athlete should also be sheltered from stimulations and excitement of social nature. A physician and training specialist must be consulted urgently to discover the cause of reaching such a training state. In the case of a mild overtraining state, when training has only to be reduced, the coach should not expose the athletes to any testing or competitions. Consequently, high intensity stimuli should be completely eliminated from both training and lifestyle. An active rest (mild exercise in a completely different environment) has to be considered even for an athlete who is in a severe overtraining state since an abrupt interruption of training may be harmful to an athlete accustomed to extensive physical involvement.

Table 14.   Symptoms which facilitate the identification of overtraining (compiled based on data from Bompa (1969), Ozolin (1971) and Harre (1982).

Psychological	Motor and Physical	Functional
A. Increased excitability B. Reduced concentration —irrational —very sensitive to criticism —tendency to isolate him or herself from the coach and teamates —lack of initiative —depression —lack of confidence C. Willpower —lack of fighting power —fear of competitions —prone to give up a tactical plan or desire to fight in a contest	A. Co-ordination —increase in muscle tension —reappearance of mistake already corrected, —inconsistency in performing rhythmical movements —reducing the capacity of differentiation and correcting technical faults B. Physical Preparation —decrease in the level of speed, strength, and endurance —slower rate of recovery —decrease in reaction time C. Prone to accidents and injuries	—Insomnia —Lack of appetite —digestive disturbances —sweat very easily —decrease in vital capacity —heart rate recovery longer than normal —prone to skin and tissue infections

Israel (1963) identifies two types of overtraining. The first one, sympathetic overtraining, or basedowoid, is the result of over-excitation or over-stressing the emotional processes. The term was borrowed from the Basedow disease, characterized by an increased metabolic rate (physical and chemical processes of the body), accelerated heart rate, sweating, nervous symptoms, irritability, restlessness, and psychic disturbances. This type of overtraining occurs mostly as a result of overemphasizing high intensity stimuli in training and the powers of concentration. The second type of overtraining, parasympathetic, or addisionoid, results in an increase in inhibition processes and is the result of an excessively high volume of training. Once again the term is borrowed from the Addison disease, characterized by progressive anemia, low blood pressure, and digestive disturbances. Either type of overtraining may occur when the load in training is abruptly increased, marked by surpassing working and adaptation capacities. Both types of overtraining states may also be deterred or facilitated by the individual's type of nervous system (Harre, 1982). The treatment of overtraining is linked with the two nervous processes, excitation and inhibition, and is presented in table 15.

Preventing the state of overtraining occurs by making sure that certain training principles (i.e., progressive increase of load in training), and a correct alternation of work with regeneration, are properly followed. In order to enhance the rate of recovery between training lessons and following competitions the individual has to continually employ recovery techniques. In addition, by frequently studying the athlete's training journal, the coach may detect exhaustion or over-training symptoms ahead of time, thus enabling him/herself to alter training programs and avoid the onset of overtraining. Frequent discussions with the athletes focusing on reciprocal confidence and trust may be another method of detecting how each individual feels and reacts to training.

Table 15. Techniques enployed for the treatment of overtraining state based on information from Israel, 1963, Ozolin, 1971, and Bucur and Birjega, 1973).

To Overcome the Excitation Processes (Sympathetic Overtraining)	To Overcome the Inhibition Processes (Parasympathetic Overtraining)
A. Special diet —Stimulate appetite through alkaline foods (milk, fruit, fresh vegetables) —avoid stimulatory substances (coffee), small quantities of alcohol permitted —increased quantities of vitamins (B-group) B. Physio-therapy —outdoor swimming —bathing 15–20 min. at a temperature of 35–37° C (but no sauna) —cold showers in the morning and brisk towelling —massage —light and rhythmical exercises C. Climatic therapy —moderate ultra-violet irradiations, but avoid intense sun radiations —change the environment, if possible alternate areas of various altitudes	A. Special diet —favour acidifying foods (cheese, meat, cake, eggs) —vitamins B-group and C. B. Physio-therapy —alternate hot-cold showers —sauna at medium temperature, alternated with short cold showers —intensive massage —active movements C. Climatic therapy —sea and sea level altitude —preferred bracing climate

CHAPTER SIX

Recovery Following Training and Competition

Most athletes, especially those of an elite class, are exposed to very demanding training often 2-3 or even more times a day. Under such circumstances the athletes may be pushed beyond physiological and psychological norms thus degenerating the body's functions and lowering work ability. The total demand placed upon the athlete is often added to by professional and private life. Each circumstance generates a physiological, and psycho-sociological stress which affects training load over a short period of time. Therefore, in order to overcome this, a good equilibrium should be maintained between training, social life, and the athlete's rate of recovery.

Following training fatigue is acquired. The greater the level of fatigue the greater the training after-effects (i.e. low recovery rate, poor coordination, decrease in speed and power of muscle contraction). Normal physiological fatigue is often accentuated by a strong emotional fatigue, especially following competitions, from which it takes even longer to recover.

In contemporary training the coach and training specialists should continually attempt to find methods which will allow an athlete to further the limiting factors in training as well as to increase performance. One of the most effective ways of achieving such goals in the employment of recovery techniques. Recovery should be so well understood and actively enhanced that it becomes a significant component in training. A coach's efforts to increase training demand, to employ higher intensity stimuli, is not often paralleled by similar efforts regarding the athletes regeneration following training and competitions. Similarly, there is a general lack of research in this extremely important area of training. And it is rather unjustified since a proper recovery accelerates the rate of regeneration between training lessons, decreases fatigue, enhances over-compensation, facilitates the employment of heavy loads in training, and even may decrease the number and frequency of injuries (when tired, co-ordination is impaired and concentration is lowered, leading to generally poor movement control.)

Both training and rest are unique and necessary components of training, and the drive for high success must assign similar importance to both. Optimally, the continuous process of training should be designed so that successive training lessons occur during the overcompensation phase of the previous lesson. Since it seldom happens that an athlete will fully recover between training lessons, the coach should consider the employment of various methods of recovery. The athlete should be equally concerned about this matter. Thus, the "unseen training", the time when the athlete is not supervised by the coach, is of significant importance and the sportsman's conscience for a well balanced life plays an important role in his/her success.

Using recovery techniques must become habitual. They must be synchronized with the biological processes of adaptation to a training demand, and the correct alternation of work with regeneration. Being habitual, recovery techniques should not be employed only following isolated training lessons and the main competitions, but rather they should be a daily concern. In this manner the athlete not only regenerates following the training session, but also benefits from the resulting preventive therapy, impeding the prospect of acute exhaustion and overtraining. Equal concern should also be given for various training cycles (i.e. micro-cycle) where the alternation of high with low intensity training lessons must be employed continuously. Similarly, when planning a macro-cycle, the coach should not disregard the principle of progressive increase of load in training, where the last cycle is a regeneration phase (figure 16). Furthermore, the transition phase in an annual plan has regeneration as the main objective prior to the commencement of a new plan, while in a four year plan, the post olympic year has similar goals.

A THEORETICAL CONSIDERATION OF THE PROCESS OF RECOVERY

The process of recovery is multi-dimensional, and as such it depends on many factors. By knowing them the coach can selectively apply recovery techniques in accordance with each individual's characteristics. Among the main factors for consideration are the following:

1. Age affects rate of recovery (Dragan and Stanescu, 1971). A younger athlete (18–22 years old) will need less time to recuperate following an intensive training or competition, since he/she has more biological reserves.

2. Experience plays an important role as well, since a more experienced athlete may adapt and adjust faster to a given stimulus. Such an athlete, based on a longer or stronger background in training, can cope better with stress, thus having a more effective rate of recovery.

3. The degree of training, and athletic shape influences the rate of recovery. An athlete who is in a higher training status has less dramatic physiological reactions to a given session, consequently the time required to recuperate may be less.

4. Sex differences affect the recovery capacity (Demeter, 1972). Female athletes apparently tend to recover at a slower rate than their male counterparts, especially following intensive training (i.e. strength training). This is primarily due to differences

in their endocrine-vegetative systems.

5. Climatic factors, altitude, and time differences may impair an athlete's rate of recovery, and the coach should consider this when planning training lessons.

Demeter (1972) also suggests that physiological recovery is dependent upon the following factors: a. the rate of replenishment at the cell level of the energetic substances (ATP-CP synthesis), b. reaching homeostasis, or the normal biological state of main body functions (i.e. circulo-respiratory, endocrine, and nervous system), and c. the elimination of metabolic by-products (burned food stuff) from the cell and body.

The dynamics of recovery is not a linear curve (Florescu, et al, 1969) but rather a curved line or an asymptote which drops abruptly during the first third (70%), and less drastically during the second (20%) and third (10%) phase. (Fig. 32)

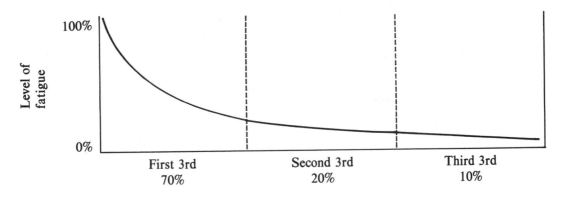

Figure 32. The dynamics of the curve recovery.

Other factors also contribute to the facilitate recovery. Thus, throughout training the coach and athletes should avoid the expression of any negative emotions or feelings such as fear, indecisiveness, and lack of will and determination. Such sensations (i.e. fear) may place extra stress upon the athlete, thus impairing recovery. During competitions with several races or games, it is rather important that the athlete not exhaust physically, or psychologically following the first trials. If this occurs, future performances will be affected. Avoidance of early exhaustion may be achieved by applying the principle of modeling in training. And finally, if a high emotional fatigue is experienced following competitions or very stressful training, changing the training environment as well as employing psychological relaxation may also be helpful.

The recovery of various biological parameters and substances occurs in a sequential manner. According to Dragan (1978) the heart rate and blood pressure recovers in 20–60 minutes following the cessation of work. Furthermore the restoration of glucides takes 4–6 hours while proteins take 12–24 hours and fats, vitamins and enzymes take over 24 hours.

The effectiveness of recovery techniques depends on when they are employed. Since recovery has to become a stereotype, certain regeneration means must be performed following each training session. However, it seems that overcompensation is better facilitated and the working capacity significantly increased when special recovery measures are taken 6–9 hours following competition or very intensive training (Talyshev, 1977). Similarly, if during the following day there is a competition, or a very important test the above claim is further enforced. On the other hand if training or competition is concluded late in the evening it is advisable that recovery techniques be employed the following morning so that sleep is not delayed. And finally, before presenting various means and recovery methods, it is important to mention that a close cooperation between coach and physician is essential to maximize the effectiveness of athletes' regeneration as well as the avoidance of misconceptions. Similarly, medical personnel may be necessary for the application of certain techniques (i.e. physiotherapy) or for advice regarding chemotherapy.

MEANS AND METHODS OF RECOVERY

Natural Means of Recovery

1. KINOTHERAPY, the therapy through movement or "active rest" is an important means of recovery and regeneration. The scientific basis of kinotherapy was revealed at the beginning of the century (1903) when Setchenov and later Weber (1914), demonstrated that a fatigued muscle can increase its rate of recovery and consequently its working capacity, if during rest another muscle group (preferably antagonistic) performs work rather that being inactive. This is explained through the compensatory effect which physical exercise has upon the fatigued centres of the CNS. By transferring the focus of excitation to another centre, the recovery of the previously over excited nervous centre is enhanced. Recovery occurs faster and more effectively than through total rest. Kinotherapy is applied during the transition phase as well as during times of emotional fatigue when other , or "defective exercises" (Asmussen 1936) ought to be employed. Similarly, this means of recovery is also employed to prevent the acquisition of high levels of fatigue in weight lifting and strength training by alternating the muscle groups. Thus, in the case of two training lessons per day, in order to facilitate recovery, one lesson may be dedicated to the upper body and the second to the lower limbs.

2. SLEEP, or passive rest is the main physiological means of restoring a person's working capacity. It is already well accepted that an athlete requires 9–10 hours of sleep, 80–90% of it during the night. The balance may be completed during the day, guided in such a way that it should not affect work or the training schedule. For day time sleep the athletes may be assisted by a psychologist as that it may be performed voluntarily, in accordance with the available free time. As far as night sleep is concerned the athlete should follow a strict schedule and should go to sleep no later

than 22:30 (10:30 PM). In order to promote a relaxed sleep, relaxation techniques, massage, and a dark, quiet, oxygenated (fresh air) room is necessary. On the other hand, being involved in emotional activities (i.e. arguments) may adversely affect sleeping.

3. LIFESTYLE, mostly related to family and peers, team atmosphere may influence the rate of recovery. A friendly team atmosphere, rich and varied leisure, and discussions with the coach may develop a sound attitude towards the problem solving process. Similarly, discussions with a sport psychologist assists the athlete to develop a well balanced lifestyle with good working and training relationships indirectly improves the rate of recovery.

Physiotherapeutic Means of Recovery

1. MASSAGE, performed through specific maneuvers (manual, mechanical, or electrical) assists the elimination of toxic substances (energy metabolism byproducts) from the tissue, reactivates peripheral circulation, accelerates reabsorption, decreases muscle tension, and increases functional and neuro-muscular activity. Zalessky (1977) implies that under water massage has a deeper and more all-around benefit to the body. Massage or self massage may be performed for 15–20 minutes before training (following a general warm-up), for 8–10 minutes following shower at the end of a training lesson, or for 20–30 minutes following a hot bath or sauna.

2. ELECTROSTIMULATION AND ULTRASOUND. Both techniques, in addition to others that a physiotherapist may suggest, are beneficial to relaxation and recovery. Electrostimulation of muscles improves local blood circulation and metabolic processes in the muscle (Zalessky, 1977). Ultrasound, both thermal and physio-chemical, acts upon deep-lying tissue, eliminates pain in the tendons and ligaments, and has an anti-inflammatory effect on minor traumas which sometimes are a side effect of intensive training.

3. BALNEO THERAPY means are applied with a prophilactic scope. Hydro-therapy (shower, bath) has a reflex effect on the nervous and endocrine systems (Zalessky, 1977) as well as a local effect on organs and tissues. Hot shower (38–42°C) for 8–10 minutes, hot bath (36–40°C) for 10–20 minutes, where medical plants may be introduced, relaxes the muscles and improves blood circulation, thus speeding up recovery. In addition, because of their relaxory effects, hot baths, saunas and showers reduce the likelihood of neurotic reactions, improve sleep, and normalize the metabolic processes, thus promoting faster removal of wastes (Serban, 1979). Thermotherapy (sauna, hot bath and shower) of higher temperatures (40–80°C) ought to be used once a week for 10–15 minutes. Thermotherapy allows for vasodilation and perspiration which facilitates recovery by eliminating the toxics from the muscle cell. If the toxics are not eliminated fatigue lingers on and affects CNS stimulation (Dragan, 1978). As Wickstrom and Polk (1961) claim such thermotherapy produces physiological effects which would ordinarily require two hours of rest to achieve.

Aerotherapy

1. OXYGENOTHERAPY. Athletes often experience O_2 debt because of the high level of O_2 consumption inherent in their training. Dragan (1978) implies that a reduction of the O_2 saturation level to 85% of normal leads to a decrease in concentration span. At 75% an athlete is exposed to a decrease in strength, and at 70% depressive states may be experienced. Therefore, in order to overcome the reduction in O_2 saturation and replenish the body, yoga and respiratory exercises should be employed. Also artificial O_2 inhalation, before, during intermissions, and following competitions and training, assists in replenishing the 0_2 level. Of great importance to the athlete is the continuous refreshing of the air in locker rooms and gymnasiums to ensure a rich proportion of oxygen.

2. AEROTHERAPY. In the atmospheric air there are particles which are electrically charged positively and negatively (positive or negative aeroions). The negative aeroions, as suggested by Dragan (1978), facilitate a fast recovery of the circulorespiratory systems, relaxes the neuro-psychic system, and serves to increase the athlete's working capacity. Such a therapy may be obtained through natural means, though high altitude cure, or a walk through parks and/or forests; or artificially by placing instruments in locker rooms which can produce negative aeroions.

3. ALTITUDE CURE, which has a visible effect on recovery, may be enhanced by either training or having 1–2 weeks of active rest at sub-alpine altitude. At this altitude (600–1000 m) the atmospheric pressure is reduced, humidity and temperature is lower and the solar rays, especially the ultra-violet rays, are of higher intensity and longer duration. Such circumstances are very favorable and help the athletes lighten the functions of the main organs, thus allowing for a quicker regeneration and an improved work capacity (Dragan and Stanescu, 1971). Following the return from the higher altitude, there is a critical phase of readaptation lasting 3–5 days, when participation in competitions is not recommended. However, the positive changes occurring in the athlete's body following an altitude cure may last up to 1–2 months (Bucur, 1979).

Reflexotherapy

1. ACUPRESSURE, evolved from the ancient Chinese method of acupuncture, is a technique by which one compresses, with the thumb and index finger the specific peripheral nerves in order to relieve discomfort. Similarly, its application by the athletes stimulates recuperation and assists to relieve psychological depressions, states of high emotions and pessimism. This technique, along with a short (5 minutes) friction massage of the same spots, may be employed before, during intermission, and following competitions and intensive training (Dragan, 1978; Bucur, 1979). It is highly suggested that a physician be asked for specialized advice on this matter.

2. VAGAL-REFLEXOTHERAPY (pertaining to the vagus nerve) uses techniques to stimulate the parasympathetic vegetative system (autonome nervous system) which

governs the recovery processes of the whole organism (Popescu, 1975). In order to increase the rate of recovery, the above author suggests employing techniques for stimulating peripheral reflexes. Ultra-thoracic pressure, or the Valsalva (an Italian physician from the Middle Ages) maneuvers performed by a physician may calm down the heart's agitated function which may be very pronounced by the end of intensive work. Similarly, slight pressure with the fingers above the eye has a calming effect. And finally a slight acupressure on both temporal arteries has the effect of calming down the circulatory system, especially the cerebral circulation.

In addition, a good sense of regeneration and functional balance may be achieved by placing a hot cloth on the athlete's face, and by blowing warm air (i.e. with a hair dryer) on the neck.

Chemotherapy

Vitamins have been suggested as an important asset to an athlete's performance (Sauberlich et al, 1974; Dragan, 1978, Bucur, 1979), and may be taken to supplement energetic needs, especially by those with a lower tolerance to work (Zalessky, 1977), as well as to enhance regeneration. Vitamins B_6, B_{12}, B_{15} seem to fulfill a catalytic role, accelerating the oxidation reaction. Vitamins H, PP, D_2, and E seem to combat fatigue, muscle soreness, anemia, and favour muscular metabolism. Vitamins in association with medicine, and medical herbs, taken under the advice of a physician have a beneficial effect on regeneration. Bucur (1979) implies that chemotherapy should be considered in accordance with the characteristics of the sport. Thus:

1. For sports of short duration, up to 60 seconds, the following holds: Vitamin B_{12} 5 mg, vitamin B_2 10 mg, potassium salt 200 mg, calcium 75 mg, magnesium 250 mg, iron 1.5 mg, and glycocol 150 mg.

2. For sports which last longer than 60 seconds: Vitamin B_{12} 10 mg, vitamin B_2 20 mg, potassium salt 500 mg, calcium 75 mg, magnesium 250 mg, iron 3.5 mg glycocol 200 mg, fructose 5 g.

3. For sports with a high psychological component: Vitamin B_{12} 10 mg, vitamin B_2 20 mg, vitamin B_6 30 mg, potassium salt 300 mg, calcium 75 mg, magnesium 250 mg, phosphorous 20 mg, iron 1.5 mg, glycocol 150 mg, fructose 5 g.

Psychological Means of Recovery

The location of fatigue is in the CNS. Since the regeneration of a nervous cell is seven times slower than the muscle cell (Krestovnikov, 1938), much attention should be paid to the neuro-psychological recovery. When the CNS, which leads and coordinates all human activity, is restored the athlete can concentrate better on the task, perform the skills more correctly, react faster and more powerfully to internal and external stimuli, and subsequently maximize his/her working capacity. The preventative measures of fatigue through psychological means has to consider: the foundation of motivation, understanding fatigue as a normal training outcome, coping with stress and frustration, model training to adapt to various competitive stressors, and the importance of a sound team atmosphere. As far as the therapy of fatigue is concerned, suggestion, self-suggestion, and psychotonic training, are efficient means which the coach may consider. A coach who is not familiar with psychological methods of recovery and relaxation should ask a sport psychologist for adequate help and instruction.

Sport Specific Recovery

Means of recovery according to the system which is affected

During training and competitions the functions of certain systems are affected to the extent of compromising future working capacity and therefore athletic performance. Unless the body recovers quickly the athlete may not be able to train adequately, perform the planned workload, or achieve expected performances. Consequently, preventive measures have to be taken by the coach or qualified personnel. Dragan (1978) and Bucur (1979) suggest that the following recovery techniques be ritualistically adhered to by all athletes.

1. FOR THE NEURO-PSYCHOLOGICAL SPHERE the following recovery techniques should be considered: psychotonic relaxation, Yoga exercises, acupressure, oxygen therapy, aerotherapy, balneo-therapy, massage, and chemotherapy.

2. FOR THE NEURO-MUSCULAR SYSTEM: balneo-therapy, massage, psychotonic relaxation, Yoga exercises, acupressure, diet rich in alkaline foods and minerals, and chemotherapy.

3. FOR THE ENDOCRINE-METABOLIC SPHERE: oxygen therapy, psychotonic training, massage, acupressure, kinotherapy, chemotherapy, and diet rich in minerals and alkaline substances.

4. FOR CARDIO-RESPIRATORY SYSTEM: oxygen therapy, balneo-therapy, massage, psychotonic relaxation, acupressure, chemotherapy, and diet rich in alkaline substances.

On the basis of the characteristics of each sport and the training demand Bucur (1979) proposes which systems and spheres are more strongly solicited for each of several sports. By knowing this the coach and qualified personnel may choose and employ adequate recovery techniques (table 16).

Means of recovery related to competition

1. BEFORE COMPETITION (1–2 days). Neuro-muscular and psychological relaxation ought to be of prime concern so that the athlete may start the competition completely regenerated. The following recovery techniques may be employed: psychotonic training, balneo-therapy, massage, active, and passive (10 hours sleep) rest. The diet has to be balanced qualitatively, with 60% carbohydrates, 20% lipids, and 20% protein (Dragan, 1978). In addition various liquids, fruits and vegetables should

Table 16. Biological parameters solicited in training for various sports.

Sport	Parameters
1. Athletics:	
—sprinting	—neuro-muscular, endocrine-metabolic, neuro-psychological
—mid distance events	—cardio-respiratory, neuro-psychologic, neuro-muscular
—distance events	—endocrine-metabolic, cardio-respiratory, neuro-muscular
—jumping events	—neuro-muscular, neuro-psychological
—throwing events	—neuro-psychological, endocrine-metabolic, neuro-muscular
2. Basketball	—neuro-psychological, endocrine-metabolic, neuro-muscular
3. Canoeing	—cardio-respiratory, endocrine-metabolic, neuro-muscular
4. Fencing	—neuro-psychological, neuro-muscular, endocrine-metabolic, cardio-respiratory
5. Gymnastics	—neuro-psychological, endocrine-metabolic, neuro-muscular
6. Handball	—neuro-psychological, endocrine-metabolic, neuro-muscular
7. Rowing	—endocrine-metabolic, cardio-respiratory, neuro-muscular
8. Rugby	—neuro-psychological, neuro-muscular, cardio-respiratory
9. Soccer	—neuro-psychological, neuro-muscular, endocrine-metabolic
10. Swimming	—cardio-respiratory, endocrine-metabolic, neuro-psychological
11. Table tennis	—neuro-psychological, neuro-muscular
12. Volleyball	—neuro-psychological, endocrine-metabolic, neuro-muscular

ensure a diet rich in minerals, alkaline substances, and vitamins. Chemotherapy as per a physician's advice may be considered.

2. DURING COMPETITION. between events, games, or even during the intermission, recovery techniques may be employed to calm not only the neuro-psychological sphere but also various psychological functions. During intermission an athlete may drink previously prepared liquids (fruit juice) with some glucose (20 g) and salt added in order to replenish what was lost during the first half of the competition. Self-massage of 5 minutes is also advisable to relax the main muscle groups involved in performance.

In between events or games a slightly different approach may be considered. The athletes should rest in a quiet place where the excitement of competition cannot reach them. During this time both psychological and neuro-muscular means of recovery should be employed. Massage, acupressure, oxygen therapy, and psychotonic relaxation are useful to accomplish the above objectives. The athlete should also be dressed in dry and warm clothing; additional blankets should be used to cover the athlete so that perspiration will be facilitated (with it, burned food stuff may be eliminated, thus enhancing recovery). Throughout the resting time alkaline liquids, which may counterbalance the athlete's acidosis state, should be taken. If the interval between events is less than four hours, only liquid nutrients should be considered, so that the digestive system is not overtaxed.

3. FOLLOWING COMPETITION. If there are only a reduced number of coaches and athletes who do pay attention to recovery, there are even less who worry about psycho-physiological regeneration following a competition. The employment of various recovery techniques makes this process thorough and fast so that the athlete's effectiveness in training may begin within the next day or two.

Physical activity does not have to be completely stopped at the end of competition. To continue a moderate exercise (i.e. jogging) is essential to eliminate excessive metabolites from the muscle cell. For sports where anaerobic processes are dominant, the O_2 debt contracted during competition is replenished during the minutes following the cessation of activity. In such cases, in addition to a light exercise of 10–15 minutes, neuro-muscular recovery is a must. The following techniques may be employed: hydrotherapy, (15 minutes), massage, aerotherapy, and psychological relaxation. For sports where the aerobic processes are dominant, the first concern will be to reach homeostasis (to stabilize the body's internal functions).This may be facilitated by 15–20 minutes of light physical activity, during which time the body is flushed of toxins, as well as the employment of recovery techniques such as: aerotherapy, hydrotherapy (15 min.), massage, and psychological relaxation. In both the above cases liquids should be ingested so that what was eliminated through perspiration will be replenished. Alkaline beverages (milk, fruit juice) enriched with minerals, glucose, and vitamins are highly recommended (Dragan 1978). An adequate relaxation which, especially through means of psychotonic training, may remove stress and eventual frustration, facilitates a desirable deep and resting sleep.

During the first 1–2 days following competition a recuperation diet has to be followed, which must be rich in vitamins and alkaline substances (salads, fruits, milk, vegetables). Meals rich in protein are not advisable during this time (Bucur, 1979).Throughout this time other recovery techniques should be employed (massage, acupressure, psychotonic relaxation, chemotherapy) and alcohol, smoking and sexual activity restricted.

PERMANENT MEANS OF RECOVERY

An effective training requires the employment of constant, permanent means of recovery. This recovery will not only facilitate a fast recuperation following training, but will also maintain a continuous state of high physical and psychological capacity to achieving training objectives. Briefly presented, the permanent means of recovery should include:

1. a rational alternation of work with regeneration phases
2. an attempt to eliminate all social stressors

3. a sound team atmosphere of calm, confident, and optimistic players

4. a rational and differentiated diet according to the specifics of the sport and the phase of training.

5. active rest and involvement in pleasant, relaxing social activities.

6. permanent monitoring of each athlete's health status.

MEANS OF MONITORING RECOVERY

Among the simple ways and means which the coach can employ to verify the athlete's state of recovery following training are:

1. observation of athletic shape, expressed through the level of effectiveness in training, in adequately accomplishing training objectives, or achieving set standards in testing sessions.

2. Being aware of the athlete's attitude. A conscientious and optimistic attitude during training, adequate relationship with team mates, and a generally positive reaction to the complexity of actions in training indicates that the load in training is proportional with the recovery capacity.

3. The athlete's health status, monitored by the physician and subjectively sensed by the athlete him/herself indicates the rate of recovery. An exhausted unregenerated individual may affect the normal functioning of the circulatory system (Bucur 1978).

4. Noting the athlete's training willingness, desire to surpass personal performances, appetite, state of sleep, and balanced emotions, indicate the recovery status.

5. Observing weight variations within ± 1 kg over 24 hours shows a normal rate of recovery. Gains or losses beyond the above figure suggests either a light load in training (gaining weight), or a load following which the athlete does not regenerate properly (weight loss).

6. Measuring heart rate, which is an important physiological indicator of the recovery status. Dragan (1978) suggests that a larger difference than 8-16 beats per minute between the resting HR taken in a laying, and in standing position represents a low rate of recovery, and as a consequence the training program should be altered.

CHAPTER SEVEN

The Theory of Planning in Training

THE IMPORTANCE OF PLANNING AND ITS ROLE IN TRAINING

The planning process in training represents a well organized, methodical and scientific procedure which assists the athlete to achieve high levels of training and performance. Thus, planning is the most important tool used by a coach in his/her endeavors of conducting a well organized training program. A coach is only as efficient as he/she is organized.

In order to be effective in his/her planning endeavors, a coach must have a high level of professional expertise and experience. The formation of a plan reflects his/her methodical inference, and is derived from the knowledge in all areas of physical education as well as a consideration of the athlete's potential and rate of development and the facilities and equipment available. A training plan must also be objective and should be based on the athlete's performance in tests or during competitions, his/her progress in all training factors and a consideration of the competition schedule. Furthermore, a training plan has to be simple, suggestive, and above all flexible, so that its contents may be modified according to the athlete's rate of progress and the coaches' improvement in methodical knowledge.

GENERAL REQUIREMENTS IN PLANNING

When a coach develops a training plan he/she must follow certain requirements, which represent the foundations of the planning process. According to Siclovan (1972) the following requirements are to be considered:

Long Term Plans Have to Be Blended with Current Plans

A long term plan represents an important requirement of the training process which is used by the coach as an objective means to guide the athlete's training. The formation of such a plan requires that both skills and performance are continuously improving. The rate of which has to be considered by the coach who should try to foresee levels to be achieved in the future, and direct his/her athlete's programs to-wards the same objectives. Following the process of forecasting future developments, the coach should then elaborate the appropriate means of training to accomplish the athlete's performance and training objectives.

The objectives of a long term plan relys on the parameters and content of training included in the annual plan's macro and micro-cycles, thus, a continuity exists between the present and future. This continuity is also reflected by the index of performance and test standards which have to be planned and achieved in a progressive manner. Such an approach is desirable not only for elite athletes but especially for children and teenagers as a guarantee of appropriate guidance.

Establish and Emphasize the Main Training Factor

During training a coach should always try to emphasize equally, or according to the athlete's needs, each factor of training as well as the underlying importance of volume or intensity. However, development is seldom proportional. Often an athlete will improve more rapidly in skill mastery, for example, or in certain biomotor functions. During competitions and testing sessions, the coach must assess the athlete's improvement and compare the achieved levels with the objectives planned for that phase. This process allows not only a conclusion regarding the gains in a particular training factor, but also (and this is even more important) a conclusion regarding the areas in which the athlete did not gain, or may even have lost some ability. Training factors which fall behind the mean rate of development are considered to be the weakest link(s) in the training chain. Following the establishment of the weakest link(s), the coach re-adjusts his/her training program, shifting more emphasis to the appropriate areas in the following phases of training. Often athletes' technical improvements (i.e., in gymnastics) depend on a high degree of strength development. Should a coach realize that his/her gymnast cannot perform a technical element because of inadequate strength, then strength becomes the weakest link which has to be stressed in the following phase of training.

Plans' Periodical Achievement

At the beginning of every phase of training, the coach should note the performance objectives or test standards to be achieved during or at the end of that particular training cycle. The objectives of each phase of training have to be accomplished periodically which, on the one hand would indicate a gradual increase of training level as well as performance ability, and on the other hand, would ensure the continuity of a sound, qualitative training program.

The establishment of performance objectives, training factors and test standards for each training phase eliminates the random approach still used by many coaches. It is not uncommon to find that this important component of an organized training program is ignored by some coaches who proceed to dramatically increase either or both the volume and intensity of training. Such actions may decrease the performance ability and even an athlete's well being. Therefore, the coach must employ the concept of periodical achievement, and must strive to achieve set standards or performance objectives in order to maximize the potential for success.

TYPES OF PLANS USED IN TRAINING

A coach's effectiveness in training is usually directly linked with his/her ability to be organized and to employ appropriate planning tools. Consequently, an organized coach may use all or some of the following training plans: Training lesson plan, micro-cycle, macro-cycle, annual plan and the quadrennial (four year) plan. Longer plans (8-16 years) often are employed in Eastern Europe especially for children selected for high performance.

When a coach commences his/her planning activity, he/she usually begins by setting up long term training parameters, which are to be achieved by the end of a long cycle such as the quadrennial plan. In a quadrennial plan the coach sets performance and training factor objectives for each year of the plan following which he/she prepares the annual plan for the current year. The general objectives of the annual plan and the competition schedule are used to establish macro and micro-cycles. The shortest term plan employed by the coach is the plan of the training lesson. Although the above approach is methodically sound, for the purpose of simplicity and progression the description of the planning chapter will be reversed, starting with the training lesson.

The Training Lesson

From the methodical point of view the training lesson is the main tool used to organize training. In it the coach shares knowledge with the athlete whose task it is to develop one or more training factors. In the methodology of training, there is a classification of training lessons based on the tasks and form of the lesson.

TYPES OF LESSONS. On the basis of its tasks, training lessons are of the following types: learning, repetition, perfection of a skill, and assessment. The main task of a learning lesson is to acquire new skills or tactical maneuvers. Such a lesson will be organized very simply so that following the introductory part when the coach explains the objectives and warm-up, the remaining time will be dedicated for skill acquisition. The last few minutes will be used to make a few remarks concerning whether the task was achieved or not. On the other hand, a repetition lesson refers to further learning, during which the athletes will try to improve their skills. Certainly such lessons are more frequent for beginners, whose limiting factor of improvement may be technique.

Training lessons whose task is the perfection of a skill are to be planned only for those athletes whose skills have reached an accepted level. Such lessons prevail in high performance training, where an athlete strives to master his/her technique, tactical maneuvers, or physical preparation. In accordance with his/her planning, on a periodical basis, the coach has to conduct assessment lessons when he/she either tests the athletes or has an exhibition competition, which is organized to estimate the level of preparation achieved in a certain phase of training. Among the main tasks of such a lesson may be to make the final selection of the team, to homogenize it, or simply to test one or more training factors.

FORMS OF LESSONS. Training lessons may be organized in several forms in order to accommodate groups of athletes and individuals.

The group lesson is organized for several athletes, and does not necessarily refer to team sports since athletes from individual sports may train together. Although such a lesson may have some disadvantages as far as the individualization of training is concerned, the main attributes are the development of team spirit (effective especially prior to important competitions) and psychological qualities.

Individual lessons have the merit of allowing the coach to stress and solve individual problems be they of physical or psychological nature. Thus, during such a lesson, the coach may rate the workload individually, adjust skills in accordance to the athlete's characteristics, and also give room to individual creative spirit. Such workouts are of great benefit, mostly during the preparatory phase, while prior to competition other forms may also be used.

As the term itself suggests, *mixed lessons* are a combination of both group and individual lessons. During the first part, all athletes perform the warm-up together, following which, according to their own objectives, they pursue individual plans. At the end of the lesson, the athletes will gather again for a cool-down and allow the coach to express his/her conclusions.

Free training lessons should be limited almost exclusively to advanced athletes. Although such a lesson minimizes a coach's control over the athlete's training, it has the great advantage that a common trust and confidence is developed between the coach and athlete. Furthermore, such a lesson develops the athlete's conscientious participation in training and stimulates the individual's independence as well as maturity in solving training tasks, which will be extremely beneficial during competitions when the coach will not be available for help.

THE DURATION of a lesson is commonly two hours, although often it could be up to 4–5 hours; from the duration standpoint, there are short (30–90 minutes), medium (2–3 hours), and long (over three hours) training lessons. The highest variety of durations may be found among individual sports, while team sports generally have greater consistency. The duration of a training lesson depends on its task, type, kind of activity and the level of the athlete's physical preparation. As far as type of training is concerned, during the competitive phase, a sprinter works approximately one hour while a marathon runner trains for three hours. In a situation of two or three training lessons per day, each would be of short duration but the sum of all lessons would be longer than 2–3 hours. The length of a training lesson also depends on the number of repetitions to be performed and on the length of the rest between repetitions.

The structure of a training lesson

In accordance with both methodical and physio-psychological rationales, a training lesson is divided into smaller parts, allowing the coach/athlete to follow the principle of progressive increase and decrease of the work applied. The basic structure consists of either three or four parts. In the first case, the lesson is divided into the following: 1) a preparation (warm-up), 2) the main body of the work-out, and 3) a conclusion. Similarly, a four-part lesson is composed of: a) an introduction, b) a preparation section, c) the main body and d) the conclusion.

The use of one of the above structures depends on the training task and content, the phase of training, and especially on the athlete's level of training. For group lessons organized during the preparatory phase, and for beginners, the four part structure is advisable, since in both cases, the explanation of training objectives and their methods of achievement described in the introduction are desirable. The three part method is mostly used for advanced athletes, especially during the competitive phase. Such athletes need less time for explanation and motivation, therefore the introduction and preparation can be condensed into one part. As will be seen from the following description, there are no major differences between the two structures except that the four part has an introduction.

1. The introduction

All training lessons should commence with a gathering of the athletes, the taking of attendance (especially for team sports) and an explanation of the objectives planned by the coach. Furthermore, the coach should give details with regard to how the objectives may be accomplished (i.e. the means and methods to be used). The coach should try to elevate the athlete's level of motivation since a higher degree of excitement for the challenging portions of the lessons may assist in the fulfillment of the objectives. Next, the coach organizes the team into smaller groups according to the specific goals of each athlete. The duration of the introduction should be between 3–5 minutes (often a little longer for beginners) depending on how long the explanation takes. However, as the athlete's level of knowledge or expertise improves the duration may be reduced.

The coach should always be well prepared for the lesson. While explaining the objective(s), the coach may use the training lesson plan, or even audio-visual aids. As far as the plan is concerned, it can be posted so that the athlete may get acquainted with it. Often a coach may have small handouts regarding portions of the plan, outlining what the athletes should do on their own. Such a method serves not only to enhance the organization of training but also to share the responsibility of the lesson with the athletes. Similarly, the athletes may also feel that the coach has confidence in their ability and maturity, assisting them to develop dependability and willpower.

2. The preparation (warm-up)

The warm-up, which is the most commonly used term for this part of the training lesson, is in fact a physiological and psychological preparation for the training tasks to come. Asmussen and Boje (1945) were among the first to conduct a study regarding the merits of a warm-up, followed by various investigators who often yielded questionable conclusions. The lack of consistency regarding the methods of investigation, type, duration, intensity and the subject's levels of physical preparation, makes the comparison of results very difficult. However, most investigations seem to arrive at the conclusion to which the practitioners have adhered for a long time, which is that a warm-up tends to facilitate performance. Ozolin (1971) claims inertia and the efficiency of the athlete's functions may not be elevated immediately. There is a certain time required to reach a state of high physiological efficiency. The purpose of a warm-up is to reach or approach this state prior to commencement of training and competition.

Resulting from a warm-up is a raised body temperature, which appears to be one of the main factors facilitating performance (Asmussen and Boje, 1945, Kaijser, 1957, Martin et al., 1975, Binkhorst et al, 1977). A warm-up stimulates the activity of the CNS which coordinates the athlete's systems (Gandelsman and Smirnov, 1971), reduces the time of motor reactions and improves co-ordination (Ozolin, 1971), therefore, motor performance is improved. In addition, during the warm-up the athlete also self-motivates or is motivated and encouraged by the coach to overcome challengeable tasks so that he/she will be psychologically ready. A good warm-up also helps prevent injuries.

Although the warm-up appears to be an integral whole, it should in fact be composed of two parts, the general and special warm-up.

During the GENERAL WARM-UP, intensity has to be increased progressively, increasing the working capacity by increasing the functions of the body, following which the whole metabolic process occurs more rapidly. As a consequence, the blood flow increases, elevating body temperatures, which in turn stimulates the respiratory centre leading to an increase in the oxygen supply of the athlete. Both the increase of oxygen and the increased blood flow seem to augment the working potential assisting the athlete to perform more effectively.

The common means used for warming up purposes is physical activity, where the athlete performs several exercises, preferably dressed in a dry, warm uniform. The most effective warm-up seems to be one of low to moderate intensity, and of longer duration. In order to determine the optimal duration the body temperature should be measured, but usually the beginning of perspiration, which signifies an increase in internal body temperature, marks the termination of the warm-up. Most athletes perform an adequate warm-up especially those participating in endurance related sports while figure skaters, divers, fencers, and ski jumpers often perform only a partial one.

The duration of a warm-up should be between 20–30 minutes, or even longer, with the final 5–10 minutes being dedicated to the specific warm-up activities. However, an athlete's physical preparation, his/her general endurance and especially environmental temperatures influence the duration. For an athlete involved in long distance events, a 10 minute run for warm-up is not demanding enough, while for a sprinter, a 10 minute warm-up run might suffice his/her needs. The temperature of the environment does affect warm-up duration, its intensity and certainly also the time required for an individual to perspire. Perspiration may commence after 12–13 minutes of uninterrupted work when the external environmental temperature is 8°C. If the temperature is 10°C, nine minutes may suffice. The environmental temperature of 14°C, six-and-a-half minutes of continuous exercise may result in perspiration while for a temperature of 16°C, the exercise period may be shortened by one minute. An intensive, uninterrupted warm-up may yield the same results after 2–3 minutes but may not ensure that the functional potential has reached an adequate level.

Although there is a general guideline and succession of body parts to be considered during a warm-up, of greater importance is that the speed of performance should be lower than that of training or competition, and also that most exercises must be specific, meaning very similar or even identical to the skill to be performed. The frequency and number of repetitions of exercises or skills must be adjusted in accordance with environmental temperature, specifics of the sport, and the athlete's level of physical preparation. A warm-up should always start with slow running of various forms (sideways, even backwards, but mostly forward) which accelerates the blood flow, thus generating a higher temperature in the whole body as well as in the muscles. Such an approach is also suggested by Barnard et al (1973) who claimed that strenuous exercises performed at the beginning of a warm-up may be associated with inadequate blood flow. Although Matthews and Fox (1976) seem to share the above reasoning, their recommended sequence, starting with stretching exercises, appears to contradict this physiological reality. Stretching exercises would hardly be regarded as a generation of blood flow. Similarly, such exercises which pull the muscle should be performed towards the end of the warm-up since a warmer muscle stretches easier.

Following 5–10 minutes of slow pace running (skating, skiing) calisthenics exercises may be performed from the top down, starting with the neck, then moving towards the arms and shoulders, abdomen, legs and back. By now the athlete may be ready for more strenuous exercises. Thus, the next group of exercises may be flexibility exercises and if the sport requires, they may be followed by some light jumping or bounding exercises. A few short sprints (20–40 m long) may complete the whole range of exercises used for the general warm-up. In between all these exercises resting and muscle relaxation (shaking the limbs) periods should be included so that a quiet and untaxing warm-up may be insured.

During this phase of the lesson the athletes also prepare themselves psychologically for the main part of the lesson or competition, trying to visualize the skills to be performed as well as motivating themselves for the difficult aspects of it.

SPECIAL WARM-UP has the main objective of tuning the athlete to the predominant type of work to be performed during the main part of the training lesson. This tuning phase of the warm-up does not refer only to mental preparation, or the co-ordination of certain exercises, but also to the preparation of the CNS and the elevation of the body's working capacity. The latter is realized by the repetition of certain technical elements and exercises of a certain intensity. The selection of exercises to be performed during the special warm-up depends strictly on the type of exercises to be performed in the main part of the lesson or competition. A gymnast, wrestler, figure skater, thrower or jumper may perform certain technical elements or parts of a routine. Similarly, a swimmer, runner or rower may repeat starts, or wind sprints with the rhythm and intensity close, sometimes even similar to what they will be required to perform after the conclusion of the special warm-up. Such an approach employed for average class athletes may reduce the intensity of the critical phase of the adaptation processes (accumulation of lactic acid which could impede performance) facilitating the onset of the second wind which is a sudden feeling of release following the distress encountered during the early part of a prolonged exercise or race.

The tuning phase of the warm-up must be performed by every athlete, especially by those whose skills are very complex. The more complex the skill the more repetitions of technical elements should be included. As for the duration of a warm-up, as a rule of thumb, the higher the volume of work or the longer the duration of the competition, the longer the warm-up should be (long distance athletes warm-up for 45 minutes). In order to warm up properly, a good general physical preparation and general endurance is required. Only very fit athletes can perform a 20–30 minute warm-up. In fact, long warm-ups are used especially during the preparatory season, as a means to develop general physical preparation.

Attempts have been made to achieve an elevated body temperature not only through active, natural athletic means, but also through passive ones such as hot shower, heated sleeping bags, electrical infra-red rays, chemicals and massage. Although there are claims that local heating, electrical means (Ozolin, 1971), and massage (Bucur, 1979) elevate body temperature, their effect upon performance is limited. An active means of warm-up, sometimes preceded by local massage, seems to be the most beneficial for the athlete.

c. The main body of the lesson

The objectives of the training lesson are fulfilled during the main or third part. Following an adequate warm-up, an athlete tries to learn the skills and tactical maneuvers, develop biomotor abilities and enhance the psychological qualities.

The content of the main body depends on many factors, among which the degree of training, kind of sport, sex, age and training phase play dominant roles. For instance, one form of training, namely interval training, is widely used which means that the coach may stress technique and develop specific biomotor abilities as well as psycho logical traits at the same time. However, as far as the lesson's content for less ad vanced athletes is concerned, the following succession is suggested:

1) at first the athlete should exert movement destined to learn and perfect technical or tactical elements, followed by
2) the development of speed and/or co-ordination,
3) the development of strength and, finally,
4) the development of endurance.

The inclusion of technical and tactical elements at the beginning of the main part of the training lesson is based on the idea that learning is more effective when the nerve cell is still rested. Should learning or perfection of a technical element be performed following speed, strength or endurance exercises, then retention would be impeded by fatigue. The reference here is to CNS fatigue, which means a loss of the capacity to respond to a stimulus. As for the composition or sequence of learning or perfecting technical and tactical elements, it is advisable that:

1) an athlete should consolidate elements and /or skills acquired in the previous lesson(s),
2) perfect technical elements and/or skills of utmost importance for the sport, and
3) apply skills in identical conditions to a competition.

If the perfection of technique requires heavy and fatiguing work then such exercises may be performed later in the lesson, usually following speed exercises. Such an approach should be used in throwing events in track and field and even in weight lifting.

Exercises used to develop and perfect speed usually are of very high intensity though the duration is quite short. Such exercises require the use of the athlete's full potential which cannot be performed but under a fresh or relatively rested condition. This is why they have to precede strength and endurance exercises. However, when the lesson's main objective is the development of maximum speed (i.e., in sprinting or starts with full velocity in other sports) then such exercises should follow the warm up. Similarly, when co-ordination is the prime objective such exercises also have to be placed at the beginning of the main body since a rested athlete can concentrate much easier on his/her tasks.

In an organized lesson, all strength developing exercises follow movements aimed at developing or perfecting technique and speed. It is not advisable to reverse the above sequence since exercises employing heavy loads impair speed.

Exercises having the objective of developing general and/or specific endurance are usually planned for the last part of the lesson. Such exercises are very demanding and fatiguing, following which an athlete would hardly be in a position to acquire skills or develop speed. However, the above sequencing should not be confused with the practice of certain drills at the end of the main part, typically for team sports, which usually are performed with a certain level of fatigue or occasionally even under the conditions of residual fatigue. In this situation the coach's goal is not for learning but rather for training under specific game conditions.

Training lessons organized for beginners should always follow the afore-mentioned sequence (technical, speed, strength, endurance), since learning is very often the dominant objective for these athletes. However, although for elite athletes such as approach should prevail, it must not be rigidly adhered to. This is because it was discovered that a few strength exercises using a moderate load (40–50% of one's maximum) increases the CNS excitability, thus enhancing the ability to perform speed work. Both Van Huss et al (1962) and Ozolin (1971) referred to the above effect, although De Vries (1980) suggested that the effect may be more of a psychological nature. Whatever the reason, the coach may explore the potential for the above for each athlete, and apply whatever yields the best results in competitions.

For each training lesson a coach should have previously planned objectives which are to be achieved during the main part. However, there should not be an excessive number of objectives. They should be linked with the micro and macro-cycle plans as well as the athlete's level of performance and his/her potential. Planning more than 2–3 objectives per lesson, however varied they might be, would be quite difficult to effectively accomplish, this slowing down the athlete's rate of improvement. Although it may be advisable to plan objectives derived from different training factors (technical, tactical, physical which may also have a psychological component) they must be chosen properly according to the needs of the sport and the athlete's abilities.

Following the achievement of daily objectives, a coach may plan 15–20 minutes of supplementary physical development, often called a conditioning program. Such a program should be considered for those training lessons which were not extremely demanding and during which the athletes did not reach a state of complete exhaustion. The program of supplementary physical development has to be very specific in accordance with the dominant biomotor abilities in the sport and the athlete's needs. Usually the limiting factor of the athlete's rate of improvement should be stressed.

4. The conclusion

Following strenuous work performed in the main body of the training lesson it is best to progressively decrease the work load at the end of the lesson so as to approach the athlete's initial normal biological and psychological rest state. At the end of the main part of a lesson, most if not all of the athlete's functions are operating at close to maximum capacity and the progressive return to a less demanding activity is necessary. The main motive is not only that an abrupt interruption of work may lead to negative physiological and psychological effects (dissatisfaction), but also through the cool down, the rate of recovery is enhanced and the accumulated lactic acid in the blood decreases more rapidly. Unfortunately, most coaches and athletes do not organize this part of the lesson, thus failing to optimize the recovery processes which means that the rate of improvement and efficiency in training may not be maximized.

The structure of the fourth part of the lesson is quite simple. During the initial part the athlete should be concerned with decreasing physiological functions. This could be assisted by 3–5 minutes of light exertion, depending on the nature of the sport. For cyclic sports this takes the form of a very low intensity performance of the skill (run, walk, row, and ski), during which the elimination of burned foodstuff is accelerated by the presence of more oxygen than would be the case during a passive rest. As far as other sports are concerned (wrestling, boxing, gymnastics), often a short and low intensity game of basketball or volleyball has good relaxation benefits. However, the game should be organized only when, during the lesson, the athletes were not exposed to high emotional experiences.

As soon as the body's functions are decreased, the athletes should perform a few breathing exercises to control and slow down the respiratory rate and they should relax the prime movers or the group of muscles mostly involved in performing the dominant skills. Light stretching exercises should be employed only by those athletes who performed strength exercises during the main part of the lesson. Such exercises artificially bring the muscle heads close to the resting length during which all metabolic functions are at their highest efficiency. By stretching the muscle, which normally takes 2–3 hours to reach its anatomical length following heavy strength training, the athlete enhances his/her physiological rate of recovery.

In the last few minutes of the fourth part of a training lesson the coach should draw his/her conclusions regarding whether the objectives were achieved or not. Although the conclusions might not necessarily be stated every time, they should be considered as an integral part of a lesson. They may have important contributions to the solution of technical, tactical, physical and psychological factors of training.

The duration for each part of a lesson

The duration of an average training lesson is 2 hours (120 minutes) which in this particular case will be used as a reference point for the duration of its parts. The division of a lesson in its parts as well as the duration for each part separately depends on many factors, among which are: age, sex, level of performance, experience, type and characteristics of the sport and phase of training. The following suggestions may be regarded by the coach as a general guideline.

For a four part training lesson the allotted time may be:

1.	Introduction	5 minutes
2.	Preparation	30 minutes
3.	Main body	75 minutes
4.	Conclusion	10 minutes
	TOTAL	120 minutes

On the other hand, the time allotted for a three-part lesson may be:

1. Preparatory   25–35 minutes
3. Main part   75–85 minutes
4. Conclusion   10 minutes
   TOTAL   120 minutes

The fatigue and methodical guidelines for a lesson

Following a demanding training session fatigue develops in the athlete causing a decrease in working capacity. Recent research indicates a number of possible causes of physical fatigue, of which energy depletion and CNS fatigue appear to be most commonly accepted. When placed under severe stress for prolonged periods of time, the CNS reacts by increasing the amount of stimulation necessary to elicit muscular contractions. As a result an individual is less reactive to internal or external stimuli which deregulates the normal nervous function.

Each sport has different physiological characteristics which stimulate the CNS disproportionately, thus fatiguing also manifests unevenly. Fatigue is often seen from the beginning of a lesson (where both O_2 intake and gaseous exchanges reach high levels), but the well-trained athlete can cope with it as long as it does not exceed his/her physiological or psychological limit. Only if these limits are exceeded will the body's working capacity be decreased.

According to Grandelsman and Smirnov (1971), fatigue has two phases, namely *latent* and *evident* fatigue. During the early part of the lesson certain functional changes occur although the work productivity and energy production is not affected. All of the athlete's functions are elevated and often the nervous system's excitability and the metabolism are intense. If such is the case, the athlete has reached the state of latent fatigue. If the activity is prolonged at the same level, the working potential may be maintained for a while but at the expense of a higher energy consumption. Should the athlete still maintain the same intensity of work to the point that he/she experiences a high degree of tiredness, evident fatigue results. As a consequence, the athlete's ability to perform maximum work will progressively decrease.

The latent fatigue could be diminished by alternative resting internals, however the coach must not forget that it does have its benefits. Training under conditions of latent fatigue prepares athletes of the cyclic-endurance sports for conditions that exist at the end of their competitions and enables them to command a stronger finish. As for the evident fatigue, it may be more easily overcome through an appropriate training lesson conclusion and the use of recovery techniques.

The power with which a stimulus acts upon the CNS is determined not only by its intensity and duration but also by its novelty. New and unfamiliar elements stimulate the CNS to a greater degree, intensifying the excitation of the nervous centres and amounting to increased muscular work and energy consumption. This places an additional stress upon the cardio-respiratory functions. Therefore, during the learning and training processes, a systematic and methodical approach should be applied carefully, following their principles and methods. The specifics of the nervous system activities requires the setting of limitations on tasks and objectives in a training lesson. Usually, the more intense an activity, the more difficult even simple problems become. An exercise or activity which requires efforts up to an individual's limits necessitates a very simply organized training lesson. Habitually, such a lesson should have an adequate warm-up and conclusion, while during the main part, the athlete should be exposed to a kind of work which maximally uses the working and willpower capacities. On the other hand, if the training lesson is of lesser intensity, the coach could plan two or even three objectives provided that each of them focuses on a different training factor (i.e., the perfection of a technical element, its incorporation into the team's tactical scheme, and tactical drills with a very high endurance component).

The coach must design each training lesson to alternate between exercises aimed at achievement of each training objective, and more importantly, between muscle groups. The former minimizes monotony, while the latter allows for regeneration of the muscle's involved. In addition, such alternation elevates the total volume of lessons where intensity of training is lower. Highly intensive training should have a very restricted number of objectives. It appears, therefore, that the intensity of training influences the duration of the training lesson and its structure. Furthermore, all three of these parameters influence the physiological changes occurring in an athlete. The easiest way of discovering the athlete's reaction to a stimulus is by measuring the heart rate. From the beginning until the end, and even following the conclusion of a training lesson, the heart rate varies. Its dynamics are a function of the intensity, duration and character of a stimulus which, when represented in a graph, illustrates the physiological curve of a training lesson (Figure 33). From the normal biological rate experi-

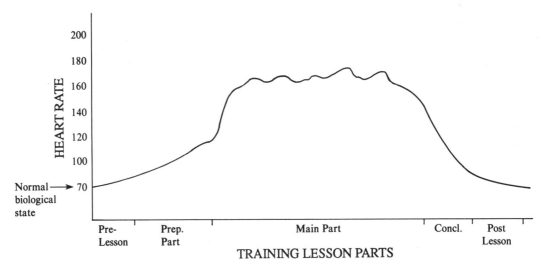

Figure 33. The dynamics of the physiological curve of the training lesson.

enced by an athlete prior to the commencement of the lesson, the heart rate curve often elevates slightly during the prestart of the lesson, mostly due to psychological factors (excitation, challenge).

During the preparation part, the cardio-vascular function raises progressively, reflecting the work which the athlete is undergoing. During the main body, the shape of the curve varies, having many ups and downs in accordance with the rate of applying training stimuli, their intensity, duration, as well as resting intervals. The heart rate drops progressively during the conclusion illustrating a decrease in the athlete's workload while in the post-lesson phase it is slightly above the normal biological level since the body's functions need some time to achieve complete recovery. The rate and duration of recovery is a direct function of the lesson's intensity, the athlete's resulting fatigue and his/her level of physical preparation.

Supplementary Training Lessons

When every athlete is trying to maximize his/her free time for training purposes, the supplementary training lessons represent one of the most effective ways of elevating the athlete's volume of training and thus improving his/her level of preparation. Such supplementary individual training lessons, and in special circumstances (i.e. camp), group training lessons are often organized for the early morning, prior to going to school or work. Usually they are performed before breakfast. However, if the duration exceeds 30 minutes, then some light food in small quantity may be desirable. The duration of these lessons varies depending on each individual athlete's time. If an athlete can afford 30–60 minutes each day, he/she can accumulate 150–300 hours per year of extra training, a volume which can be a determinant addition to his/her degree of training and athletic potential.

Such training lessons are to be performed at home, indoors or outdoors, by each individual athlete. However, they must be part of the general training plan made by the coach. The coach suggests the content and dosage of each lesson in accordance with the athlete's objectives, weaknesses and phase of training. Basically, through supplementary training lessons, an athlete may improve his/her general endurance through running 20–40 minutes, general or specific flexibility and even general strength or specific strength of certain muscle groups. One of the main goals might be to work and thus improve the athlete's weaknesses so that the rate of improvement of certain abilities may be accelerated.

A basic supplementary lesson consists of three parts, with the time allotted per part as follows: 1) Preparatory 5–10 minutes, 2) Main 20-45 minutes, and 3) Conclusion 5 minutes, which amounts to 30–60 minutes. The goal and format of each part follows the same concept as the regular training lessons. However, for the main part attention should not be focused on more than two objectives, one being more realistic and thus desirable considering the time available.

TRAINING LESSON PLAN NO. 148

DATE: June 14th _____

PLACE: York Stadium _____

OBJECTIVES: Perfect the start; specific
endurance; power training.

EQUIPMENT: Starting block; barbells _____

PART	EXERCISES	DOSAGE	FORMATIONS	NOTES
I	—describe the lesson's objectives and how to achieve them. —what the athletes are expected to stress during training	3 min		John: Pay attention to arm work
II	—warm up	20 min		Rita: put on two warm up suits
	—jogging	1200 m		
	—calisthenics —arm rotations —upper body rotations	$8 \times$ (8 times) $12 \times$		
	—hip flexibility	8–$10 \times$		Stress hip flexibility
	—ankle flexibility	8–$10 \times$		
	—bounding exercises	4×20 m		Stress the weak leg.
	—wind sprints	4×40–60 m		
III	—Starts	12×30 m Rest(1) = 2 min		Stress arm work
	—Specific endurance	$\dfrac{8 \times 120 \text{ m}}{3/4 \ (14 \text{ sec})}$		Maintain a constant velocity throughout all repetitions
	—power training	$\dfrac{60 \text{ kg}}{8\text{–}10 \text{ reps}}$ 4 sets		In between exercises relax arms and legs
IV	—jogging	800 m		Light and relaxing
	—massage	5 min		work with a partner

Figure 34. A sample of a training lesson plan for a sprinter.

The Training Lesson Plan

The format of a training lesson plan should be simple and functional, meaning that the plan has to be an important tool for the coach in his/her training endeavors. As can be seen from figure 34 on the left hand side at the top, the date and location should be specified, while on the right hand side, the coach will specify the objectives and equipment needed for the lesson, so that he/she should briefly write all exercises and/or drills to be used in each part of the lesson. In the dosage column the coach inserts the duration of each part, exercise/drill as well as distance and number of repetitions per exercise. The intensity and load of the exercises also can be specified (figure 34 part III.). As for the formations column, the coach, especially in team sports, would draw the most difficult drills to be performed during the lesson. The last column is reserved for brief notes, remarks which the coach would like to emphasize throughout the lesson.

The length of a plan differs from sport to sport, as well as with the coach's experience. Inexperienced coaches are advised to be as specific as possible, writing down everything that he/she intends to do with the athletes. The plan must then be followed closely to ensure that nothing will be missed. As for the experienced coaches, a general training lesson outline will suffice.

The plan can be briefly presented to the athletes during the introductory part. If the coach so chooses, and the facilities permit it, the plan can be posted in advance, enabling the athletes to become acquainted with it before training. One advantage of such an approach is that the athletes would have time to prepare psychologically for any demanding lessons.

CHAPTER EIGHT

Short Term Planning

THE MICRO-CYCLE

The etymology (the study of derivation of words) of the term micro-cycle can be traced from both Greek and Latin languages. The Greek term, "mikros", means small, while in Latin, "cyclus", refers to a sequence of phenomenon which succeeds regularly. Thus, in the methodology of training, a micro-cycle refers to a weekly training program, which in an annual program succeeds in a certain fashion according to the needs of peaking for the main objective (competition) of the year.

A micro-cycle is probably the most important and functional tool of planning in training, which, through its structure and content, determines the quality of the training process. Not all training lessons of a single micro-cycle are of the same nature. They do alternate according to training objectives, volume, intensity, and methods, any of which may be dominant in a given phase of training. Furthermore, the physiological and psychological demands placed upon the athlete can not be steady but on the contrary must change depending on the working capacity, needs of recovery and regeneration, and the competition schedule.

Criteria for a Micro-cycle

The main criteria used for a micro-cycle is derived from the general goal of training, which is the improvement of training factors and the elevation of athletic performance. The improvement of abilities is very closely linked with the changes of various kinds of training factors so that a correct mixture will prevail. Thus, the efficiency of a lesson aiming at developing a technical element is a function of the type and content of training performed previously. If the former training lesson was devoted to the development of endurance or if it utilized highly intensive stimuli, the following lesson should not aim at perfecting technique since the athlete and especially the CNS will probably not have adequate time to recover. The reverse sequence seems to be more effective, meaning that the development of endurance seems to be more effective when it follows a training lesson having the objective of developing speed.

The criteria of deciding the sequence of training lessons in a micro-cycle has to consider the dominant factors or biomotor abilities specific to the sport. According to Ozolin (1971) the optimal sequence is as following:

— learn and perfect technique with medium intensity
— perfect technique at submaximum and maximum intensity
— develop speed of short duration (up to one's limit)
— develop anaerobic endurance
— improve strength using a load of 90–100% of the individual's maximum
— develop muscular endurance using medium and low load
— develop muscular endurance with high and maximum intensity
— develop cardio-respiratory endurance with maximum intensity
— develop cardio-respiratory endurance with moderate intensity

The above suggested sequence should be considered as a general guide and should be applied in accordance with the specifics of the sport's and the athlete's training needs. The intensity that increases progressively, concludes in the middle section, while toward the end endurance development prevails.

The above sequence has strong similarities to the one advocated during the main part of the training lesson: 1) technique and/or tactical elements; 2) develop speed and/or power; 3) develop strength, and 4) develop general endurance.

Methodical Parameters for the Construction of a Micro-cycle

Often, in order to have a training effect, training lessons of similar objectives and content must be repeated 2–3 times during the same micro-cycle. The repetition of similar exercises several times is an essential plight for learning a technical element or developing a biomotor ability (the Romans used to say that "repetitia mater studiorum est", repetition is the mother of study). However, during a micro-cycle, exercises designed to develop biomotor abilities have to be repeated with varying frequencies. Thus, the development of general endurance, flexibility, or strength exercises designated for a large group of muscles lead to better results if repeated every second day. Strength training of large muscle groups has cardio-vascular components which, as opposed to smaller muscle groups where training is localized, is more exhaustive and therefore requires a longer recovery period. As for the development of specific endurance of submaximum intensity, three training lessons per week will suffice, while specific endurance of maximum intensity during the competitive phase should be planned twice a week with the remaining days being dedicated to lower intensity training. Similarly, two lessons per week are for the maintenance of strength, flexibility and speed. Finally, an optimal frequency for bounding exercises used to develop leg power and exercise for speed performance under strenuous conditions (snow, sand), seems to be 2–3 times per week.

The alteration of work with regeneration is of great importance and must be maintained when planning a micro-cycle. Work reaching an athlete's limits should not be planned more than twice a week, while an active rest, incorporating low intensity, relaxing activities should be planned once a week. However, days planned for active rest ought to follow a lesson that demands maximum effort from the athlete.

The concept of repeating the same lesson 2–3 times during a week of training may also be valid for the micro-cycle themselves, especially during the preparatory phase. Throughout a macro-cycle a micro-cycle of the same nature (i.e., content, methods) may be repeated 2–3 times, following which a qualitative improvement based on the athlete's adjustment to a lesson may be observed. However, especially for advanced athletes, the nature of the micro-cycle may be constant, but both components of training may vary, meaning that either or both the volume and intensity of training should be increased for each cycle.

Criteria to Construct a Micro-cycle

Although an organized coach would use long term plans from which he/she would extract term plans like macro and micro-cycles, a detailed training program should not be prepared for more than two micro-cycles into the future. This is due to the fact that the dynamics of the athlete's improvement is quite difficult to foresee. However, the coach could compile his/her athlete's macro-cycle, but be quite flexible in applying it in the sense that the last micro-cycle could be considered as a general guideline and thus be altered if requested in accordance with the athlete's rate of improvement.

As far as the construction of a micro-cycle is concerned, there are many factors to consider, among which the following are of prime importance:

—set the micro-cycle's objectives, especially for the dominant training factors.
—set the absolute level of work to be used in training, such as the number of training lessons, volume, intensity and complexity of training.
—set the relative level of work for the micro-cycle: how many peaks and alterations with less intensive training lessons.
—decide on the character of training, referring to the kind of methods and means of training to be employed per lesson.
—set training or competition days, if applicable, which are derived from the annual plan.
—a micro-cycle very often commences with low or medium intensity training lessons and progresses with increasingly intensive ones.
—prior to an important competition, a micro-cycle may be used with one peak only, which should be reached 3–5 days before the competition commences.

In addition to the above, the coach also has to determine whether his/her athletes should perform one or more training lessons per day as well as the time and content of each lesson. And finally, each micro-cycle should be preceded by a short meeting between the coach and athletes.

During the meeting the coach may discuss:

1) Objectives for each training factor and eventual performance or test standards to be reached during that micro-cycle; 2) Methods and means used to achieve the objectives; 3) Details of the program (time of each training lesson, volume and intensity of training, the difficulty of certain lessons and eventual priority, and special remarks for individual athletes); 4) Miscellaneous information. Should the micro-cycle end with a competition, the coach must give the athletes all details about it and motivate them to meet the goals set for the competition. Similarly, following the last training lesson of the micro-cycle, the coach should conclude with a short meeting where he/she must:

1. Analyze whether the objectives were achieved;
2. Analyze negative and positive aspects regarding the athlete's training behavior, motivation, etc.;
3. Let the athletes make their own comments regarding the past micro-cycle;
4. Outline changes to be considered for the future and which may be reflected in the following micro-cycle.

Such meetings, during which everything is directly and honestly stated are important ingredients in training, a very practical vehicle for communication during which the coach/athletes may learn aspects regarding their athletic endeavors, and which may assist them to make the appropriate changes so that future athletic improvements may be enhanced.

The Classification of Micro-cycles

The above suggested criteria may be used in structuring micro-cycle, which, according to different circumstances, could lead to certain variations. In addition, the dynamics of a micro-cycle also depend on the phase of training, the priority of certain training factors (whether the technical or the physical factor should prevail), and more importantly, it should reflect and evolve around the athlete's individual progress and training capacity. Consequently, the coach should try to eliminate standardization and rigidity. A certain degree of flexibility should give room to certain alterations which mirror all information gathered by the coach regarding his/her athlete's and opponent's progress.

A micro-cycle may be structured in accordance with the number of training lessons planned in a particular week. Obviously, the number of training lessons depends on the athlete's level of preparation as well as whether he/she follows a general club program or takes part in a camp. The availability of training time certainly plays an important role. Figure 35 illustrates a micro-cycle with 8 training lessons which maximizes the use of the athlete's free time on the weekend. The T symbols suggests when training takes place while the diagonal line illustrates a rest time.

In a camp situation or during a holiday, the structure would be altered in accordance with the time available for training. Under such circumstances and considering the athlete's training potential, different variations may be organized. Figure 36 illustrates a 3 + 1 structure which suggests that the athlete trains successively in three half days while the fourth is set aside for rest.

	M	T	W	Th	F	Sat	Sun
AM						T	T
PM	T	T	T	T	T	T	

Figure 35. A micro-cycle with eight training lessons.

	M	T	W	Th	F	Sat	Sun
AM	T	T	T	T	T	T	
PM	T		T		T		

Figure 36. A 3 + 1 structure of a micro-cycle.

A slightly altered structure may be considered for athletes whose training potential corresponds with a more demanding micro-cycle. A 5 + 1 (five training lessons followed by one-half day rest) or a 5 + 1 + 1 suggesting that the end of the cycle would incorporate 5 lessons plus a half-day rest followed by another half day of work are illustrated by figures 37 and 38 respectively.

A micro-cycle may also be structured according with available time and the kind of training to be performed. Figure 39 illustrates an example where during early morning, a supplementary training lesson (ST) is organized, while in the evening the athlete performs the main training of the day (T) followed by a weight training (WT) program.

The dynamics of training throughout a micro-cycle is not uniform, but rather of various intensities, depending on the character of training, the type of micro-cycle, climate and environmental temperature. As far as the dynamics of intensity is concerned, there is a certain alternation between high (H), or 90–100% of maximum, medium (M), or 80–90%, and low (L), or 50–80%, often followed by rest (R) on

	M	T	W	Th	F	Sat	Sun
AM	T	T	T	T	T	T	
PM	T	T		T	T		

Figure 37.   A micro-cycle with a 5 + 1 structure.

	M	T	W	Th	F	Sat	Sun
AM	T	T	T	T	T	T	T
PM	T	T		T	T		

Figure 38.   A micro-cycle with a 5 + 1 + 1 structure.

	M	T	W	Th	F	Sat	Sun
7:00	ST	ST	ST	ST	ST	ST	ST
17:00	T	T	T	T	T	T	
19:00	WT	WT		WT	WT		

Figure 39.   A micro-cycle illustrating various kinds of training.

Sundays. For an intensive micro-cycle, a coach may plan either one, two, or occasionally even three peaks of high intensity.

Certainly, the elevation of intensity and the planning of the number of peaks have to be managed progressively following the principle of progressive increase of load in training. Altitude, temperature, long travel and time difference as well as climatic factors also influence the intensity and number of peaks employed in the training program of a micro-cycle. During high altitudes, or following long travel involving a 5–8 hour time difference, a peak may only be planned in the second micro-cycle with the first being for adaptation. Similarly, in a hot and humid climate a coach should rarely employ more than one peak, which usually should be at the beginning of the week when the athlete has more vigor.

From the methodical point of view, in a micro-cycle with only one peak, that peak should be planned for one of the three middle days of the week. As for the two peaks structure, they could be placed towards the two ends of the cycle, being linked with one or two regeneration days. An exception to this may occur when the coach applies model training. Two peaks may be planned on adjacent days to simulate a competitive situation.

The following seven figures (40–46) illustrate various structures of micro-cycles with one and two peaks. Other combinations may be made by the coach depending on specific particularities and training needs.

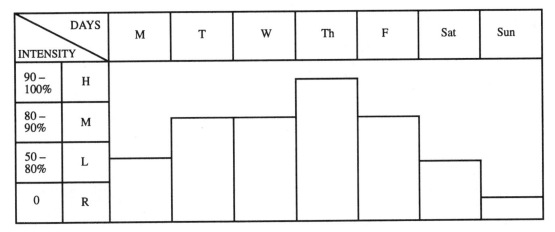

Figure 40. A micro-cycle with one peak.

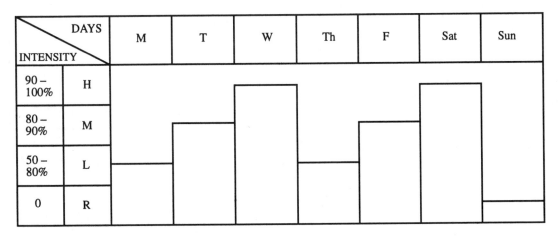

Figure 41. A two-peak micro-cycle.

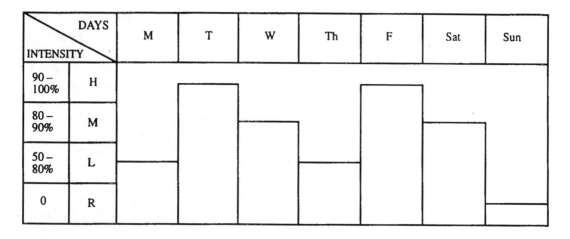

Figure 42. Another version of the two-peak micro-cycle. Its proponents suggest that the athletes can easier tolerate a H intensity day following a L one. Although this is true, the advocates of this type of load fail to understand that following a H intensity day one should normally plan a L one in order to facilitate regeneration and overcompensation. If a H intensity is followed by a M one, the residual fatigue makes the M intensity more difficult to cope with, transforming it from M to another H intensity day. Furthermore, this affects the L intensity, where the training demand is much higher than the planned one. As such the curve of intensity is much higher throughout the week, resulting in increased levels of fatigue.

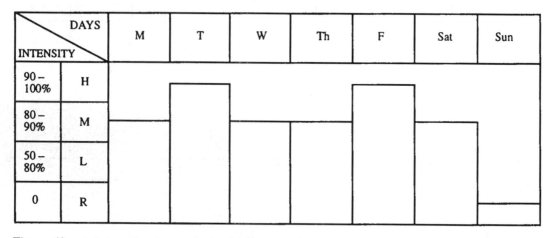

Figure 42. A two-peak micro-cycle but higher demand.

DAYS
INTENSITY
M
T
W
Th
F
Sat
Sun
90 – 100%
H
80 – 90%
M
50 – 80%
L
0
R

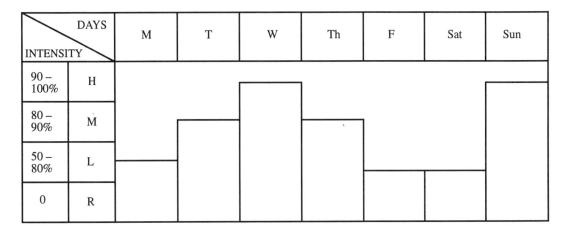

Figure 44. A two-peak micro-cycle, where the second one is a competition, preceded by two unloading training lessons.

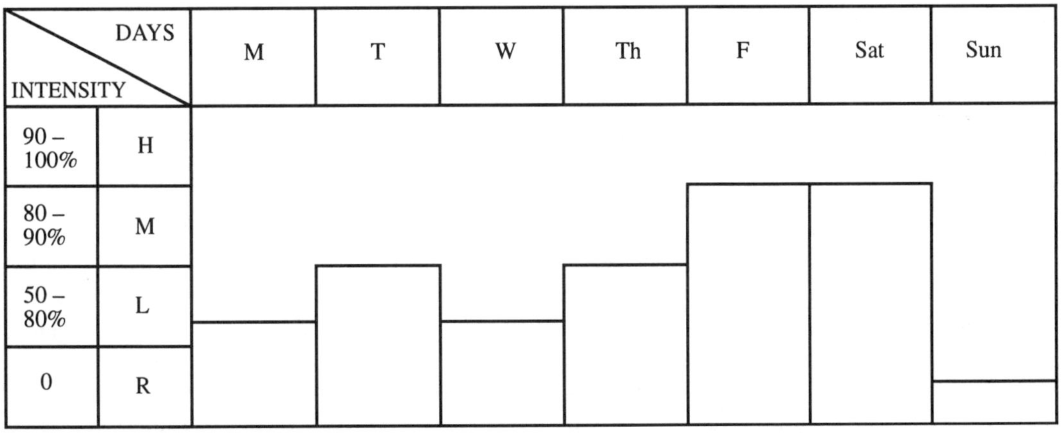

DAYS
INTENSITY
M
T
W
Th
F
Sat
Sun
90 – 100%
H
80 – 90%
M
50 – 80%
L
0
R

Figure 45. Two adjacent peaks of a model training micro-cycle.

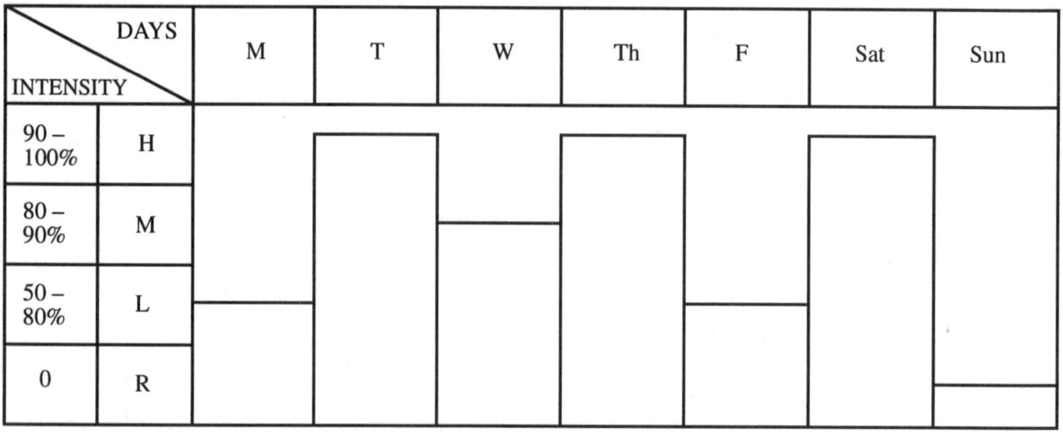

DAYS / INTENSITY		M	T	W	Th	F	Sat	Sun
90 – 100%	H							
80 – 90%	M							
50 – 80%	L							
0	R							

Figure 46. A three-peak micro-cycle alternated with lower intensity training lessons.

The micro-cycle has to be a functional plan and, therefore, as simple as possible. Figure 47 exemplifies a plan from the competition phase. The plan itself should specify the date, objectives, and content for each training lesson. Obviously, the content has to be expressed in a brief form, but citing the major items of each training lesson.

Numeric Symbols of Intensity Used for Planning a Micro-cycle

In all athletic programs the intensity of training must be changed throughout every micro-cycle in order to enhance both the athlete's physiological adaptation to a certain load as well as his/her regeneration following a demanding workout. Based on physiological characteristics of a sport a coach may identify 4–5 intensities of training. Each intensity should correlate with a certain rhythm of activity, type and method of training as well as a certain heart rate, plus or minus a few beats per minute. Also, a specific ergogenesis, or the percentage of each energy system used must characterize each level of intensity. Then, as illustrated in figure 48, the coach must plan the percentage of each intensity of training to be employed in the micro-cycle. The highest percentage of training should be allocated to the development of the dominant ability of the sport.

Both figures 48 and 49 exemplify the above concept as well as its practical application in a micro-cycle used by the Canadian National Rowing Team (Bompa, 1975). As suggested by figure 48 it was considered that for the sport of rowing, intensities 3 and 4 are dominant, and comprise 70% of the total training for the competitive phase of the annual training plan. The same two intensities predominate the following example of a micro-cycle (Figure 49) which shows the linkage between the concept and its practical application in training.

SPORT/EVENT: Javelin

MICRO-CYCLE NO:29

DATE: 20.07–27.07

OBJECTIVES: — Performance: 67.00 m
— Perfect the rhythm of the last three strides under higher velocity conditions
— Develop the ability to concentrate for the morning competition
— Maintain leg and arm power

TIME	M	T	W	Th	F	Sat	Sun
A.M. 10:00–11:00	—warm-up: 15 min —sprints 20,30,40 m $\frac{6}{2/4;\,3/4}$	—competition warm-up —6 throws		As Tuesday	—competition warm-up	—competition 10:45	
P.M. 17:00–19:30	—warm-up: 20 min —sprints $\frac{30\ m}{4/4}$ 3 —Technique last 3 strides —30 throws with baseball —15 medicine ball throws —2×30 m bound.	—competition warm-up —6 throws 4/4 —15 throws 3/4 with short approach —7 min spec. warm-up —30 min wt. training —5 min flex. exercises —10 game	Basketball game: 2 × 15 min	As Monday	—competition warm-up —15 thrown med. appr. —15 min walk & throw at different spots in the grass —special exercises for relaxation	Basketball game: 2 × 15 min	

Figure 47. A competition phase hypothetical micro-cycle plan.

153

SYMBOL	CHARACTERISTICS OF TRAINING	RHYTHM OF ACTIVITY	STROKE RATE	TYPE OF TRAINING	HEART RATE/MIN	ERGOGENESIS		PERCENTAGE OF TOTAL VOLUME OF TRAINING
						AEROBIC	ANAEROBIC	
1	Endurance of speed	Maximum	> 40	Starts and sprints of up to 15 seconds Rest = 1.5 minutes	> 180	20%	80%	10%
2	Endurance of strength	Very high, over the racing rate and rhythm	37–40	Repetitions of 250–1000 m Rest = 3–10 min	170–180	35%	65%	
3	Specific (racing) Endurance	Rapid, Find out the optimal rhythm and ratio	32–36	Races and controlled races Interval training of 3–4 min Rest = 4–5 min	150–170	75%	25%	70%
4	Aerobic endurance of medium distances	Moderate. Lower than the racing rhythm	24–32	Long repetitions. Variable rate and variable power Long distance rowing intercalated by sprints of 30–60 secs	120–150	85%	15%	
5	Aerobic endurance of long distance	Low	< 24	Long distance (steady state) Technique	< 120	95%	5%	20%

Figure 48. Numeric intensity symbols used in rowing (Bompa, 1975).

TRAINING TIME	M	T	W	Th	F	Sat	Sun
7:00–8:00		10 km tech. (5)	10 km Aerobic endurance (5)	10 km Aerobic endurance (5)	10 km tech. (5)	10 km speed pl. (4)	
9:30–11:30	24 km Long reps: 8 × 2 km (4)	20 km I.T. 10 × 2 min R = 3 min (3)	24 km Aerobic endurance (long dist.) (5)	24 km Variable rate variable power (4)	20 km I.T. 6 × 3 min R = 5 min (3)	24 km Aerobic endurance and 3 × 1 min (4)	
16:00–18:00	20 km Model training 1 × 250 m 2 × 500 m 2 × 1000 m 2 × 500 m 2 × 250 m (2)	24 km Variable rate and variable power (4)		20 km Sprints: 500 total strokes R = 1.5 min (1)	24 km Long reps. 3 × 6 km R = 5 min (4)	20 km Model training 1 × 250 m 6 × 1000 m 2 × 500 m 2 × 250 m (2)	
18:00–19:00	Weight train. Max. strength	W.T. musc. endur.		W.T. max. str.	W.T. musc. endur.		

Σ km = 294

Figure 49. Numeric intensity symbols used as a guideline to construct a micro-cycle rowing training program. Note the intensity symbols in the upper right-hand corner.

155

The Daily Cycle of Athletic Training

Figure 49 shows that the daily training schedule, especially in a camp situation, is very heavy. In order to maximize the time for training purposes, the daily schedule has to be organized very carefully and effectively. Athletes want to train hard but they also need free time for their own purposes, relaxation and fun. Therefore, training programs as well as other activities from the general daily consensus have to be extremely well organized and adhered to. Suggested below are activities for three and four daily training lessons applicable to elite class athletes in a camp situation:

A daily program with three training lessons:

6:30 — wake up
7:00–8:00   — first training lesson (low intensity)
8:30–9:00   — breakfast
9:00–10:00   — rest
10:00–12:00 — second training lesson
12:00–13:00 — recovery techniques and rest
13:00–14:00 — lunch
14:00–16:00 — rest
16:00–18:00 — third training lesson
18:00–19:00 — recovery techniques and rest
19:00–19:30 — dinner
19:30–22:00 — free program
22:00 — sleep

As for the daily program with four training lessons, the following may be considered:

6:30 — wake up
7:00-8:00   — first training lesson
8:30-9:00   — breakfast
9:00-10:00   — rest
10:00-12:00 — second training lesson
12:00-13:00 — recovery techniques and rest
13:00-14:00 — lunch
14:00-16:00 — rest
16:00-17:30 — third training lesson
17:30-18:30 — recovery techniques and rest
18:30-19:30 — fourth training lesson
19:30-20:00 — recovery techniques
20:00-20:30 — dinner
20:30-22:00 — free program
22:00 — sleep

In camp situations some coaches and athletes prefer to have two lessons per day but of longer duration, often 3–4 hours. However, on the basis of personal experience and also considering the general practice employed by most East European specialists, it seems that the breakdown of 5–6 hours of training into 3–4 training lessons is more effective. Training lessons of longer duration than two and a half hours seem to be less effective since fatigue is acquired which hinders learning and limits the furthering of certain biomotor abilities. However, as illustrated by figure 49, even during a camp situation the athletes may have a half day free time on Wednesday afternoon as well as the entire day of Sunday. This is sufficient for both rest and fun.

The Model of a Competition's Micro-cycle

The entire annual training program is composed of many micro-cycles, most of which have the goal of developing skills and specific abilities required by a sport. However, during the competitive phase the entire training program becomes strictly dependent on the goal of a successful performance in the major competition of the year. In order to facilitate a good performance, the structure of the last micro-cycle is modified in accordance with the specific needs of the competition and the athlete's physiological and psychological adjustment to it. Based on specific information regarding the competition the coach develops the micro-cycle which becomes a model to be repeated several times prior to the main contest. This model should incorporate training lessons of various intensities, where training alternates with active rest and recovery, and where the daily cycle should be identical to that of the day of competition.

Often major competitions have qualifying rounds, frequently followed by finals in the same day (i.e., Friday 10:00 and 15:00). This type of program is not uncommon in track and field and swimming. In the model developed for the competition, the coach regards the day of Friday as the main training day in which he/she would plan two very intensive training lessons at the times of the scheduled competitions. In some sports, like team sports, boxing, tennis, and wrestling athletes are exposed to 3–4 days of consecutive contests; a situation which has to be reflected in the model of the competition's micro-cycle and repeated several times before the tournament starts. However, the model cannot feasibly be repeated consecutively but rather at an interval of 2–3 weeks so that in between developmental micro-cycles may be planned.

In some sports (team sports, boxing, wrestling) tournaments for the Olympic games, World championships or other top international competitions are organized over 4–9 days which hardly may be reproduced in training, especially because of the time factor involved and the high demand placed upon the athletes. In order to overcome this deficiency and gain experience for larger tournaments, the coach should enter his/her athletes in tournaments of shorter duration, 2–3 days, where they may be exposed to 4–5 contests. However, the general characteristics of the big tournament to come could be reflected in the developmental micro-cycles, especially with regard to the daily cycle, which will be modeled accordingly. Furthermore, the athletes could be familiarized with the competition schedule by simulating the rhythm of alternating contest and free days, thus applying the model training concept. Training lessons falling on the same day as a competition in the upcoming tournament should be very demanding while those falling on a day of no competition should be of a lower intensity.

Ozolin (1971) considers that the alternation of simulated competitive days with days of rest is an important factor in the athlete's adaptation to the competition schedule. He claims that generally the athletes do not favour free days between two competitions, such as preliminary heats and finals, since sometimes performance during the second day of competition is not as good as expected. The eventual drop in performance seems to be based on post competition psychological reactions (i.e. overconfidence, conceit) rather than on accumulation of fatigue. However, such negative athletic behaviors may be overcome by introducing model micro-cycles in all macro-cycles planned for the competitive phase. If the competitive phase is short, the same model may be introduced during the last part of the preparatory phase. Such a program would develop a stereotype which would enhance the athlete's performance throughout future competitions.

During the competitive phase, athletes take part in other competitions which may not occur on the same day of the week or at the same time of day as the main competition. It is advisable that the model micro-cycle not be altered, especially if the competitions do not pose a serious problem in qualifying the athletes for the main competition.

When the competition commences, the athlete must be completely recovered, both physiologically and psychologically, from the last cycles and lessons of training. The athlete should feel in optimal physical and psychological condition, a status which may be enhanced in two ways. First, reducing the volume and especially the intensity of training during the 5–8 days preceding the competition in order to ensure that all the energy spent during training is replenished. Alternatively, the coach may use a double micro-cycle for unloading purposes. This means that in the first cycle, intensity will be maintained above the medium level and for 1–2 training lessons will be high, while during the second cycle it will be much lower, averaging well below the medium level. While the first cycle may be quite demanding, the eventual fatigue will disappear during the second micro-cycle. This should lead to both a physiological and psychological state which will favour optimal performance. This first alternative may be adequate for sports requiring dynamic performance, while the second may meet the needs of sports where endurance is dominant.

THE MACRO-CYCLES

The term, macro, is derived from the Greek word, "makros", which signifies something of large size. In the methodology of training a macro-cycle represents a phase of training with a duration of between 2–6 weeks or 2–6 micro-cycles. During the preparatory phase, a macro-cycle commonly consists of 4–6 micro-cycles while during the competitive phase it will usually consist of 2–4 micro-cycles, depending on the competition schedule.

Criteria Used to Establish the Duration of a Macro-cycle

Although there may be some similarities, the criteria used to establish the duration of a macro-cycle often differs from sport to sport. However, the following points maybe of some assistance when dividing the annual plan into macro-cycles.

For the preparatory phase the main criteria are the objectives and type of training used in different parts of this training stage. The time necessary to develop or perfect a technical element may be considered as a macro-cycle. The same may be valid for certain tactical maneuvers. As far as the development of biomotor abilities is concerned, the time needed to perfect an ability or its components may also be an adequate criterion to decide the length of a macro-cycle.

Should the coach decide to have some exhibition competitions towards the end of the preparatory phase, the date of competition is also a decisive factor in determining the macro-cycle length. If the coach is able to select the competitions at his/her will, they should be scheduled for the end of a macro-cycle so that specific information with regard to the progress made by the athletes in that particular training stage may be obtained.

MONTH	DEC.	JAN.	FEB.	MAR.	APRIL
Macro-cycle	1	2		3	4
OBJECTIVES	—testing —general strength —prepare the muscles, tendons and ligaments for heavy load training	Maximum strength		Power Maintain maximum strength	Power Maintain maximum strength

Figure 50.   A hypothetical strength training program for a long jumper where the objectives of training are the criteria for defining the macro-cycles.

As for the competitive phase, the establishment of each cycle depends mainly on the competition schedule. If the athlete is of international caliber, the schedule of trials and international competitions are the chief factors in deciding the duration of a macro-cycle. The competitive phase especially for individual sports should be divided in such a way that, if possible, each competition should fall at the end of a macro-cycle. Often, it happens that during the competitive phase, especially for team sports, there are several competitions schedules, sometimes 2–4 per month. In this case the coach should decide which is the most important competition and should prepare the athlete accordingly with less attention given to the other competitions. The main competition should occur at the end of a macro-cycle.

The Components of a Macro-cycle

As any other phase or cycle of training, a macro-cycle must have objectives which are derived from and concord with the annual plan. While the objectives of the plan refer to the general direction of training for years to come, those of a macro-cycle should be functional, specific, and characteristic to that cycle. These objectives aim at improving performance in competitions and/or specific tests, as well as training factors planned for the macro-cycle. Often a specific objective of a certain cycle is linked with and precedes others which have to be achieved in the following phase of training. For instance, if a gymnastic coach plans for his/her athlete to acquire a technical element which requires a great deal of strength in macro-cycle No. 5, then in the preceding cycles among the main objectives should be the development of the required strength of the primary muscles involved as well as a progressive introduction of specific exercises leading up to execution of that element.

Now that the coach has set the objectives for the macro-cycle in order of importance, he/she should make the decision regarding which method of training is most appropriate to accomplish the objectives. If the gymnast from the above example is deficient in strength, then the coach should select training methods in consideration of this fact. Isometric, isokinetic or weight lifting methods are alternatives from which he/she can choose. The third step is for the coach to consider the alternative means of training. In order to develop a gymnast's strength, the coach must employ the most effective means of training. Two questions that must be answered follow: Should the gymnast use only training methods with direct effect or should he/she use means with indirect effect? Are there special apparatuses available to develop specific strength or must simple barbells suffice?

Following the decisions made in the above three steps, the coach constructs the plan for the macro-cycle. For sports which have constant training conditions (performed indoors), the plan may be subject only to minor changes as opposed to those performed under variable conditions (outdoors) where rain and wind often are important training impediments.

And finally, as is the case of every training phase, at the end of the macro-cycle the coach has to analyze whether the objectives were achieved or not, as well as specific remarks concerning the athlete's rate of improvement and psychological behavior during training and competitions. All these observations and the conclusions of the coach's analysis should be actively used to draw the objectives for the following macro-cycle. The coach's analysis and subsequent conclusions should be inserted in his/her training book. An example of such an analysis is offered below and refers to a javelin thrower.

> The performance objective (i.e., 67.00 m) was achieved. The athlete trained well with a high level of determination and conviction. The athlete's body adapted well to training loads. In the following cycle much attention must be paid to the perfection of technique under increased velocity of the approach and transition. For competition purposes and achievement of a high performance level the most efficient micro-cycle seems to be: Monday: technique and speed development; Tuesday: strength and power; Wednesday: technique, flexibility and co-ordination; Thursday: model training (a repetition of the day of competition); Friday: rest; Saturday: competition; Sunday: rest.

As observed from the above suggested analysis, the coach has to be brief, summarizing the main features of a program, and indicating future objectives which might be different or slightly altered from the ones which were previously planned.

Structural Consideration Regarding a Macro-cycle

The structure of a macro-cycle should be based on specific objectives and the competition schedule. However, the methical principle of progressive increase of load in training ought to be considered as a constant guideline for every coach. The increase of load in training is made in steps, and figure 51 schematically illustrates the dynamics of intensity in each micro-cycle (in an average macro-cycle of 4 weeks).

The first three micro-cycles are developmental, where the intensity increases progressively throughout. The fourth micro-cycle is a maintenance one at the end of which is a short unloading phase to allow the athlete to overcompensate prior to a hypothetical competition on the weekend. In situations where the last micro-cycle does not end with a competition, the cycle still has to be maintenance, where the components of training are of lower intensity than the previous micro-cycle. Such a short unloading phase with lower physiological and psychological demands is necessary in order to enhance regeneration and to eliminate most, if not all, fatigue symptoms which were accumulated following stressful training. Furthermore, it provides an adequate methical foundation to start another developmental phase.

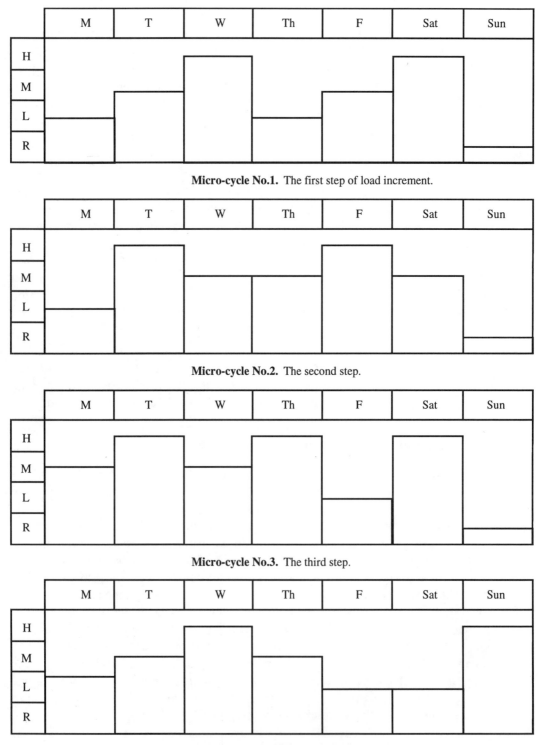

Micro-cycle No.1. The first step of load increment.

Micro-cycle No.2. The second step.

Micro-cycle No.3. The third step.

Micro-cycle No.4. The fourth step.

Figure 51. The classical structure of a macro-cycle, where in the first three micro-cycles the load in training is increased whereas in the fourth the load is decreased prior to a competition (Sunday).

D A Y S

Training content	1	2	3	4	5	6	7	8	9	10	11	12	13	14	15	16	17	18	19	20	21	22	23	24	25	26	27	28	29	30
Physical preparation																														
Uniform running 5000 m	x																													
Variable running 3000 m			x																											
Fartleck 4000 m (4)					x			x														x			x					
Interval training																														
long intervals: 1200 m											4													4						
medium intervals: 400 m																						8								
short intervals: 60 m																		12												10
Strength training																														
max. strength: 16 tons												x					x										x			
12 tons										x						x														x
8 tons									x															x		x				
Muscular endurance:																														
30 tons							x																							
25 tons		x		x																										
Power training: 8 tons																				x			x							
6 tons																									x			x		
Flexibility:	x	x	x	x	x			x	x	x	x	x		x	x	x	x	x	x				x	x	x	x	x			
Cross Country Skiing						x							x								x								x	
Basketball					x							x							x							x				

Figure 52. A hypothetical example of a macro-cycle for the preparatory phase, for a football team.

Below are a few suggested variations of macro-cycles which the coach may use in his/her training endeavours (figure 53–56)

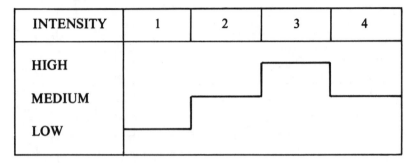

Figure 53. The step-type approach: three developmental micro-cycles followed by an unloading/regeneration one.

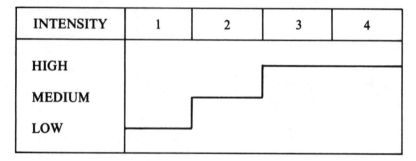

Figure 54. A structure of a macro-cycle used in the loading portion of the preparatory phase.

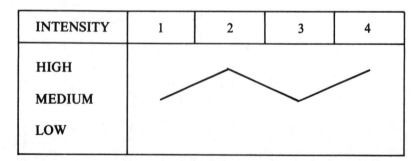

Figure 55. A two peak or wave-like structure. Following a regeneration micro-cycle, the fourth one reaches the highest intensity.

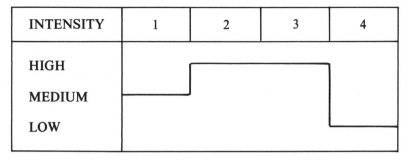

Figure 56. Another variation with two peaks followed by a regeneration micro-cycle, at the end of which a competition may be planned.

The structure of a macro-cycle may assume many different forms. Often it may happen that most if not all micro-cycles have a uniform intensity, especially in learning phases (i.e. in diving, and in figure skating). On the other hand, in other sports (i.e. weight lifting) the load in each cycle may increase continuously. It appears that the macro-cycle's structure changes in accordance with the coach's needs, the phase of training, and the competition schedule. During the preparatory phase, the vast majority of micro-cycles composing a macro-cycle ought to be of a developmental nature. On the other hand, specific to the competitive phase there are macro-cycles which always should conclude with a peaking micro-cycle regardless of whether or not a competition is scheduled.

CHAPTER NINE

The Annual Plan

INTRODUCTION

The annual plan is the tool used by the coach to direct and guide athletic training over a year. It is based on the concept of periodization (the division of an annual plan into phases of training) and the principles of training. A training program organized and planned over a year is necessary in order to maximize the improvement in an athlete's performance. As a general principle this means that an athlete must train continuously for approximately 11 months while during the last one he/she should perform only a reduced amount of work. This work should vary from that of regular training in order to facilitate physiological, psychological and CNS rest and regeneration prior to the beginning of another year of training.

As previously stated, the main objective of training is to reach a high level of performance at a given time (which usually is the main competition of the year), based on a correct development of athletic shape. Good athletic shape occurs when the degree of training is high and the psychological status enhances a high level of performance. In order to achieve such a performance, the entire training program has to be properly periodized and planned so that the development of skills, biomotor abilities and psychological traits follow in a logical and sequential manner. Well organized and planned training is a goal not often achieved by a coach. In fact, Matveev (1965) found that from a large group of Russian athletes, swimmers and weight lifters participating in the Olympics and World Championships, only 15–25% of them did the top performance coincide with the major competition. The remaining percentage of athletes achieved their best performance prior to or following the planned date, which illustrates inadequate knowledge and experience in planning.

In the methodology of training, one of the most challenging and complex problems is to achieve the peak of athletic shape on the planned date. As concluded above, often an athlete's peak, and for that matter, highest performance, is achieved prior to the main competition, which seems to be the result of pushing the athlete too much to reach a high level of athletic shape, with an inadequate alternation of work with short regeneration phases. On the other hand, the peak is often reached following the top competition as a result of a deficient preparation or an inadequate load or demand placed upon the athlete. A typical example of inferior planning occurs sometimes in gymnastics when some routines are finalized just prior to an important competition.

Planning has to be done by the coach, especially for inexperienced athletes. As for the athletes with a rich background and much experience they should join the coach in setting objectives and the plan outline for the following year. In this way the athletes may have a say in the design of their program while the coach can use their feedback in a positive manner.

PERIODIZATION

Periodization is a process of dividing the annual plan into small phases of training in order to allow a program to be set into more manageable segments and to ensure a correct peaking for the main competition(s) of the year. Such a partition enhances a correct organization of training, allowing the coach to conduct his/her program in a systematic manner. Though not all coaches are familiar with all the details of periodization, the concept is not very new. It has existed in a very unrefined form for an unknown length of time. However, it is very difficult to trace out who initiated it. Probably, though in a very primitive form, it was used even by the Greek Olympians.

The annual training cycle, in most sports, is conventionally divided into three main phases of training: preparatory, competitive, and transition. Both the preparatory and competitive phases are also divided in two subphases since their tasks are quite different. The preparatory phase, on the basis of different characteristics of training, has both a general and a specific subphase, while the competitive phase usually is preceded by a short pre-competitive subphase. Furthermore, each phase is composed of macro, and micro-cycles. Each of these smaller cycles have specific objectives which are derived from the

	THE ANNUAL PLAN					
PHASES OF TRAINING	P R E P A R A T O R Y			C O M P E T I T I V E		TRANSITION
SUB-PHASES	GENERAL PREP.	SPECIFIC PREP.	PRE-COMPET.	COMPETITIVE		TRANSITION
MACRO-CYCLES						
MICRO-CYCLES						

Figure 57.   A schematic illustration of the division of an annual plan in its phases and cycles of training.

general objectives of the annual plan. Figure 57 illustrates the division of the annual plan into phases and cycles.

High levels of athletic performance are dependent upon the athlete's adaptation, psychological adjustment to the specifics of training and competitions, and the development of skills and abilities. On the basis of these realities, the duration of training phases depends heavily on the time needed to increase the degree of training and athletic shape. The main criteria of calculating the duration of each phase of training is the competition schedule. The athlete trains for the competitions for many months aiming at reaching his/her highest level of athletic shape at those dates. The accomplishment of such a goal assures very organized and well-planned annual training, which should facilitate psychological and physiological adaptations. Organization of an annual plan is enhanced by the periodization of training and the sequential approach in the development of athletic shape. However, an optimal periodization for each sport and precise data regarding the time required for an optimal increase of the degree of training and athletic shape, is not exact yet. This difficulty is further expressed by athlete's individual characteristics, psycho-physiological abilities, diet, and regeneration.

Improved planning ability may be facilitated by developing a model plan which, based on yearly observations, may be continuously improved.

The Needs of Periodization

The needs for different phases of training were inflicted by physiology since the development and perfection of neuro-muscular and cardio-respiratory functions, to mention just a few, are achieved progressively over a long period of time. The athlete's physiological and psychological potential also needs to be considered, and that athletic shape cannot be maintained throughout the year at a high level. Any increase of the required training work above a previously established highest level ought to be preceded by an unloading phase, when the level of training is decreased. Usually, during the preparatory phase the coach attempts to develop the physiological foundations of his/her athlete's systems, while throughout the competitive phase he/she strives for perfection in accordance with the specifics and needs of competitions.

The methodology of developing skills, strategical maneuvers and biomotor abilities also require a special approach, specific for each phase of training. The learning of a skill requires time and is achieved in a sequential manner throughout training phases. The above is also valid for strategical maneuvers. The closer to perfection a skill is, the more sophisticated strategical tools a coach can use. Periodization is also a decisive factor in the development and the needs of a sequential approach in the perfection of a biomotor ability. As for the enhancement of athletic shape both the volume and intensity of training have to be increased in an undulatory manner as proposed by the principle of progressive increase of load in training.

Climatic conditions and the seasons also play a deciding role in the needs of periodizing the training process. Often, the duration of a phase of training depends strictly on the climatic conditions. Seasonal sports such as skiing, rowing, and soccer are very much restricted by the climate of a country. For many sports, winter is always the preparatory phase, while the competitive phase is in the summer (rowing) or spring and fall (soccer).

Each competition and the highly intensive training which is specific to the competitive phase has a strong component of stress. Although most athletes and coaches may cope with stress, a phase of stressful activities should not be very long. There is a high need in training to alternate phases of stressful activities with periods of recovery and regeneration, during which the athletes are exposed to much less pressure. Such a phase (usually the transition) facilitates the creation of a favorable mood and generates the athlete's potentials, thus providing a solid ground for a following period of heavy work.

The Classification of Annual Plans

Although annual plans differ depending on the specifics of the sport, their classification depends on the number of competitive phases incorporated in a plan. For seasonal sports (skiing, canoeing, football) or for those sports having only one major competition during the year, only one competitive phase is prevalent. Such an annual plan is called a mono-cycle, meaning that there is only one competitive phase, therefore, one peaks only for one major competition (figure 58). Such a plan is divided into the three classical phases of training: preparatory, competitive, and transition. While the preparatory phase includes the general and specific preparation, the competitive phase is subdivided into smaller subphases. The pre-competitive subphase, which usually includes exhibition competitions only, precedes the subphase of main competitions, where all official competitions are scheduled. Prior to the main competition, the most important one in that year, two shorter phases are planned. The first one is an unloading phase (also named tapering-off) during which both the volume and intensity of training are lowered so that the athlete may regenerate prior to taking part in the main competition. A special preparation phase which could be organized either separately or together with the unloading phase follows, during which the coach may make some technical, and especially tactical changes. This phase may also be used for relaxation and psychological preparation for the competition(s).

Although it may differ in accordance with the specifics of the sport, during the preparatory and beginning of the competitive phase, the volume of training is emphasized, while intensity reaches only relatively low levels. This suggests that the quantity of work should be dominant, as opposed to the competitive phase where intensity, or quality, of work is emphasized.

A completely different approach is taken in those sports which have two separate competitive seasons as is the case with track and field where an indoor and outdoor

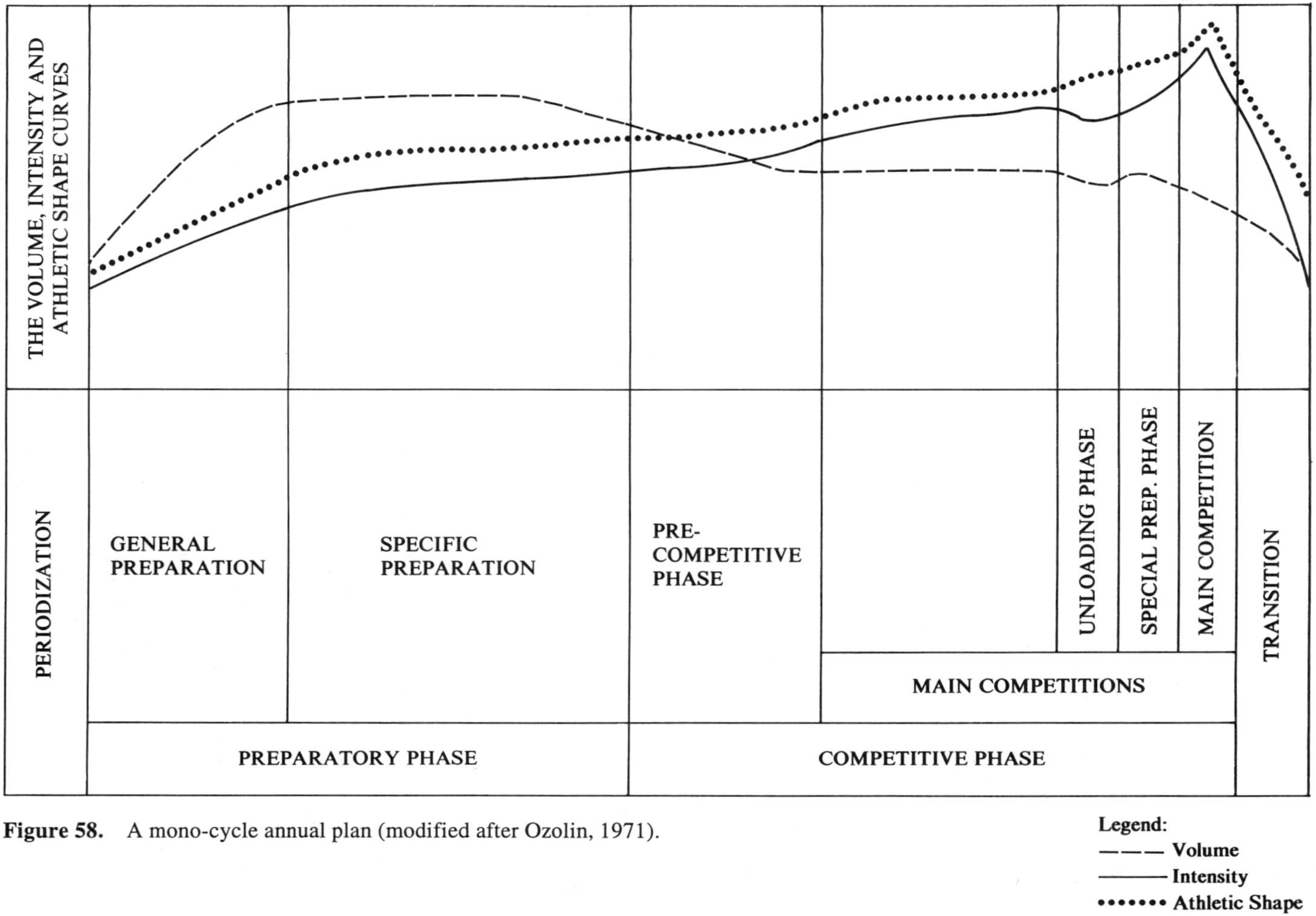

Figure 58. A mono-cycle annual plan (modified after Ozolin, 1971).

171

season is common. Owing to the fact that there are two distinct competitive phases such a plan is called a bi-cycle (bi in Latin refers to having two of something). Figure 59 represents a schematic illustration of a bi-cycle, which incorporates the following phases of training:

> —preparatory phases I which usually is the longest of the two preparatory phases
> —competitive phase I
> —a very short transition (1 week) linked with a preparatory phase II. The beginning of this phase may be an unloading phase for recovery purposes.
> —competitive phase II
> —a transition phase

As may be observed from figure 59, a bi-cycle is composed of two short mono-cycles linked together through a short unloading and preparatory phase. For each cycle the approach may be similar, except for the volume of training which in the longer preparatory phase I is of much higher magnitude than in preparatory phase II. Also, the level of athletic shape may be lower in the competitive phase I, since in our example, track and field, the outdoor championships usually are more important. This is appropriately illustrated by the curve of the athletic shape which is planned to reach the highest values during competitive phase II.

And finally, it is not unusual for sports such as boxing, wrestling or gymnastics to have three very important competitions during the same annual plan (i.e., national championships, qualification meet for a big international competition and the competition itself). Assuming that each competition is 3–4 months apart, an athlete would have three competitive phases and the plan would be called a tri-cycle (Latin tri—meaning three).

As illustrated by figure 60 a tri-cycle incorporates the following sequence of training phases:

> —a long preparatory phase I
> —competitive phase I
> —a short unloading, transition and/or preparatory phase II
> —competitive phase II
> —unloading, transition and/or preparatory phase III
> —competitive phase III
> —transition

When a coach plans a tri-cycle, the most important competition of the three should occur during the last cycle. On the other hand, of the three preparatory phases, the first one should be the longest, during which the athlete(s) should be building the physical foundation which will foster the following two cycles. As may be observed from figure 60, the curve of volume is the highest, reflecting the relative importance of volume of training in the preparatory phase I as opposed to the following two preparatory phases.

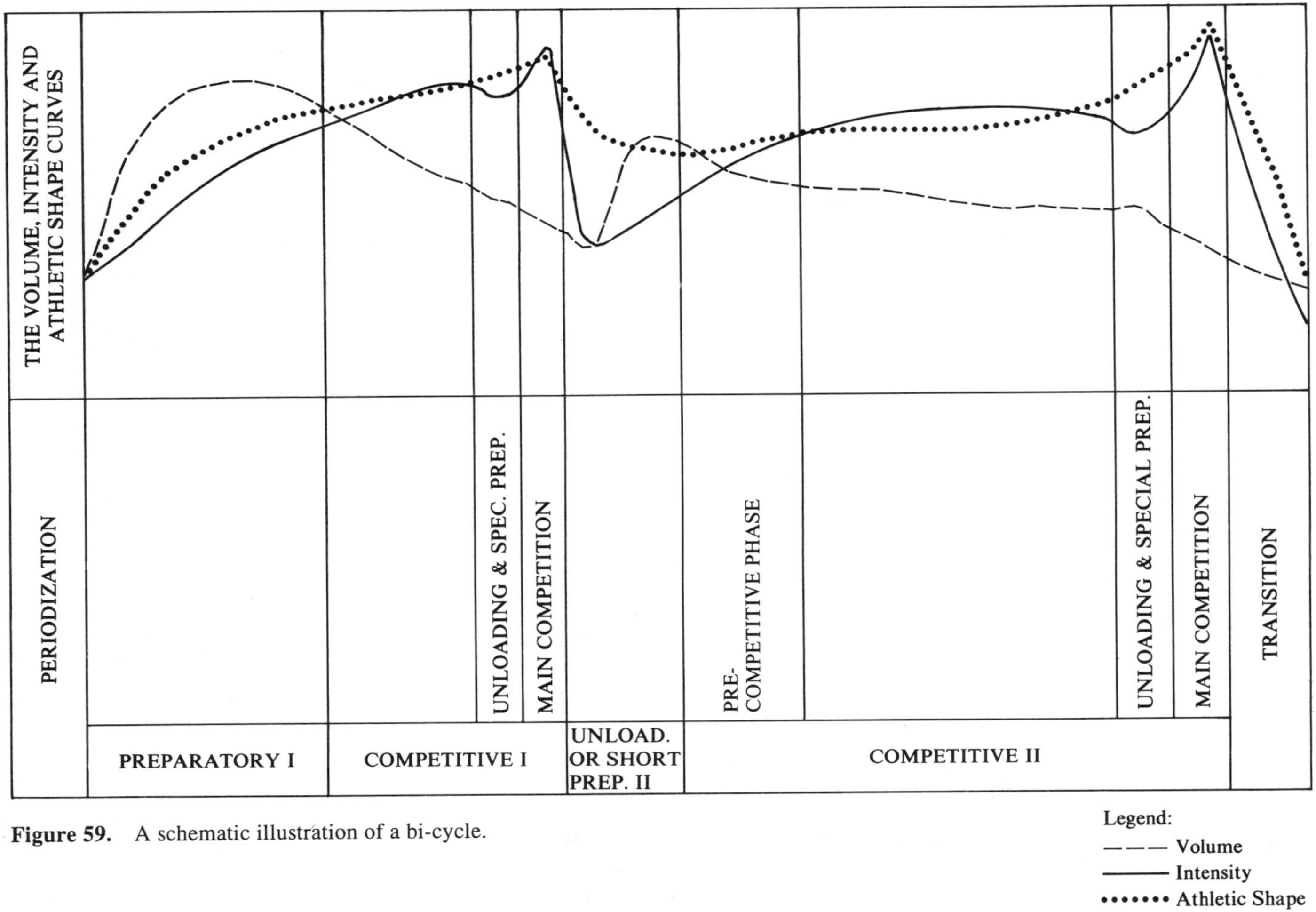

Figure 59. A schematic illustration of a bi-cycle.

Legend:
- – – – Volume
- ——— Intensity
- ••••• Athletic Shape

173

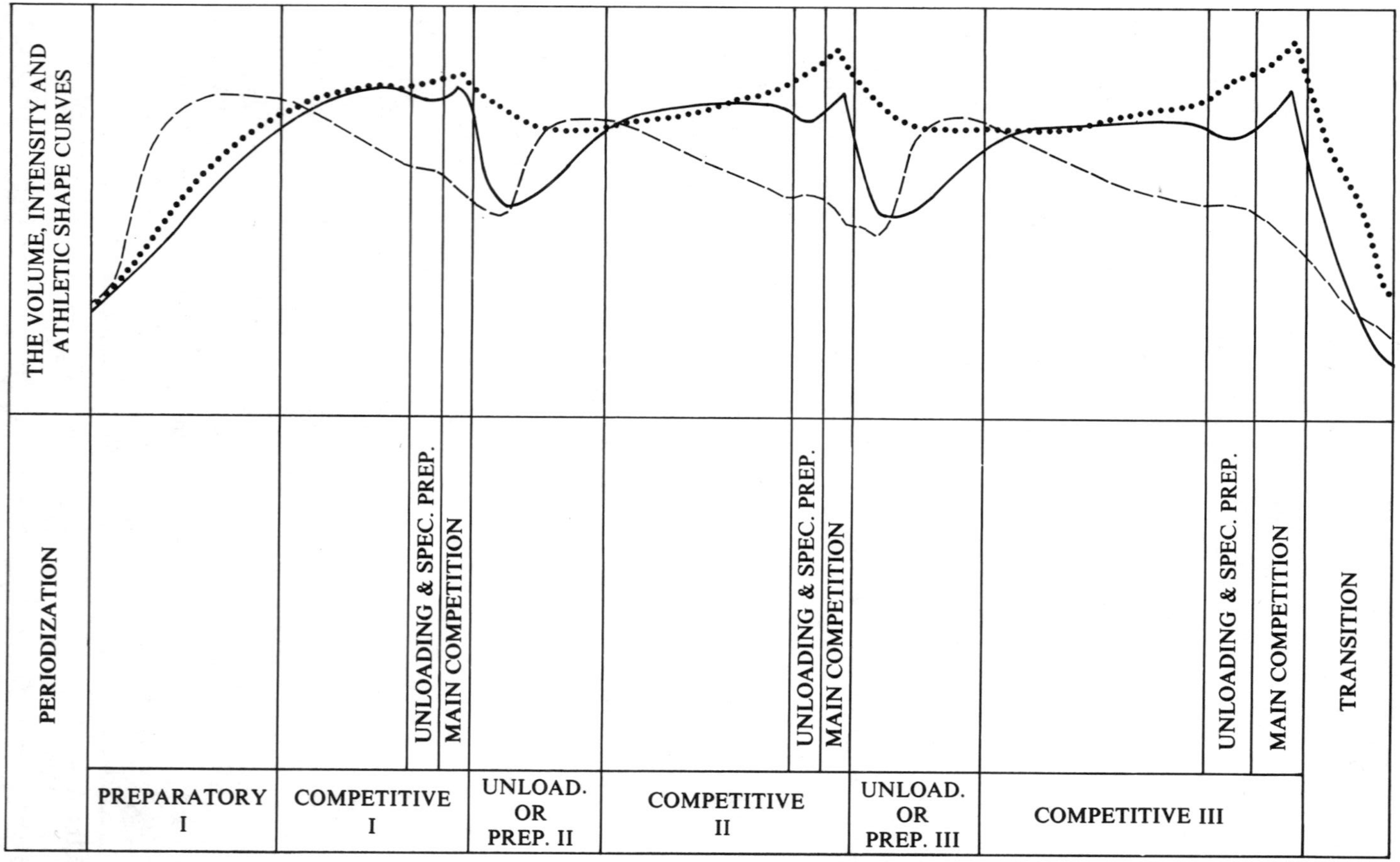
THE VOLUME, INTENSITY AND ATHLETIC SHAPE CURVES
PERIODIZATION
PREPARATORY I
COMPETITIVE I
UNLOADING & SPEC. PREP.
MAIN COMPETITION
UNLOAD. OR PREP. II
COMPETITIVE II
UNLOADING & SPEC. PREP.
MAIN COMPETITION
UNLOAD. OR PREP. III
COMPETITIVE III
UNLOADING & SPEC. PREP.
MAIN COMPETITION
TRANSITION

Figure 60. A schematic illustration of a tri-cycle.

Legend:
- – – – Volume
- ——— Intensity
- ••••••• Athletic Shape

The curve of intensity follows a pattern similar to that of a mono-cycle for each of the cycles. Both the volume and intensity curves drop slightly for each of the three unloading phases preceding the main competitions. As far as the curve of athletic shape is concerned, the coach would plan the highest peak for the third cycle, which is assumed to correspond with the main competition of the year.

Stress: Its Planning and Periodization

Stress is a significant by-product of training and competitions which often, if not manipulated properly, may affect an athlete's performance and behavior in training and competitions. Since training deals primarily with biological and psychological components, stress is considered to be the sum of these phenomena elicited by internal and adverse external influences.

Throughout training and competitions, the athlete is exposed to several stressors of biological, psychological and sociological natures. The competition, audience, peers, family, coach's pressure to perform well, and intensity of training are among the main stressors with which the athlete has to cope. Therefore, a wise coach should consider these athletic by-products and, on one hand train the athlete to cope with them, while on the other hand plan the stress properly throughout the annual plan. Once again, the concept of periodization is an important tool in properly planning stress. As shown in figure 61, the curve of stress does not have the same magnitude throughout the annual plan, and this appears to be one of the most distinctive advantages of the concept of periodization. The shape of the curve is very low during the transition phase, and progressively elevates throughout the preparatory phase and fluctuates during the competitive phase, as a consequence of alternating stressful activities (competitions) with short regeneration periods. During the preparatory phase the magnitude of the stress curve is the outcome of the relationship between the volume and intensity of training. While the volume, or the quantity of training is high, the intensity is lower since it is difficult to emphasize both a high amount of work and an elevated intensity simultaneously, with an exception probably being made in weight lifting. Since intensity of training is one of the prime stressors and, as mentioned above, throughout most of the preparatory phase it is emphasized less than the volume of training, the curve of stress is low as well. However, one exception may be the testing dates which could place some stress upon some athletes especially those who find it difficult to meet the standards. Similarly, since coaches in team sports select the team during the preparatory phase, the dates and days prior to selection are often considered stressful as well.

The curve of stress throughout the competitive phase has an undulatory structure, as a consequence of alternating competitive with developmental micro-cycles. Thus, it appears quite evident that the number of competitions and their frequency represent the cause of an elevated stress curve. The more frequent the top competitions are the more stress the athlete is exposed to. In such cases, following competitions, the coach has to plan a few days of regeneration and only when the athlete is almost fully

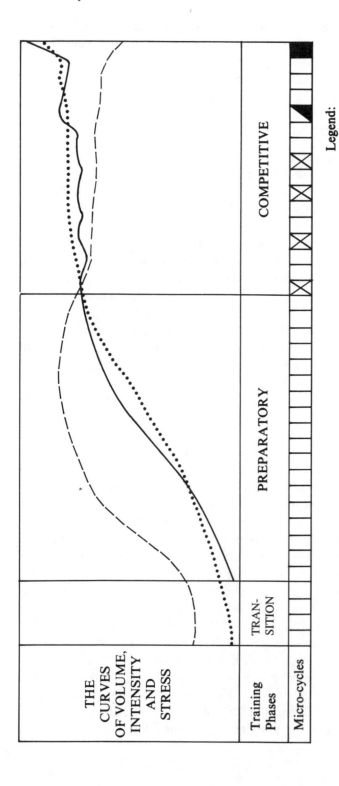

Figure 61.   The stress curve during a mono-cycle.

recovered would he/she be again exposed to intensive training lessons. Similarly, prior to important competitions the coach would be wise to plan a short unloading period (2–3 days).

Apart from alternating high with low stressful activities, the coach may also use relaxation techniques so that the athlete may cope more easily with stress. However, in athletics there are various types of athletes, some with a natural ability to cope with stress, others being less gifted. Although for the second category motivational and relaxation techniques may be of some assistance, some athletes may require more work in dealing with their stressors. Therefore, when the coach selects athletes for the sport, he/she should consider psychological tests which may sort the candidates in accordance with the needs of high performance athletics.

THE PERIODIZATION OF BIOMOTOR ABILITIES

The utilization of the concept of periodization is not limited only to the structure of a training plan or the type of training to be employed in a given training phase. On the contrary this concept should also have a large application in the methodology of developing the dominant biomotor abilities of the chosen sport.

While in some sports, mostly individual, there is a loose structure of periodization especially of endurance, in most team sports the periodization of dominant abilities allows for some room of improvement. Similarly, when the periodization of endurance is compared with strength, it is often seen that strength training does not properly follow the concept of periodization.

In many sports the dominant biomotor ability is power. Recognizing this, some coaches can often be seen employing exercises aimed at developing power throughout the year, from the early preparatory to the beginning of the competitive phase. Such an approach may be the result of misunderstanding both the concept of periodization as well as the principle of specificity which some physiologists suggest. Power is the product of maximum strength and maximum speed. This product could reach a much higher level when actually needed, namely prior to the start of the main competitions, if the strength component is developed separately and then converted into power (figure 62).

PERIODIZATION OF STRENGTH TRAINING

The objectives, content and methods of a strength training program changes throughout the training phases of an annual plan. Such changes occur in order to reflect the type of strength a sport/event, or individual athlete requires so that optimal performance improvement may be enhanced.

ANATOMICAL ADAPTATION. Following a transition phase, when in most cases athletes do not particularly do much strength training, it is scientifically and methodically sound to commence a strength program aimed at adapting the anatomy of the athlete to a new strength program. Thus, the main objective of this phase is to in-

	PREPARATORY		COMPETITIVE			TRANSITION
	GENERAL PREPARATORY	SPECIFIC PREPARATORY	PRE– COMPETITIVE	MAIN COMPETITIONS		TRANSITION
STRENGTH	ANATOMICAL ADAPTATION	MAXIMUM STRENGTH	CONVERSION: – POWER – MUSCULAR ENDURANCE – OR BOTH	MAINTENANCE C	REGENERATION	
ENDURANCE	AEROBIC ENDURANCE	DEVELOP THE FOUNDATION OF SPECIFIC ENDURANCE		SPECIFIC ENDURANCE		AEROBIC ENDURANCE
SPEED	AEROBIC AND ANAEROBIC ENDURANCE	DEVELOP THE FOUNDATION OF SPEED		SPECIFIC SPEED, AGILITY AND REACTION TIME		

Figure 62.   The periodization of main biomotor abilities.

volve most muscle groups to prepare the muscles, ligaments, tendons, and joints, to endure the following long and strenuous phases of training. A general strength program, with many exercises (9–12), performed comfortably, without "pushing" the athlete, is desirable. A load of 40–60% of one's maximum, 8–12 repetitious, in 2–3 sets, performed at a low to medium rate, with a rest interval of 1–1:30 minutes between exercises, over 4–6 weeks will facilitate to achieve the objectives set for this first phase. Certainly, longer anatomical adaptation (8–12 weeks) should be considered for junior athletes, and for those without a strong background in strength training.

MAXIMUM STRENGTH PHASE. Most sports require either power (i.e., long jumper), muscular endurance (i.e., 800–1500 m swimming), or both (i.e., rowing, canoeing, wrestling, team sports). Each of these two types of strength are affected by the level of maximum strength. Without a high level of maximum strength, power cannot reach high standards. Therefore, since power is the product of speed and maximum strength it is rather logical to first develop maximum strength and then convert it into power. During this phase the goal is to develop maximum strength to the highest level of the athlete's capacity. The duration of this phase (1–3 months) is a function of the sports/events, and the athlete's needs. For a shot putter or football player it may be quite long (3 months) as opposed to an ice hockey player who may allocate only a month for the development of this type of strength.

THE CONVERSION PHASE. According to the needs and characteristics of the sport/event, maximum strength has to be converted into either power or muscular endurance, or both. By applying the adequate training method for the type of strength sought, and through the application of training methods specific to the selected sport (i.e. speed training) maximum strength is gradually converted. Throughout the duration of this phase (1–2 months), a certain level of maximum strength still has to be maintained, otherwise towards the end of the competitive phase power may slightly decline.

For sports where power or muscular endurance is the dominant strength component, the appropriate method has to be prevalent in training. When both power and endurance are required, an adequate training time and method(s) should reflect the optimal ratio between these two abilities. For instance, for a wrestler the ratio has to be almost equal. In a canoer's (500 m) program power should dominate, while for a rower (duration of race 6–8 minutes) muscular endurance should prevail.

While the maximum strength phase is specific to the preparatory phase, the duration of the conversion period commences towards the end of preparatory and continues on through the beginning of the competitive phase (pre-competitive phase).

THE MAINTENANCE PHASE. As the term suggests the main objective of strength training for this phase is to maintain the standards achieved during the previous phases. Once again the program followed during this phase is a function of the specific requirements of the sport. The ratio between maximum strength, power, and muscular endurance has to reflect such requirements. For instance, a shot putter and linemen in football may plan two sessions for maximum strength and two for power, while a jumper may consider one for maximum strength and three sessions for power respectively. Similarly a baseball player, a wide receiver in football, or a 100 m swimmer may plan one session for maximum strength, two for power and one for muscular endurance, while a 1500 m swimmer may dedicate the entire strength program to perfect muscular endurance.

The number of sessions dedicated to the maintenance of the required strength has to be between 2–4, depending on the athlete's level of performance, and the role played by strength in the skill (i.e., pole vault) and performance. Considering the objectives of the competitive phase, the time allocated to the maintenance of strength is rather secondary. Therefore, the coach has to develop a very efficient and specific program. Two to a maximum of four exercises involving the prime movers may suffice the needs of maintaining previously reached strength levels.

THE CESSATION (C) PHASE. Prior (5–7 days) to the main competition of the year the strength training program is ended, so that all energies are saved for the accomplishment of a good performance.

THE REGENERATION PHASE completes the annual plan and coincides with the transition phase from the present to the next annual plan. While the objectives of the transition phase are through active rest, to remove the fatigue and replenish the exhausted energies, the goals of regeneration are more complex. For the injured athlete, this phase of relaxation also means to rehabilitate and restore injured muscles, tendons, muscle attachments, and joints, and should be performed or aided by specialized personnel. Whether parallel with the rehabilitation of injuries, or afterwards, before this phase ends all the athletes should follow a program to strengthen the stabilizers, the muscles which through a static contraction secures a limb against the pull of the contracting muscles. Neglecting the development of stabilizers, whether during the early development of an athlete, or during his/her peak years of activity, means to have an injury prone individual, whose level of maximum strength and power could be inhibited by weak stabilizers. Therefore, the time invested on strengthening these important muscles means a higher probability of having injury free athletes for the next season.

PERIODIZATION OF ENDURANCE

During an annual plan of training, the development of endurance is achieved in several phases. Considering as a reference an annual plan with one peak, endurance training is accomplished in three main phases: 1) aerobic endurance, 2) develop the foundation of specific endurance, and 3) specific endurance (figure 63).

A similar approach is suggested also for a long term training plan. Assuming that a young athlete commences training at the age of 12, the development of endurance would follow the phases suggested by figure 63.

AGE		
12–16	**17–18**	**19+**
Aerobic endurance	Develop the foundation of specific endurance	Specific endurance

Figure 63. Periodzation of endurance in a long training plan.

Each of the suggested phases has its own training objectives:

1. AEROBIC ENDURANCE is developed throughout the transition and early preparatory phase (1-3 months). Although each sport may require slight alterations, the accomplishment of the goals of aerobic endurance could be achieved through the uniform and steady state method with a moderate to medium intensity. As a general consequence of such a program, the athlete's working capacity, the cardio-respiratory system, progressively improves. Parallel with the athlete's adjustment to training the workload has to be elevated, especially the volume of training.

2. THE DEVELOPMENT OF THE FOUNDATION FOR SPECIFIC ENDURANCE has an extremely important role in achieving the objectives set for endurance training. Throughout this phase, representing a transition from aerobic endurance to a type of endurance specific for each sport, the aerobic endurance is still emphasized. Elements of anaerobic activity are introduced, depending on the specifics of the sport and in accordance to the ergogenesis of each activity. Certainly for team sports, the rhythm of activity and the pace of specific drills are progressively becoming sport specific. An intensive training specific to the competitive phase may fail unless the foundations of endurance are not solidly developed during the second phase. Uniform, alternative, and long and medium interval training (towards the end of this phase) are the prevailing methods. The volume of training reaches the highest levels during the aerobic and this phase of the annual plan.

3. SPECIFIC ENDURANCE coincides with the competitive phase. The selection of the appropriate methods depends strictly on the ergogenesis of the sport and the athlete's needs. However, for many sports the intensity of training has to be emphasized, where it often exceeds the racing intensity. The alternation of various types of intensities should facilitate a good recovery between training lessons, thus leading to a good peak for the final competition.

THE PERIODIZATION OF SPEED

The periodization of speed training is dependent upon the characteristics of the sport, the athlete's level of performance, and the competition schedule. Therefore, the periodization of speed training will be different for team sport athletes and sprinters.

The first group of athletes usually follow a mono-cycle annual plan, while sprinters, who in most cases participate in an indoor and outdoor season, will follow a bi-cycle.

Whether for individual or team sports, the periodization of speed may follow these training subphases:

1. AEROBIC AND ANAEROBIC ENDURANCE should be considered as the training base for the other phases to come. Whether through tempo (i.e. sprinters) or simply through steady state-type of training for the other sports, this first subphase of the preparatory phase is a necessity to build a solid aerobic foundation on which speed training has to rely.

Training progressively incorporates more specific means of activities, using standard methods of that sport. At the beginning of this subphase, fartlek (speed play) followed later on by various types of intervals, and repetition training, are used in order to build a strong anaerobic base, which represents one more step closer to specific speed.

2. DEVELOP THE FOUNDATION OF SPEED. As the competition phase approaches, training becomes more intensive, more event-specific, refined, and specialized. Specificity of training, both methods and specific exercises, prevails.

3. SPECIFIC SPEED, AGILITY AND REACTION TIME. Specific methods and drills are largely dominant not only for the scope of developing specific speed, but also in order to refine other related abilities such as agility and reaction time.

During the competitive phase the intensity of training is elevated both through specific training methods and also through participation in competitions. While exercises specific to the chosen sport prevail, general means of training, games and play for fun, relaxation, and active rest should also be incorporated. A correct ratio between these two groups of exercises would lower stress and strain in training. Since many sprinters and team sports, as a result of high intensity training are prone to injuries, the alternation between various means and intensities represent not only a training deterrent, but also an important training requirement.

Illustrations of periodization of training for various sports are represented by figures 64-68.

THE ANNUAL PLAN TRAINING PHASES
AND THEIR CHARACTERISTICS

As has been mentioned, an annual plan has three types of training phases: preparatory, competitive, and transition. Whether they are repeated several times, as in a bi or tri-cycle, or not, the objectives and characteristics of training are the same. It is of great importance to the athlete's success that the suggested duration, sequence, characteristics and emphasis which is placed upon each phase of training be followed. This will ensure that he/she may reach the highest athletic shape for the planned competition.

Figure 64. The periodization of strength training for gymnastics (mono-cycle).

DATES	SEPT	OCT	NOV	DEC	JAN	FEB	MAR	APR	MAY	JUNE	JULY	AUG
COMPE-TITIONS					Detroit	L.A.	Toronto	PROV. ORILLIA		NAT. CH. VANCOUV.		
PERIOD-IZATION	PREPARATORY				COMPETITIVE						TRANSITION	
PERIOD-IZATION	GEN. PREP.		SPECIFIC PREP.		PRE-COMP	MAIN COMPET.					TRANSITION	
PERIOD OF STRENGTH	ANAT. ADAPT.		MAX STRENGTH		CONVERS. TO POWER	MAINTENANCE (MX. STR. AND POWER)					REGENERATION	

Figure 65. The periodization of dominant abilities for figure skating (mono-cycle).

DATES	JUNE	JULY	AUG	SEPT	OCT	NOV	DEC	JAN	FEB	MAR	APR	MAY
COMPE-TITIONS								DIVIS. CHAMP.	NAT. CHAMP.	WORLD CHAMP.		
PERIOD-IZATION	PREPARATORY						COMPETITIVE				TRANSITION	
PERIOD-IZATION	GEN. PREP.			SPECIFIC PREP.			PRE-COMP	MAIN COMPET.			TRANSITION	
PERIOD OF END.	GEN. END. (Run, Bicycle)			DEV. FOUND SPECIFIC ENDURANCE (Run, Skate)			SPECIFIC ENDURANCE				GEN.END.	
PERIOD OF STRENGTH	ANATOM. ADAPT.			MAX STRENGTH			CONVERS.: —MUSC. END —POWER	MAINTENANCE POWER: MUSC. END.			REGENERATION	

Figure 66. The periodization of dominant abilities in synchronized swimming (mono-cycle).

	SEPT	OCT	NOV	DEC	JAN	FEB	MAR	APR	MAY	JUNE	JULY	AUG
COMPE-TITIONS						PROV. CHAMP.		DIVIS. CHAMP.		NAT. CHAMP.		
PERIOD-IZATION	PREPARATORY					COMPETITIVE					TRANSITION	
PERIOD-IZATION	GEN. PREP.		SPECIFIC PREP.		PRE-COMP	MAIN COMPET.					TRANSITION	
PERIOD OF END.	AEROB. END.		DEV. FOUND OF SPEC. END. (SWIM; APNEA)			SPECIFIC ENDURANCE					GEN.END.	
PERIOD OF STRENGTH	ANAT. ADAPT.		MAX. STRENGTH		CONVERS.: —MUSC. END —POWER	MAINTENANCE					REGENERATION	

Figure 67. Periodization of dominant abilities of a hypothetical baseball team (mono-cycle).

	NOV	DEC	JAN	FEB	MAR	APR	MAY	JUNE	JULY	AUG	SEPT	OCT
COMPE-TITIONS								LEAGUE GAMES				
PERIOD-IZATION	PREPARATORY						COMPETITIVE				TRANSITION	
PERIOD-IZATION	GEN. PREP.		SPECIFIC PREP.				PRE-C.	LEAGUE GAMES			TRANSITION	
PERIOD OF STRENGTH	ANAT. ADAPT.		MAX. STR.		CONVERS.: —MUSC. END —POWER			MAINTEN: POWER; MUSC. END.			REGENERATION	
PERIOD OF SPEED	AEROB. END.		DEV. THE FOUND. OF SPEED				SPECIFIC SPEED, REACTION TIME, AND AGILITY				—	
PERIOD OF END.	AEROB. END.		DEV. THE FOUNDATION OF SPECIF. END.				PERFECT SPECIFIC ENDURANCE				AEROB. END.	

184

DATES	OCT	NOV	DEC	JAN	FEB	MAR	APR	MAY	JUNE	JULY	AUG	SEPT
COMPE-TITIONS					WINTER CHAMP-IONSHIPS						SUMMER CHAMP-IONSHIPS	
PERIOD-IZATION (phase)	PREP. I			COMPET. I		T	PREP. II			COMPET. II		TRANS.
PERIOD-IZATION (sub)	GEN. PREP.		SPEC. P.	PRE C.	MAIN. C.	T	GEN. P.	SPEC. PREP.		PRE C.	MAIN C.	TRANS.
PERIOD OF STRENGTH	ANAT. ADAPT.	MAX STRENGTH	CONV. POW. M-E.		MAINTAIN POW.: M-E.		ANAT. ADAPT.	MAX STRENGTH	CONVER. POW.: M-E.		MAINTAIN POW.: M-E.	REGEN.
PERIOD OF SPEED	AEROB. ENDURANCE		ANAER. END.		SPECIF. SPEED		AEROB. ENDURANCE		ANAER. END.		SPECIF. SPEED	GAMES

Figure 68.   The periodization of dominant abilities for swimming (200m) with a winter and summer National Championships (bi-cycle).

The Preparatory Phase

The preparatory phase has an enormous importance for the entire year of training since throughout this period the general framework of physical, technical, tactical and psychological preparation for the competitive phase is developed. An inadequate amount of training performed during this period would have visible repercussions during the competitive phase which would not be improved by any other form of training. A high degree of training, based especially on an increased volume, in the long run, would result in a relatively low level of fatigue following training and may also enhance recovery. Therefore, throughout the entire phase, especially during its initial part, a high volume of training is essential to create the basis of an adequate body adaptation to the specifics of training.

Ozolin (1971) illustrates, though in very general terms, the orientation and specifics of training in this phase by proposing the following objectives:

1. acquire and improve general physical preparation;
2. improve the biomotor abilities required by the sport;
3. cultivate specific psychological traits;
4. develop, improve, and/or perfect technique;
5. familiarize with the basic strategical maneuvers to be employed in the following phase;
6. improve the athlete's knowledge regarding the theory and methodology of training specific to the sport.

The preparatory phase could last between 3–6 months, depending on the characteristics of the sport and the type of annual plan employed. For individual sports the duration should be between 1–2 times as long as that of the competitive phase. However, for team sports, it may be shorter but not less than 2–3 months.

For methodological purposes, the preparatory phase is divided into two subphases; l) general and 2) specific preparation.

The GENERAL PREPARATORY subphase has the objectives of developing the athlete's work capacity, general physical preparation and the improvement of technical elements as well as basic tactical maneuvers. However, the foremost objective should be the development of a high level of physical conditioning, which will facilitate future training and, thus, future performance. This is a must for all sports, and the use of general exercises as well as those specific to the sport should have a higher priority than just performing the specific skills of the sport. For instance, in gymnastics, the first 2–3 micro-cycles should be almost totally dedicated to the development of general and special strength of those muscle groups which will be involved in learning or just performing certain technical elements in the following cycles of training. The same is valid for other sports as well, where certain physical components represent a limiting factor in technical progress. Often coaches wonder why their athletes do not acquire a skill according to their expectations. In such instances, the coach is well advised to test the athlete in order to determine whether or not he/she possesses adequate physical support for the technical performance of that particular element or skill.

Throughout this subphase, a high volume of training must be emphasized through the incorporation of exercises requiring extensive efforts both of general and especially of a specific nature. Such a program aims at improving the athlete's working capacity along with his/her psychological drive (determination, perseverance, willpower), thus progressively adjusting him/her to the specific effort requirements of the sport. For sports where endurance is the dominant ability or has an important contribution to the final performance (i.e. running, swimming, rowing, cross-country skiing), the development of aerobic endurance is the main objective. According to Harre (1982) 70–80% of the total training time should be allocated to the development of aerobic endurance, this should be evidenced by the number of kilometers covered in training. As for the sports where strength is an important attribute (i.e., weight lifting, gymnastics, wrestling, throwing events), general and maximum strength development should be the main objectives of the subphase. Increasing weight lifted in training would be an objective means of increasing an athlete's working capacity and specific adaptation to the needs of the sport.

Along with the development of the physical basis of training, athletes involved in team sports must allocate substantial time to the development of technical and tactical skills. However, this should not dominate to the extent of neglecting the improvement of endurance, strength, and speed as the physical groundwork for further performance accomplishments.

In most sports, the type of training performed in the preparatory phase, especially in the general subphase, represents an influencing factor for the competitive phase and the quality of results achieved. An insufficient emphasis on the volume of training during this subphase may account for poor performance, lack of consistency of performance throughout the competitive phase, and a decrease in performance during the last competitions of the year. Therefore, the time allocated to this subphase ought to be about one-third of the total time of the annual plan.

As seen from the previous figures, the intensity of training is of secondary importance throughout the preparatory phase, especially during the general preparatory subphase. However, intensive training may be continually employed, but its ratio should not exceed 30–40% of the total amount of training, particularly for juniors and beginners. Gandelsman and Smirnov (1970) explain this by suggesting that the impulses coming from the muscles during intense exercise are very strong and this irradiation in the CNS burdens the perception and reaction to a stimulus, leading to the performance of imprecise, uncontrolled skills. A less intensive or lower rate of performing an exercise allows the CNS to be more selective in the type of reply to a stimulus, thus enabling the athlete to have better control over his/her skills.

Considering the objectives of this subphase, it is not advisable to participate in any competitions throughout this period of heavy work since an athlete will not be ready to test his/her skills or abilities against those of an opponent. Usually, the technique is not stabilized yet, and poor results often affect the psychological sphere of the athlete. In addition, competitions may adversely affect whole training programs or, more specifically, the amount of work which has to be performed, which, is the main goal of this training phase.

The SPECIFIC PREPARATORY, or the second part of the preparatory phase, represents a transition towards the competitive season. Though the objectives of training are quite similar to those of the general subphase, the character of training becomes more specific. Although the volume of training is still high, most (70–80%) work is directed towards the specific exercises related to the skills and/or technical patterns of the sport. Towards the end of this subphase the volume tends to drop progressively, allowing an elevation of the intensity of training. For sports where intensity is an

Table 17. The specifics of training objectives for each subphase of the preparatory phase.

Sport	Dominant Training Factors	General Preparatory	Specific Preparatory
Gymnastics	Physical	General and maximum strength	Specific strength and power
	Technical	Technical elements	Elements, half and skeleton of full routine
Rowing	Physical	Aerobic endurance	Aerobic endurance
		General and maximum strength	Muscular endurance
Swimming (100 m)	Physical	Aerobic endurance	Anaerobic and aerobic endurance
		General and maximum strength	Maximum strength and power
Swimming (800 m)	Physical	Aerobic endurance	Aerobic and anaerobic endurance
		General and maximum strength	Muscular endurance
Team sports	Technical	Technical elements	Apply them in game situation
	Tactical	Individual and simple team tactics	Team tactics
	Physical	Aerobic endurance	Anaerobic endurance
		General and maximum strength	Power

important attribute (sprinting, jumping, team sports), the volume of training could be lowered by up to 20–40%.

For sports where technique and the perfection of co-ordination (sports such as figure skating, diving and gymnastics) are predominant, an athlete should continue to improve and perfect technical elements, but also to put them together in different combinations so that by the end of the preparatory phase he/she will have at least a skeleton of the routine prepared.

The improvement and perfection of technique and tactical elements should be one of the main goals of this subphase. The fulfillment of such a goal requires the performance of specific exercises involving the prime movers, exercises which simulate or are similar to the technical pattern of the skill. The basic theory which should prevail is that every exercise must be of high quality and have a maximum training effect. In this way, an optimal link between skills and biomotor abilities is facilitated, leading to a development of technique and abilities required to perform successfully in competitions. As for exercises of an indirect nature, only a few of them, up to a maximum of 30%, should be maintained in the program, mostly in order to fulfill the needs of alternating exercises of various patterns, to avoid boredom, enhance multilateral development, active rest and fun. An increase in proportion to specific exercises of direct effect facilitates an easy transition to the competitive phase.

Following this shift in the proportion of specialized training, the athletes should progressively show an improvement not only in their test scores but also in their performance. At the conclusion of this subphase, involvement in a competition of secondary importance or an exhibition game will provide important feedback. The type of training performed throughout the preparatory phase is specific for each sport, and is distinctive for each subphase as well. This assertion is supported by table 17 which illustrates some distinctive objectives of training for the general and specific preparatory subphases.

The Competitive Phase

Among the main tasks of the competitive phase is the perfection of all training factors, thus enabling the athlete to improve his/her abilities and thus compete successfully in the main competition or championship meet. Among the general objectives of the competitive phase are the following:

1. the continuous improvement of the biomotor abilities and psychological traits in accordance with the specifics of sport;
2. the perfection and consolidation of technique;
3. to feature and perfect tactical maneuvers and gain competitive experience;
4. to maintain general physical preparation;
5. to improve the level of theoretical knowledge.

Physical preparation still seems to remain the basis on which an athlete's performance is dependent. During the preparatory phase, it was the dominant training factor that was used to develop a foundation for future training. Throughout the competitive phase, the level of physical preparation must be maintained at the level achieved by the end of the preparatory phase as a constant and continuous support for the other training factors, and for performance as well. From the total amount of physical preparation planned in training, 90% has to be with direct action, while only 10% at the most would be dedicated to exercises with indirect action; the last group of exercises may be used especially for active rest and fun (games, team sports).

The objectives of the competitive phase are achieved through training, by performing specific skills and exercises, and competitions. A relatively high weight given to the specificity of training ensures improvement, stabilization, and performance consistency. Consequently, training becomes more intensive while the volume of training decreases. For sports where speed, power, and maximum strength are dominant and consequently determinant in the performance (i.e., sprinting, jumping and throwing events, weight lifting), the intensity of training increases dramatically as opposed to the volume which is reduced progressively. On the other hand, in sports where the dominant ability is endurance (distance running and swimming, cross-country skiing, canoeing, and rowing), the volume of training may be held constant or slightly lower than during the preparatory phase. An exception to this is the competitive micro-cycle where the intensity drops according to the number of races and the opponent's level.

During the competitive phase, it is obvious that an athlete's performance has to improve, as a result of well-planned training programs. However, should the performance improvement stagnate or even decrease, then the coach may conclude that in the second part of the preparatory phase the amount of work was reduced excessively as the intensity was increased. Discovering the correct ratio between intensity and volume of training is an artful job and those who can not handle it properly should prepare for some disappointments.

The duration of the competitive phase could be between 4–6 months, depending on the sport (team sports usually have a longer competitive phase) and type of annual plan. However, an excessively long competitive phase requires proportionately longer preparatory and transition phases which might shorten the duration of the next preparatory period.

Another important factor is to determine the date at which the competitive phase is to begin. A guideline proposed by Harre (1982) may be of some assistance in this matter and includes the following parameters:

1. The number of competitions required to reach the highest performance. Gandelsman and Smirnov (1970) claim that on the average, an athlete must partake in 7–10 competitions before achieving very high results;
2. The interval between competitions;
3. The duration of eventual qualifying meets;
4. The time required for special preparation prior to the main competition of the year; and
5. The time needed for recovery and regeneration.

For methodical and organizational reasons, the competitive phase may be divided into two basic subphases: 1) the pre-competitive; and 2) the phase of main competitions.

The OBJECTIVE OF THE PRE-COMPETITIVE phase is participation in various unofficial or exhibition meets so the coach can objectively assess his/her athlete's level of preparation in all factors of training. Everything that was accumulated during the preparatory phase, namely technique, tactical skills, physical and psychological preparation, ought to be tested in the real world of athletic competition. The participation in competition, especially for elite athletes, should not significantly change the training program since these meets represent just testing grounds for the next phase, where the athlete participates in official contests. However, as early as possible during the pre-competitive phase, the coach should draw thorough conclusions concerning necessary alterations to his/her athlete's training programs in order to maximize performance improvements for the main competition.

The PHASE OF MAIN COMPETITIONS is dedicated strictly to the increase of the athlete's potentials to the optimum, thus facilitating a superior performance in the main contest(s). The number of training lessons should reflect whether the athletes are exposed to a loading or a regeneration (unloading) micro-cycle. In the first case there may be up to 10–14 lessons per week, while in the second fewer lessons will prevail to permit an unloading phase prior to a competition. The content and means of training for the vast majority of training programs ought to be very specific including exercises directed to physical development of a direct nature. However, once a week, especially during an unloading phase, exercises of an indirect nature (games) may be used.

While the volume of training may be still high for sports where one of the dominant abilities is endurance, for sports where co-ordination, speed and/or power has to be perfected, it may be reduced by as much as 50–75% of the level reached during the preparatory phase. On the other hand, the intensity is increased continuously, reaching the highest level 2–3 weeks prior to the main competition, and then dropping continuously and progressively throughout the unloading phase. During the entire subphase, training lessons of maximum intensity should not occur more frequently than 2–3 times per micro-cycle.

During the competitive phase the stress curve is also elevated as a result of the increased intensity of training and the participation in competitions. The stress curve should be of an undulatory form reflecting the alternation of stressful activities (competitions and intensive lessons) with short phases of regeneration. The harder, more stressful a competition, the higher the stress curve and the longer the necessary compensation phase during which the curve decreases.

As far as the competitions are concerned, if possible, they should be arranged progressively in their order of importance, concluding with the main competitions. Another possibility may be the introduction of hard with a few lighter competitions, where the athlete competes without making drastic alterations in his/her training program. Although this may be feasible for individual sports, for team sports basically there exists an official game's schedule which can not be changed by the coach.

Some 6–8 micro-cycles prior to the main competition, the whole training program and daily cycle can be modeled according to the specifics of that competition. Under these circumstances the physical, technical, tactical and especially the psychological preparation for the main competition would be thorough. Should the coach predict and develop every single habit of the athlete in agreement with pre, during and post-competition specifics, the athlete may not be exposed to any surprises. During the presentation of the periodization concept, it was revealed that the main competition is preceded by an unloading and then followed by a special preparation phase.

The UNLOADING phase's objectives, which usually follows a long period of hard training and participation in competitions, is to regenerate all of the bodily functions, especially that of the CNS and the athlete's psyche, prior to participation in the main competition of the year. This is usually attained through a reduction of the volume and intensity of training so that the athlete may rest, replenish his/her energy reserves and let the body rebound and be fresh before entering the annual plan's top priority competition.

The enhancement of psychological well-being which generates positive emotions towards competition, is a major reason for the existence of the unloading phase. The time needed for physiological and psychological regeneration must dictate its duration. An early discovery (Krestovnikov, 1938) suggests that following an intensive stimulus, the CNS suffers the most fatigue and that the nervous cell recovers seven times more slowly than a skeletal muscle cell. This finding is the foundation of further demonstrations in the area of the needs and techniques of psychological regeneration during, prior, and post competition periods (Bompa, 1969). However, the duration of this phase should not exceed two weeks, during which time the coach should try to lessen the impact of every stressor upon the athlete, especially those of a psychological nature. The approach to be used differs in accordance with the characteristics of the sport. For sports where the dominant ability is endurance, the main stressor, intensity, is reduced (figure 69).

In the first week of unloading the intensity of training is reduced. Also, the number of training lessons is reduced to a maximum of two per day. The number of high intensity lessons may not exceed two per micro-cycle and their duration should be reduced to a minimum, meaning that outside of the three parts of the training lesson all other activities would be eliminated so that the remaining free time may be used for recovery techniques. Weight training programs may also be reduced to two sessions per cycle to be performed following aerobic endurance training lessons. The content may consist of muscular endurance, which is the least stressful of all weight training methods, where 2–3 sets of maximum 20–25 repetitions would suffice. The volume of training may be as in previous micro-cycles or slightly reduced. However, as far as the content of training is concerned, it should incorporate mostly medium and low intensity methods where the aerobic component is clearly dominant. Such a program has a dual importance: it is the least stressful activity but at the same time satisfactory as far as the needs of maintaining the level of physical preparation. In the

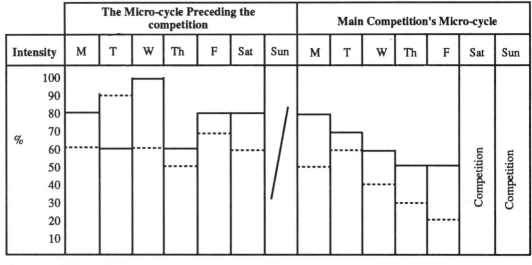

Figure 69. The dynamics of the volume and intensity during the unloading phase for sports where endurance is the dominant ability.

second week, or the main competition's micro-cycle, both the intensity of training and weight programs are completely removed from the schedule. If in a camp situation, the athletes should still perform two lessons per day mostly for the reason of keeping them pre-occupied with training rather than worrying about the competition.

The same approach may not be used by those sports where speed, power, or co-ordination is the dominant ability. As illustrated by figure 70 in the first micro-cycle, the volume of training ought to be reduced to approximately 50% of the previous level. A two peak micro-cycle may be used but the intensive training lessons should have long recovery intervals between repetitions, so that the level of stress is diminished. Most exercises performed during the intensive training lessons should be dynamic in nature but of short duration and not heavily loaded. The dominant intensities, outside of the two intensive lessons, ought to be submaximal alternated with moderate or low intensity lessons. Weight training programs should be excluded completely so that all the energy is saved for the competition.

During the main competition's micro-cycle, the volume of training continues to fall while the intensity, which also is progressively reduced, may have one peak in the first part of the cycle, but not of a high intensity. This micro-cycle, even in a camp situation, may be of 3 + 1 format, which means that after every three half days of work there will be a half day of rest where psychological relaxation may be a priority.

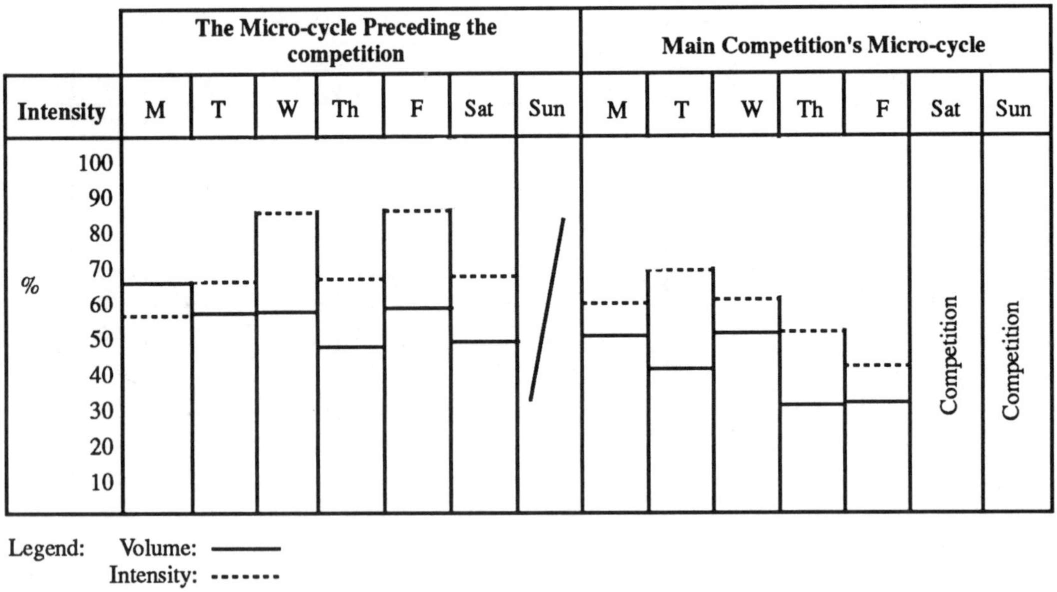

Figure 70. The dynamics of the volume and intensity for the unloading phase for sports where speed, and/or power are dominant abilities.

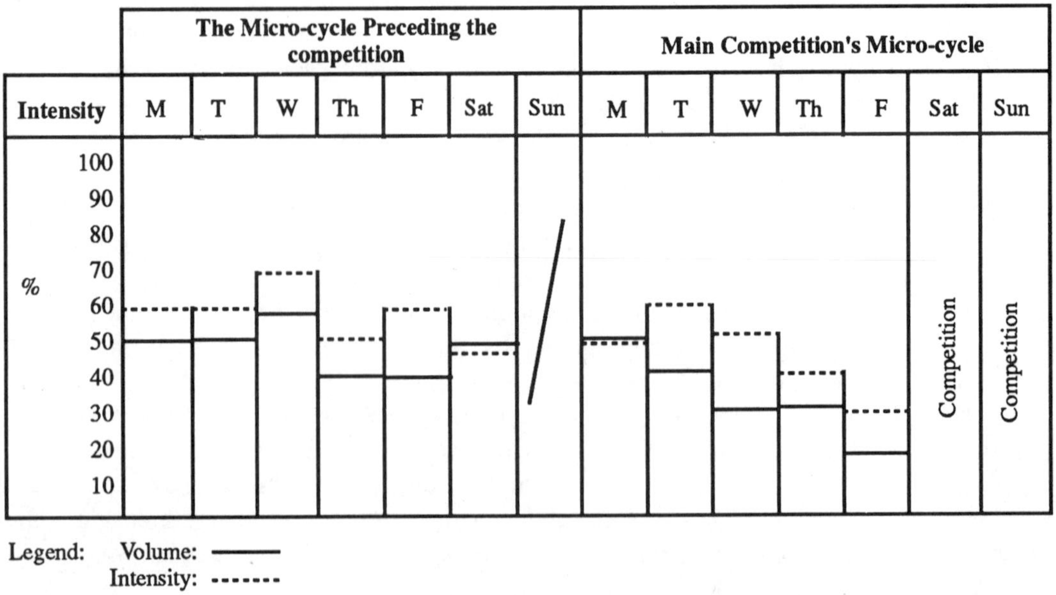

Figure 71. The dynamics of volume and intensity for the unloading phase for team sports where both the aerobic and anaerobic energy systems have an almost equal contribution.

Figure 71 suggests the approach which may be considered for sports in which both the volume and intensity of training have relatively equal importance (i.e., team sports). In the first week, unloading is produced by reducing the volume of work. Only one peak may be necessary during the week. Intensity is progressively reduced, but the coach can still have two intensive training sessions of 60 and 50 per cent of the maximum. In the second week, both curves of intensity and volume taper down. Volume falls to a lower point than intensity. However, even during this week, a micro-cycle with two peaks may be planned. The first peak should be 30 to 40 percent of maximum and the second 25 to 30 percent. Two days before the main competition, training is still scheduled, but it must be short and of low intensity (see figure 71). During these sessions, enjoyment, confidence-building, optimism and team spirit should be strived for.

The SPECIAL PREPARATION period, which may be organized separately or in conjunction with the unloading phase, refers to eventual activities arranged by the coach to facilitate a successful participation in an important competition. Its duration could be between 3–7 days, depending on the specific needs and characteristics of the competition. During this entire phase, the coach may alter certain training aspects, especially those of a tactical nature, in concordance to the latest information collected with regard to future opponents and/or the competition schedule. Most training lessons would follow the model training concept with the purpose of enhancing the athlete's preparation for the competition to come. A crucial aspect with important implications for the final result, is the special psychological preparation which has to consider both the relaxation and promotion of confidence as well as motivation of the athletes for the contest. However, the coach has to be very careful of the way he/she uses psychological techniques, since often overemphasizing them leads to negative results. Each athlete is different and all training aspects have to be applied individually to each athlete. Often, some athletes do not require any of the above and a casual approach might be the most successful.

The Transition Phase

Following a long period of preparation, hard work and stressful competitions when the athlete's determination, motivation, and willpower are very often challenged and tested, the athletes acquire a high degree of fatigue, physiologically and especially psychologically. Although the muscular fatigue may disappear in a few days, the fatigue of the CNS and the psyche could be sensed through the athlete's behavior for a much longer period of time. The more intense the training and the greater the number of competitions the athlete is exposed to, the higher the fatigue level. Under these circumstances, it is hard to believe that an athlete may be able to immediately commence a new annual training cycle. Before starting to train again for another season of competitions, rest is necessary, so as to physically and especially psychologically refresh the athlete. When the new preparatory phase commences, the athlete will be completely regenerated and will participate in training with pleasure. In fact, following a successful transition phase the athlete should feel a strong desire to train again. Removing the CNS fatigue is considered by Hahn (1977) as the major goal of the transition phase. In order to minimize fatigue, a special psychological preparation and treatment (see chapter six on body recovery) should be taken throughout the annual program and especially during the transition phase. If the stress of the previous season cannot be eliminated and its negative elements cannot be identified and compensated for, then throughout the following preparatory phase negative elements of stress may be experienced again.

The transition phase, which is often inappropriately called the "off season", represents a linkage between two annual plans. Its major objectives are to facilitate psychological rest, relaxation and biological regeneration as well as to maintain an acceptable level of general physical preparation (40–50% of the competitive phase). The transition phase lasts between 3–4 weeks and sometimes even longer but should not exceed five weeks under normal circumstances. During this time athletes should train 3–5 times per week depending on their level of involvement in athletics.

In athletics there are two common approaches to the transition phase. The first and incorrect approach encourages complete rest without any physical activity; the term "off season" fits perfectly to its followers. The abrupt interruption of training and the resulting passive rest, or complete inactivity, certainly would lead to a dissipation of most gains in training resulted from hard work over the previous eleven months. In addition, as Ozolin (1971) suggests, the sudden shift from intensive work to a complete passive rest may be harmful to one's organism, reflected through insomnia, loss of appetite, and eventual perturbations of the digestive system. Passive rest may also cause the athlete to be unable to begin the new training cycle at a higher level than in the previous year, which is an important requirement if a continuous performance improvement is expected from year to year. Astrand and Rodahl's (1970) assert that less effort is required to maintain a certain level of preparation than to develop it in the first place. If complete inactivity prevails throughout the transition phase, the first macro-cycle of the new annual plan will be wasted to reach a level which otherwise could have been easily maintained through an active rest.

From a methodical point of view, a different (second) approach is desirable, where activities of a different nature than those used during regular training should be emphasized. This will enhance active rest, or, more specifically, psychological relaxation and rest along with a level of physical activity proportional with maintaining a good level of fitness. Apparently, athletes who followed this concept were found to be psychologically vigorous and physically, adequately prepared at the beginning of the new preparatory phase (Ozolin 1971; Harre, 1982).

The transition phase must be well planned by the coach and athletes together. Throughout this period athletic ethics should be followed. Being physically active does not mean lifting bottles of beer. An overindulgence of alcohol is harmful even during the transition phase. On the other hand, a correct athletic regimen also means an adequate diet. Weight gain of more than 2–4 kg is undesirable.

The activity during the transition phase should be planned immediately following the main competition. During the first week both the volume and intensity of work have to be progressively reduced and exercises of a different nature than those regularly used in training should be emphasized. If some athletes want to postpone completely any physical activity because of either a need for special medical treatment or a high degree of nervous exhaustion, it has to occur in the second week, following the first week of detraining. After total rest, the following 2–3 weeks should consist of an active rest, fun and general enjoyment including physical involvement. Although the activity performed throughout this phase ought to be planned by the coach, or in the case of elite athletes, by the athlete and approved by the coach, all activities must be performed by the athletes without the coach's presence. The athletes have to be comfortable, do what they want and have fun, and in some cases the coach might be an impediment. Besides, the coach also needs his/her own relaxation period.

During the entire phase of active rest changing the environment and means of training have a positive effect upon the relaxation of the CNS and psychological sphere. Gymnasts should perform everything outdoors since for 11 months they train indoors, while athletes who perform their skills in a water environment should find a completely different surrounding for activity. The same is valid for other athletes (wrestlers, weight lifters, and gymnasts) where a holiday at the seashore or at least some swimming and game activities would be very relaxing and enjoyable. In addition to the above activities, other means of training (exercise for flexibility, general strength) may be performed in order to maintain the general level of physical preparation. As part of the general activities, Hahn (1977) suggests that the athlete practice his/her hobby which is often neglected during times of intense training.

The transition phase also has to be used to analyze past programs and to compile the plan for the following annual cycle. The most appropriate time for the analysis would be the first week of the transition phase when many aspects of the past activities are still fresh. The analysis should be made by the coach and the athletes where a positive criticism should prevail. The idea is that everyone involved should learn from past mistakes in order to avoid repeating them in the future. During the same time a medical control examination would be appropriate, the physician should make precise remarks with regard to the athlete's health states and eventual treatment to follow. Throughout the transition phase the coach should make the outline of the training plan for the following year, so that during the first days of the new preparatory phase he/she would be in a position to present it to the athlete.

THE CHART OF THE ANNUAL PLAN

Assuming that by now the reader is familiar with the periodization concept and the main objective of each training phase and sub-phase, the time has arrived to acquire the methodology of making and using the chart of the annual plan. The compilation of a chart requires adequate knowledge of the relationship between the components of training and to what degree they represent an important source of stress upon the athlete. One must also know the ratio between training factors as well as the appropriate emphasis to place on each during every macro-cycle. If a coach handles all the

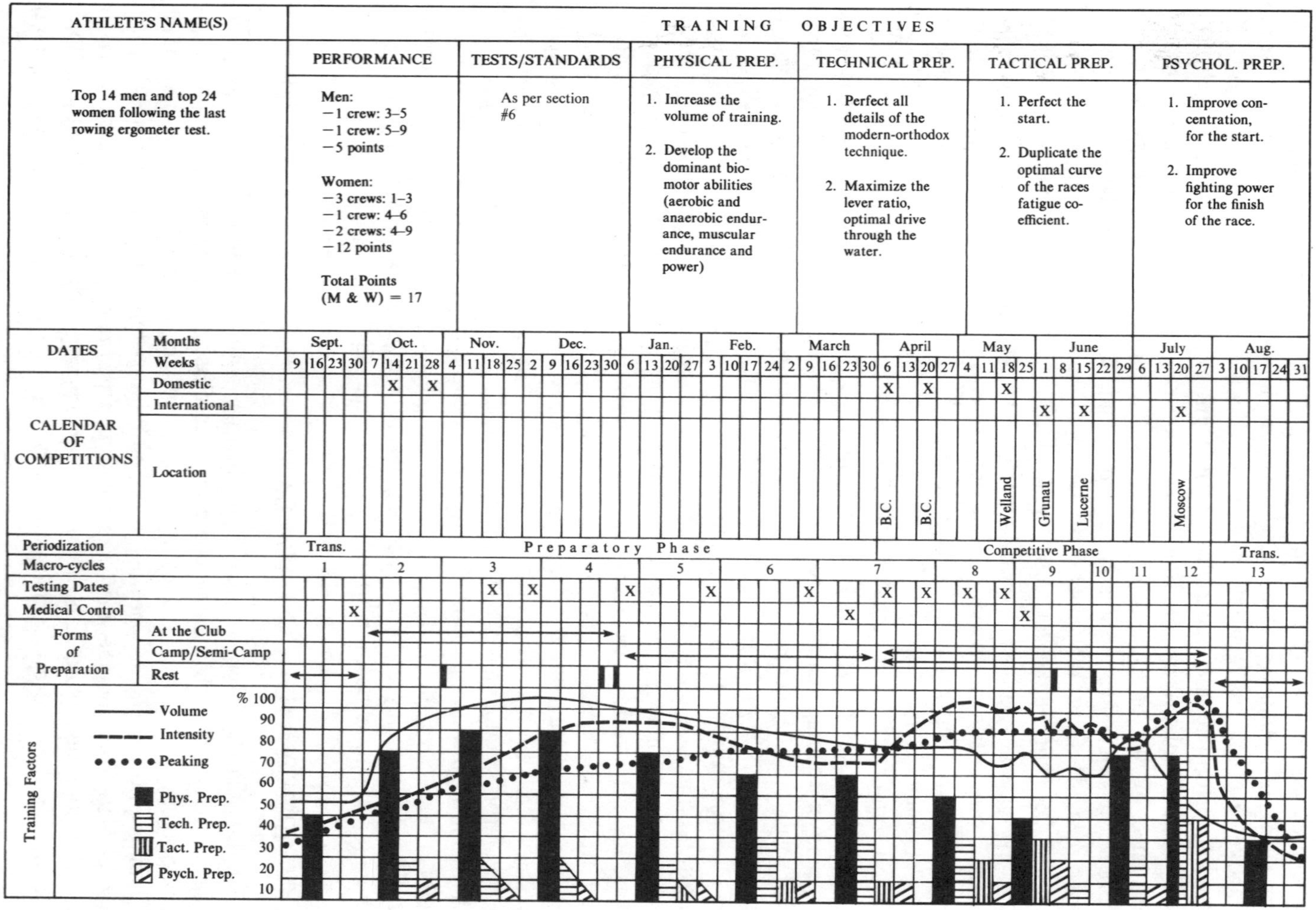

Figure 72. The chart of the annual plan for the 1980 Olympic Games.

198

above aspects correctly he/she may assume that he/she is an adequate planner of training. Consequently it is justifiable to claim that the process of planning an annual plan represents the highlights of one's knowledge in the area of training.

The compilation of an annual plan differs from sport to sport, and its synthesis is expressed in graphical forms as suggested below. The reader will be exposed to various forms of charts and he/she should choose to utilize the chart which suits him/her the best. For experienced coaches just the chart alone, without listing other factors as presented in the section on the compilation of an annual plan, may represent a very effective planning tool.

The Chart of a Mono-cycle

The first chart, illustrated in figure 72 is one of the simplest forms presented in this book. It is a mono-cycle and it was intended to be used by the Canadian Rowing Team for the Moscow Olympic Games. Using this chart as a reference, the methodology of the production of the chart of an annual plan will be explored.

In the top part of the chart the coach may list his/her athlete's name(s) followed by a brief statement of objectives set by the coach (sometimes in consultation with the athletes) for the athletes or team. The first objective to be set is the performance objective. It could be expressed as a measurable performance (i.e., 11.8/110 m-dash), place to achieve or both (i.e., winning 6 games and placing 4 in the junior championships). Tests and standards also ought to be presented very briefly as suggested in section 6 of this chapter. Next, the coach has to specify the main objectives set for each training factor. Of course these objectives, tests and standards, and performance objectives have to be strongly related. The achievement of the standards for each test and objectives for each training factor should represent a strong guarantee that the performance objectives will be achieved. Therefore, the objectives of each training factor must aim at improving all the athlete's weaknesses which the coach is aware of. If the chart is included in a project where the objectives are listed separately then it may be redundant to specify them again in the chart.

Below the objectives are the dates and the schedule of competitions. The latter is the most important training parameter required in planning. Without knowing the precise dates of competitions the coach can not commence a planning program for the year. Therefore, it is necessary that each sport governing body or national sports federation inform the clubs of the schedule of competitions for the following year immediately after the completion of the current year's championships.

The chart of the annual plan must be constructed from right to left around the competition dates. The main competition of the year, be it provincial, national, world championships, or Olympic games, is placed on the right hand side of the chart allowing room (3–4 weeks) for the transition phase. That date (in our example July 20) determines how the months and weekends are written in their own boxes. There are 52 boxes, one for each weekend when, in most cases, competitions are organized. In our example the Olympic finals were on July 20. To the right of that date, the whole month of August was planned as a transition phase. Then all the other months and weekends were listed from right to left, suggesting that under normal circumstances the preparatory phase may commence in September. To the left of the main competition of the year, the coach should then list all the other contests he/she plans to enter the athletes in. The symbols used to illustrate a competition ought to be very suggestive, enabling the coach to discriminate between the main, important and exhibition competitions. The most visible symbol or color should be used to illustrate the main championships of the year.

Should the athletes only participate in domestic competitions, then all the symbols would be placed in that particular line. Otherwise the line for international competitions would be used to show when such competitions are planned. Below the dates of competition there is a space provided where the location for each competition is indicated.

By now the coach knows the dates and the location of competitions. Paramount to the process of dividing the whole year into training phases are the dates of competitions. Once again the process is performed from right to left. The line designated for periodization will be divided into the three classical training phases. In our example, the whole month of August was planned as a transition phase. All competitions of the year will be incorporated in the competitive phase. Figure 72 suggests that the competitive phase is 16 weeks in length, from April 6 to July 20. The remaining part of the year is a long preparatory phase. The space left for each phase could be colored separately or just divided by a line with the name of the phase indicated.

In order to divide the annual plan into macro-cycles, two criteria may be used: 1) the schedule of competitions and 2) the objectives of training and the similarities of the methods employed to achieve the objective. As illustrated in our example (again from right to left) the transition itself is a separate macro-cycle. Although the main competition (or tournament) is of a short duration, athletic preparation, especially psychological preparation during the days or week before, is sufficiently unique to warrant a separate macro-cycle. Furthermore, the whole period preceding the main competition (in our example 3 micro-cycles) is another macro-cycle, since the coach, through specific means and methods, attempts to elevate the athlete's athletic shape to the highest reachable levels. Another macro-cycle of very short duration is specified for the week following the two competitions attended in Europe, namely, Grünau and Lucerne. At the end of these competitions where the athletes will meet some of the finest competitors in the world, they will be fatigued and therefore will need a few days of recovery and regeneration before starting an important cycle of training for the Olympics. The two international races are approached in a cyclic manner, each time having one micro-cycle for training and one for unloading and participation in the competition. Since there is such a similarity between these four micro-cycles, they will be incorporated into a single macro-cycle. The following cycle is again four weeks long culminating with a time trial race in Welland, which is preceded by three micro-cycles of special training for the competition. Prior to this macro-cycle is the longest of all, being composed of six micro-cycles where aerobic endurance is the main objective. During this cycle the athlete participates in two long distance regattas in British Columbia (B.C.) The macro-cycle organized for most of February and March is also quite long, and has as the main objective the conversion of maximum strength to muscular endurance. Both cycles prior to this have some similarities, specifically, the development of maximum strength and aerobic endurance. However, there is a small difference which leads to the decision of dividing these nine micro-cycles into two macro-cycles; that is the means through which the aerobic endurance is to be developed. During the cycle which includes most of the month of December, the above objective will be achieved through running and cross-country skiing. General development, general strength, and aerobic endurance are among the main objectives of both cycles. And finally, after the division of the entire year in macro-cycles was completed, the coach numbers them from the first to the last one. Whenever the coach refers to a macro-cycle he/she specifies its number; in addition, these numbers are useful to refer to when a project is compiled.

The dates for testing and medical control are to be set next. The first test ought to be organized, especially for prospective athletes, at the beginning of the first macro-cycle of the preparatory phase. Data collected from them may be used as a reference in computing the optimal load, number of repetitions, and the amount of work the athlete should be exposed to in training. For top athletes, with adequate information from the past years, often the first date of testing is planned at a later date, towards the end of the general preparation subphase. However, it is more advisable to test all athletes at the very beginning of a new training program to know where they are starting from. As far as the other testing dates are concerned, it is suggested that since each macro-cycle has specific objectives, a testing date should be planned at the end of each cycle to find out whether the objectives were achieved or not. Obviously, this refers mostly to the preparatory phase since during the competitive phase the coach has available the optimal means of testing which is the competition itself. As is the case of our example from figure 72, certain competitions, organized especially during the pre-competitive phase may be considered as testing dates, since their goal is in fact to obtain objective information about the athlete. As for the dates of medical control, 3–4 per year are sufficient. The first has to be organized prior to the beginning of the preparatory phase to know the health status of each athlete. Unhealthy individuals would either not be considered or if necessary, committed to a prolonged regeneration and resting phase. Other dates for medical control may be set prior to the commencement, and following the termination of the competitive phase. A long competitive phase may require at least one extra date to monitor the athlete's health status. All these medical controls ought to be performed thoroughly by a good physician, if possible, by one who has some background in sports. Medical information collected during the last control may influence the length and type of transition phase set for each individual. Often some athletes require special treatment prior to the beginning of a new annual training program, and the physician should indicate which care is appropriate.

The following heading is employed to indicate forms of preparation for the team/athletes during the annual plan. Thus the coach, either by using different colours or by simply drawing an arrow (as exemplified by the chart) would point out the training time consumed at the club or in camps and semi-camps. The length of rest, including the transition phase, has to be indicated as well. If the only day off is on Sundays, it is not necessarily shown on the chart. However, when 2–3 days are used for a holiday or rest (i.e., Christmas, or following a very important competition) it may be indicated by a narrow stick in the appropriate box.

By now the coach has noted in the chart most of his/her athletes' activities. What still remains to be expressed is the percentage of each training factor per macro-cycle. Following this, the curves of the components of training and peaking will be drawn. In order to distinguish quickly between each training factor, the coach may use different colors or symbols.

The emphasis placed on each training factor depends strictly on the specifics of the sport, the strengths and weaknesses of the athlete, and the phase of training. However, as far as the first macro-cycle is concerned, most sports if not all, should emphasize physical preparation. If during the first cycle general physical preparation is stressed, during the second one specific physical preparation directly related to the demands of the sport should prevail. The above reality is more valid for individual sports since team sports would also have the objective of technical improvement. For sports where technique is quite simple, especially in cyclic sports, physical preparation will be dominant throughout all training phases. In any case, regardless of the type of sport the coach is involved in, during macro-cycles, where physical preparation prevails, training should be geared towards hard work and a positive attitude. Such an approach would strengthen the athlete's psychological preparation and improve their perseverance, tenacity and determination. These psychological traits would be converted during the competitive phase into willpower, combativity, and fighting power.

Another important factor to be considered when deciding what weight to place on each training factor, is the athlete's level of performance. The limiting factor of improvement for beginners and prospective athletes is technique, especially for team sports. As for elite athletes, physical preparation, particularly specific physical preparation seems to be a limiting factor in performance improvement. Therefore, each year the coach should emphasize the factor(s) which seems to restrict athletic advancement.

The percentage of work with which an athlete starts the new annual training program may be between 30-50, depending on his/her level of performance. However, those who allow themselves lower training parameters to start with, should not expect more than a low level of improvement. Therefore, the curve of the volume of training should not drop below the above values. In a year following the Olympic games participating athletes may allow themselves a longer rest period. Therefore, the curve of volume for the new plan may start between 20–30%. On the other hand, an annual training program preceding the Olympics should commence with the curve in the neighborhood of 40%. This curve then elevates progressively throughout the preparatory phase, reaching its summit at the end of general preparation and the beginning of specific physical preparation. During the competitive phase the endurance curve lowers progressively to allow the elevation of intensity. As for the intensity curve, throughout the preparatory phase it trails the volume of training curve but surpasses it by the mid-part of the competitive phase. Both curves have a more undulatory shape during the macro-cycles with many competitions. The intensity is higher in the micro-cycle preceding a competition, and it decreases in the competitive cycle to allow the athlete to rest and regenerate his/her body before the competition starts. As a general rule of thumb one may state that where volume is high the intensity is lower, since the athlete may hardly perform many repetitions at a very fast pace simultaneously.

During the macro-cycle preceding the main competition, the volume increases, reflecting an emphasis on the quantity of work. The volume lowers again in the last two micro-cycles prior to the next macro-cycle. The intensity of training behaves differently. At first it is slightly below the volume of training for a very short period of time, and then elevates progressively as the competition approaches. However, during the unloading subphase, both curves may drop slightly depending on the specifics of the sport. For sports, where endurance is dominant, the intensity does not elevate much, allowing the coach to stress almost equally both volume and intensity. Contrary to this, in sports which are characterized by a dynamic performance, the intensity may elevate above the curve of the volume of training. As for the short subphase of participation in competitions, the volume is down and intensity up, signifying that most competitions are of an intense nature.

The peaking curve, which is a direct result of the interplay between volume and intensity, trails both curves throughout the preparatory phase and elevates substantially during the precompetitive, and especially the competition subphases. The magnitude of the curve of peaking is also very heavily dependent on the psychological preparation which the coach undertakes with his/her athletes prior to important competitions.

In simple charts of an annual plan (as is the case in our example) the magnitude and not the percentage of each curve signifies the emphasis placed by the coach on the volume and intensity of training. Their expression in percentage form rather than in relation to each other is more complicated, therefore it may be utilized by coaches with greater experience, who are training elite athletes. Similarly, the curve of stress was not included in the chart since habitually its shape is affected by (and therefore quite similar to) the curve of intensity as well as the vicinity of, and participation in a competition.

Figure 73 also illustrates a mono-cycle, but for a hypothetical volleyball team. The team is involved in the provincial/state championships (⊠ signifying all the league games). One of the main performance objectives is to qualify for and win the finals of the provincial/state championships (◰). As a consequence, the team will qualify

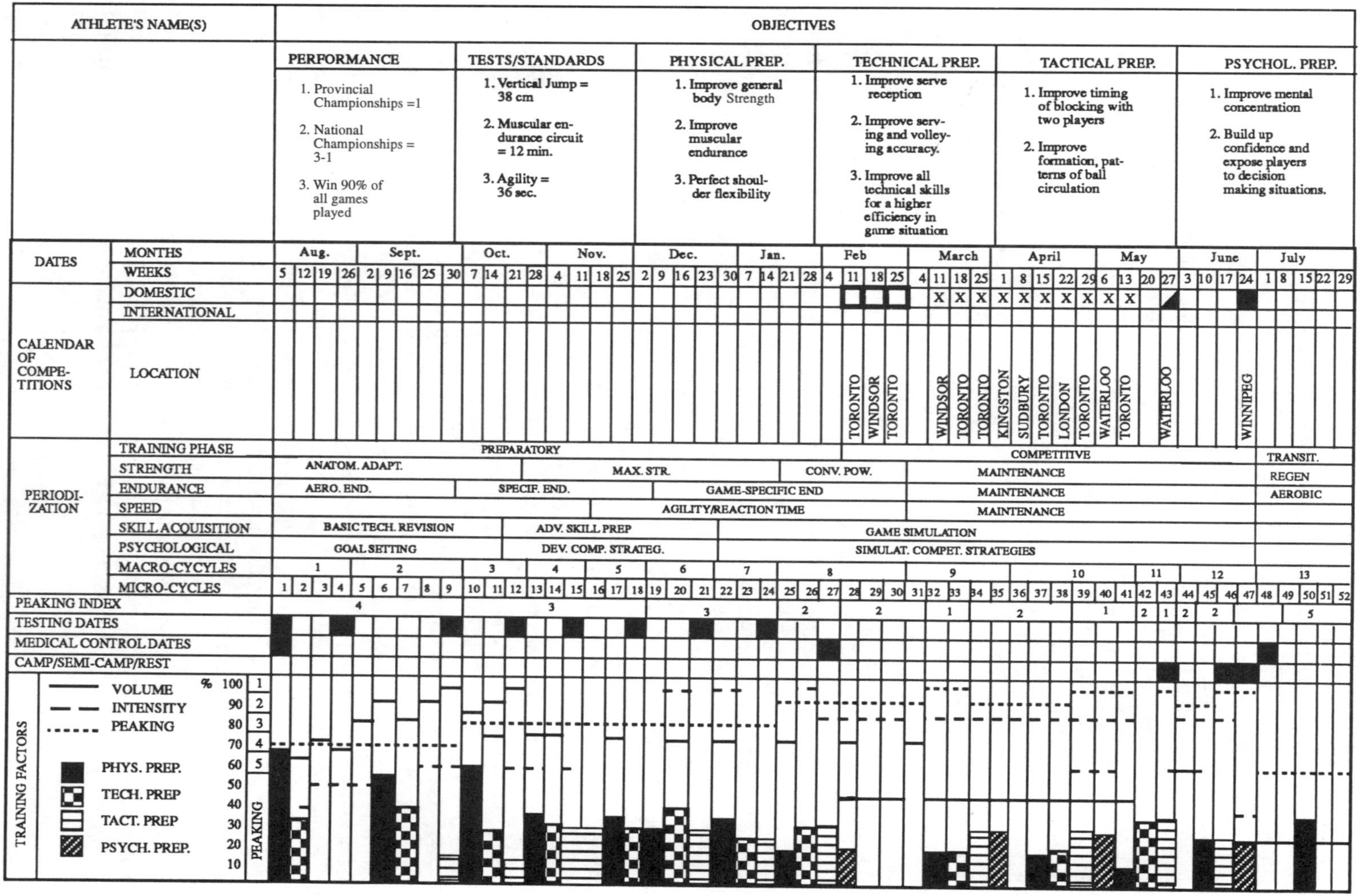

Figure 73. A mono-cycle annual plan for a volleyball team.

for the national championships (■), where the objective is to place in the top three teams (third being a more realistic objective). Prior to the league games there are three exhibition games (☐) scheduled which are also considered as a means of specific testing of the team's abilities.

Because of the specific requirements of a team sport, the ratio between the training factors is different than in the previous example. In this example technical and tactical preparation plays a more important role. However, as should be the case in most sports, and especially in light of the very long preparatory phase speculated in this chart, in the first macro-cycles physical preparation is the dominant factor, since a physical foundation of training has to be developed first. Without such a solid physical support, certain technical maneuvers may not be perfected (i.e., without powerful legs an athlete should not expect adequate spiking and blocking). Similarly, the relationship between the curve of volume and intensity, both presented in horizontal lines to better illustrate their percentage as compared to figure 72 when curves were used, since the intensity component must be stressed at a much earlier stage in the team's preparation. Throughout the first four macro-cycles the volume of training prevails, while from the fifth one, the magnitude of the intensity curve elevates higher than in the adjacent cycles, to reflect that during that period maximum strength is developed, and that game specific endurance and agility/reaction time are stressed as well. Throughout the competitive phase the intensity remains higher to suggest not only the activity in training but also the stress of competitions.

The Peaking Index

Compared to previous examples, the present chart (figure 73) introduces a new parameter, namely the peaking index. It reflects the athlete's state of mind, physical, technical, tactical and psychological readiness at a given time. Thus, the concept of a peaking index refers to the idea that competitions should be approached with varying emphasis according to the preparation level of the team/athlete, the importance placed on the competition and the opponents' athletic abilities. With the exception of high priority competitions, competitors, especially elite athletes/teams, do not necessarily have to push themselves for each competition with equal drive, or peak evenly for every single competition included in the annual plan. In those sports where the competitive phase is very long or have many competitions, to peak equally for each competition is not only very stressful but may also be very difficult to maintain. An athlete must not be worn out by the date of the championship meet, which occurs at the end of the competitive phase. Therefore, elite athletes especially those involved in team sports, may approach certain competitions with a lesser drive, resulting in a lower peak and less stress. Peaking for a competition is usually preceded by an unloading phase and special psychological preparation. Repetitive unloading phases (say for 40 games) lowers significantly the volume and intensity of training performed throughout the competitive phase, which may result in an inadequate level of physical preparation for the final games. As for the recurrent psychological preparation and high concentration for each game, it may lead to an inability for the athlete to maintain concentration power until the very end of the competitive phase. By using the peaking index, it does not mean that the athletes do not focus carefully on each game, but rather that they approach some of them differently, with a much shorter unloading phase and less tension.

Peaking index 1 may be used by the coach when his/her team meets one of the top three strongest opponents of the league. For such games the team must reach their highest physical and psychological potential which should give a solid ground for victory. Therefore, peaking index 1 should be equated with 100% of the athlete's physical and psychological potential. Peaking index 2 may be used when playing opponents in the top 2/3 of the league, excluding the top 3–5 teams. It equates with 90% of one's maximum potential. Peaking index 3 should be reached when playing the much less threatening teams in a league game or during the pre-competitive games. For the pre-competitive games, however, certain technical or tactical objectives may be emphasized, rather than the victory itself. This same level of physical and psychological potential may be required to be achieved in the special preparation subphase of a bi or tri-cycle. Peaking index 3 suggests 70–80% of one's potential. Peaking index 4 represents the state of preparedness during the preparatory phase, when the athlete does not participate in any competitions (60% of maximum). Peaking index 5, the lowest of all, refers to the athlete's physical and psychological state during the transition phase, when the competitive potential is decreased to 50% of maximum.

The above approach was used in figure 74 where the peaking index line symbolized the appropriate index used for each macro-cycle. At the bottom of the chart there also exists a special column for the peaking indices which was used as a guideline to draw the curve of the peaking index. Although the curve is symbolically expressed through a straight horizontal line to signify the curve index and magnitude for each macro-cycle, in reality the peaking curve should be drawn more undulatory.

The Chart of a Bi-cycle

The following chart, figure 74 illustrates a bi-cycle for a hypothetical team/athlete where both technical and tactical preparation are of significant importance in training.

The whole annual plan has two main competitions. The first priority is the competition on August 26th. The other major competition, February 25th, is also important but of a slightly lesser magnitude. The first preparatory phase is of longer duration, where volume is the most significant component of training. In comparison to the second preparatory phase, the first one places less emphasis on the intensity of training to allow the athletes to acquire a very solid base level of endurance and strength. Also, during the first cycle the competitive phase is of much shorter duration. Its duration and number of competitions may also suggest that the coach does not over-emphasize the attainment of outstanding performances for the first half of the

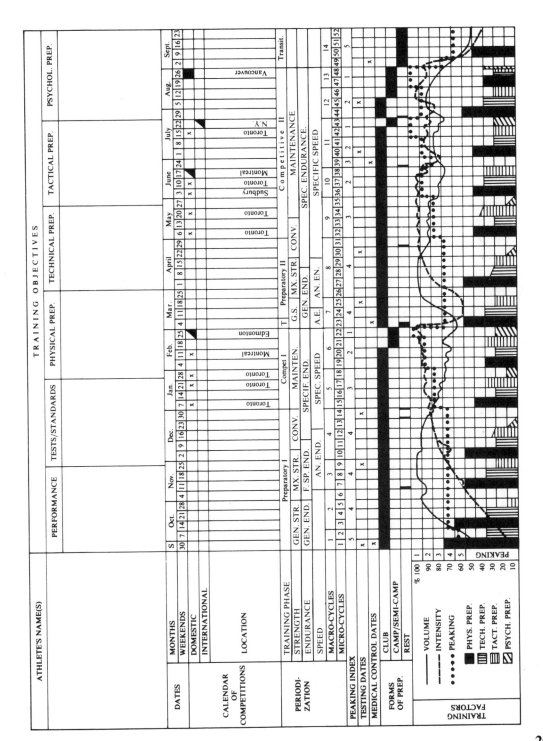

Figure 74. A hypothetical example of a bi-cycle.

training year. However, the gains in physical preparation, along with technical and tactical improvements in the first cycle, are expected to measure favorably upon the athlete's potential during the second competitive phase.

During the second cycle the volume of training, though dominant for six micro-cycles, is of slightly less importance for the remaining 19 micro-cycles. This is the consequence of a longer competitive phase, throughout which the intensity is the most emphasized component of training. Once again, the undulatory shape of both the volume and intensity of training signifies the stress placed on the athletes during each micro-cycle, as well as the short unloading phases organized prior to each important competition. As far as the competitions are concerned, it is evident that during competitive phase I they are organized in a cyclic manner while for the second cycle the grouping approach was used. This allows the coach to divide the whole competitive phase II into periods of training and competitions. Following the first group of competitions (June 3, 10, and 17) the coach may make important observations regarding the athlete's preparation and may attempt to correct eventual shortcomings during the following three micro-cycles which precede the two competitions in July. A similar approach may be considered for the last part of the competition phase II.

As far as the periodization is concerned an additional line is included in the chart, specifying the 52 micro-cycles of the year. This new parameter is of great significance, especially during the retrospective analysis of the previous year's training program (please see the following section of this chapter). Analysis of the previous year's program, can help determine which micro-cycle the best performance was achieved and therefore know how many cycles were needed to reach it. Consequently, the following year's program will be designed either to accommodate this finding or to alter the program in such a way that the highest performance will be reached either earlier or later as necessary.

The Chart of a Tri-cycle

Figure 75 illustrates a chart of a tri-cycle, or an annual training plan where three main competitions govern the entire training program. Such a program, where the athletes peak three times during an annual plan, could be used for many sports (i.e., boxing, wrestling, swimming) provided that the competitions are spread out relatively evenly throughout the year.

The chart illustrates a hypothetical example without any specific reference to a sport, consequently no training objectives were set. However, it was assured that all training factors play an almost equal role. The first main competition (April 26) was assumed to be a qualifying meet for the following two international competitions (say Pan American Games on August 2nd and World Championships on December 13th). Therefore, since in this hypothetical case the athlete/team will qualify without any difficulties (probability 90%), for the first competition a peaking index 2 was assumed to be adequate. As for the following two competitions the coach plans to reach peaking index 1.

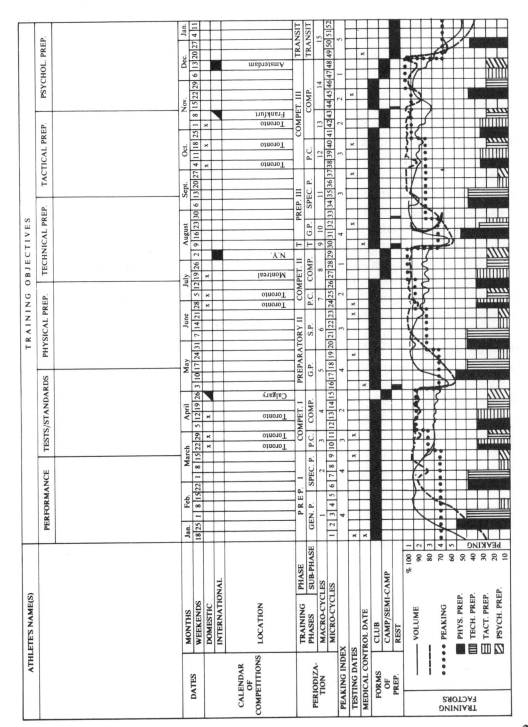

Figure 75. A hypothetical example of a tri-cycle.

For each competition an adequate periodization is organized with the classical phases and subphases of training. However, since for the first competition a peaking index 2 was assumed to be adequate, which did not expose the athlete to a very stressful training, following the qualifying meet (April 26) a transition phase was not considered necessary. Instead, following three days of active rest, the athletes commenced a new preparatory phase to prepare themselves for the August 2nd international competition. A short transition phase (or full micro-cycle) follows the above competition, and once again the athletes are exposed to a new preparatory and competitive phases. Prior to the December 13th competition (World Championships) the participation in an invitational international meet (Frankfurt, November 8th) was considered as being essential for the athletes to gain European experience.

Of the three preparatory phases, the first is of slightly longer duration, where the volume of training is stressed over the longest period of time. The foundation of physical preparation developed in this phase as well as in the following two preparatory phases, is considered to be adequate, providing a base and allowing the intensity of training to be stressed throughout each of the three competitive phases. The ratio between the training factors illustrates the same concept. For each of the three preparatory phases, physical preparation appears to be dominant. In the following macro-cycles, especially during the competitive phase, the ratio is altered to illustrate a more balanced interplay between the four training factors.

Figure 76 illustrates the training program for an Olympic sprinter, where in addition to the periodization of the dominant abilities, skill acquisition and psychological periodization can be specified. The latter intends to bring forth the need of a year-round concern for psychological preparation, which often is misinterpreted as being essential only prior to important competitions.

Another substantial addition is the incorporation of the volume of specific endurance in meters per week. The curve of this activity evolves in accordance to the phase of training, following as well the concept of periodization. Similarly, since the volume of specific endurance per week is expressed in precise amounts, it adds the critical element of objectively planning the load of training.

A similar element of objectivism in defying the volume and intensity of training is exemplified by figure 77. This plan, a bi-cycle, illustrates the volume in the number of kilometers swum per week, while intensity (in this case the speed) is calculated in percentage of maximum.

Such a plan could be used as an example for all the sports where the load in training can be objectively measured (running, skiing, canoeing, rowing, cycling, weight lifting). Similarly, sports such as gymnastics could also quantify the load in training by specifying the number of half and full routines to be performed per week.

The Chart of an Annual Plan for Gymnastics

For the sports where the perfection of co-ordination and skills is one of the prime objectives, a slightly different chart of the annual plan may be employed. Although

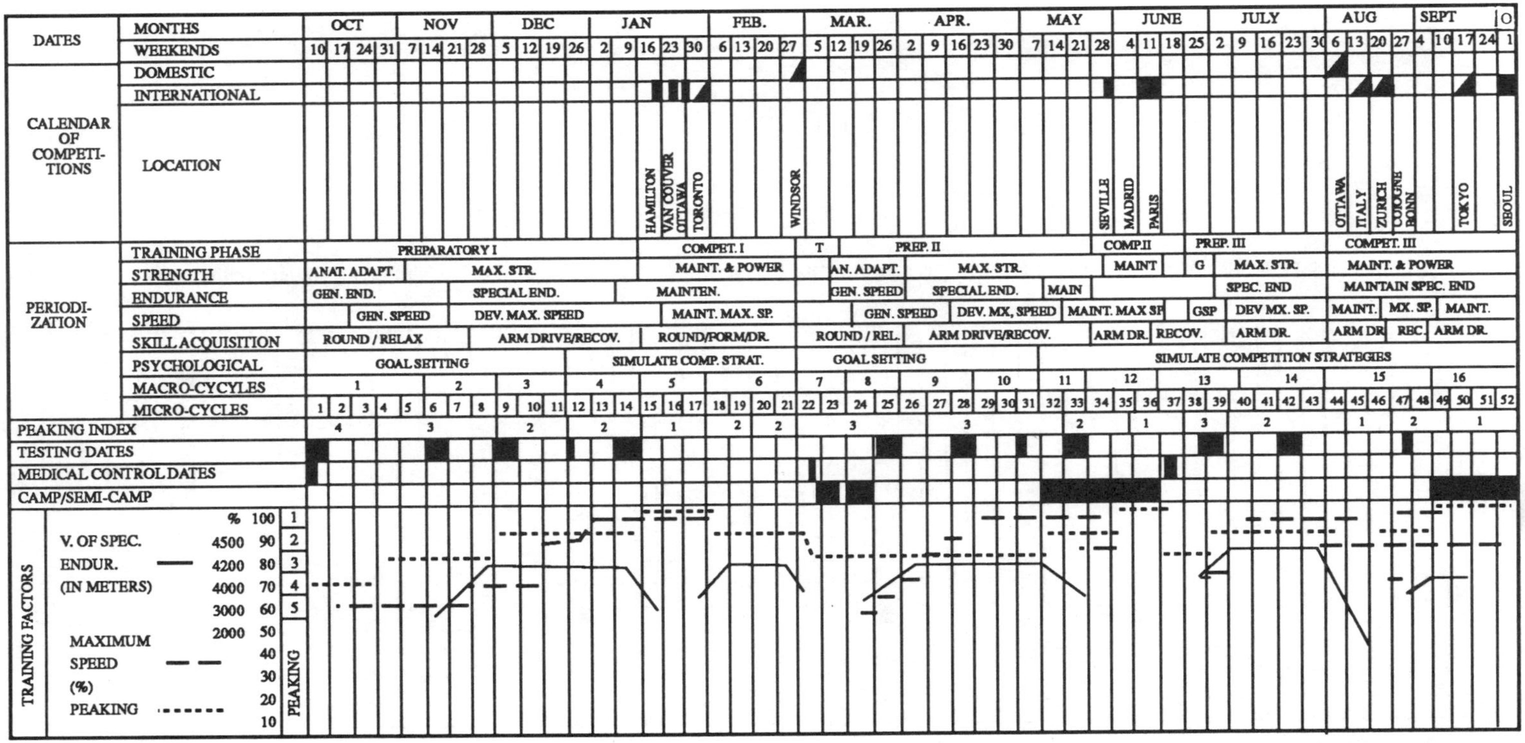

DATES	MONTHS	OCT				NOV				DEC				JAN				FEB.				MAR.				APR.				MAY				JUNE				JULY				AUG				SEPT			O
	WEEKENDS	10	17	24	31	7	14	21	28	5	12	19	26	2	9	16	23	30	6	13	20	27	5	12	19	26	2	9	16	23	30	7	14	21	28	4	11	18	25	2	9	16	23	30	6	13	20	27	4	10	17	24	1

Calendar of competitions:
- DOMESTIC
- INTERNATIONAL
- LOCATION: HAMILTON, VAN COUVER, OTTAWA, TORONTO, WINDSOR, SEVILLE, MADRID, PARIS, OTTAWA, ITALY, ZURICH, COLOGNE, BONN, TOKYO, SEOUL

Periodization:

TRAINING PHASE	PREPARATORY I	COMPET. I	T
	PREP. II	COMP.II	PREP. III	COMPET. III
STRENGTH	ANAT. ADAPT.	MAX. STR.	MAINT. & POWER	AN. ADAPT.	MAX. STR.	MAINT	G	MAX. STR.	MAINT. & POWER
ENDURANCE	GEN. END.	SPECIAL END.	MAINTEN.	GEN. SPEED	SPECIAL END.	MAIN	SPEC. END	MAINTAIN SPEC. END
SPEED	GEN. SPEED	DEV. MAX. SPEED	MAINT. MAX. SP.	GEN. SPEED	DEV. MX. SPEED	MAINT. MAX SP	GSP	DEV MX. SP.	MAINT.	MX. SP.	MAINT.
SKILL ACQUISITION	ROUND / RELAX	ARM DRIVE/RECOV.	ROUND/FORM.DR.	ROUND / REL.	ARM DRIVE/RECOV.	ARM DR.	RECOV.	ARM DR.	ARM DR	REC.	ARM DR.
PSYCHOLOGICAL	GOAL SETTING	SIMULATE COMP. STRAT.	GOAL SETTING	SIMULATE COMPETITION STRATEGIES
MACRO-CYCLES	1	2	3	4	5	6	7	8	9	10	11	12	13	14	15	16
MICRO-CYCLES	1 2 3 4 5 6 7 8 9 10 11 12 13 14 15 16 17 18 19 20 21 22 23 24 25 26 27 28 29 30 31 32 33 34 35 36 37 38 39 40 41 42 43 44 45 46 47 48 49 50 51 52

PEAKING INDEX	4 3 2 2 1 2 2 3 3 2 1 3 2 1 2 1
TESTING DATES	
MEDICAL CONTROL DATES	
CAMP/SEMI-CAMP	

TRAINING FACTORS:
- V. OF SPEC. ENDUR. (IN METERS): % 100/1, 4500 90/2, 4200 80/3, 4000 70/4, 3000 60/5, 2000 50
- MAXIMUM SPEED (%): 40, 30
- PEAKING: 20, 10

Figure 76. The chart of an annual plan for an Olympic sprinter.

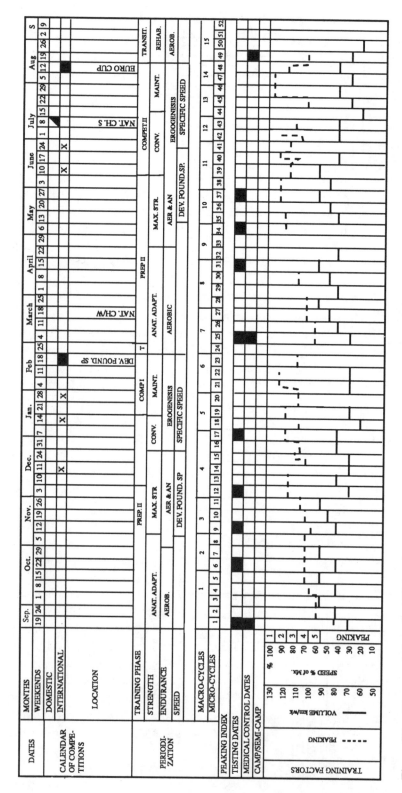

Figure 77.   The annual plan of a 100 m swimmer where both the volume and the intensity of the training can be objectively planned.

such a plan could be a mono, bi or tri-cycle, depending on the number and distribution of competitions, the middle part of the chart is unique. Here the coach may prescribe and plan the adequate time required to assimilate compulsory and optional exercises and skill acquisition. Also, the time when the gymnast should learn, repeat, and perfect half or full routines may be specified. Although figure 78 exemplifies a chart of an annual plan for gymnastics, the same approach is suggested for other sports such as figure skating, diving, and synchronized swimming.

The type of plan illustrated in figure 78 hypothesizes a bi-cycle since there are two major competitions: the Olympic games (July 20) and the World Cup (October 24–26). Prior to both major contests, it is assumed that a competition to select the team or individual gymnasts is organized. As part of a normal progression, a few exhibition meets are also planned during the precompetitive subphase, one of which may be an international meet (May 25). Following the Olympics a short transition phase is planned, during which total rest of 3–4 days followed by light work is advisable.

As both the objectives and the compilation of the chart is based on hypothetical data, the phase and data when technical elements, exercises, and routines have to be learned or perfected, are also strictly supposition. Obviously, new elements/routines normally ought to be acquired a year prior to a meet such as the Olympics or World Cup. As for the skill acquisition, where the perfection of an element starts, the coach should retain only those elements which are incorporated in the final routine. And as a rule of thumb, from that point on the coach should not look for, or teach the gymnast new technical elements. It may be too late to perfect them for the major competition. The coach should confirm in his/her mind at least one year in advance which elements are to be learned, and therefore remain as potentials to be included in a routine. Only under special circumstances, like the invention of a new element or the discovery of a new skill that does not pose a learning problem or place stress upon the athlete, should the coach consider introducing a new skill to his/her athlete close to a major competition. Strangely enough, some coaches are unsatisfactorily organized and planned and it has happened that a routine is finalized days prior to a major competition. Obviously, under such circumstances the responsibility should not be put on the gymnast's shoulders.

The ratio between training factors is unique for gymnastics (as may be the case for the other sports included in this group) in the sense that tactical preparation plays a very minor role, therefore it very rarely appears on the chart. In the first macro-cycle physical preparation should be by far the dominant training factor. During this cycle of training the coach seeks to develop and/or improve the dominant biomotor abilities required in gymnastics with special emphasis placed upon specific strength. If the strength is not developed appropriately, the gymnast will not be able to acquire certain technical elements. From the second macro-cycle on, technical preparation assumes the leading role, along with an appropriate physical preparation. This is valid

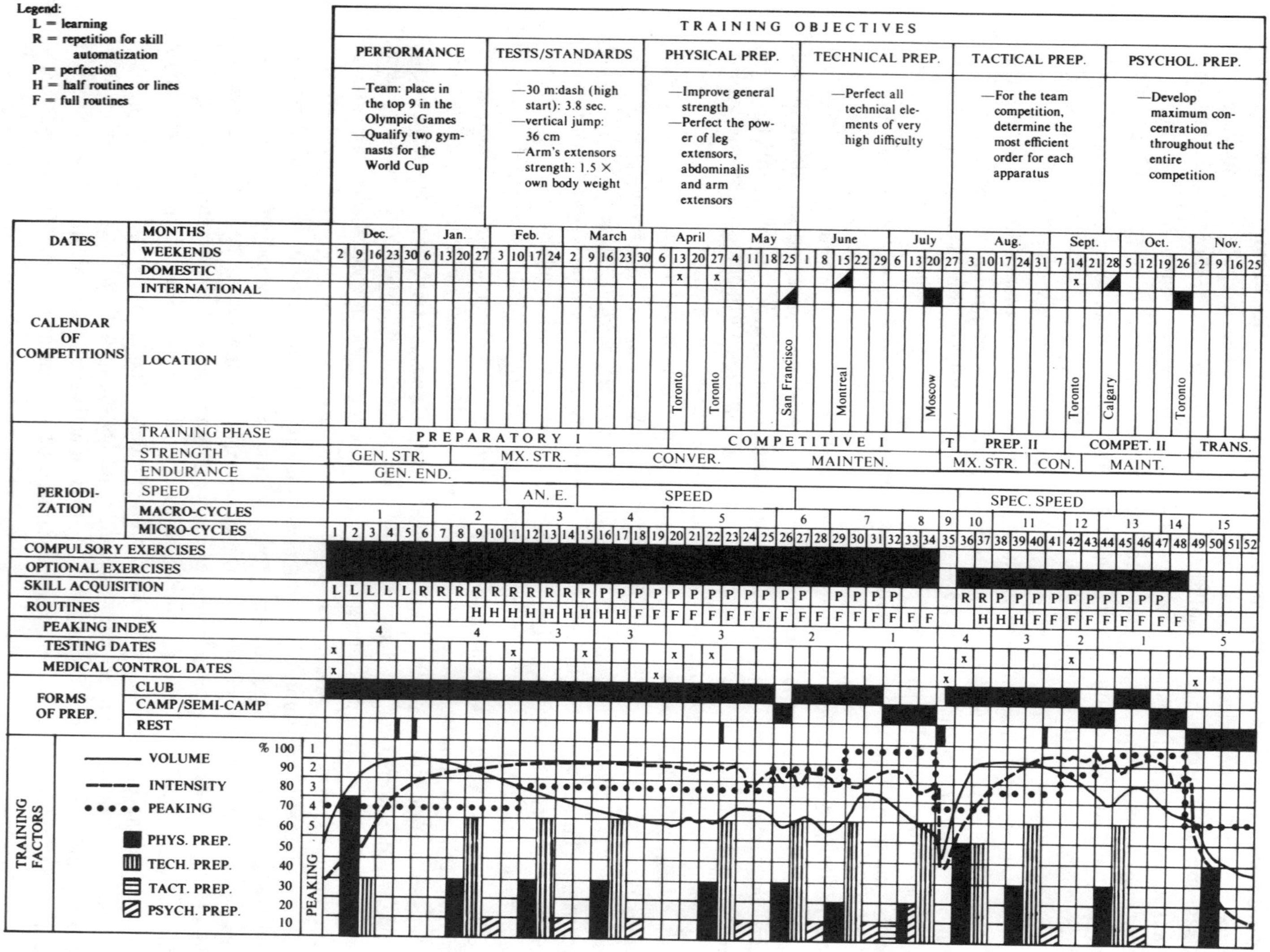

Figure 78. A hypothetical example of an annual plan for gymnastics.

214

for all cycles of training except the 10th, which marks the beginning of the second part of the annual plan. The transition phase should be regarded as a maintenance phase for the physical preparation.

The curves of the volume, intensity and peaking follow the same concepts which were presented in the previous charts, with their shapes depending strictly on the phase of preparation and content of training.

Individual Annual Training Plans

Most of the annual plans previously represented could be used for either individual athletes or teams. They represent in specific terms the guidelines to follow in preparing a year of training. However specific they may be, such a plan can not discover individual quantities of work to be performed by each athlete, and this is a very significant factor in training. Therefore, the employment of the individual annual training plan as outlined in figure 79 may be considered. Such a plan will assist the coach to monitor each athlete's training plan in very precise terms, since it incorporates all the means of training employed by an individual athlete, and the number of repetitions/mileage for a year of training.

When compiling such a plan the schedule of competition must be known. Based on this data the coach sets the periodization of the plan and the objectives for each macro-cycle. They are expressed for each training factor in accordance with the phase of training. For instance, in figure 79 where a hypothetical individual program for a high jumper is illustrated, during the first subphase of training, general strength (G.S.), power (P) and maximum strength (M.S.) are abilities which were planned for development. As the program advances, or approaches the competitive phase, other factors such as technique (T) receive more emphasis. During the transition phase, general physical preparation (G.P.P.) prevails.

The intensity of training has to be stated for each macro-cycle which governs the amount and quality of work to be performed by the athlete. The intensity of training could simply be expressed on a scale of low (L), medium (M), or high (H) as is the case in our example, or more precisely by the following scale: 1. Up to one's limits; 2. Maximum; 3. Sub-maximum; 4. Great; 5. Medium and 6. Low.

One of the highlights of the plan in a practical sense is the area where the means of training are listed. In this section, the coach lists the dominant technical skills or drills as well as exercises utilized to develop specific biomotor abilities. Adjacent to each means of training the coach will specify the number of repetitions, distance/time, or kilogram force meters (kgm) to be performed during the whole year of training. These figures are then divided per each macro-cycle, depending on the objectives and importance placed on each of them in the succeeding macro-cycles. Some exercises are part of the entire year of training (i.e., ankle flexions) while others (exercises with medicine balls) are specific for the preparatory and pre-competitive phases only. Similarly, all weight training exercises are expressed in kgm, while the other exercises,

Athlete's Name: _____

Event: __High Jump__

Performance Obj. : 2.10 m

YEAR: _____   Coach: _____

	Nov.	Dec.	Jan.	Feb.	March	April	May	June	July	August	Sept.	Oct.
Month / Weekends	4 11 18 25	2 9 16 23 30	6 13 20 27	3 10 17 24	2 9 16 23 30	6 13 20 27	4 11 18 25	1 8 15 22 29	6 13 20 27	3 10 17 24 31	7 14 21 28	5 12 19 26
CALENDAR of COMPETITIONS — Domestic / International / Location			Toronto	Toronto · Edmonton	Montreal		Toronto · Toronto	Regina · Quebec City	Vancouver	Toronto · Unc.	Sudbury · Transition	
Periodization — Training Phase	Preparatory I			Competitive I	T	Preparatory II		Competitive II			Transition	
Sub Phase	Gen. Prep.	Spec. Prep.		Comp.	T	G.P.	S.P.	Pre-C.	Competitive		Unc.	Transition
Macro-Cycles	1	2	3	4	5	6	7	8	9	10	11 12	13
Training — Objectives	G.S.	M.S.;P M.S.	M.S.;T. P.	T;P. M.S.	T	G.S. M.S.	M.S.;T.	M.S.;T P.	T;M.S. P.	T;P.	T;P. T;P.	G.P.P.
Intensity	M	M	H	H	L	M	M	M	H	H	H M	L
Performance Objectives		2.06		2.06				2.06	2.08		2.10	
Forms of Preparation		Club		Cmp.		Club		Club	Camp		Camp	Holiday

Means of Training

	Nov.	Dec.	Jan.	Feb.	March	April	May	June	July	August
Jumps 600	15	30	35	60		40	50	100	150	100
Technic. Drill 800	25	70	50	85		60	60	130	200	100
Weight Train. (KGM):										
— Leg Press 342.000	30.000	60.000	30.000	60.000	20.000	50.000	20.000	30.000	20.000	5.000
— Jump ½ Squat 90.000	6.000	12.000	10.000	15.000	5.000	15.000	5.000	6.000	7.000	7.000
— Power Lift 266.000	20.000	45.000	20.000	40.000	15.000	50.000	14.000	14.000	15.000	4.000
— Ankle Flex. 109.440	7.220	15.000	10.000	16.220	8.000	20.000	6.500	8.000	10.500	
Bounding Ex. 35.700	2.200	3.800	3.200	3.400	1.850	5.000	2.400	4.200	5.200	3.600
Exer. Benches 3.340	280	480	360	360	500	800	560			
Exer. Gym Box 1.280	160	200	140	200	140	260	180			850
Exer. Med. Balls 4660	300	1.400	600		200	1.600	300			

Tests and Standards

	Nov.	Dec.	Jan.	Feb.	March	April	May	June	July	August
— 30 m. dash 3.3 sec	3.7	3.5		3.4		3.5	3.4		3.3	3.3
— stand. high j. 62 cm	54	58		60		60	60		62	
— stand. pent. j. 15.20m	14.00		14.80			14.80			15.20	
— leg press 260 kg	00	220	240	260	230	250		260		
— power lift 90 kg	65	70	75	90	68	90		70		
— back flex. 70 cm	60	65								

Figure 79. A hypothetical individual training plan for a high jumper.

aiming at developing power, in number of repetitions (i.e., power lifting was calculated as follows: 3800 repetitions/year x 1 m, or distance traveled by the bareball x 70 kg, or the average load = 266,000 kgm). At the bottom of the chart the tests and the corresponding standards are listed as well as the progression planned to achieve those standards.

The utilization of the individual annual training plan is advocated for both individual and team sports. Although in some instances it may appear that this plan is more suitable for individual sports, especially for those with objective means of measurement, such an approach should be employed for team sports as well. A coach can easily plan the number of repetitions of specific skills or tactical maneuvers. As for physical preparation and test and standards, there should not be any discrepancies.

The Practical Significance of the Chart of the Annual Plan

The chart of the annual plan represents the basic guidelines for most of the training activities organized by the coach throughout a year of training. While such a plan is constructed around the competition schedule, the ratio between training factors, and the shape of the curves of the components of training and peaking, the annual training plan is a specific tool which governs the athlete's program. From the chart of the annual plan the coach can extract the emphasis to be placed upon each training factor in a given training cycle. Having this as a basis the priorities can be set for a macro-cycle (i.e., 50% physical, 40% technical, etc.). Also by concerting the above with the magnitude of volume and intensity, as well as the quantity of work planned per cycle in the individual annual training plan, the coach can plan precisely the training program for a macro and then for a micro-cycle.

CRITERIA FOR COMPILING AN ANNUAL PLAN

The compilation of an annual plan is of great importance for both the coach and athlete since it will represent the guideline on which the coach will conduct his/her training for the following year. The ideal time to compile it is at the end of the transition phase. Following the main competition of the past year's plan, the coach can reflect and analyze the program as well as the athlete's general improvement, rate of progress in both competitive performance and tests and psychological behavior during training and competitions. This analysis should terminate by drawing the main conclusions which should influence the objectives set for the next year's plan. Such observations along with the competition schedule represent the most important parameters used in the compilation of the next annual plan. The schedule of the following year's competitions, including both national and international events is set by the national federation. Based on this schedule, each regional organization sets their own competition dates. These dates should be known to all coaches by the transition phase of the previous annual plan. Otherwise the coach can not objectively compile the follow-ing year's plan since periodization depends strictly on the competition schedule. The compilation of an annual plan and the quality of the plan reflects the coach's meth-odological knowledge, his/her experience, as well as the latest theoretical gains in the field of training. The first plan ever made has to be improved with time to reflect all the above aspects, so that progressively the coach will develop a model of an annual plan which, on a yearly basis, will reflect both the progress in knowledge and his/her gains in experience. After making the annual plan, the coach may compile training programs for individuals or small groups of athletes to reflect their specific needs. All the formulation and the language used has to be very clear, concise and technical. There is no room for rhetorics in an annual plan.

Training Parameters Used in the Compilation of a Model of an Annual Plan or Project

Every organized coach should compile his/her own annual plan. A coach is only as efficient as he/she is organized. Coaches involved at the national level may be asked by the national sports association or funding organizations to submit a model (project) of the program to be followed in the next year. Such a program has to be well compiled, justified and must comprise the main parameters of training. Below is a model of an annual plan or project which consists of all the needed elements.

1. Introduction

In the introduction the duration of the plan should be specified (i.e., September 15, to August 16, 19–) as well as personal or team information: 1. sport, 2. sex, 3. age, 4. height, 5. weight, and eventually 6. somatotype (body type). This data may be just listed without any specific comments. Then, especially for a project, there should be some explanation of the scientific and methodological characteristics of the sport from which the needs of training are determined. Such a presentation may be exem-plified as follows: As an individual sport, women's gymnastics is characterized by a high level of co-ordination, along with much demand for maximum strength, power, muscular endurance and flexibility. Rhythm and the sense of music are also signifi-cant. The duration of activity ranges from 4–5 seconds in vaulting to 1.30 minutes in a balance beam routine, consequently the ergogenesis in gymnastics is 80% anaerobic and 20% aerobic. The major sources of energy includes the ATP-CP stored in the muscle for activities lasting less than 30 seconds and the anaerobic metabolism sys-tem, which produces the byproduct lactic acid, for parts, half routines and routines of 30 seconds—1.30 minutes duration.

2. Retrospective analysis

In order to provide a proper elaboration of both the performance predictions and objectives for the following year, the coach has to analyze the athlete's performance

		PLANNED	**ACHIEVED**
	PERFORMANCE	**51.50m**	**52.57m**
OBJECTIVES	TESTS: 1. 30 m Dash	4.8 sec	4.7 sec
	2. Standing long jump	2.40 m	2.36 m
	3. Chin-Ups	8	7
	4. Baseball throw	60.00 m	61.36 m

Figure 80.   The presentation of a hypothetical performance analysis of a women's javelin throw.

and behavior in the past year very thoroughly. The performance achievements refer to the performance as well as tests and standards, and could be presented in a table as suggested in figure 80.

After analyzing the past year's objectives of performance and the tests and standards, the athlete's state of preparation has to be determined by analyzing each training factor separately. As far as physical preparation is concerned the coach has to analyze whether the indices of general, specific and biomotor ability development did correspond to the specific needs of the sport and whether they adequately supported the technical, tactical and psychological preparation. Such information should be collected from competitions as well as from the results of the specific tests. Any improvement or decline in the athlete's technical or tactical performance has to be linked with his/her rate of progress or regress as reflected in test scores. Often it may happen that improvement prevails during the preparatory phase but regression occurs during the competitive phase as a result of inconsistent and inadequate physical preparation. Thus, specific physical preparation ought to be not only continued throughout the competitive phase but should be tested consistently in each macro-cycle in order to collect objective data regarding the dynamics of physical preparation.

The analysis of technical preparation should focus on the fineness of performing technical elements and to what extent they affected the overall performance. The effectiveness of past technical elements must be assessed to determine whether or not they should be employed in the future. The amount of time dedicated to the improvement of technical elements directly reflects the athlete's level of technical proficiency and the fineness of skill acquisition.

An analysis of tactical preparation should mirror whether tactical maneuvers employed by the team or individual athletes were properly chosen, suited to the characteristics of the team and whether they led to the solution of game problems. As a final conclusion of the retrospective analysis, the coach should indicate which, if any, of the past year's strategical tools should be eliminated, or maintained as part of the

	Performance (minutes) and place			
EVENT	I	II–III	IV–VI	VI–IX
Eight	5:38	5:41	5:45	5:50
Quad	5:51	5:55	5:59	6:04
Coxless four	6:05	6:09	6:13	6:17
Coxed four	6:13	6:17	6:21	6:26
Double scull	6:23	6:27	6:31	6:36
Coxless Pair	6:43	6:46	6:50	6:55
Single Scull	7:03	7:07	7:11	7:16
Coxed Pair	7:08	7:12	7:16	7:21

Figure 81. Performance predicted for the various places of men rowers in the Olympic Games (events listed in speed order).

team's strategies and which remain to be perfected so that the team's efficiency will improve in the following year.

And finally, the coach also has to investigate the athlete's psychological preparation and behavior and how it was reflected in the final performance. He/she has to consider positive and negative aspects of the whole process and whether it led to an optimization of competition performance. To assess the athlete's behavior one has to consider not only what happened during training but also during all other times since very often the unseen training has important implications in training and competitions.

The coach also has to reflect upon eventual collaboration with training specialists and psychologists to determine what should be altered in the future in order to improve the athlete's performance. The final conclusions of the retrospective analysis are the basis for predicting future progress and performance, as well as for setting the specific objectives for the new annual plan.

3. Performance prediction

Among the more important abilities of the coach is the ability to forecast the rate of progress and the trend of skills, abilities and general performance to be achieved between the date of planning and the main contest. Then, having the performance prediction as a reference, the coach may draw his/her athlete's objectives and tests' standards. Achieving these objectives and test standards throughout the progression of training represents a guarantee that the athlete will reach the highest possible level of performance. For instance, a gymnastics coach predicts that in order for an athlete to place in the top six in the women's national championships, she will have to score a routines and technical elements to see whether they are difficult enough to warrant a

EVENT	PERFORMANCE	PLACE
Eight	5:45	VI–VIII
Quad	5:58	VI–VIII
Coxless four	6:12	III–V
Coxed four	6:20	VII–IX
Double Scull	6:30	III–V
Coxless pair	6:50	V–VI
Single Scull	7:10	VII–IX
Coxed pair	7:15	VII–IX

Figure 82. Minimum performance prediction and placing expectation in Olympic Games Regatta (Bompa, 1979).

9.4 average score. Following such an analysis, the coach, based on the gymnast's realistic abilities, decides what kind of technical elements have to be incorporated in the following year's routines in order to score as predicted. Unlike the individual sports, performance prediction of team sports is a very difficult task. Among the few aspects which the coach may predict are the kind of technical elements, tactical maneuvers or level of physical ability the players must acquire in order to achieve a higher performance in the following year.

For sports where performance is objectively and precisely measured, performance prediction is an easier task. In such cases the coach has to contemplate the best results achieved in the past year, and, on the basis of the rate of performance improvement, he/she predicts the level to be reached in the following year. On such a basis, the performances for men rowing in the 1980 Olympic Games Regatta (Bompa, 1979) were predicted as illustrated by figure 81. Then considering his/her own athlete's realistic abilities and potential for further improvement the above author set the standards for his crews and the placing expectation for the Olympic Games (figure 82). On the basis of performance prediction the coach sets realistic objectives for each training factor and prepares the chart of the annual plan (see the following sections).

4. Objectives

In both the annual plan and the planning project the coach has to state the objectives in a precise, and concise language as well as in a methodological sequence. The basis of the objectives setting process are the past performances, standards achieved in each test, the rate of improvement of skills and performance in a sport, and the dates of the main competition. In setting objectives, the coach has to consider the dominant training factor of a sport and the factors which are most poorly developed and thus limiting to the athlete. Then the methodological order of priorities in training must be decided in accordance with the limiting factors (i.e., is the physical preparation the main limiting factor or is technical or psychological preparation?).

The methodological sequence and order of presentation of each training factor is as follows:

1. Performance objective
2. Physical preparation (strength, speed, endurance, flexibility and co-ordination)
3. Technical preparation—offensive skills
   —defensive skills
4. Tactical preparation —individual tactics—Offensive
   —Defensive
   —team tactics   —Offensive
   —Defensive
5. Psychological preparation
6. Theoretical preparation

However, this does not mean that the coach should stress each factor in the above sequence. Priority must be given to those factors in which the athlete is proportionately underdeveloped and those which are of primary importance to all athletes participating in the sport.

While the coach sets the objective he/she must also consider and state the probability (percentage chance) of achieving them, especially the performance objective. Although this process has to rely on concrete and objective facts the coach may also consider subjective methods of assessment, like the athlete's reserves and improvement potential, and psychological traits. Below are the objectives of a hypothetical volleyball player:

The objectives for the 19-plan.
A. Performance:
   1. First place in the national junior championships.
      Probability of achievement: 80%
   2. Place in the top six in the senior national championships.
      Probability: 50–60%.
B. Training Factors:
   1. Physical preparation
      a. Strength: improve leg strength for higher and more contested jumps.
      b. Speed: Improve speed to facilitate quicker footwork for blocking and defence.
      c. Endurance: Improve muscular endurance required in long games and tournaments
      d. Flexibility: Perfect shoulder and improve ankle flexibility.

2. Technical preparation:—improve serving consistency,
—improve spiking accuracy
3. Tactical preparation:
   a. offence: improve spiking variety in a 6–0 system
   b. defence: improve timing and quickness of blocking
4. Psychological preparation: develop the ability to play calmly and with confidence following a mistake
5. Theoretical preparation: Know all penalties which may be called by the referee.

5. Calendar of competitions

A detailed presentation of competitions and their importance in athletics is presented in the following chapter. However, since in this section the methodology of setting up the schedule/calendar of competitions for the annual plan is discussed certain relevant aspects ought to be mentioned.

The schedule of competitions is set by the coach. In fact he/she should choose those competitions which suit the athletes, their level of performance and skills, and their psychological traits. Although the coach may take into consideration the athlete's opinions, especially the elite class athletes whose experience and judgment represent an important element in the competitions selection process, it is advisable that the coach, based on his/her experience, assumes the decisive role. Some coach's practice of asking the athletes to make the final decision seems fallacious.

The determinant factor in both periodization and the process of setting up the competition's schedule is the major championship, sometimes referred to as the main objective of the year. Of secondary importance but still of concern are other official competitions the coach chooses to participate in, and unofficial competitions, whic¡h are sometimes scheduled to provide an opportunity to assess the athlete's level of preparation. They are spread throughout the competitive phase, but are most prominent during the precompetitive subphase. Sometimes exhibition competitions are planned for the last micro-cycles of the special preparatory subphase. No competitions should be scheduled early in the preparatory phase since during that time the coach and athletes are concerned with the acquisition of physical preparation and skills rather than performance. Consequently, major competitions have to be integrated with competitions of secondary importance. The alternation of such competitions may be ideal though not often possible. Unlike team sports, where there are many leagues, or official games, in some individual sports competitions are often scarce. In order to maintain the unity of the annual training plan, throughout the competitive phase, it is advisable to organize preparatory competitions as an integral part of the training plan.

The arrangement of competitions in an annual plan has to take into consideration the principle of progressive increase of load in training, where preparatory and therefore secondary important competitions have to lead official, challenging ones. However, this is not always possible, especially in team sports, where the calendar is set by sport governing bodies. In such instances, the subphase.

A determinant factor in achieving the performance objectives of the year is the number of competitions in which the athlete participates. A heavy schedule of demanding competitions, as often occurs in team sports, may speed up the process of reaching a high level of athletic shape, and may decrease the team's efficiency for the important competitions occurring during the end of the competitive phase. On the other hand, an extremely reduced number of competitions may lead to the same end result, that is a lower athletic shape for the main objective of the year. Two important criteria for determining the number of competitions are the characteristics and the nature of the demand of the sport as well as the athlete's performance level. For sports where the effort is very intense, as well as for athletes with low performance capabilities, 15–25 competitions per year may suffice their needs. A higher number of contests (30) may be planned for elite athletes involved in most other sports.

Once the competition schedule is made, no changes, especially for the major competitions should be considered since the periodization of the entire annual plan is based on this schedule. No competitions, especially important ones, should be planned during examination periods for high school and university students. Similarly, during the last macro-cycle prior to the main competition no official or demanding contests should be engaged in. During this last cycle of training the athletes ought to be trained in a quiet atmosphere, where a few changes may be operationalized in accordance with the conclusions drawn from the previous competition. During each contest an athlete is highly solicited, not only physically, but mentally and psychologically as well. The athlete needs time to rest, relax and to rebuild mental toughness and concentration power for the main competition of the year. By not respecting such psychological and physiological needs, a poor showing in the last contest of the competition schedule will result.

6. Tests and standards

The importance of knowing more about the athletes and their athletic potential implies an organized, systematic, and consistent evaluation. A sound methodology of training requires athletic evaluation to be an intrinsic part of the planning process. All evaluation procedures and means of testing should aim at objectively quantifying the athlete's evolution, stagnation or eventual performance deterioration.

A test is an instrument requiring performance by the individual being tested while evaluation refers to the process of determining the status of that person related to a standard utilized as a reference. The evaluator should always be the coach and not an athlete, though the latter may often be an important assistant.

A test has to be objectively measured, thus guaranteeing comparable results. According to Meyers (1974) the functions of measurement are: 1) to ascertain the status or capacity in a given ability or skill, and 2) to provide the basis for a) determining achievement or progress, b) diagnosing particular weaknesses and c) predicting further improvements.

The same author implies that a test and measurement program should serve the following functions:

1. to determine the status of skills and level of abilities, which can be utilized to plan a training program;
2. to facilitate the determination of the athlete's training content;
3. to determine specific strengths, weaknesses, and limitations of the athlete's abilities
4. to measure improvement in motor skills and tactical maneuvers to be used in the future;
5. to act as a guide to better body mechanics and the development of specific psychological traits;
6. to guide the establishment of appropriate standards in all training factors, and
7. to act as a motivating device for effective learning, development of specific skills, and evolvement of psychological traits.

It appears that tests utilized in training have to be diversified in order to measure and therefore provide information regarding status of each training factor. To test just one factor, say the strength of a wrestler, would be insufficient, thus making the whole process very limited. Consequently the coach has to aim at measuring all the determinant training factors, but most of all a test must detect the limiting factors of the athlete's improvement.

Throughout the training process a coach should be concerned with two basic categories of tests. The first category includes tests for athletic selection purposes, aiming at tracing out genetic abilities which are specific and dominant in a certain event or sport. The second category includes tests that provide information about the athlete's adaptability to the training program, as well as his/her evolution of skill acquisition, and performance improvement.

As far as the test employed for selection purposes is concerned, they ought to be simple, without requiring any technical sophistication or high degrees of co-ordination from the testee (except for co-ordination tests). Such tests should not be trained for, except for a very short period of time sufficient to learn the simple technique of performing them. As for the tests utilized to discover an athlete's adaptability and performance evolution, they have to be selected or designed very specifically in order to provide valid, useful information to the coach. These tests should be selected in such a way that they duplicate and possibly develop those abilities at which the coach aims through the training program. Ideally, some exercises or means of training would be utilized as a testing tool. For instance most jumpers in athletics or for that matter most athletes from team sports should use bounding exercises to develop leg power. Penta (five) and deca (ten) triple-jump-like-steps are common exercises. The same exercises lend themselves nicely as testing devices and should be used as such

throughout the annual training cycles. Such a test is trainable, has a very high correlation with the specificity of the event or sport, and most importantly motivates the
athlete to train since the exercise serves not only as a testing tool but also as a
means to develop a necessary ability.

When developing a battery of tests, the coach should be very selective, choosing
only those which incorporate the majority of abilities required by a particular sport.
For instance, in rowing the rowing ergometer test is highly regarded since in one test
it measures the athlete's specific endurance, strength, speed, pacing, and will power.
Often the concept of having a battery consisting of only a small number of tests is
not followed by the coach. In some sports (i.e., volleyball) there are coaches whose
battery of tests numbers 18! If the coach tests a team of 12–16 players in each
macro-cycle, one may wonder if he/she has any time left for training! Considering the
above it is advisable to keep the number of tests to a minimum (4 to maximum 8)
but making sure that all tests have a high degree of validity. Ideally, the coach (who
could employ the advice of a testing specialist) should compute the correlation between
each available test and the specifics of the sport, and then select only those tests
which have the highest correlation coefficient. This is the most scientific way to select
an appropriate battery of tests.

It was mentioned above that as far as choosing a test is concerned, the coach
should be selective, meaning that he/she should choose a test which embodies many
abilities. Also, the test must facilitate a fair discrimination between athletes and must
have an objectively measurable standard. For instance, push-ups is still overwhelming
utilized to evaluate the elbow flexors strength. However, the tester omits the fact that
arm length varies from person to person, therefore a comparison between individuals
is far from being adequate. If no other sophisticated tools are available to measure
elbow extensor strength, it is more accurate to use bench press and compute the kilogram force meters (Kgm) of each testee and make comparison between athletes.
(Kgm = limb's length x load x number of lifts. i.e.: 0.60 m arm length x 50 kg x
10 lifts = 300 Kgm). Coaches requiring assistance for their athlete evaluations may
ask the advice of a testing specialist or consult a test and measurements book available on the market.

Often testing and training specialists and coaches question whether or not a test
should be trained for. The answer to this is both positive and negative. Yes, a test
may be trained for if it is one of many exercises/means of training used in the training program (i.e., penta jump). Similarly, an athlete may train for a test utilized for
selection purposes for a short period of time to learn the eventual technical pattern of
a skill. All other types of tests must not be trained for. Prior preparation or training
for a test distorts its purpose. As has already been stated, most tests have the purpose
of measuring the effect of previous training at a given time. A test is not a formality;
it should not limit the scope of the athlete's preparation. In this context one should
understand that a VO_2 max test should not be trained for specifically since by doing
so the athlete would not gain much. On the contrary, the aerobic and anaerobic en-

durance would improve much more through different kinds and methods of training where the general volume of training is stressed. The test should not be a scope in itself.

For any annual training program or project, the coach has to decide and plan in advance all testing dates. It is advisable that the first date of testing be planned for the first micro-cycle of the preparatory phase. Such a test would give the coach an opportunity to evaluate the athlete's level of preparation, which will influence the development of the new annual program. An organized coach should plan to achieve certain training objectives in each macro-cycle. The accomplishment of such objectives has to be verified. Consequently, at the end of each macro-cycle the coach should plan 1–2 days of testing to collect information regarding the athlete's progress. If consistent improvement is indicated, the training program will be maintained as originally planned. Otherwise the program for the next cycle should be altered to reflect the reality of the athlete's training status. Therefore, testing dates have to be planned periodically for the end of each macro-cycle but only during the preparatory phase and eventually the precompetitive subphase. It is obvious that evaluation of the athlete's preparatory status during the above phases is needed to monitor training programs based on objective data. Similarly, regular testing may serve as a motivating tool in the absence of competitions as well as a means of developing specific psychological traits. During the competitive phase, testing sessions will be planned only if the time period between two competitions exceeds 4–5 weeks. During this phase the competitions themselves serve as an ideal form of evaluating all training factors.

Although testing dates ought to be scheduled throughout the annual plan, the coach may occasionally opt for an ad hoc evaluation. Since the athlete does not have time to prepare psychologically for the test, the results are often quite surprising. Those who fail to perform adequately do so mostly because of a lack of psychological support. Though such an approach may reveal certain weaknesses in the athlete's preparation this method should not be abused. Once, or a maximum of twice a year would be acceptable. Testing scores should be accurately recorded by each athlete in his/her training journal as well as in the coach's records.

In the descriptive part of a plan or project the test for each training factor should be expressed by using different colours or symbols (i.e., ⊠ for technical, ■ for psychological, and ☰ for physical). Standards for each test, especially for physical and technical factors are established during the compilation of the annual plan. The standards of the previous year are regarded as a reference point. The planned progression toward achieving each standard ought to reflect the athlete's adaptation to a program as well as their rate of improvement. For athletes just beginning an organized program, the scores of the first test could be used as a reference point for further planning.

However, the coach has to be very careful when planning the standards since they represent an incentive for both preparation and progress. Standards have to be difficult enough to present a challenge and realistic enough to be achievable. For athletes aiming at high levels of performance, their standards have to bear resemblance to other top athletes from the same or other countries.

Basically, there are two types of standards:

1. evolutionary standards, with a stimulative character, which therefore are slightly superior to the athlete's potential in a given time; and
2. maintenance standards, which aim at preserving an optimal level of preparation.

Standards for sports from the second group are more common and should prevail in a training program, while those for sports from the first group represent the highlights of the preparatory phase. The progression of these standards is such that a maximum of 2 macro-cycles may be included in each step. If the athlete has not achieved the standard by this time the coach must try to determine why.

Both tests and standards should be set for each training, with more emphasis being placed on the dominant ones. Since athletes' unspecific (through testing as opposed to specific or the event) evaluation is conducted mostly during the preparatory phase and since one of the prime goals of this phase is the improvement of biomotor abilities, each ability has to be trained but also tested regularly. For the sake of simplicity both the tests and standards could be presented in a chart form as suggested in figure 83.

NO.	TEST	STANDARDS			
		DEC. 23	JAN. 28	MARCH 4	APRIL 1
1	30 m Dash with high start	4, 3	4, 3	4, 2	4, 1
2	Standing long jump	2,60m	2,70m	2,73m	2,75m
3	Standing penta jump	13.50m	13.60m	13.80m	14.00m
4	Leg press (one attempt)	340kg	360kg	370kg	380kg

Figure 83.   Tests and standards for the preparatory phase for a hypothetical male junior long jumper.

7. Periodization model

The periodization of the annual plan should be conceived in such a way that it represents a model to follow. Having the competition schedule as a foundation, the coach should decide what type of annual plan is most suitable (mono, bi, or tricycle). Following this, the phases of training must be designated with the duration of each phase specified precisely. Continuing the same process, the coach then specifies the macro-cycles stating their number, date, location for training, objectives set for each cycle and the methods of training to be employed to meet these objectives. Then the coach proceeds with one of the most difficult tasks in planning. That is, the insertion of all athlete (team) activities into the chart of the annual plan. The methodology of compiling the chart is explained in Section 4 of the planning chapter.

TRAINING PARAMETERS	SYMBOL/UNITS	VOLUME %	% CHANGE OVER PREVIOUS YR.
The type of annual training plan	mono-cycle		
Periodization:			
—duration of the annual plan/days	322	100	
—preparatory phase/days	182	56.5	> 8
—competitive phase/days	119	37	< 5
—transition phase/days	21	6.5	< 3
Macro-cycles	9		
Micro-cycles	46		
—at the club	41		
—national camp	3		
—travel abroad	2		
Competitions	7		
—international	2		
—national	4		
—regional	1		
Number of training lessons	554		> 6
Number of hours of training	1122		> 8.4
Number of tests	16		
Number of medical controls	3		
Activity milieu:			
—specific training/days	266	82.6	> 3
—swimming/km	2436		> 6
—non-specific training/days	14		> 2
—running/km	640	4.4	> 2
—weight training/kgm	460.000		> 14
—games/hours	28		> 1
—rest/days	42	13	< 8

Figure 84. A hypothetical preparatory model for a 400 m swimmer.

8. The preparation model

The preparation model is in fact a synopsis of the entire annual training program. It comprises the main qualitative, and quantitative parameters used in training and the percentage increment per parameter between the current and previous annual plan. The preparation model has to be closely linked with the whole structure of the annual plan and its objectives. An experienced coach might predict quite accurately the duration of and number of workouts required to develop the necessary skills and abilities to accomplish the set objectives. However, a preparation model could be structured as per figure 84.

A hypothetical preparation model of a male 400 m swimmer is presented in figure 84. It is assumed that in order to reach a higher performance level the athlete has to increase his aerobic endurance and muscular endurance. This will be accomplished through elevating the volume of training by prolonging not only the preparatory phase but also the total number of training lessons and, thus, the total hours of training.

The ratio between different methods and types of training will be also modified in order to enhance the development of muscular and especially aerobic endurance.

In order to improve both aerobic endurance and muscular endurance (through weight training and special water exercises) the training content will be altered, using the following guideline as a model (figure 85).

CONTENT	%	% OF CHANGE
Anaerobic endurance-speed (AE)	2	< 6
Muscular endurance (ME)	16	> 2
Racing tempo endurance (RTE)	32	=
Aerobic endurance over medium distance (EMD)	24	> 2
Aerobic endurance over long distance (ELD)	20	> 2

Figure 85. The model of the training content for the annual plan and the alteration of weighing each means of training as compared to the previous year's plan.

Using the above model as a guideline, the breakdown per training phase may be as in figure 86.

CONTENT	% PREPARATORY PHASE	% CHANGE	% COMPETITIVE PHASE	% CHANGE
AE	5	< 4	8	< 2
ME	10	> 2	16	> 3
RTE	20	< 2	36	< 2
EMD	30	> 3	20	> 2
ELD	35	> 5	20	> 4

Figure 86.   The alteration of the training content and its percentage per training phase between the past and the following annual plan.

In addition to the above sections of an annual plan, the team/club's budget should also be considered when designing the program. Therefore, a complete outline of a training program may be as follows:

1. Introduction
2. Retrospective analysis
3. Performance prediction
4. Objectives
5. Calendar of competitions
6. Tests and standards
7. Periodization model
   a. The chart of the annual plan
   b. The macro-cycles
8. Preparation model
9. Athlete's/team's organization and administration model
   a. Athlete's/team's budget
   b. Equipment needs

CHAPTER TEN

Long Term Planning

Long term planning is one of the characteristics and requirements of modern training. A well-organized and planned training program over a long period of time greatly increases the efficiency of the preparation for major future competitions. In addition, it encourages a rational utilization of means and methods of training and facilitates a concrete, specific assessment of the athlete's progress. Long term planning has to rely on the knowledge accumulated from both scientific and empirical informations. Being aware of and using the advancement in the science of training in sports as well as the experience gained by top coaches and training specialists in the field will aid in perfecting one's training.

It is not uncommon for a coach in Eastern Europe to compile a long term plan of 8–16 years for a young prospective athlete. In fact without such, the coach may find him/herself involved in a random training program, which may not meet their expectations. The achievement of high performance may be facilitated by the following sequential approach to training:

The approach suggested by figure 87 refers to the fact that a youngster who was scientifically selected for the sport based strictly on his/her specific qualities, and

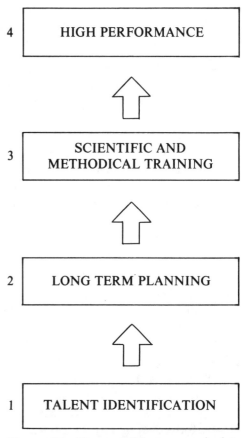

Figure 87. The essential steps required to achieve high performance.

233

who follows a precise long term training program, undoubtedly will have a higher probability of reaching top performance than those involved in the natural programs. In fact such an approach is not really a novelty. In most East European countries, it is a common reality. Many Western specialists were overwhelmed by rumours stating that the East German swimming miracle, Cornelia Ender (5 golds in Montreal) was, from the beginning, meant to be an Olympic champion. The truth of the matter is that Cornelia, like Romania's Nadia Comaneci and many other great athletes, was selected for the sport because of her outstanding abilities. Becoming a champion was just the normal outcome of a long term, well organized and scientifically monitored training program. And such an approach should not be the prerogative of certain countries. It is possible to be just as well organized in almost all countries.

A long term training plan has to establish its direction and its general and specific objectives, which have to be organized over several years. The construction of such a plan has to consider the following four factors:

1. the number of systematic training years necessary for a prospective athlete to obtain high performance;
2. the age at which, on the average, top performance is achieved;
3. the level of natural abilities the prospective athlete starts with;
4. the age at which one starts specialized training starts.

As illustrated by table 3, on the average, the number of years necessary to reach high performance is 5–7. However, this figure may be affected by the age of the prospective athlete when he/she started the systematic program, as well as the number of years left until athletic maturation occurs in the chosen sport (table 2). If a swimming program began at the age of 12, there would be just a few years left until maturation in swimming is attained. Therefore, the long term training program of such an athlete should be drastically altered to accommodate his/her needs. And even so, although not impossible, such an athlete would have a lower probability of reaching a high level of performance as opposed to one with equal abilities but who started a systematic program at an earlier age.

During an athletic life, the dynamics of physical and psychological evolvement alters quite frequently and the motor and physiological functions reach an optimal level between the age of 25–30 for men, and about 3–5 years earlier for women (Ozolin, 1971). However, one may not claim that the above age is also optimal for maximal performance in all sports. For instance, according to the same author, optimal performance in sports requiring maximum speed is achieved by athletes around the age of 20–24. Similarly, activities requiring a great deal of strength and endurance are performed optimally by athletes approaching the age of 30 and quite often even a little older. On the other hand, sports in which success depends on the mastery of movement which could be acquired at an early age, the optimal age is drastically lower (figure skating at 16–20, while gymnastics at the age of 14–16 for the girls and 18–24 for boys). However, although Olympic medals have been won by athletes older than indicated above, it may be fair to say that the victory for older athletes is an exception rather than a common occurrence.

When compiling a long-term plan, it must be done so in light of the fact that the rate of an athlete's improvement, as shown by figure 88, is not linear. The dynamics of the athlete's improvement is much higher at the beginning and during the phase of specialization, and tends to slow down throughout the phase of high performance. Obviously, the shape of the curve is more undulatory and is the product of the correlation between one's physiological and psychological abilities and the type of work, volume, and intensity performed in training. This reality ought to be considered by the coach when setting long term objectives, especially performance objectives and standards for tests. As reflected by figure 88, the highest increase in performance abilities are expected to be reached in the first years of training. A long term plan should have two general phases: 1. preparatory and 2. specialization.

During the preparatory phase the content of training should focus on a multilateral physical development, during which the physical (both anatomical and physiological),

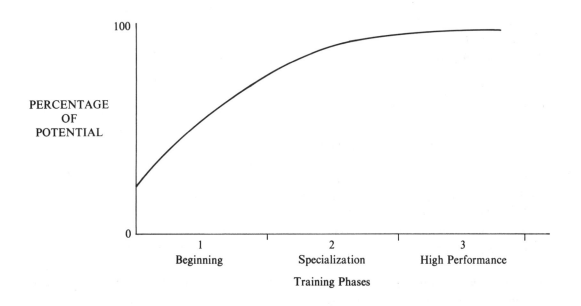

Figure 88.   The curve of the athlete's improvement from the beginning to the phase of high performance.

technical, tactical and psychological premises necessary for specialized training should be developed. Among the main tasks to be considered are the following:

1. Through the use of a high variety of exercises the athletes should experience multilateral development enabling their bodily functions to adjust to different kinds of stimuli.
2. Through the employment of exercises specific to the chosen sport, a base required for training in the specialized sport should develop.
3. Acquisition of simple skills of other sports, especially those which are closely related to the sport of primary interest.
4. Acquisition of the technique of the chosen sport with adjustments to emphasize the individual's qualities/abilities.
5. Exposure of the athletes to diverse types of competition (in various events/sports) so that they will learn to cope with stress.
6. Development of the athlete's determination, firmness, and willpower to pursue an objective.

Obviously, the younger the athlete, (i.e., in swimming or skating they may be 4–6 years old) the fewer and simpler the tasks must be.

For the specialization phase the following tasks may be considered:

1. Improve the level of general physical preparation.
2. Develop and improve the foundations of specific physical preparation.
3. Perfect the technique of the selected sport.
4. Improve the tactical maneuvers of the sport.
5. Improve psychological traits specific to the sport.
6. Learn the theoretical aspects related to the training of the practiced sport as well as the utilization of a training diary.

The development and construction of a long term plan has to take into consideration the athlete's age. For the younger athletes such a plan could be of 6–8 years duration. For juniors (over 16) and elite athletes, a 4–year plan is recommended. However, long term plans, especially for young athletes, have to be linked with the abilities that were discovered when he/she was selected for the sport.

A comprehensive illustration of a long term plan for a prospective athlete (6 years) and a junior (4 years), as well as the emphasis placed upon various types of training, are presented in figure 89. Regardless of the duration of the plan, each of them is solidly based on a multilateral physical preparation, on top of which is built the foundation of specialized training which facilitates a very highly specialized training in accordance with the specifics and needs of the selected sport. It may also be observed that the work is increased in steps on a yearly basis. Similarly, as the

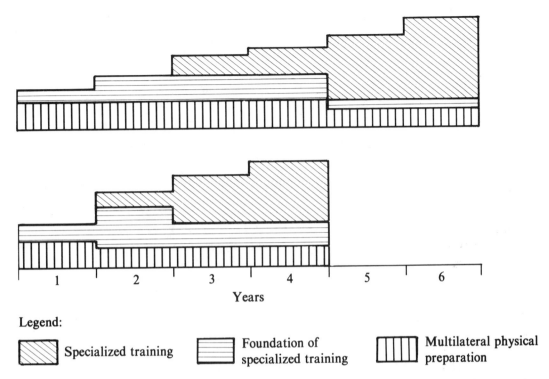

Figure 89.   An illustration of the interrelationship between different types of training employed in a long term plan.

program progresses, the ratio between the three types of training is changed. Whether for an individual or team sport, the coach can make two types of plans: 1) a comprehensive plan for the whole group of athletes; and 2) a plan for each individual athlete. However, prior to the construction of either plan, the competition schedule has to be set for the whole training period. Obviously, this refers to major competitions only (i.e., national championships, which often have a traditional date).

The comprehensive plan should contain the data concerning the whole group and the objectives common to all the athletes. On the other hand, the individual plan focuses strictly on the needs, objectives, and specifics of each athlete.

The construction of a long term plan should entertain the following methodical premises:

1) The athlete's performance objectives has to relate to factors specific to the sport, and their dynamics should reflect the ascending tendency valid for every sport. Furthermore, the coach should be aware of the dynamics of performance in his/her own country as well as the entire world.

2) As the athlete progresses, the coach should increase the number of training lessons and training hours per year, as well as the number and frequency of competitions. However, for highly advanced athletes the number of competitions, especially major ones, may be leveled off.

3) A long term plan should forecast the annual increase for both the volume and intensity of training according to the dominant component of the sport and the athlete's needs. For those sports in the first, third and fourth groups of the sports classification, the intensity of training should be elevated towards the end of the plan.

For most of the other sports, especially those from the second group, in addition to increasing the intensity, there should be a continual elevation of the volume, as the dominant component of training.

4) On a yearly basis, especially for the best athletes, the coach has to alter the emphasis placed upon various exercises employed in training. While at the beginning of the program a high variety of exercises is suggested, towards the end a limited but very specific scope (exercises with direct action) should prevail. Such an approach would enhance the athlete's adaptation to the specifics of the selected sport.

5) The plan must specify the tests and, if possible, standards which ought to be passed every year. This would assist the coach to continually assess and thus discover the strongest and weakest link in the athlete's training. Tests and standards, if correctly selected, represent an important stimulant for the athletes. Tests and standards should be implemented in accordance with the following regulations:

a. select a small number of tests;
b. tests ought to be very specific and reflect the characteristics of the sport;
c. ensure consistency by employing the same tests over a longer period of time during the same phases of training;
d. demand higher standards every year to reflect the demand and improvement of all training factors. Medical controls ought to be an integral part of the athlete's health and training assessment.

6) A long term plan should incorporate all the particularities of a sport. For instance, in acyclic sports, technical and tactical elements have to be reflected by specific indices, such as:

a. the number, grade, and variety of technical elements;
b. the number, grade of difficulty and variety of tactical maneuvers;
c. the degree of general and specific physical preparation;
d. the standards of a test have to reflect the physical requirements of a good technique;
e. performance predictions.

7) And finally, the progression of the number of training lessons and training hours per year should be shown in the plan. As far as the training lessons are

concerned, one may start from approximately 200–250 training lessons per year for the first few years, increasing towards the end of the plan to around 400 per year. For elite athletes the number may be elevated to 500–650, especially for those who participate in individual sports. The number of hours of training should follow a similar pattern: between 400 for beginners, and 1000–1200 for world class athletes.

Forms of Long Term Plans

All long term plans must be compiled with the specifics of the sport in mind. Although all sports differ to some degree, the following general guidelines should be of assistance when compiling a long term plan:

1. A brief outline of the athlete(s) strong and weak points in training, tests and standards and any other relevant information should be included.
2. The scope and objectives of the long term plan must be clearly specified.
3. Performance predictions must be recorded.
4. The competitions schedule and the phases of training must be decided upon. Each year may be considered as a separate phase.
5. General training guidelines for each year (phase) of training should be noted. Each training objective is given a specific weight or priority. These may be presented in the following chart form:

OBJECTIVES	WEIGHT PER TRAINING PHASE					
	19–	19–	19–	19–	19–	19–

6. Physical preparation and its prospective improvement may be specified in the following chart:

MAIN PHYSICAL DEFICIENCIES	OBJECTIVES TO IMPROVE AND PERFECT THEM	MEANS OF IMPROVEMENT

7. Technical preparation and its prospective improvement should be outlined as above.

8. Tactical preparation and its prospective of improvement should be presented as above.

9. Psychological preparation and its prospective of perfecting each trait (specific to the sport) could be noted in the chart that follows:

PSYCHOLOGICAL TRAIT	MEANS OF IMPROVEMENT

10. A periodization model (per each training phase) could be presented as below:

	MONTHS											
	OCT	NOV	DEC	JAN	FEB	MAR	APR	MAY	JUNE	JULY	AUG	SEPT
Number of Competitions												
No. of Competition days												
No. of training hrs.												
No. of days of rest												

11. Tests and standards should be itemized as follows:

TESTS	STANDARDS					
	19–	19–	19–	19–	19–	19–

12. Medical control (type and frequency) must also be planned.

Once the long term plan, and for that matter any single plan, is made, it must not be considered as an inflexible doctrine. Throughout the athlete's preparation, the coach collects information regarding the dynamics of this improvement which may command alterations in the plan. Changing the training plan does not indicate weaknesses on the part of the coach. On the contrary, it proves that he/she is rather flexible and understands the athlete's needs. It shows that the coach is a knowledgeable person with a strong ability to assess the athlete's training. He/she has to solve in a creative and wise fashion all the complex aspects which may arise in the very complex framework of long term planning.

The Olympic Cycle, or Quadrennial Plan

The Olympic cycle, or the quadrennial plan (comprising four years), should be regarded as a segment of the long term planning. The perpetration for the Olympic Games every fourth year necessitates a special planning for sports and athletes included in the Olympic program. Although for such athletes the Olympics is the zenith of the Olympic cycle plan, non-olympians may also use a quadrennial plan as a tool to better organize their long term training programs.

Classification of Olympic Cycle Plans

As for the organization and planning of an Olympic cycle, there are two methodological approaches. The first one is a mono-cyclic approach, where all training factors and components of training are increased progressively every year in a step-wise manner, culminating with the Olympic Games (figure 90). Although such an approach appears to have a built-in progression, it has the disadvantage of placing upon the athletes a continuous elevation of stress, without a year where a longer unloading phase may be planned. The same is not true though for the second approach or the bi-cyclic concept. As illustrated by figure 91, such an approach allows the coach to increase the load in training in an undulatory way. Often, during the post-Olympic year, when a new cycle starts, the intensity and stress of training are lowered so that a relative regeneration is achieved.

During this year the coach builds the basis for the second year when the intensity will elevate, by stressing the volume of training.

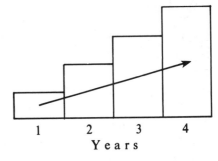

Figure 90. The illustration of a mono-cyclic approach.

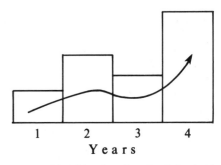

Figure 91. The elevation of training load and the curve of stress in the bi-cyclic approach.

Similarly, during the second year very demanding competitions may be planned when high performances must be reached following which the coach makes a thorough assessment (the midquadrennial analysis) of the athlete's ability. Such an analysis is valid mostly for Olympic sports, although the concept may be applicable to any other sport. The analysis should, among other things, consider: 1) whether the performance and the objectives for each training factor were achieved, and, 2) based on number 1, make adequate corrections in the plan (objectives, standards of each test, etc.). The third year, although the level of work is higher than in the first, may be considered as an unloading year, in preparation for the following year when the Olympics will be held. Although the volume of training may be quite high, the intensity, and the number of stressful competitions may be lowered. This would enhance a regeneration phase on which basis the extremely demanding training program for the Olympics may be built. As for the fourth year, the coach attempts to maximize the athlete's performance through wisely using the athlete's talent and knowledge.

The bi-cyclic approach should be considered only for those athletes who have reached the optimal age for a particular sport and who, based on a strong background, are planning to compete in the Olympic games. For younger athletes, who have not yet reached the above level, the mono-cyclic approach is more advisable since their objective is a perpetual improvement up to the maturation age in the chosen sport. However, since elite athletes may have intermediate goals, like a successful performance in the world championships, the approach utilized in the Olympic cycle plan may be monocyclic (several sports do have world championships on an annual basis). In such circumstances careful attention must be paid to thorough regeneration periods, usually organized during the transition phase. On the other hand, the percentage of the total amount of work with which the preparatory phase may be slightly altered to allow an undulatory approach. Thus, for the post-Olympic year (year 1 in the plan), one may start with a workload equal to 30% of the previous year's most demanding level. In the second year the total load may begin around 40% while the third year 30% again to allow a better regeneration. Finally, the plan for the Olympics may commence with a workload equal to 50% of the previous year's most demanding level.

The Compilation of an Olympic Cycle Plan

The compilation of an Olympic cycle or Quadrennial plan may follow similar headings as the annual plan, such as:

1. retrospective analysis, where the coach analyzes:
   —the athlete's dynamics of physical development—results of competitions
   —tests and standards for each training factor
   Such an analysis has to be made in conjunction with an analysis of the dynamics of the sports development at the national and international level. Based on such

an analysis, the coach may make the appropriate conclusions and set realistic objectives.

2. Performance predictions for each year, concluding with the Olympic year.
3. Objectives set for each training factor in accordance with the dynamics, and tendencies of development in the world.
4. The calendar of major competitions (i.e., National Championships and main international competitions).
5. Tests and standards to reflect the conclusions of the retrospective analysis. These are linked with the performance predictions and objectives set for each training factor.
6. The chart of the Olympic cycle plan.
7. A basic periodization model for each year of training.
8. A preparation model (general outline).

The Chart of the Olympic Cycle or Quadrennial Plan

The chart of the Olympic Cycle Plan should be regarded as a synopsis of the whole plan, which mirrors the main training objectives planned to be achieved on a yearly basis. The chart may also be considered as a working tool which the coach uses when he/she extracts the data necessary to construct the current year's annual plan.

Figure 92 illustrates a chart of a Quadrennial plan for a hypothetical junior athlete, which incorporates the dynamics of all objectives (performance, training factors, and tests and standards), as well as the ratio of all training factors and the curves of the components of training.

The objectives are assigned separately for each of the four years composing the plan. Their sequential set up should reflect the overall flow of training from year to year.

For instance, as far as physical preparation is concerned, initially general physical preparation and aerobic endurance are emphasized, leading to a very specific physical preparation and anaerobic endurance towards the end of the four year period. The same approach is employed for technical preparation, most of which (considering our example of a cyclic skill) has to be acquired in the first part of the program. As for the standards of each test, they are expected to be improved annually reflecting the general improvements of the athlete's abilities. As for the shape of the curves of the components of training and peaking, their magnitude should signify the general ascending tendency from year to year. There is no relationship between the percentage scale (which refers to training factors only) and the curves magnitude. Furthermore, the interrelationship between the curves of volume and intensity reflects the same concept as in the annual plan. Volume dominates the preparatory and the beginning of the competitive phase (note—the specifics of an event like 800 m), and is surpassed by intensity in the second part of the competitive phase, as a result of the emphasis placed on anaerobic endurance. The magnitude of the peaking curve also holds an ascendent trend, signifying the athlete's predicted performance evolution.

CLUB: _____

ATHLETE: _____

EVENT 800 m

OBJECTIVES

	19 –	19 –	19 –	19 –
PERFORMANCE	2:14	2:06	2:01	1:58–1:59
PHYSICAL PREP.	—Develop general physical preparation —Develop aerobic endurance	—Improve gen. phys. prep. —Dev. muscular endur. —Improve aerobic endur. —Develop anaerobic endurance	—Improve specific phys. prep. —Improv. musc. endurance —Perfect aerob. end. —Improve anaerob. end.	—Perfect spec. phys. prep. —Perfect aerob. endur. —Perfect anaerob. endur.
TECHNICAL PREP.	—Correct arm carriage —Correct position of head	—Efficient stride length —Minimum vertical bouncing	—relaxed running —efficient technical movement	↑ ↑
TACTICAL PREP.	—Steady pace throughout the race	—Fast, alert in the first 400 m. —Steady pace in the body of the race	—Take a good position before the finish —Perfect the start	—Cope with various strategies —Perfect the finish
PSYCHO-LOGICAL PREP.	—develop mental awareness and the resulting consequence —attempt to modify the above	—develop self concept.	—Identify anxieties and stressors and how to handle them —relaxation techniques	↑ ↑
TESTS AND STANDARDS	100 m = 12.4 400 m = 57.00 1500 m = 4.22 VO₂ Max = 3.08 ℓ	12.0 55.5 4:16 3.7 ℓ	11.7 53.0 4:09 4.1 ℓ	11.5 51.5 4:04 4.5 ℓ

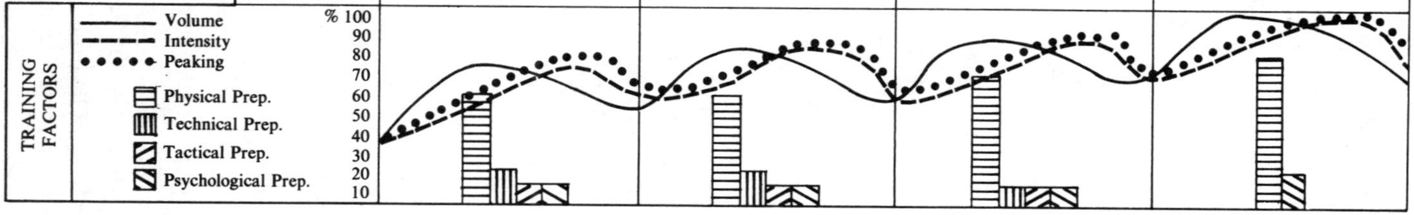

% 100 90 80 70 60 50 40 30 20 10

Legend:
- —— Volume
- –·– Intensity
- •••• Peaking
- ▦ Physical Prep.
- ▥ Technical Prep.
- ▧ Tactical Prep.
- ▨ Psychological Prep.

TRAINING FACTORS

Figure 92. The chart of a hypothetical Olympic cycle or Quadrennial plan.

METHODS AND FORMS OF EVIDENCE

The concept of using specific methods and forms of evidence should be viewed by the coach as an integral part of the planning process. Without precise data collected from the athletes throughout all training phases, one may not plan and make a retrospective analysis based on concrete evidence. By utilizing the forms of evidence as a reference, one may factually pursue the athlete's dynamics of physical development, and his/her improvement in tests and athletic performance.

The following are some of the more simple but crucial forms of evidence suggested for consideration:

Athlete's personal data

NO.	NAME	DATE AND PLACE OF BIRTH	ADDRESS	TELEPHONE
1	Joe Morgan	15.03.70	21 Lancer St., Maple	494–5981

Training lesson's attendance

NO.	NAME	NOVEMBER	
1	Joe Morgan		28

Biometric data

NO.	NAME	HEIGHT			WEIGHT			RESTING HEART RATE	BLOOD PRESSURE	VITAL CAPACITY
		JAN	MAY	AUG	JAN	MAY	AUG			
1	Joe Morgan	1.83	1.83	1.84	70	71	71	56	10.5/8.0	4800

Performance in competitions
a) for individual sports

NO.	NAME OF COMPET.	DATE	PLACE	RESULTS	NOTES
1	All comers meet	Aug. 12	Bolton	6.36 m	Medium head wind

b) for team sports

NO.	TEAM	1	2	3	4	5	POINTS	STANDING
1	The Barons		6–1	2–0	3–3	9–2	7 (20–6)	1
2	The Blues							3
3	Centennial W.P.C.							5
4	R.R.T.							4
5	The Eagles							2

Tests and standards

NO.	NAME	TEST	OCT. 16		JAN. 9		MAR. 20		NOTE
			PLANNED	ACHIEVED	PLANNED	ACHIEVED	PLANNED	ACHIEVED	
1	Joe Morgan	Leg Press	160 kg	170	180	180	200	190	

Medical Control

NO.	NAME	DATE	DIAGNOSIS
1	Joe Morgan	Oct. 4	
2			

Evidence of Accidents

NO.	NAME	DIAGNOSIS	CAUSE	TREATMENT	NOTE

The above charts include information of a general nature, but others may be added, especially for the biometric data, since the charts should be made in such a way that the specifics and needs of the sport are considered. However, in the field of training, other charts of a more comprehensive nature are available. An example of a chart with the objective to synthesize a year of training is presented in figure 93. However hypothetical, the reader may note that the standards are presented in a format where a comparison between the planned (P) and achieved (A) objectives is obvious. Similarly, the performance achievements are presented in a graphical form so that the difference may be visualized immediately.

The planning process in training has to be perceived as one of the top priorities among the coach's activities. One's effectiveness in training depends a great deal on his/her abilities and knowledge to organize a short and long term program. In order to compile a comprehensive training program a high level of knowledge is required. In fact, when a coach plans the athlete's training program, he/she utilizes all the knowledge acquired from the assimilation of training principles, emphasis of training factors and the components of training up to the skills of correctly interpreting the athlete's behaviour and training assessment. The greater the knowledge in the theory and methodology of training the more sophisticated the planning can be.

PERFORMANCE OBJECTIVE FOR 19 –

	Planned	Achieved
PERFORMANCE OBJECTIVE	52.00 m	53.14 m

MAIN CONCLUSIONS

1. Several technical elements were improved
2. As a result of abdomen and back muscle's strength gains the last phase of throw was improved.
3. Gains in mental awareness

FUTURE OBJECTIVES

1. Perfect the power position.
2. Improve maximum strength (arm and shoulder)
3. Develop self concept as a means to improve consistency in training and competitions.

PERIODIZATION

PREPARATORY		COMPETITIVE		TRANSITION

MONTHS / WEEKENDS

	Nov. 1 7 14 23		Dec. 1 7 14 21 30		Jan. 6 13 20 27		Feb. 3 10 17 24		Mar. 2 9 16 23 30		April 6 13 20 27		May 4 11 18 25		June 1 8 15 22 29		July 6 13 20 27		Aug. 3 10 17 24 31		Sept. 7 14 21 28		Oct. 5 12 19 26

Plan(P)/Achv(A)	P	A	P	A	P	A	P	A	P	A	P	A	P	A	P	A	P	A	P	A	P	A	P	A
30 m Dash(sec)	5	5.1			4.8	4.9			4.7	4.8			4.7	4.8	4.7	4.7						A		
Stand. Long Jump	2.20	2.23			2.25	2.31			2.30	2.38			2.40	2.43							2.40	2.41		
Chin-Ups	6	4	7	5	9	8	10	10	12	13	14	15	14	15					4.7	4.8		
Leg Press(Kg)	180	170	190	180	210		210	210	220	220	220													
Baseball Throw (m)									60	57	63	61.7	68	67.3										

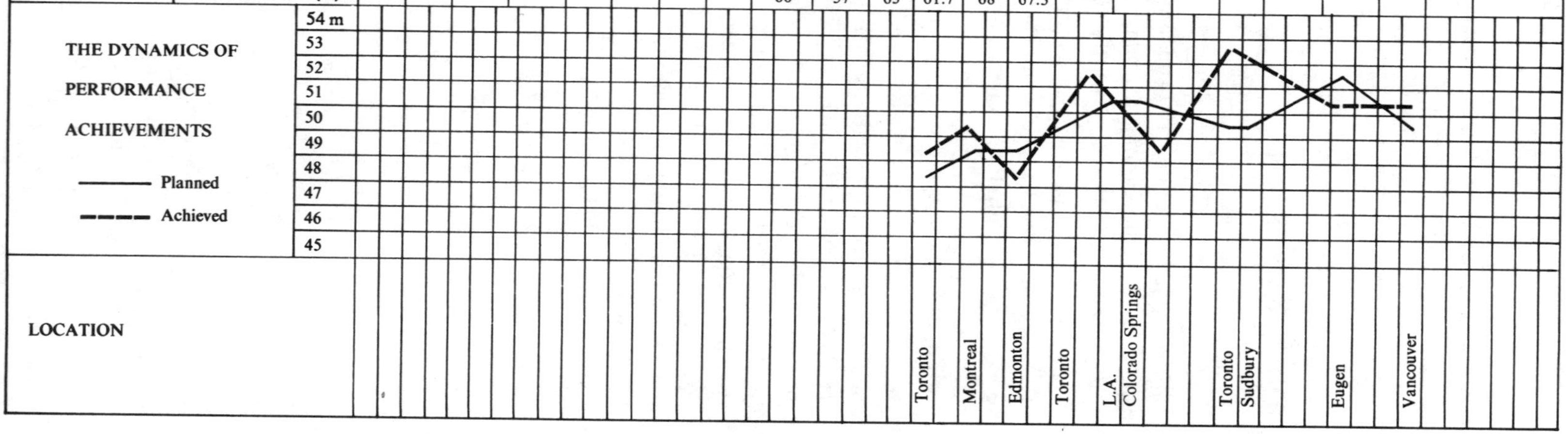

THE DYNAMICS OF PERFORMANCE ACHIEVEMENTS

54 m
53
52
51
50
49
48
47
46
45

——— Planned
– – – Achieved

LOCATION: Toronto, Montreal, Edmonton, Toronto, L.A. Colorado Springs, Toronto Sudbury, Eugen, Vancouver

Figure 93. The synthesis of the performance analysis of a hypothetical woman javelin thrower.

CHAPTER ELEVEN

The Athletic Competition

It is obvious that the main goal of an athlete's training is to take part in competitions, to challenge other athletes for a top spot in the competition hierarchy, and to achieve a high level of performance. The importance of competitions extends beyond these goals. A competition is also considered as the most important and specific means of assessing an athletes' progress. Many coaches maintain that an athlete's level of preparation is also elevated by participation in competitions. Although this is true to a certain extent, it should not be expected that a degree of training and correct peaking can be achieved through competition only, as is often attempted in some professional sports. Participation in competitions, especially during the precompetitive phase when exhibition contests are planned, does assist the athletes to reach a high state of readiness for the main competition of the year. During such competitions, the athletes have the opportunity to test all training factors in the most specific way. However, to consider the competition as the only means of improvement lessens the whole philosophy of training, and consequently disturbs the main cycle of activity: training → competition → regeneration (figure 94).

Often coaches become captivated by participation in many exhibition competitions and overlook proper training. They stress intensity at the expense of volume and, as a result, the athletes peak much earlier than originally planned. Therefore, a natural

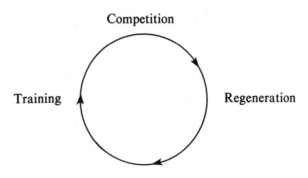

Figure 94. The cycle of activities in training.

consequence is a poor show towards the end of the competitive phase when the main competitions are planned. One should never forget that training accumulation during the preparatory phase is not a bag without end. On the contrary, the bag must always be replenished so that adequate physical and psychological support will last until the end of the competitive phase.

An important outcome of participation in competitions, especially for prospective athletes, is the gaining of competitive experience. However, all competitions included in an annual plan must be subordinated to, and must enhance the achievement of the main performance objective of the year which usually is expected to be accomplished during the main competition of the year. Therefore, the selection and planning of competitions is an art of its own.

A competition is the real testing ground for an athlete's preparation. During such a contest, the athlete can test his/her level of improvement on a given date, consolidate the technique and test tactics against direct opponents, learn how to spend energy effectively, improve psychological traits such as will power, and perseverance. However, prior to participating in any competition specific objectives to be achieved must be planned. The objectives are to be oriented and determined according to the type and characteristics of the competition in which the athlete takes part.

CLASSIFICATION AND CHARACTERISTICS OF COMPETITIONS

Most competitions may be classified into two groups: 1. official or main, and, 2. preparatory or exhibition competitions.

1. THE OFFICIAL OR MAIN competitions are considered to be determinant for qualification or in defining the final standing in a championship. They are of paramount importance, and customarily athletes strive to achieve a high or the highest possible performance (in heats or qualifying rounds highest performance is not always necessary for further levels of competition). Main competitions, especially for individual sports, may serve as a guideline to segregate the annual plan into macro-cycles.

2. THE PREPARATORY OR EXHIBITION competitions are customarily planned to test and to attain feedback from athletes/teams regarding certain aspects of training. Such competitions are an integral part of a micro-cycle, and therefore the coach should not alter or unload his/her normal training plan. However, although victory should not be the only objective, in such competitions the athletes may endure maximal intensity, deplete energy reserves, surpass physical and psychological capacities, overcome emotions and acquire experience against known and unknown opponents, so that they will arrive at an adequate state of readiness prior to beginning the official competitions.

Consequently, all competitions in athletics have the following characteristics and orientations:

VICTORY in a competition captivates each athlete from early involvement in training. But to be a victor in a competition requires long hours of hard work. Talent in athletics is an important asset, but hard work is a requirement. There are no short cuts for hard work in the pursuit of becoming a winner.

RECORD, which can be closely linked to victory, is the dream of many athletes. To surpass one's own and previously scored records, means that under specific, ideal conditions, one defeats one's own weaknesses both physiologically and psychologically.

Although records are not always beaten as planned by a coach in a particular phase, such competitions are usually organized during the mid part of the competitive phase. No such meets should be organized within 2–3 weeks of the main competition of the year since they exhaust the athlete's physical and psychological capabilities.

TEST competitions are organized with the scope of verifying an athlete's potential and qualities on a given date. The objectives in such competitions are to test the athletes physically as well as psychologically and to validate their technique or tactical maneuvers. In team sports, since such competitions are informal, the coach may decide to stop the game from time to time and suggest various tactics to be tested against opponents.

ADJUSTMENT TO SPECIFIC CONDITIONS of future competitions plays an important role in an athlete's abilities to perform adequately. Therefore, the coach may choose to compete in a place which would familiarize the athletes with facilities and the quality of the equipment to be experienced in a future major competition. Such a competition may be considered as an exhibition, therefore, the coach should not stress victory, but rather adaptation and adjustment to the specifics of the facilities.

PLANNING THE COMPETITION

The competition schedule is usually set by the sport governing bodies. However, since in their decisions they are concerned with the championship or league competitions only, according to the time available and specific objectives the coach may decide to select preparatory/exhibition contests also. The selection and planning of competitions is a paramount process in training which may enhance or adversely affect peaking for the major contest(s).

As far as the selection procedures and the coach's role in the decision making process goes, there often exist some misinterpretations. Some coaches follow the belief that an athlete has to participate with all possible effort in every available competition. Obviously, in such a case, the athletes are constantly exposed to stressful activities which might not lead to an optimal season climax (please refer to the peaking index). Similarly, such a heavy game/contest schedule requires many regeneration dates, disturbing the normal course of training. Also of concern is the intense psychological stress required for an athlete to reach an adequate state of arousal for each competition. Neglecting these two aspects may facilitate undesirable consequences, reflected through a poor peaking for the main competition of the year.

Another unusual procedure referring to the process of selecting competitions is the fact that some coaches tell the athletes to make the decision. Obviously, in most

TRAINING PHASE	COMPETITIVE PHASE																					
DATES	MAY					JUNE				JULY					AUGUST				SEPT.			
	1	8	15	22	29	5	12	19	26	3	10	17	24	31	7	14	21	28	4	11	18	25
MACRO-CYCLES	6			7			8				9					10				11		
CALENDAR OF COMPETITIONS			x	x						x	x	x										

Figure 95.　Planning the competitions based on the grouping approach.

cases the athletes do not have the knowledge to use the proper methodological guideline for selecting and planning a competition. Consequently, in such cases the leadership should come from the coach who may decide to employ one of the two basic methods of planning the calendar of competition for the entire annual plan as discussed below:

　　1. THE GROUPING approach refers to the method of planning 2–3 weeks in a row during which the athletes take pan in tournaments or competitions where they participate in several events or races per weekend. As illustrated by figure 95, such a phase is usually followed by a macro-cycle of training only, allowing the athletes to train for another 2–3 weeks of group competitions.

TRAINING PHASE	COMPETITIVE PHASE																					
DATES	MAY					JUNE				JULY					AUG.				SEPT.			
	1	8	15	22	29	5	12	19	26	3	10	17	24	31	7	14	21	28	4	11	18	25
MACRO-CYCLES		7					8					9						10		11		
CALENDAR OF COMPETITIONS		x		x		x	x	x	x	x	x	x	x	x	x	x						

Figure 96.　A hypothetical example of a cyclic approach for a team sport.

　　The hypothetical example illustrated by figure 96 suggests that at the end of May the athlete/team takes pan in a group of competitions spread out over two weeks. In each case, it may happen that races/games are organized over 2-3 days during each weekend. The first micro-cycle following these competitions is a lower intensity cycle, with one peak at the end. The first part of the cycle (2-3 days) is dedicated to regeneration, where low intensity, non-stressful training lessons are organized. The next two and a half micro-cycles are planned for hard training, followed by a short unloading phase (2-3 days) and again three weeks of competitions. August 21st is hypothesized to be the qualifying (regional) competition for the main championships of the year held during the weekend of September 25th. As far as training is concerned, the macro-cycles preceding the qualifying and final championships follow the same pattern as the previous ones.

The grouping approach is most suited to individual sports, where the only two official competitions are planned in a manner similar to the above example. For team sports, such an approach may be used only for international competitions, where the grouping concept is a typical model training for an official international tournament.

2. THE CYCLIC APPROACH may be employed by both individual and team sports. The term itself refers to competitions that are planned in a repetitive, cyclic manner (figure 96).

The competitions during macro-cycles 8 and 9 are league games planned for each weekend. Then at the end of macro-cycles 10 and 11 the regional and final championships are planned. Since each micro-cycle ends with a game, each may be structured with one peak only, which usually should be on Tuesday or Wednesday. One or two days prior to the game, there is a progressive unloading phase to enhance overcompensation for the day of the game.

As for individual sports where there are no league competitions but only the qualifying and finals (main competition of the year), the cyclic approach may be considered as in figure 97. In such circumstances, the coach decides to take part in other competitions organized by various clubs. Assuming that there are several competitions to choose from, the coach plans to take part only in those which facilitate a cyclic approach. Consequently, athletes will compete every second weekend, with the time between competitions devoted to training. Such an approach is rather advantageous because the coach can modify training programs according to the feedback received during competitions. Naturally, this will enhance an ideal preparation for the main competition.

As far as the structure of micro-cycles for the cyclic approach is concerned, the micro-cycle following a competition must be of low intensity during the first half, to enhance recovery, and of higher intensity during the second half. The micro-cycle prior to the competition is structured oppositely: the athletes train harder during the

TRAINING PHASE	COMPETITIVE PHASE																		
DATES	November					December				January				February				March	
	1	8	15	22	29	5	12	19	26	3	10	17	24	31	7	14	21	28	4	11	18
MACRO-CYCLES	7					8								9					10		
CALENDAR OF COMPETITIONS	x			x		x		x		x		x									

Figure 97.   A hypothetical example of a cyclic approach for a cross-country skier.

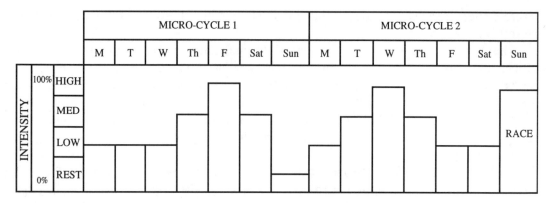

Figure 98.   The curve of peaking the load in training during the interval between copetitions.

first half (highest peak on Tuesday or Wednesday), unloading during the second half of the week (figure 98).

The reader may correctly assume that a pragmatic coach can employ a combination of both methods of selecting and planning for competitions. It may very well happen that in a certain pan of the competitive phase a certain method prevails, while the other will remain for the balance of the year.

The planning of the main competition, normally performed by the national association/federation should be on the date of future Olympic games so that coaches may experience several annual cycles before the games. Such experimentation will hopefully lead to an ideal annual plan which then has to be duplicated for the Olympic year. This is a very important concept which the national federation should consider and follow.

THE NUMBER AND FREQUENCY OF COMPETITIONS

Individual characteristics, experience, age, and characteristics of the sport are among the determinant factors when deciding upon the frequency and number of competitions to be included in the annual plan. An additional and important factor which has to be considered as well is the duration of the competitive phase. The longer the phase, the greater the number of competitions. The characteristics of the sport must be considered as the paramount guideline when deciding the number and frequency of competitions. Athletes participating in sports of short duration (i.e., sprinting, jumping, diving) where the physical demand is lower, experience a higher rate of recovery. Consequently, the frequency and implicitly the number of starts (races, events) could be quite high. Ozolin (1971) suggests that in such sports, elite athletes may take part in 40–50 starts per year. On the other hand, sports demanding high energy and nervous expenditure, where endurance, strength, and muscular endurance are either dominant or an impor-

Table 18.   The suggested number of competitions per year in athletics.

Event	Beginners and Prospective Athletes		Elite Athletes	
	Winter	Summer	Winter	Summer
Sprinters, hurdlers, jumpers and throwers				
—specialized event	3–4	12–16	3–5	16–20
—other events/sports	2–3	4–6	1–3	3–5
Mid distance				
—800–1500m	—	4–8	2–3	10–16
—shorter distances	2–3	8–10	2–4	8–10
Distance running and walking				
—marathon	—	1	—	2–3
—50 km walk	—	6–8	—	8–10
Combined events				
—decathlon	—	1–2	—	2–3
—heptathlon	—	2	—	2–4
—individual events	2–4	10–12	3–5	12–16

tant component of training (i.e., swimming, mid and long distance running, cross-country skiing, rowing, cycling, boxing, wrestling, etc.) the number of competitions should be much lower, 15–25 (table 18). Athletes participating in team sports often take part in more than 30 games per year. As far as frequency is concerned, the time required for recovery should be considered which, in the case of the latest group, is quite long.

During the competitive phase the athletes should be entered in 2–4 main competitions which, in most cases, are qualifying meets for the main contest of the year, and the main competition. In addition, other competitions of lesser importance are included in the calendar of competitions. However, as suggested by table 19 between the preparatory (exhibition) competitions, planned for the precompetitive subphase, and the main competitions, a short period of training has to be planned.

It is not necessary for a competition to be organized only in a specialized sport/event. Often, especially during the preparatory phase, special competitions could be organized to enhance general physical development. Such competitions are intended mostly for beginners and prospective athletes; those whose technique is not yet properly acquired. Quite often such competitions are organized for elite athletes as well. In Eastern Europe it is quite common to see gymnasts and weight lifters competing in a 30 m dash and standing high jump while rowers, cyclists, canoeists compete in cross-country skiing, etc. There is not only a psychological but also a physical advantage to such competitions. Since the athletes are competing in activities which are part of their training, or have certain similarities with their particular event, the athletes will be more highly motivated to work hard for the improvement of their general or specific physical preparation.

As far as participation in the interval between competitions is concerned, Bompa (1970) and Harre (1982) recommend that a coach consider the following aspects:

1. an athlete should take part in a competition only when he/she is capable of achieving set objectives for each training factor: physical, technical, tactical, and psychological.
2. each competition should be selected carefully, in such order that the level of difficulty is increased progressively.
3. unchallengeable competitions do not motivate an athlete.
4. do not avoid opponents of much superior capabilities.
5. too many competitions, especially roads trips, diminishes the coach's possibility to properly dose both competitions and training. The end result will be a decrease in the athlete's physical and especially psychological potential.
6. a correct planning of the competition schedule should ensure the best peaking for the main competition.
7. the main competition of the year is the only one which establishes an athlete's hierarchy in a sport. The other ones (except for league games) are just progressive steps which bring the athlete to that level.

Table 19. Guiding objectives for the competitive sub-phase.

TRAINING PHASE	COMPETITIVE			
Subphases	**Pre-Competition**	**Spec. Prep. for League Compet.**	**League/Official Competition**	**Special Preparation**
OBJECTIVES	—improve performance —gain competitive experience —determine main strengths and weaknesses —test technique and tactics under competitive circumstances	—correct deficiencies shown during the pre-competition sub-phase —alter techniques and methods to improve athlete's competitive effectiveness	—reach high athletic potentials —prepare for qualifying competitions	—take part successfully in the main competition
MEANS OF IMPLEMEN-TATION	—competitions of progressively increasing difficulty —Increase density of competitions —decrease slightly the volume of training	—extensive training —increase volume —some competitions without affecting training	—reduce volume and increase intensity according to the needs of the sport —take part in more demanding competitions	—Special preparation for the main competition

CHAPTER TWELVE

Biomotor Abilities and the Methodology of Their Development

BIOMOTOR ABILITIES: A GENERAL VIEW

Almost all physical movements incorporate, to a certain extent, the elements of force, quickness, duration, complexity and a range of movement. Further, one may distinguish individual motor aspects as well as physiological components like strength, speed, endurance and co-ordination. From the training point of view, there will likely be more interest in perfecting the athlete via these physiological components, more commonly referred to as biomotor abilities, rather than in perfecting the skill.

The ability of an individual to perform an exercise is considered to be the cause, while the movement itself is just the effect. Therefore, the ability to control the cause in order to perform a successful effect is required. The biomotor abilities which are the foundations of a cause are largely genetic, or inherited abilities. Therefore, in this chapter one's ability to perform an exercise will be referred to as a basic, natural ability and the outcome of the combination of certain biomotor abilities. Although flexibility is not a natural ability but rather an anatomical quality of the locomotor organ, it will also be considered since it has high importance in training.

A biomotor ability is strongly linked with and dependent upon its quantitative sphere, where the magnitude of the strength, speed, and endurance levels limit physical work given the qualitative demands. Each exercise has a dominant ability, and when the load is maximized it is called a strength exercise. When in a given exercise quickness and high frequency is maximized it is called a speed exercise. Furthermore, when distance, duration or the number of repetitions is maximized one is exposed to an endurance exercise. And finally when in a given exercise a high degree of complexity is required it is known as a co-ordination exercise. However, in training an exercise is rarely dominated by only one ability. Rather a movement is often the product or combination of two abilities. As illustrated by figure 99, when strength and

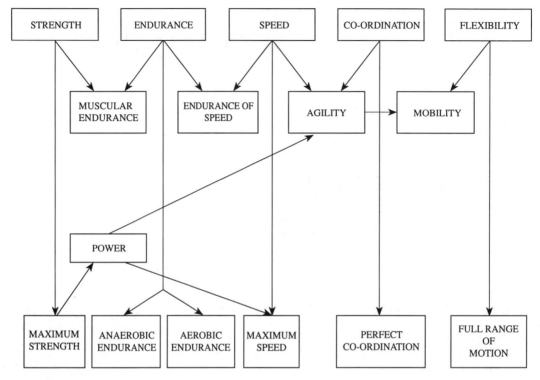

Figure 99. An illustration of the interdependence between the biomotor abilities.

speed are almost equally dominant, as in jumping and throwing events in athletics, or spiking in volleyball, the product is called power. Furthermore, the combination of endurance with strength produces muscular endurance (swimming, canoeing, wrestling and others). The product of endurance and speed (events around 60 seconds) is often called speed-endurance or endurance of speed, while in some sports the highly acclaimed agility is a combination of speed, power and co-ordination. And finally, when agility and flexibility join together the result is called mobility, or the quality of performing a movement quickly, well timed and co-ordinated throughout a wide range of movement (in diving, floor exercises in gymnastics, karate, wrestling, and team sports).

Among strength, speed and endurance there is a relationship of high methodical importance. During the initial years of involvement in training, all abilities have to be developed in order to build a solid foundation for specialized training. This latter phase is specific to national level and elite athletes whose program aims for a precise, specialized training effect. Thus, as a result of employing specific exercises, the adaptation process occurs in accordance with one's specialization. For elite class athletes the relationship between the magnitude of strength, speed and endurance, as the three

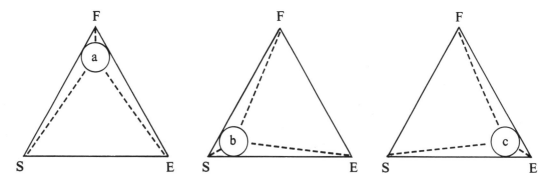

Figure 100. A graphical illustration of the relationship between the main biomotor abilities, where strength (a), speed (b) and endurance (c) are dominant (from Florescu et al., 1969).

more determinant and difficult to develop biomotor abilities, are dependent upon the particularities of the sport and the athlete's needs. Figure 100 illustrates such a relationship, where in each example strength or force (F), speed (S), or endurance (E) is dominant. In each case when one biomotor ability is strongly dominant the other two do not share or participate to a similar extent. However, the above example is just pure theory, which may only be directly applied to a very few sports. In the vast majority of sports the combination between the three biomotor abilities leads to a different outcome in which each ability has a greater input. Figure 101 exemplifies a few sports where the circle represents the dominant composition between strength, speed and endurance.

The contribution of the biomotor abilities to the attainment of high performance is determined by two factors:

1. the ratio between them as a reflection of the specifics of the sport; and
2. by the level of development of each ability according to its degree of participation in performing the sport/event.

Therefore, the appropriate selection of the means of training to meet the needs of the sport is crucial. This refers to both the selection, in relationship to the dominant composition of biomotor abilities, and phase of training. The exclusive utilization of technical elements or specific skills leads to a correct composition of abilities, but the improvement of each ability to the required level of high performance is slow. The ratio of such a development is much higher when the biomotor abilities are developed by employing specific exercises (refer to Physical Preparation in chapter 3).

The development of a biomotor ability is very specific and related to the method employed. However, even when a dominant ability is developed (e.g., strength), it has an indirect effect upon the other abilities (speed and endurance). Such an effect de-

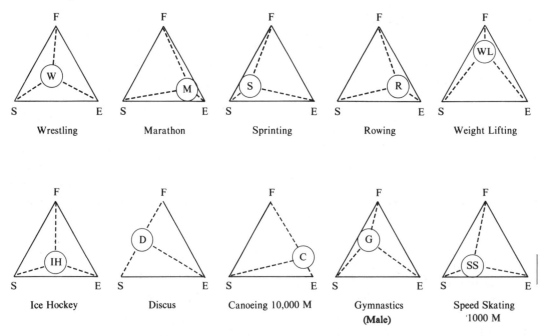

Figure 101.   The dominant composition between the biomotor abilities for various sports.

pends strictly on the degree of resemblance between the methods employed and the specifics of the sport. Thus, the development of a dominant biomotor ability may have a positive or negative transfer. When one attempts to develop strength there may be a positive transfer to speed, and to a certain degree even to endurance. On the other hand, a weight training program designed to develop maximum strength may have a negative transfer to the development of aerobic endurance such as the one required in marathon running. Similarly, a training program aiming exclusively to develop aerobic endurance, under certain circumstances (i.e., training for marathon) may have a negative transfer to strength and speed, while specific training for speed always has, what Florescu et al (1969) calls a "neutral effect."

In the area of biomotor abilities there is a vast amount of information referring to both the scientific foundations and the methodology of their development. The methodology of developing the biomotor abilities concerned training specialists for centuries. The first information regarding these abilities were written in the methodical literature (Uhov, 1875; Lagrange, 1892; Schmidt, 1925; Novikov, 1941 and others) and only later on did the physiologists attempt to investigate them. Since such an enormous amount of information exists, and considering the objective and size of this book, this chapter will be reduced to a minimum possible size. However, the area which will be stressed in particular is the practical or methodical area which may be the most beneficial to a coach.

STRENGTH TRAINING

In simple terms, strength is defined as the ability to apply force. Its development should be the prime concern of anyone who attempts to improve an athlete's performance. Although strength development in primitive forms was employed by athletes preparing to compete in the ancient Olympic games, there are still many coaches who do not take advantage of its benefactory role. Using several strength development methods seem to lead to a faster growth, by up to 8–12 times, as compared to the employment of only skills available for a certain sport, (i.e., a volleyball player may develop a faster jumping ability for spiking by using weight training, rather than simply by performing several spikes during a volleyball practice). Therefore it seems that strength training is one of the most important ingredients in the process of "making" athletes.

From the theoretical viewpoint, force may be referred to as both a mechanical characteristic and a human ability. In the former case force is the object of studies in mechanics, while in the latter it is the scope of physiological and methodical investigation in training.

Force as a Mechanical Characteristic

Force could be determined by direction, magnitude or the point of application. According to Newton's second law of motion force is equal to mass (m) times acceleration (a), or:

$$F = m \cdot a$$

Consequently, an increase in strength may be achieved by changing one or both of these factors (m or a). Such changes result in quantitative alterations which must be kept in mind when developing strength. The following two equations used in mechanics may illustrate this point:

$$F_{mx} = m_{mx} \cdot a \ (1)$$
$$F_{mx} = m \cdot a_{mx} \ (2)$$

where F_{mx} is maximum force; m_{mx} is maximum mass and a_{mx} means maximum acceleration.

In the first equation maximum force is developed by using the maximum mass (or load) possible, whereas the same result is achieved in the second equation by using the maximum speed of movement. The force that an athlete can apply and the velocity at which he/she can apply it maintain an inverse relationship (which was demonstrated above). This is also true for the relationship between an athlete's applied force and the time period over which one can apply it. The gains in one ability is at the expense of the other. Consequently, although force may be the dominant characteristic of an ability, it cannot be considered in isolation because the afore-mentioned speed and time component will directly affect its application.

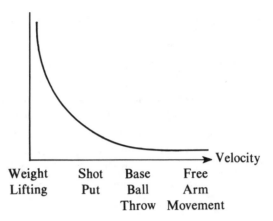

Figure 102. The force-velocity curve (adapted from Ralston et al., 1949).

The force-velocity inverse relationship was demonstrated by Hill (1922) and Ralston et al (1949). An adaptation of Ralston's force-velocity curve is illustrated by figure 102 which demonstrates that when the mass is low, the acceleration is high given maximum effort by the participant. As the mass increases (from baseball throw to shot put and weight lifting) the acceleration decreases, up to no movement at all (or static muscular contraction for mass heavier than one's maximum force).

The magnitude of the force is directly related to the magnitude of the mass. This relationship is linear only at the beginning when the force increases as the mass of the moving object increases. A continuous elevation of a mass will not necessarily result in an equally large increase in applied force. Therefore, the per gram force which the athlete applies against a shot (shot putting in athletics) will be greater than that applied when he/she lifts a barbell. As suggested by Florescu et al (1969), in order to put a shot of 7.250 kg 18.19 m an athlete displays a power of 6.9 h.p. (horse power) or 5147 Watts, while to snatch (weight lifting) 150 kg requires only 4.3 h.p, or 3207 Watts.

The Physiological Characteristics of Strength

Strength may be defined as the neuro-muscular capability to overcome an external and internal resistance. The maximum strength that an athlete can produce depends upon the biomechanical characteristics of a movement (i.e., leverage, the degree to which larger muscle groups may be involved) and the magnitude of contraction of the muscles involved. In addition, maximum strength is also a function of the intensity of an impulse (which dictates the number of motor units involved) and its frequency. According to Zatsyorski (1968) the number of impulses per second, may be elevated from 5–6 at rest up to 50 during the lift of a maximum load.

Following a strength training program a muscle enlarges itself (Morpurgo, 1897), or hypertrophies as a result of the following factors:

1. the number of myofibrils (the slender threads of a muscle fiber) per muscle fiber increases (hypertrophy),
2. an increased capillary density per muscle fiber,
3. an increased amount of protein,
4. and an increased total number of muscle fibers.

All these occurrences lead to the general increase in a muscle's cross-sectional area. (Golberg et al., 1975; McDongall et al. 1976, 1977, and 1979; Costill et al. 1979, Gregory, 1981; and Fox et al, 1989).

Zatsyorski (1968) considers that strength magnitude is a function of the following three factors:

1. Intermuscular co-ordination, or the interaction of various muscular groups during performance. In a physical activity which requires strength there has to be an adequate co-ordination between the muscle groups which take part in the action. Often the muscles are involved in a certain sequence. For instance in clean and jerk (weight lifting), at the start and during the early part of the lift the trapezius muscle has to be relaxed. This muscle, however, should take part in the jerking phase. Very often though, even some elite athletes contract the trapezius from the beginning of the lift. This lack of co-ordination results in an alteration of the technical pattern of the lift, and consequently in an ineffective performance. Similarly, in sprinting events often the contraction of shoulder muscles has a negative effect upon the sprinter's performance. Therefore, it seems that the consequence of inadequate intermuscular co-ordination is a performance below one's potential, and both the coach and athlete should pay attention to it. Relaxation techniques seem to lead to an improvement in the co-ordination of muscular contractions.

2. Intramuscular co-ordination; an athlete's force output depends also on the neuromuscular units which simultaneously take part in the task. According to Baroga (1978) if during an arm curl the muscle biceps brachii has a maximum force output of 25 kg, electrical stimulation of the same muscle may result in an elevation of the muscle's force capacity by 10 kg. It is therefore apparent that the athlete often is not capable of involving all of the muscle fibers in any particular activity. This phenomenon is called by Kuznetsov (1975) the "force deficit" and may be improved by the employment of maximum load or other training methods (forthcoming in this chapter) which result in the recruitment of more neuromuscular units.

3. The force with which the muscle reacts to a nervous impulse. A muscle reacts to a training stimulus with only about 30% of its potential (Kuznetsov, 1975). The employment in training of the same methods or loads only leads to a proportional training adaptation. In order to elevate or bring about a superior threshold of adaptation higher intensity stimuli have to be used since maximum stimuli results in maximum effect. Therefore, one of the consequences of a systematic training is the progressive

improvement of the nervous impulses synchronization, and the intensive activity of the antagonistic muscle (a muscle that acts in opposition to the action of another muscle) with the agonistic muscle (prime mover). A training program will also enable muscle fiber groups to alternate so that when one group of muscle fibers exhaust, another group will start to contract, thus resulting in strength improvement.

It should be noted that the ability of an athlete to exert force is also dependent upon the angle of the joint. Research performed in this area has yielded conflicting results. While some findings suggest that maximum strength is achieved when the joints are in full extension, or very close to it (Hunsicker, 1955; Elkins et al. 1957; Zatsyorski, 1968 etc.) others reported higher muscular efficiency when the joint is flexed 90–100 degrees. As Logan and McKinney (1973) put it, a muscle must be placed at its longest length in order to exert its greatest force. However, the muscle is contracting in the direct line of movement when the joint is flexed at 90° and is thus working at a greater mechanical efficiency. In fig. 103 (A) below, contractions start from a more open angle (arrow #2). In figure 103 (B), muscle contractions start from a more acute angle (arrow #3). It seems safe to say that the athlete can produce more force from an open angle joint than he/she could if the same joint was acute.

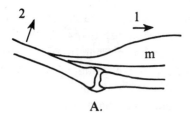

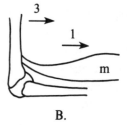

Figure 103. Joint angle and muscle efficiency.

Types of muscle contraction
Muscle contraction or tension can be generated by using the following means:

1. force of gravity
2. isokinetic apparatus
3. fixed resistance
4. electrical stimulation

A brief discussion of each of the above means may enhance the reader's specific comprehension of this topic.

1. The force of gravity
When free weights are used, usually the athlete exerts force against the force of gravity which increases proportionally to the mass (load) of an object. Tension in the

muscle can be attained by either overcoming gravity, or opposing or resisting it. In either case there occurs a dynamic contraction which often is incorrectly called *isotonic* (the Greek word isos means equal, while tonikos is tension, or in other words isotonic means equal tension which is inaccurate since the muscle tension is a function of the angle of flexion).

DEFEATING THE FORCE OF GRAVITY results in a type of contraction which is commonly called *concentric* (Latin com-centrum means having a common centre) and denotes the case where the muscle length shortens. Concentric contraction or defeating the force of gravity is the common training technique employed by most athletes using free weights.

RESISTING THE FORCE OF GRAVITY is a means of developing strength which is less frequently used, although extremely effective. This simply means that instead of lifting a weight (defeating the force of gravity) one lowers it, slowly yielding to the force of gravity. During such an *eccentric* contraction the muscles actually lengthen during the phase of stimulation. Such is the case when the shock of impact is absorbed after jumping down from a high object.

2. Isokinetic apparatus

Several types of machines (Nautilus, mini-gym, Cybex) have recently been developed and used for strength development. In all cases an isokinetic (equal or constant movement) contraction occurs, during which the resistance of the apparatus is held constant throughout a full range of movement. During the movement which combines both concentric and eccentric contractions, the machine provides a resistance which is equal to the force performed by the athlete.

3. Fixed resistance

A muscle can develop tension, often higher than that developed during a dynamic contraction, via static or isometric condition. The application of an athlete's force against specially built immobile frames or objects that will not yield to the force generated by the athlete, make the muscle develop high tension without altering its length.

4. Electrical stimulation

Although not yet adequately investigated, it seems that electrical stimulation could lead to gains in a muscle's strength. Sources suggesting such improvements are mostly from Russia (Webster, 1975; Kots, 1977) and Japan (Ikai and Yabe 1909). According to Webster, Russian weight lifters improved their maximum strength as a result of employing electrical stimulation. Kots (1977) claims that the use of electrical stimulation increases the muscle's hypertrophy and that gains were found to be not only in strength but also in endurance. Ikai and Yabe used a frequency of stimulation three times higher (up to 150 impulses/second) than the physiological frequency (1–50 impulses/second) claimed that strength increases were found to be 31% higher than those realized through voluntary maximum contractions.

Factors Affecting Strength Performance

The display of maximum strength depends on three main factors:

1. MUSCLE POTENTIAL   This is the sum of forces performed by all the muscles involved in a movement. According to Kuznetsov (1975) and Baroga (1978) the potential to perform force is 2.5–3 times higher than the contemporary performances in weight lifting. Thus, on the basis of these claims an athlete should be able to lift a weight of up to 800 kg, which obviously is much above current performances.

2. THE UTILIZATION OF MUSCLE POTENTIAL   This refers to the ability to utilize simultaneously many muscle fibers, both central and peripheral. The ability to elevate the utilization of muscle potential is substantially facilitated by employing specific exercises of both natures: defeating and opposing gravity. In addition, exercises performed in a rhythm superior to that of a competition, a high volume of work, and a wise utilization of isometric with dynamic contractions are considered effective.

3. TECHNIQUE   A muscle that has an in vitro potential to lift 100 kg is physiologically limited to 30% of its potential (Baroga, 1978) or 30 kg. As previously suggested, from a theoretical potential of 800 kg a weight lifter may lift a load of about 240 kg. However, through a specific training aimed at improving the utilization of muscle potential, technique used as an intermediary, may serve to improve athletes' ability to lift a weight up to 80% of his/her maximum potential. As a result, weight lifters should be able to lift 640 kg and high jumpers to perform 2.60 2.70 m. It seems that the possibility to achieve such performances lies on the ability to involve simultaneously in activity, central and peripheral muscle fibers (Kuznetsov, 1975).

Types of Strength and Their Significance in Training

There are various types of strength which the coach has to be aware of in order to conduct more effective training. For instance, the ratio between body weight and strength has an important consequence to the extent that it allows comparison between individual athletes, and indicates whether or not an athlete has the ability to perform certain skills. Therefore, the following types of strength should have important meaning to a coach:

1. GENERAL STRENGTH refers to the strength of the whole muscular system. As this aspect is the foundation of the whole strength program, it must be highly developed, with a concentrated effort during the preparatory phase, or during the first few years of training beginner athletes. A low level of general strength may be a limiting factor for the overall progress of an athlete.

2. SPECIFIC STRENGTH is considered to be the strength of only those muscles that are particular to the movement of the selected sport (concerns the prime movers). As the term suggests, this type of strength is characteristic for each sport, therefore any comparison between the strength level of athletes involved in different sports is invalid. Specific strength, which has to be developed to the maximum possible level,

should be progressively incorporated toward the end of the preparatory phase for all elite class athletes.

3. MAXIMUM STRENGTH refers to the highest force that can be performed by the neuromuscular system during a maximum voluntary contraction. This is demonstrated by the highest load that an athlete can lift in one attempt.

4. MUSCULAR ENDURANCE is usually defined as the muscle's ability to sustain work for a prolonged period of time. It represents the product of stressing in training both strength and endurance.

5. POWER is the product of two abilities, strength and speed, and is considered to be the ability to perform maximum force in the shortest period of time.

6. ABSOLUTE STRENGTH (AS) refers to the ability of an athlete to exert maximum force regardless of own body weight (BW). In order to be successful in some sports (shot put, heaviest weight categories in weight lifting and wrestling) absolute strength is required to reach very high levels. Although it may be measured by using dynamometers, in training it is very significant to know the maximum amount of weight that can be lifted in one attempt, on which basis the load in training may be calculated. Considering that an athlete follows a systematic training, absolute strength increases parallel with gains in body weight.

7. RELATIVE STRENGTH (RS) represents the ratio between an athlete's absolute strength and his/her body weight. Thus:

$$RS = \frac{AS}{BW}$$

Relative strength is very important in sports where the athletes travel during performance, or are divided into weight categories (i.e., wrestling, boxing). For instance a gymnast may not be able to perform the iron cross on the rings unless the relative strength of the muscles involved is at least 1.0, which means that the absolute strength must be at least sufficient to offset the athlete's body weight. Table 20 illustrates a comparison of the relative strength of two record holders in weight lifting.

Table 20. The relative strength of the weight lifting record holders (clean and jerk) from the lightest and heaviest weight categories.

NR	Weight Category/Kg	World Record/Kg	Relative Strength (Kg Force Per Kg Body Weight)
1	52	140	2.7
2	>110	255	2.3

Table 21.   A comparison of relative strength of some of the two Soviet high jumpers (from Zatsyorski, 1968).

Name	Standing Vertical Jump/cm	Absolute Strength/Kg (Full Squats)	Relative Strength/Kg
BRUMEL	104	174	2.21
DYK	81	135	1.73
GLASKOV	78	130	1.83

From table 21, it is evident that as the body weight increases relative strength decreases. This reality is of high significance for sports where power is the dominant ability. According to the data provided by Zatsyorski (1968) the former world record holder in high jump, Valeri Brumel, had the highest relative strength among Soviet jumpers (table 21).

From the data provided above, the conclusion that may be drawn is that the increment of relative strength is a function of weight loss. However, if weight loss is a requirement for performance improvement it has to be done under the supervision of a physician and the guidance of a nutritionist. Above all, the coach should not forget that a systematic training is the ideal means of increasing relative strength.

8. STRENGTH RESERVE. Although at this point in time it is inadequately investigated, strength reserve is regarded as the difference between absolute strength of an athlete and the amount of strength required to perform a skill under competitive conditions (Bompa, 1978). For instance, strength gauge techniques used to measure rowers maximum strength per stroke unit revealed values of up to 106 kg while the mean strength per race was found to be 56 kg (Bompa et al, 1978). The same subjects were found to have an absolute strength in power clean lifts of 90 kg. Subtracting the mean strength per race (x = 56 kg) from absolute strength (90 kg) one will find the strength reserve which in our example is 34 kg. The ratio of mean: absolute strength is 1:1.6. Similarly, other subjects were found to have a higher strength reserve with a ratio of 1:1.85. Needless to say, the latter subjects were capable of achieving higher performances in rowing races, thus allowing one to conclude that an athlete with a higher strength reserve is capable of reaching higher performance. Although the concept of strength reserve may not be meaningful to all sports it is hypothesized to be significant in sports such as swimming, canoeing, rowing, jumping, and throwing events in athletics.

The Methodology of Strength Training

General guidelines

Strength may be improved by overcoming internal (i.e., attempt to flex an arm while opposing it with the other one) or external resistance. The following means of training, listed in a progressive sequence; may be considered among the main sources of external resistance:

—individual body weight (i.e., push-ups) exercises with a partner (i.e., grip the hands and perform arm pulls against partner's resistance)
—medicine balls (i.e., lifts, throws, etc.)
—elastic bands and cords (either fastened to solid object or held by partner. As cord stretches resistance increases)
—dumbbells
—barbells exercises with or against apparatus
—fixed resistance (isometric contraction)

Since most strength training programs are performed with free weights (barbells) the coach should consider the following rules:

1. a strength training program should use free weights in connection with other means of training (medicine balls, apparatus, bounding, etc.) since the training effect is more complex, they compliment each other, and therefore are more beneficial to the athlete.

2. weight training exercises may use both analytic and synthetic exercises since their training effects are different. An analytic exercise involves a small group of muscles or a body limb, and as a consequence the effect is strictly local. The main advantage of such an approach is that muscle groups can be alternated continuously, and as such the summation of training loads could reach high levels. However, although local strength may be improved dramatically, it has a low transfer effect to the individual's general endurance. Therefore, sports requiring an endurance component should consider synthetic exercises, which simultaneously involve several limbs and muscle groups. Such exercises may not permit equally high amounts of work but do provide a superior general and specific functional component.

3. Before working the active limb, the passive segment should be exercise. In other words, before strengthening the arms, the muscles and ligaments of the supporting segments (the vertebral column, and the scapulo-humeral girdle) must be exercised. This concept is also valid for the warm-up prior to a weight training lesson.

4. Before developing muscular strength good flexibility should be developed in order to avoid eventual joint rigidity. Flexibility exercises should not be incorporated only during the second pan of the warm-up (please refer to the planning of a training lesson in Chapter Eight) but also during the rest periods between weight training exercises. This will facilitate a faster recovery in the muscle because the muscle will reach its normal resting length more quickly when flexibility exercises are employed (Pendergast, 1974). In addition, the efficiency of a movement does not depend only on the force of the active muscles but also on the degree of relaxation of the antagonistic muscles.

Methodical parameters relevant to strength training

Strength is one of the most important biomotor abilities and its role in an athlete's training is often paramount. A correct understanding of the methodology of developing it is of prime importance since it affects both speed and endurance. The construction of a strength training program has to consider several parameters (explained below) which are paramount to any successful program.

Number of exercises

The key to an effective program is adequate selection of exercises. The establishment of an optimum number of exercises is often overlooked by some coaches. In their desire to develop most muscle groups coaches select too many exercises. Obviously the outcome is an ineffective and fatiguing training program.

The selection of exercises has to be done in light of the aspects explained below:

1. AGE AND LEVEL OF PERFORMANCE One of the main objectives of a training program designed for juniors or beginners is the development of a solid anatomical and physiological foundation. Without such an approach consistent improvement will certainly be less likely. Therefore, as far as strength training is concerned, the coach should select many exercises (9–12) which are addressed to the main muscle groups of the body. The duration of such a program may be up to 2–3 years, depending on the age of the athlete and the expected age of high performance (table 3). Considering the above circumstances one of the coach's high attributes is patience.

Training programs designed for advanced or elite class athletes should follow a completely different approach. For such athletes a main objective of training is the elevation of performance to the highest possible levels. Strength training has its own role in accomplishing such an objective. Therefore a strength program for elite class athletes (especially during the competitive phase) has to be very specific, directed precisely to the prime movers, and containing only a few exercises (3–6).

2. NEEDS OF THE SPORT Exercises selected for strength training, especially for elite class athletes, ought to be selected to meet the specific needs of the sport. Thus, an elite class high jumper may perform only 3–4 exercises, while a wrestler has to elevate the number up to 5–8 so that all prime movers are adequately strengthened.

3. PHASE OF TRAINING During the commencement of the preparatory phase a general strength training program is desired. Following the transition phase the coach starts a new annual plan the beginning of which ought to be designed to build the foundation of training to come. Since such a program has to involve most muscle groups, the number of exercises for strength training during the early preparatory phase has to be high (9–12) regardless of the specifics of the sport. As the program progresses the number of exercises is reduced, concluding with the competitive phase when only the very specific, essential exercises are performed.

The succession of strength training exercises in a training lesson

Strength training exercises were found to be more effective when they follow exercises aimed at developing speed (Baroga, 1978). Apparently powerful stimuli, like those applied during speed training, seem to arouse the athlete's body and CNS for strength development. Often, this concept is applied by weight lifters from Eastern Europe, although in most cases strength training programs begin with exercises aimed at developing strength.

The load of training

Load refers to the mass or amount of weight used in developing strength. As suggested by figure 104 the following loads may be employed in training:

SUPERMAXIMUM or a load which exceeds one's maximum strength. In most cases loads between 100–175% should be used by applying the eccentric, or opposing (known also as negative) gravity method. Elite class weight lifters often employ 105–110% of maximum strength two-three times per week by employing the concentric

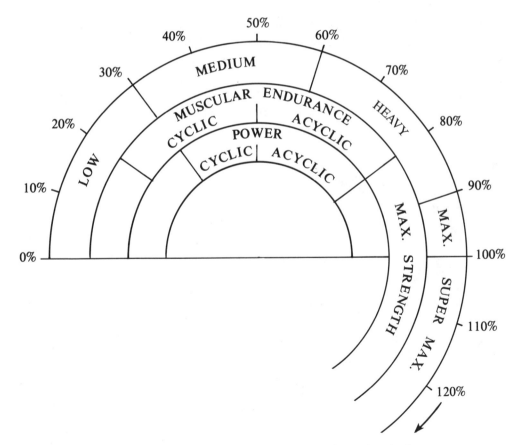

Figure 104.   The load magnitude and abilities developed by employing various loads.

(or positive) method. When supermaximum loads are used it is advisable to have two individuals, one at each end of the barbell, to assist or guard the performer so that accidents are avoided. (i.e., in bench press employing the negative method a barbell may fall on the performer's chest).

Supermaximum loads are to be used during maximum strength development by only those athletes with a strong background in strength training. Most other athletes should be restricted to a load of up to 100%.

MAXIMUM load, as indicated by the outer circle (fig. 104), refers to a load of 90–100% of one's maximum.

HEAVY load is used when one employs a load between 60–90% of one's maximum.

MEDIUM load refers to a percentage between 30–60% of one's maximum.

LOW is considered to be any load below 30% of one's capacity.

Muscular endurance, both cyclic and acyclic (to which further reference will be made below) is developed when the load is between 20–80%, while for power one has to employ a load between 30–80%.

The number of repetitions and the rhythm of execution

Both the number of repetitions and rhythm or speed of execution are a function of load; the higher the load the lower the number of repetitions and rhythm of execution. As illustrated by figure 105, for the development of maximum strength (90–175%) the number of repetitions is very low (1–3) and is performed slowly. For exercises aimed at developing power (30–80% of maximum) the number of repetitions

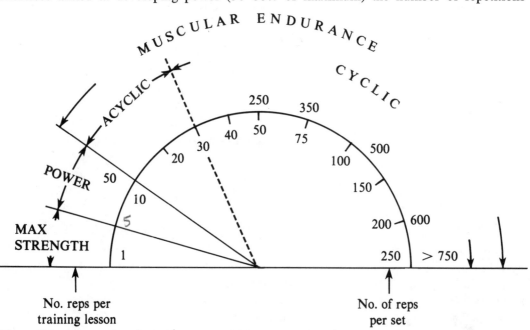

Figure 105. The number of repetitions required for the development of various types of strength.

is moderate (5–10) and they are performed dynamically. As for muscular endurance, the number of repetitions is high, sometimes up to one's limits (250 or more), performed in a slow to medium rhythm. For acyclic muscular endurance the number of repetitions is between 10–30 while for cyclic it approaches one's limits.

The rhythm of breathing ought to be in harmony with the rhythm of performing a movement. Usually one inhales prior to the lift. During the movement the athlete should hold his/her breath (apnea), and exhale towards the completion of the lift.

The number of sets

A set consists of a number of repetitions of an exercise followed by a rest interval. Between the training demand (load and number of repetitions in our case) and number of sets, there is an inverse relationship: as training demand increases the number of sets must decrease. The number of sets is also a function of the following factors: the athlete's abilities and training potential, the number of muscle groups that must be trained (a higher number of sets is necessary when few muscle groups are involved), the number of exercises composing a training lesson, and the phase of training. For instance, a high jumper who is in a very specialized training program may use only 3–5 exercises, could employ 6–10 sets per lesson. On the other hand, a wrestler who is interested in developing most muscle groups may plan only 3–6 sets. Similarly, during the competitive phase, when in special circumstances an athlete is interested in maintaining only a certain strength level will employ a lesser number of sets as compared to the preparatory phase, when the main objective was the development of strength. Therefore, the conclusion is that the number of sets may vary between 3–8 depending on specific training circumstances.

The notation of load, number of repetitions, and number of sets are expressed as follows:

$$\frac{\text{Load}}{\text{\# Reps}} \text{ (\# Sets), } \quad \text{For example: } \frac{100}{8} \text{ 4}$$

where the numerator (100) refers to the load to be employed, the denominator (8) represents the number of repetitions and the multiplier (4) illustrates the number of sets.

The rest interval and activity during rest

As a general guideline the rest interval is progressively reduced as the athlete adjusts to training stimuli. However, the rest interval is prolonged as the load increases. The rest interval also depends on the type of strength sought, the athlete's training status, the rhythm and duration of performance, and the number of muscles involved. Ozolin (1971) suggests that for exercises aiming at developing maximum strength the rest interval should be between 2–5 min. However, longer rest may be recommended (between 5–10 min.) for all out exercises. As for exercises whose objective is to develop muscular endurance the rest interval is shorter, often being

Table 22.   A summary of the dominant parameters in strength training and the emphasis to be placed upon each according to the needs of developing a certain ability (H = High; M = Medium; L = Low).

	EXERCISES FOR:		
	Maximum Strength	Power	Muscular Endurance
LOAD	H	M → L	M → L
# REPETITIONS	L	M	H
# SETS	H	M	L
RHYTHM OF PERFORMANCE	L	H	L → M
REST INTERVAL	H	H → M	L → M

1–2 minutes. Scholich (1974) considers that the rest interval, especially for circuit training, has to be associated with the physiological response to a stimuli as indicated by one's heart rate. When the rate of the heart decreases to 120 bpm, another set may be performed. And finally, it is important that the coach consider the individual rate of recovery since each individual reacts differently to similar training stimuli. First study and get to know the athlete and then prescribe precise training programs.

In order to facilitate a quicker recovery between sets, the coach should advise the athlete as to the type of activity to be performed during the rest interval. Relaxation exercises (i.e., shaking the legs, arms and shoulders) and light massage seem to be effective means of facilitating a faster recovery between sets. Baroga (1978) claims that relaxation exercises are indicated especially since heavy load exercises increase the quantity of myostromin (a protein occurring within the framework of a muscle tissue) in muscles which causes muscle rigidity.

The selection means and methods of training as well as the load, number of repetitions, and number of sets are essential to the success of a strength training program. A summary of these training parameters is presented in table 22.

Using table 22 as a reference, it can be seen that the load exercises aiming at developing maximum strength is high, for power it is medium to low, and for muscular endurance it is medium to low. On the other hand, the opposite part of the table suggests that in order to enhance maximum strength the rest interval has to be high, while for power it is high to medium, and for muscular endurance low, to medium, since such exercises place a lower demand upon the body.

The total volume of training for strength development
The total volume of strength training depends on the needs and specifics of the sport. It is quite common for weight lifters to lift 30 tonnes (33 short tons) per

Table 23. The volume (tonnes) of strength training for various sports (men) (modified from Bompa, 1960, and Baroga, 1978.).

No.	Sport/Event	Volume Per Microcycle in Training Phases			Volume/Year	
		Preparatory	Competitive	Transition	Minimum	Maximum
1	Shot Put	24–40	8–12	4–6	900	1450
2	Downhill Skiing	18–36	6–10	2–4	700	1250
3	High jump	16–28	8–10	2–4	620	1000
4	Ice Hockey	15–25	6–8	2–4	600	950
5	Speed Skating	14–26	4–6	2–4	500	930
6	Basketball	12–24	4–6	2	450	850
7	Javelin	12–24	4	2	450	800
8	Volleyball	12–20	4	2	450	700
9	Sprinting	10–18	4	2	400	600
10	Gymnastics	10–16	4	4	380	600
11	Boxing	8–14	3	1	330	500

lesson. Since most international class weight lifters train a minimum of 1200 hours per year (the Bulgarian athletes train 1600 hours per year, this being probably one explanation of why they are among the very best in the world) then lifting 40,000 tonnes (44,000 short tons) per year is a medium volume of work.

The duration of a strength training lesson may vary between 2–4 or even more hours, depending on the specific strength requirements for the chosen sport as well as other factors such as age, sex, sport classification, and phase of training. Table 23 may be considered as a guideline for the volume of strength training for various sports/events.

The above figures, specific for sports/events requiring strength or speed refer to elite athletes. The total volume of strength training for sports where muscular endurance is an important component is drastically altered. Thus for sports like wrestling, swimming, canoeing and rowing, the yearly tonnage may be 3–6 times higher. For instance canoers and rowers may lift as much as 20,000 tonnes (22,000 short tons) per year. One of the highest volumes of strength training per lesson ever recorded was that of an athlete involved in rowing; 118 tonnes, or 129 short tons, (Bompa, 1979).

The methodical sequence of developing a strength training program

A strength training program must be developed with consideration of the following systematic sequence:

1. The coach should select the exercises which will be employed in the program.

2. Test the maximum strength in one attempt, or one repetition maximum (1RM), to determine the athlete's prime movers' 100% strength. The coach should know each individual athlete's maximum strength in at least the dominant exercises composing a training program. Often it happens that the load and number of repetitions are chosen randomly, or by following other athletes' programs instead of using objective data of the individual. This data is valid only for a certain cycle of training (usually a macro-cycle) since the athletes' degree of training and their potential alter continuously.

3. Now that the coach knows the individual's maximum strength, he/she must decide (according to the characteristics of the sport, the athlete's needs, and the type of strength sought) the range of percentage of loads to be used in training. For example, a basketball coach may decide to develop leg power by employing 75% of each player's maximum strength. Thus, if player AB has a maximum strength for leg press of 220 kg then the load employed in training would be 165 kg (or 75% of maximum strength). Obviously the percentage of load to be employed in training depends on the type of strength sought to be developed (see figure 104).

4. The next step is to test the athlete's maximum number of repetitions with the selected load. Let 12 be the maximum number of repetitions which player AB per-formed with 165 kg. Now the number of repetitions (NR) to be performed in a given training lesson can be calculated by using the following equation:

$$\frac{RM(\%)}{100} = NR$$

where RM represents repetitions maximum performed with the selected load, and % refers to the percentage of load (the selected load) of 1RM.

By employing the figures from the above example, the following NR to be used in training will be found:

$$\frac{12(75\%)}{100} = 9$$

Thus the NR to be used for the basketball player in a given phase of training is 9.

5. Develop the training program and apply it in a given phase of training. By now the coach knows the exercises to be performed, the athlete's maximum strength, the percentage of load to be used in training, and the number of repetitions for each exercise. All of this data has to be used to make the training program for a macro-cycle. But this program cannot be the same for each macro-cycle. Progressively the training demand has to be increased so that the athletes will adjust to an elevated work load which will be translated into an increase in strength. The training demand may be increased by any of the following means: increase the load, decrease the rest

interval, or increase the number of repetitions. In the latest case the following equation may be used:

$$\frac{RM}{DC} + PC = NR$$

where the numerator represents the repetitions maximum (in our example 12) and the denominator is a dividing constant (DC). The progression constant (PC) will be added to the product in each micro-cycle so that the training demand will be increased continuously.

Both DC and PC are a function of the athlete's classification and potential (Table 24).

Table 24.   The DC and PC are altered in accordance with the athlete's classification.

NR	Athlete's Classification	DC	PC
1	Elite class	1.2	2
2	National level	1.5	2
3	Prospective athletes	1.8	1
4	Juniors and beginners	2	1

Let RM be 12, DC 1.5 and PC 2. By substituting these figures into the equation the following number of repetitions in a given phase of training will be found:

$$\frac{12}{1.5} + 2 = 10$$

The PC increment will be cumulatively added from the second micro-cycle only. Therefore, considering the above figures, the number of repetitions will be as follows: 12, 14 and 16. However, this progression does not have to be followed rigidly, but rather should be adjusted to suit the athlete's rate of improvement.

6. Test to recalculate the maximum strength, and number of repetitions per selected percentage of maximum strength. This new test is required prior to a new macro-cycle to ensure that progress prevails and that training demand is adequate.

Any strength training program has to be written on a free sheet of paper, or even better in the training journal. An example of a format to express a strength training program is illustrated by table 25 and 26.

Table 25.   The headings of a chart used to present a strength training program.

NR	Exercise	Load/Kg	Number of Reps.	Number of Sets	Rhythm	Rest Interval	Activity During Rest
1	Leg Press Etc. . . .	120	20	6	Moderate	90 sec	Relaxation and breathing exercises

Table 26.   A more condensed chart suggested to present a strength training program.

NR	Exercise	Load, # Reps, # Sets	Rhythm	Rest Interval	Activity During Rest
1	Leg Press Etc. . . .	$\frac{120}{20}$ 6	Moderate	90 sec	Relaxation

Methods Used to Develop Strength and Its Components

1. Characteristics of developing maximum strength

The main characteristic of a maximum strength training program is the involvement in exercise of all or at least most of the neuro-muscular units. Therefore everyone aiming to develop maximum strength has to employ maximum and supermaximum stimuli very frequently.

Among the sports requiring maximum strength development are weight lifting, shot put, discus, and hammer throw. Other sports requiring power or muscular endurance may benefit from maximum strength development at least during certain parts of the preparatory phase.

Since the strain placed on an athlete's body is very high, especially when employing maximum or supermaximum (negative method) loads the alternation of muscle groups for each training lesson seems to facilitate a higher volume of work as well as a better rate of recovery between lessons. Therefore in one lesson the legs may be worked, while the next the arms and shoulders.

2. Characteristics of developing power

The principal stimulus in power training is the performance of a movement very dynamically linked with the force magnitude taking place in the same exertion. For instance during sprinting an athlete's force of leg impulsion is 3.5 times that of his/her own body weight while the force used to throw a javelin is much smaller (Ivanova and Weiss, 1969). Thus the force of acceleration is the main stimulus for power training. In acyclic sports (i.e., jumping events) power is the determinant ability to achieve a good result. On the other hand, in cyclic sports (i.e., sprinting) power is brought into action repetitively and very rapidly. These general characteristics of the sports requiring power has to be considered and reflected in one's strength training program.

Acyclic power

Throwing and jumping events in athletics, most gymnastics elements, fencing, diving, and every sport requiring a take-off (i.e., volleyball) are among the main beneficiaries of developing acyclic power. For these sports or athletic elements power performed acyclicly is the dominant factor in the performance. Although maximum strength is an important element of progression, exercises using lower loads but being performed extremely quickly (i.e., exercises with medicine balls) ought to be part of the program as well.

Most strength training exercises are from the weight lifters repertoire (power clean, snatch, clean and jerk) but this does not exclude other exercises like weight belts and vests, various jumps, and the like (i.e., deep jumps, over benches, bounding exercises). The load for acyclic power is between 50–80% (fig. 104, page 273), the movement is performed very quickly, and 4–6 sets are recommended with a rest interval of 3–5 minutes for an almost full recovery. Adequate recovery is paramount because only an almost completely recovered body can perform acyclic power exercises efficiently.

Cyclic power

A characteristic of sports requiring cyclic power (sprinting in athletics, swimming, speed skating, and cycling as well as all sports requiring speed) is that their relationship with speed is extremely pronounced. The strength component of a strength training program employs slightly reduced stimuli (load: 30–50%). The improvement of cyclic power has to be linked with sprinting endurance, which assists the athlete to avoid a decrease in stride frequency towards the end of a race.

The load for cyclic exercises is recommended to be 30–50% of one's maximum (fig. 104), performed in a very dynamic rhythm, with up to 10 repetitions, and a long recovery interval (5 minutes). Relaxation exercises throughout a training program, and the alteration of contraction with relaxation is a mandatory requirement, since rigidity may affect the rate of a muscle's contraction.

3. The characteristics of developing muscular endurance

Acyclic muscular endurance

Acyclic muscular endurance can be improved by either repeating parts of elements (routines of the sport) with an intensity slightly higher than that employed in competition, or by using weight training. In the latter case a load between 50–80% of one's maximum should be employed with a number of repetitions between 10–30 (fig. 105, page 274). Those involved in gymnastics, wrestling, and martial arts are among the athletes who may benefit the most from this method. Considering the fact that the needs of the athletes often are very complex, they have to combine the development of acyclic muscular endurance with the development of other strength components, which calls for the employment of other methods.

Cyclic muscular endurance

All cyclic sports that have a performance time in excess of 2 minutes ought to regard the development of cyclic muscular endurance as one of the main factors which would lead to performance improvement. Thus, sports like swimming (400–1500 m), canoeing (1,000–10,000 m), rowing, speed skating, and cross-country skiing, can evidently benefit from the perfection of this strength component. In order to model a strength training program to the specifics of the sport, the exercise has to be selected and performed in such a way that phases of muscular contraction are alternated with a phase of relaxation. The load for this type of duration is 20–50% of the maximum.

In most of the sports/events listed above, aerobic endurance is an important if not dominant component. Strength, especially muscular endurance is also a key element, since in most of the above sports the athletes perform against water resistance. A strength training program has to be related to the distance and therefore to the objective requirements of the event. Consequently, for events of shorter duration (i.e., 400 m swimming, 1,000 m in canoeing) the load may be between 40–50% or even higher. The number of repetitions should be between 30–100. For events of longer duration the load is slightly lower while the number of repetitions increases (up to one's maximum). The frequency or rhythm of repetitions again has to be related to the dynamics of the event, but generally between 30–50 repetitions per minute is adequate. The heart rate, as a guidelines to the physiological reaction to training demand, has to be, as suggested by Schroeder (1969), between 150–160 bpm.

As a summary of the means and methods employed in strength training, the reader is invited to study table 27 which was proposed by Harre (1982). Although Harre holds slightly different opinions than those explained in the present section, one still may gain a better comprehension of the subject from the table.

Training Methods for Strength Development

The selection of a strength training method has to be related to the type of strength sought. Thus, there are training methods designed to develop maximum strength, power, or muscular endurance; methods which are very briefly presented below:

Maximum strength methods

The weight lifting method

Although maximum strength may be developed through static, isokinetic or electrical stimulation methods, the weight lifting method using free weights or other instruments is still the most common. The main element of progression is the intensity of stimulation realized through the load increment. As suggested by Baroga (1978) four variants may be considered to develop one's maximum strength. The progression suggested by each variant refers to a training lesson. The selection of a variant depends upon its effectiveness according to individual particularities.

Variant A: the load increases continuously
    80%–90%–100%–110%
Variant B: the load increases in steps
    80%–80%; 90%–90%; 100%–100%; 110%–110%
Variant C: the load increases and decreases continually (pyramid)
    80%–90%–100%–100%–100%–90%–80%
Variant D: the wave-like increase of load
    80%–90%–85%–90%–100%–95%–100%–90%

Table 27. The dosage and methods employed in strength training (Harre, 1982).

Percentage of Maximum Strength	No. of Repetitions Per Set	Rhythm of Performance	Rest Interval	Number of Sets	Method	Applicability
100–85%	1–5	Moderate	2–5 min	Beginners: 3–5 Advanced athletes: 5–8	$\frac{85\%}{5} + \frac{95\%}{2\text{–}3} +$ $\frac{100\%}{1} + \frac{95\%}{2\text{–}3}$	To improve maximum strength for acyclic sports
85–70%	5–10	Moderate to slow	2–4 min	3–5	$\frac{70\%}{10} + \frac{80\%}{7} +$ $\frac{85\%}{5} + \frac{85\%}{5}$	To improve maximum strength. Basic method for cyclic sports requiring maximum strength
50–30%	6–10 at a maximum speed	Explosive	2–5 min	4–6	$\frac{30\%}{10} + \frac{40\%}{10} +$ $\frac{50\%}{10} + \frac{40\%}{10}$	To improve power under conditions of enhancing maximum strength
75%	6–10	Very fast	2–5 min	4–6	$\frac{75\%}{10} + \frac{40\%}{10} +$ $\frac{75\%}{10} + \frac{75\%}{10}$	To improve power as maximum strength
60–40%	20–30 (50–70% of maximum # of repetitions)	Fast to moderate	30–45 sec	3–5	Circuit training	To improve muscular endurance
40–25%	25-50% of maximum number of repetitions	Moderate to Fast	Optimal	4–6	Circuit training	As above but for sports which do not require overwhelmingly this quality

The number of exercises used in a training lesson is between 4–8, the number of repetitions is between 1–5. Since the number of sets has to be related to one's abilities, but also to the total number of exercises, an exercise may be repeated in 4–10 sets. The rhythm of performing an exercise depends on the load. High loads do not allow a rapid rhythm. However, the athlete should strive for a dynamic rhythm regardless of load.

The weight lifting method is beneficial to all athletes requiring maximum strength, but especially to weight lifters, and throwers in athletics.

Static (isometric) contractions

Although the concept was improperly used for some time, Hettinger and Muller (1953) and again Hettinger (1966) scientifically justified the merits of static contractions in the development of maximum strength. This method reached its climax in the sixties and has since faded in popularity. Although static contraction does not have a marked functional effect (i.e., for muscular endurance) it still can assist the development of maximum strength and therefore may be used by weight lifters and throwers in their strength training efforts. Static conditions may be realized through three techniques:

1. by attempting to lift a weight heavier than one's potential.
2. by applying force (push or pull) against an immobile object.
3. by applying force with one limb and opposing it with another.

Static contractions could be performed in various limb positions and angles from a muscle which is completely elongated to one which is fully shortened. When using this method, the following methodological aspects may be regarded:

1. static contractions are efficient when using 70–100% of one's maximum strength.
2. employ the method primarily in the training of mature athletes with a good background in strength training. If used in junior's training, use low intensity.
3. training dosage is intensified by increasing the number of exercises and not the effort per contraction.
4. the duration of a contraction is between 6–12 seconds with a total of 60–90 seconds of contraction per muscle group per training lesson.
5. during the rest interval (60–90 seconds) relaxation and breathing exercises are recommended. The latter is a compensatory necessity since static contraction is performed in apnea (breath hold). In addition, the intrathoracic pressure is elevated restricting circulation and thus the oxygen supply.
6. for a more effective program alternate static with isotonic contractions, especially for sports requiring speed and power. A variant of the static contraction, the intermediary contraction, where the lifted object may be stopped several times (for 48 seconds) throughout the performance, seems to be more acceptable than the strictly static method.

Power training

Developed by Belgian R. Molette (1963) this method aimed as developing power by employing three groups of exercise:

1. free weight exercises, mostly similar to those used by weight lifters,
2. exercises with medicine balls, and
3. tumbling and flexibility exercises.

The main elements of progression are:

1. increase the number of repetitions, and
2. increase the speed of performance.

The load is determined by the amount of weight the athlete can lift correctly six times. The speed of execution is then improved. When the speed of execution is satisfactory the number of repetitions is increased from 6 to 12. When the speed for 12 repetitions is satisfactory then the load is increased until only six repetitions can again be completed. When exercises can not be performed correctly training has to stop.

The rest interval is 2–3 minutes when exercising with a load below 85% maximum, and 3–5 minutes when the load exceeds this amount. The program is composed of 12 exercises divided into four groups of three: one with barbells, one with medicine balls, one again with barbells, and finally one with simple tumbling and flexibility exercises. Following each group of exercises a rest interval is taken.

Exercises performed with medicine balls have to be performed with a high speed, the main elements of progression being the enlargement of distance between two performers, and the increase and decrease of weights of balls. Power training may be used for sports requiring power or complex biomotor abilities: jumping, throwing events in athletics, alpine skiing, most team sports, boxing, and wrestling.

Methods to develop muscular endurance

Circuit training

At Leeds University, Morgan and Adamson (1959) developed a fitness and training method which proved to be successful for many decades. Because all stations of the program were arranged in a circle this method was called circuit training. A similar concept was used in training prior to World War II, where the main merit was the alternation of muscle groups. This concept was also employed in circuit training. During the following years several other publications on this topic were printed. However, the books written by Jonath (1961) and especially by Scholich (1974) managed to further the scientific knowledge of this method.

Although circuit training was initially used to develop general fitness, progressively it was improved and became a very complex method. Thus, by considering various strength training methodical parameters a circuit training programs may be designed to develop strength, speed and co-ordination as well as combinations of abilities like power and muscular endurance. In developing a circuit training program the following characteristics may be considered:

1. a circuit may be short (6 exercises), normal (9 exercises), or long (12 exercises), therefore its total duration may vary between 10–30 minutes. Usually, a circuit may be repeated three times. However, its duration, the number of repetitions and the rest interval depend on the athlete's background and the ability sought.
2. the physical demand has to be elevated progressively and individually.
3. because there are set stations, arranged prior to training, many athletes may be involved simultaneously. Thus, this method has an organizational advantage.
4. the circuit has to be arranged to alternate muscle groups, thus body segments may be exercised as follows: leg, arms, abdomen, and back.
5. the training demand can be precisely managed by indicating the precise time or number of repetitions to be performed. However, variations of circuit training exist where:
    a. one can perform a circuit without having rest intervals or time limits.
    b. one must perform all exercises without rest intervals but with a time standard for one or three circuits.
6. as an element of progression, the time to perform a circuit may be reduced without altering the number of repetitions or the load, or there may be an increase in the load, or number of repetitions.
7. the rest interval between circuits is about 2 minutes but may change according to the demand placed upon the athletes. The heart rate method could be employed to calculate the rest interval. When the rate falls to about 120 bpm another circuit may be started (Scholich, 1974).

According to the needs of the sport Scholich (1974) suggests two variants of strict circuit training:

1. Circuit training intensive with interval. This may be used to develop acyclic muscular endurance. As the term suggests the rhythm of repeating an exercise is dynamic, with a load between 50–80% of maximum and between 10–30 repetitions. The rest interval is 2–3 times higher than the execution time. This variant may be used for sprinting events (athletics, swimming, speed skating), wrestling, boxing, football and other team sports.
2. In contrast, circuit training extensive with interval, employs a lower load (20–50%), but an extensive number of repetitions (up to one's limits). The rhythm of performance is medium to slow, with a rest interval shorter than in the intensive variant. Such a program is indicated for sports requiring cyclic muscular endurance, distance running, swimming, cross-country skiing, rowing, etc.

Specificity Vs. a Methodical Approach

By attempting to develop an optimal strength training program some coaches, based on their experience, suggest that the program has to be specific. This concept was then developed by some physiologists (i.e., Matthews and Fox, 1976) into a principle of training. By strictly following this principle, throughout an athletic career one has to simulate the movement pattern used while performing a skill and develop to perfection only that type of strength which is dominant in the selected sport.

This concept is correct if applied only to elite athletes and during the competitive phase. If the same rule is followed by children and beginners from their first day of training throughout their entire athletic career and throughout all training phases then the principles of training are misunderstood and violated.

An optimal strength program has to be developed in conjunction with the determinant and prevalent biomotor abilities of the selected sport. Furthermore, the selected exercises ought to simulate the plane, direction, and specific angle in which the skill is performed. Strength development exercises have to involve the prime movers. However, these realities are to be considered for elite athletes and during the conversion and maintenance phases of an annual plan regarding strength training. Consequently, periodization is the leading concept in planning a strength training program. On the other hand, children's strength training program has two main phases:

1. General and multilateral strength training, during which the coach develops all the muscle groups of a child, ligaments and tendons, thus strengthening and developing the base for future heavy loads and specific training. Such an approach is not only desirable from the methodology of training point of view but would also be more likely to lead to an injury free athletic career. The duration of this phase may be between 2–4 years, depending on the athlete's age and abilities. Throughout this phase the coach's patience is a desirable attribute. To look for a quick return in training is an unhealthy approach.

2. The specific phase. Following the development of the foundations of strength training the coach may start the specific phase which will be considered for the rest of the athlete's career. However, this does not mean that a strength training program specific to the needs of the sport will be followed throughout all phases of an annual training plan. It rather has to consider the concept of periodization of strength training, which always starts with a build-up, or general strength development phase.

ENDURANCE TRAINING

Classification of Endurance

Endurance refers to the limit of time over which work of a given intensity may be performed. The main factor which limits and at the same time affects performance is fatigue. Thus, a person is considered to have endurance when he/she does not easily fatigue, or when a person has the ability to continue work in a state of fatigue. An athlete is capable of doing that if he/she is adapted to the specifics of the work performed. Endurance depends on many factors such as: speed, muscle force, technical abilities of performing a movement efficiently, the ability to economically use physiological potentials, and psychological status when performing work.

Considering the needs of training there are two kinds of endurance:

1. GENERAL ENDURANCE is considered by Ozolin (1971) to be the capacity of performing a type of activity which involves many muscle groups and systems (CNS, neuro-muscular and cardio-respiratory system) for a prolonged period of time. A good level of general endurance, regardless of the sport's specialization, facilitates success in various types of training activities. However, athletes involved in sports where endurance, especially aerobic endurance, is dominant, do have a high level of general endurance suggesting that there is a strong relationship between general and specific endurance. On the other hand, athletes taking part in sports of short duration or of high technical sophistication do not hold a good level of general endurance. General endurance is vigorously needed by each athlete. It assists the athletes to successfully perform a high volume of work, to overcome fatigue in competitions of long duration, and to recover faster following training or competitions.

2. SPECIFIC ENDURANCE, which often is referred to as endurance of playing, sprinting, and the like, is dependent on the particularities of each sport, or the many repetitions of the motor acts of each sport. Although specific endurance is imprinted in the characteristics of certain sports, it may be affected by the excitement of competitions, the performance of difficult athletic tasks, or the type of training per-formed. Also, as Teodorescu (1975) put it, a very demanding tactical game often affects an athlete's specific endurance, thus the athletes may be subject to various technical and tactical faults during the second part of the contest. Consequently, the stronger the specific endurance which is developed from a solid base of general endurance, the easier the athletes may overcome various training and competition stressors.

The types of endurance presented above refer and are paramount to a successful performance in each sport. However, as far as cyclic sports are concerned, the follow-ing classification is often suggested (Pfeifer, 1982).

1. ENDURANCE OF LONG DURATION, is required for sports that endure for more than eight minutes. Energy is supplied almost exclusively by the aerobic system, and the cardiovascular and respiratory systems are highly involved. During an endurance race falling in this category, the heart rate is very high (over 180 bpm), the heart's minute volume (the volume of blood pumped by the heart in one minute) is between 30–40 litres, and the lungs ventilate 120–140 litres of air per minute (Pfeifer, 1982). Obviously for long duration races (i.e., marathon) these values are lower. The O_2 supply is a determinant factor for a good performance. Therefore, the vital capacity and the minute volume of the heart represent limiting factors for high athletic results. They also reflect the athlete's adaptation to the stress of such activities. Work of

medium intensity seems to favour the body's adaptation and capillary vascularization so vital for the supply of O2 to the muscle cells (Mader and Hollmann, 1977).

2. ENDURANCE OF MEDIUM DURATION is specific for sports/events where work is performed over a duration of 2–6 minutes. The intensity is higher than in sports requiring endurance of long duration. The O_2 supply cannot totally meet the body's needs; therefore, the athlete develops an O_2 debt. The energy produced by the anaerobic system is proportional to the speed magnitude. Pfeifer (1982) claims that for the 3000 m run the anaerobic system supplies approximately 20%, and for 1500 m up to 50% of the total energy required by the athlete. As in the above case, the O_2 absorption has a determinant role in performance.

3. ENDURANCE OF SHORT DURATION are sports which travel a distance which is covered in a duration between 45 seconds–2 minutes. For sports which are classified in this category, the anaerobic processes partake intensely in supplying the energy required to perform the athletic task. Strength and speed play an important role in producing high results. The O2 debt is quite high, and according to Pfeifer (1982) the anaerobic system provides 80% of the required energy for a 400 m and 60–70% for the 800 m run. The basis for the development of the anaerobic capacity is the aerobic capacity. Consequently, a high aerobic capacity has to be developed even for sports/ events which compose this category.

4. MUSCULAR ENDURANCE, which was referred to in strength training, is facilitated by a high strength development blended with an adequate endurance. Sports like rowing, swimming, and canoeing, are the main beneficiaries of this combined ability.

5. ENDURANCE OF SPEED represents the resistance of the athlete's to fatigue under conditions of maximum intensity. Most of the work is done in apnea, requiring from the athlete both maximum speed and strength (also refer to speed training).

Factors Affecting Endurance

The central nervous system (CNS)

During endurance training the CNS adapts to the specifics of the training demand. Thus, as a result of training the CNS increases its working capacity and improves the nervous connections required for a well and co-ordinated function of the organs and systems. Fatigue, which often impairs training, occurs at the CNS level. Thus decrease in the CNS working capacity is a major cause of fatigue. The struggle against fatigue is a battle engaged by the nervous centres in order to maintain their working capacity.

The increment of the CNS endurance and its optimal status ought to be one of the main concerns in training. The coach may facilitate this by selecting adequate and optimal means of training. Uniform work with moderate intensity improves and strengthens the entire activity of the CNS; namely, its neuro-muscular co-ordination specific for endurance activities. Similarly, long duration endurance activity performed under increasing levels of fatigue increases nervous cell resistance to stressful work (Ozolin, 1971).

Athletic willpower

Willpower is a paramount ingredient in endurance training. It is mostly required when work has to be performed in a state of fatigue, or when the level of fatigue increases as a result of prolonged activity. This is even more obvious when intensity is an important component of training. The required level of intensity cannot be maintained unless the athlete's desire and will order the nervous centres to continue the work or even increase it (i.e., at the finish). Human beings do hold a great deal of endurance reserves. Such reserves may be maximized only by appealing to the athlete's will to defeat his/her weaknesses which may often result from fatigue. Thus, an important training objective is to increase pain tolerance so that the athletes can psychologically tolerate the hurt, pain, and agony of training and competitions.

Aerobic capacity

The aerobic potential, or the body's capacity to produce energy in the presence of O_2, determines the athlete's endurance capacity. Aerobic power is limited by the ability to transport O_2 within the body thus the O_2 transportation system should be developed as part of any program designed to improve the endurance capacity. A high aerobic capacity is not vital to training only but also between and after training to facilitate a faster recovery. A rapid recovery allows the rest interval to be reduced and the work to be performed with higher intensity. As a result of shorter rest intervals the number of repetitions may be elevated, thus facilitating an increase in the volume of training. A fast rate of recovery which is enhanced by a high aerobic capacity is also important in other sports where a high number of repetitions of a skill (i.e., jumping events) or an increased number of bouts in team sports (i.e., hockey, football) are necessary.

During endurance training the organs and especially the system which supplies the oxygen (respiratory system) become well developed. In fact certain organs are developed in accordance to the training method employed. Thus, interval training strengthens the heart, while high altitude or long duration training increases the O_2 utilization capabilities (Ozolin, 1971). However, the aerobic capacity relies on the development of the respiratory system and correct breathing.

As far as breathing is concerned, it plays an important role in endurance training. It has to be performed deeply and rhythmically, where an active exhalation is critical for an adequate performance. Most athletes have to learn how to exhale, to evacuate from the lungs as much air as possible from which the O_2 had already been extracted. Otherwise the concentration of O_2 in the freshly inhaled air will be diluted and performance will be adversely affected. A forceful exhalation is even more important during the critical phase of a race/game, when an adequate supply of O_2 enables one to overcome the difficulty.

A high aerobic capacity positively transfers to the anaerobic capacity. If an athlete improves his/her aerobic capacity the anaerobic capacity will also improve since he/she will be able to function longer before reaching an O_2 debt, and will recover more quickly after building up an O_2 debt (Howald, 1977). This finding is of significant importance for most sports where the anaerobic capacity is an important component. By improving aerobic capacity most team sports would maximize their technical and tactical knowledge. Therefore the improvement of aerobic endurance must be a permanent goal for the vast majority of athletes.

A strong aerobic capacity also stabilizes speed. During the competitive phase of many sports anaerobic capacity is emphasized. But very often the consistency of anaerobic performance is affected by exaggerated stressful, intense work. Thus, in order to prolong a successful performance when anaerobic capacity is an important component of training, aerobic types of activities have to be introduced in training. In such cases training lessons stressing aerobic, long duration endurance, play the role of alternating activities of various intensities. Under this new circumstance the body can regenerate and thus increase the durability of anaerobic power. The same concept is also valid for the unloading (tapering) phase. Prior to important competitions when the athletes reduce their training demands, training lessons of aerobic activity ought to be introduced to replace stressful intensive activities. As a result, the body will regenerate since the load is lighter while the degree of training is not affected. Howald (1977) implies that there is a definite trend showing that athletes using long duration submaximum training do have higher anaerobic thresholds (the blood level of lactic acid rises above the resting level) than those using a higher percentage of high intensity endurance and interval types of training. Consequently, on the basis of the above realities coaches should revise their training concept and introduce into their training programs a much higher percentage of aerobic activities.

Anaerobic capacity

For sports which demand maximum exertion, and during the initial stages of those requiring sub-maximum exertion, energy is produced in the absence of O_2 by the anaerobic system. Energy contributed by the anaerobic system is directly related to the intensity of the performance. For example, if an athlete runs a 400 m race and a velocity of 7.41 m/s the ergogenesis (the production of energy) is 14% aerobic and 86% anaerobic while running the same distance with a velocity of 8.89 m/s the ratio is 7.7% aerobic and 92.3 anaerobic (Razumovski, 1968). Therefore, it appears that the utilization of the two energy systems is dependent not only on the distance of the race but also on the classification or the level of performance of an athlete. From the above example, it is also obvious that the two systems can provide energy in various proportions. The proportion of the aerobic component increases as the distance increases and the intensity decreases.

Ozolin (1971) claims that the body's anaerobic capacity is affected by the CNS processes which facilitate an athlete to continue intensive work, or work under exhausting conditions. It is also suggested that the anaerobic capacity is affected by hyperventilation, or the provision of extra O_2 prior to the start by inhaling additional O_2 through increasing the rate of respiration.

Specific training in the respective sport is the best method of improving the anaerobic capacity. However, as explained above, anaerobic training has to be often alternated with aerobic training. For sports which endure longer than 60 seconds, aerobic training should predominate. The anaerobic type of training, like the overemphasized interval training in North America, will not necessarily make an athlete (competing in sports of a duration longer than 2 minutes) faster, that is helpful for the first part of the race only

The speed reserve

One of the factors which affects endurance, especially specific endurance, is the speed reserve. Its importance in cyclic sports may often be determinant, although many coaches are still unaware of it, or disregard it. However, speed reserve is considered to be the difference between the fastest time achieved on a distance much shorter than the racing distance (i.e., 100 m) and the time achieved over the same short distance during a longer race (i.e., 800 m) . In order to have any validity the test has to be performed during the same period of time. If an athlete is capable of covering a short distance very fast, he/she will be able to travel longer distances at a lower speed more easily. Under such circumstances, an athlete with a higher speed reserve would spend less energy to maintain a given speed as compared to others with a lower reserve.

A speed reserve test may be performed as follows: At first the coach should determine the distance to be tested. For mid distance running events, a standard speed distance (100 m dash); for swimming, either 25 or 50 m (or one length of the pool); while for rowing 500 m and canoeing 250 m. Then the athletes should be tested to determine the maximum speed with which they can cover the standard distance. The following step should be to test the athlete's speed over the standard distance (i.e., 100 m) while he/she competes or is tested over the distance in which he/she is specialized.

Let 11 seconds be the maximum speed over 100 m and 12.4 seconds the time achieved over 100 m while running 400 m. The difference (1.4 seconds) is considered to be the speed reserve index. The larger the difference, the higher the speed reserve. A good speed reserve and a systematic specific endurance training will lead to high performance in the chosen event. Similarly, provided that the athlete has a good speed, the smaller the index the better the specific endurance. Therefore, although this aspect of training is inadequately researched, it is obvious that there is a strong interdependence between speed reserve and the athlete's abilities to reach a high performance. An athlete running 100 m in 10.6 seconds even without too much specific training would cover 400 m in 50 seconds (a speed reserve of probably 1.8 seconds and a mean speed of 12.5 seconds). However, an athlete with a speed of 12 seconds/100 m would have a hard time, or may even be unable to perform a similar time over 400 m. Therefore, speed in general, and a speed reserve in particular may be a limiting factor in an athletic progress.

The Methodology of Developing Endurance

In order to improve endurance, the athlete must learn to overcome fatigue and this is done by adapting to the training demand. Any degree of adaptation is reflected in the improvement of endurance.

According to the specifics of the sport/event the two types of endurance, aerobic or anaerobic, have to be primarily developed. The development of these two types of endurance is dependent upon the type of intensity and the methods used in training. Although in training other classifications of intensities are used the absolute intensity in endurance training is linked with the energy supply systems. Thus, Zatzyorski (1980) considers the following three intensities:

1. The subcritical intensity, when the speed is reduced, with a low energy expenditure, and the O_2 demand is below the athlete's aerobic power. The O_2 supply meets the physiological demand; therefore the work is performed under the steady state condition.

2. The critical intensity is achieved when the speed is elevated, and the O_2 demand reaches the O_2 supply capacity. The critical intensity is performed in the anaerobic threshold zone, thus the speed is directly proportional to the athlete's respiratory potential.

3. Supra critical speed refers to the types of activities which are above the critical speed. The work is performed under O_2 demand usually increases faster than the speed of performance.

Training parameters for aerobic endurance

The physiological threshold of various organs and systems involved in aerobic activity increases and apparently is more efficiently developed when training consists of low intensity, long duration work. If the activity is continuous, the maintenance of O_2 consumption, so specific for aerobic endurance, is a difficult task for an athlete's body. Usually, the duration of work under maximum O_2 consumption cannot exceed 10–12 minutes except for highly trained athletes (Zatzyorski, 1980). Elite class athletes from sports like running, cross-country skiing, rowing, swimming, etc., may maintain a velocity close to the critical level for between 1–2 hours (heart rate: 150–166 bpm).

As a general outline, the following training parameters are significant for the development of aerobic endurance.

1. THE INTENSITY of training has to be below 70% of the maximum velocity (Herberger, 1977). As a criteria to follow, the intensity may be measured by the time of performance per a given distance, the velocity in meters per second, or the heart rate (140–164 bpm). Training stimuli which does not elevate the heart rate above 130 bpm does not significantly increase the aerobic capacity (Zatzyorski, 1980).

2. THE DURATION of an isolated stimuli (i.e., one repetition) has to be of several varying magnitudes. While sometimes it must be around 60–90 seconds in

order to improve anaerobic endurance which is an important component during the beginning of a race, very often long repetitions (3–10 minutes) are used and needed for the perfection of aerobic endurance. However, the general composition of a training program depends on the phase of training, the characteristics of the sport, and the needs of the athlete.

3. RESTING INTERVALS have to be calculated in such a way that the following stimulus occurs during the period of favorable changes provoked by previous work. According to Reindel et al. (1962) it has to be between 45–90 seconds. However, for aerobic endurance the resting interval should definitely not exceed 3–4 minutes because during a longer rest the capillaries (the blood vessels that connect the arteries with veins) shrink, and during the first minutes of work blood flow is restricted (Hollmann, 1959). The same author suggests that the heart rate method may also be considered for the calculation of the rest interval. Usually when the rate drops to 120 bpm working commences.

4. ACTIVITY DURING THE REST INTERVAL is normally of a very low intensity to stimulate biological recuperation. In athletics a walk or jog (for very well trained athletes) is the familiar activity.

5. THE NUMBER OF REPETITIONS is determined by the athlete's physiological capacity to stabilize O_2 consummation at a high level. If this stabilization does not occur at a sufficiently high level the aerobic system will be unable to meet the energy demands. Consequently, the anaerobic system takes up the slack putting a severe strain on the body and resulting in the onset of fatigue. As suggested by Zatzyorski (1980) the heart rate may be a good indication of the level of fatigue. As fatigue develops the heart rate increases while performing equally strenuous repetitions. Once above 180 bpm or so, which is reflective of a high level of fatigue, the heart actually has less power of contraction resulting in the delivery of less O_2 to the working muscles. At this point, or shortly before, training should be ceased.

Training parameters for anaerobic endurance

Most of the means utilized for the development of anaerobic endurance are cyclic in nature and are performed with high intensity. The brief presentation that follows may be used by the coach as a general guideline in training:

1. THE INTENSITY may range from submaximum up to maximum limits. Although in training, a variation of intensities is employed, for the purpose of the improvement of anaerobic endurance, intensities around 90–95% of maximum ought to prevail.

2. THE DURATION of work may be between 5–120 seconds, depending on the type of intensity employed.

3. THE REST INTERVAL following an activity of very high intensity must be long enough to replenish the O_2 debt. Since the interval of recuperation is a function of the intensity and duration of work it may be within the limits of 2–10 minutes. For a more efficient recuperation and replenishment of fuel to provide the required

Table 28.   The four zones of effort based on the LA method.

Zone No.	Zone	LA Composition
1	Compensation	0—23 mg
2	Aerobic	24—36 mg
3	Combined	37—70 mg
4	Anaerobic	71—300 mg

energy, it is advisable to divide the total number of repetitions into a few series of 4–6 repetitions. The longest rest interval (6–10 minutes) is planned between the sets so that the accumulated lactic acid will have sufficient time to oxidize and the athlete may start the new set almost totally recovered.

4. ACTIVITY DURING REST has to be light, relaxing. Total rest, (i.e., lay down) is unadvisable since the excitability of the nervous system may decrease to unacceptable levels (Zatzyorski, 1980).

5. THE NUMBER OF REPETITIONS must be low since the work aimed at developing anaerobic capacity is of an intense nature and can not have many repetitions without accumulating lactic acid (LA). If work continues the glycolytic resources become exhausted and the aerobic system has to assume the responsibility of providing the required energy. Under this circumstance, the velocity is decreased, and consequently the work will not benefit the anaerobic capacity. Therefore, it seems that the best method is to divide the planned number of repetitions into several sets, say 4 sets of 4 repetitions. The rest interval between repetitions may be that which was planned (i.e., 120 seconds) but the rest between sets has to be long enough (i.e., up to 10 minutes) to replenish the O_2 debt and consequently to oxidate LA.

Directing endurance training programs based on the lactic acid method

Contemporary training is very complex, and in order to direct adequate programs the coach often needs to find out very precisely the internal dosage and how the body responds to training stimuli. The LA method refers to detecting the quantity of LA present in the blood as a result of training. Although the method is not very complicated it requires the scientific assistance of a physiologist. To put it simply, a blood sample is taken from the ear lobe and analyzed to determine the LA concentration. According to the LA concentration the effort in training is divided into four zones (Marasescu, 1980), illustrated in table 28.

The first zone refers to the type of work which is easier than aerobic endurance exercises of the second zone. Activities such as jogging for warm-up, compensation activity performed between repetitions, and light activities employed at the end of a

Table 29. Combinations of activities, according to the objective of endurance training.

Combination Number	Training Objective	Type of Activity	Percentage
1	Improve endurance	Aerobic Combined and anaerobic Compensatory	≥ 50% ≤ 25% Remaining percent
2	Improve speed	Aerobic Combined and anaerobic Compensatory	≤ 50% ≥ 25% Remaining percent

training lesson lie in this zone. The third zone is a typical program where aerobic and anaerobic programs are combined, while the last zone refers strictly to intense, anaerobic activities.

Data interpretation is very simple. By comparing the LA concentration to the figures of table 28, required alterations in the program can be made depending on the type of training required. Often a coach's intention is an aerobic type of workout but the reality, based on the LA method, may be that the athlete worked harder, performing an activity either of the third of fourth zone. As a result, the program has to be changed. The LA method may also illustrate other features of the athlete's training. Thus, the lower the LA concentration following a harder work the better the athlete's training capacity. On the other hand the higher the LA concentration following an anaerobic type of training the better the anaerobic mechanism was mobilized.

The correct combination in training of work from the four zones (table 28) may lead to an objective method of directing a program. Table 29 illustrates two types of combinations which could be used as a guideline for a correct program in a given training phase.

The combination of activities employed for endurance training and especially the percentage per combination represents additional proof to the importance of the aerobic component in any endurance training program.

Methods Used to Develop Endurance

Throughout all phases of development, especially the phase of perfecting endurance, the body's adjustment to physiological limitations of endurance training is crucial. Physiological limitations (i.e., tissue adaptation to work under the conditions of insufficient O_2, hypoxia, an excess of carbon dioxide) are always accentuated when the athletes reach a high state of fatigue. In order to further the body's adaptation to a higher endurance demand, in addition to classical methods which briefly will be described below, other techniques may also be considered. Breathing at a lower rate than the body and rhythm of performance demands may artificially create a state of hypoxia (i.e., to breath once at every 3–4 swimming strokes). Training at a medium or high altitude, which many East European athletes do twice a year for 2–4 weeks, where the partial pressure of O_2 is lower, also leads to the same result, that is to train under the conditions of hypoxia. Another positive result of employing the above two techniques is the increase of hemoglobin content of blood. Hemoglobin is an iron-containing protein pigment present in the red blood cell, functioning primarily in the transport of O_2 from the lungs to the muscle tissue.

Long distance training methods

One of the characteristics of all training methods incorporated in this category is the fact that work is not interrupted by rest intervals. The most commonly used methods are as follows: a. uniform or steady state, b. the alternative, and c. the fartlek method.

1. THE UNIFORM METHOD is characterized by a high volume of work without any interruptions. Although it is used throughout all annual training phases, this method is dominant during the preparatory phase. It is highly recommended for most sports requiring aerobic endurance, but mostly for cyclic sports of which the duration is 60 seconds or more. The duration of one training lesson may be between 1–2.5 hours. The intensity may be properly calculated by employing the heart rate method, and it is suggested to be between 150–170 bpm.

The main training effect is the improvement and perfection of aerobic capacity. Similarly, the steadiness of performance leads to a consolidation of technique (i.e., speed skating, swimming, canoeing, rowing) while the working efficiencies of the body's functions are improved.

A variant of this method is the progressive increase of speed from a moderate to a medium intensity throughout a training lesson. For instance, the athlete may perform the first one-third of the training distance at a moderate speed, increasing it to a intermediate, and finally to a medium intensity for the last one-third. This progressive elevation challenges the athlete both physically and psychologically, thus being considered an effective method of developing aerobic endurance.

2. THE ALTERNATIVE METHOD is considered as one of the most effective methods of developing endurance. Throughout the lesson, the athlete changes the intensity of performance over a predetermined distance. The intensity of work varies frequently from moderate to sub-maximum without any interruptions. These variations of intensities may be determined by external factors such as terraine profile (for running, cross-country skiing and cycling) or by internal (athlete's will) or planned factors (coach's decision regarding portions of distance to alter the intensity). The peak velocity of a duration between 1–10 minutes ought to be alternated with moderate intensity, which will allow the body to recuperate slightly prior to another increase. For high velocity stimuli the heart rate may reach values around 180 bpm while the restoration phase may have the rate around 140 bpm (Pfeifer, 1982), but not much lower than that. The rhythmical, wave-like approach in altering the intensity facilitates a high volume of work, where the cardio-respiratory and CNS capacity improves significantly. In addition, this method promotes a flexible adaptation of the body's processes resulting in a strong development of general endurance.

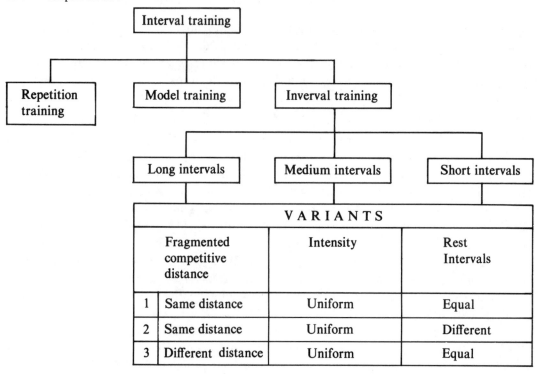

Figure 106. Variations of training with a rest interval.

This method may be applied not only by those involved in cyclic sports (pre-competitive, and competitive phase), but also by others (team sports, wrestling, boxing) during the preparatory, and pre-competitive phase.

A meritous variant of this method is the organization of the entire training program into sets. Instead of performing an uninterrupted work of, say, 90 minutes, it may be divided into three sets, having an active rest (i.e., walk) in between each set.

3. THE FARTLEK, or speed play, method was developed by the Scandinavian and German runners in 1920–1930. While performing it, the athlete inputs his/her own contribution in the sense that uniform training is alternated at will with short portions of higher intensity performance. Such sprints are not planned, and rely mostly on the athlete's subjective feeling and judgment. The use of the fartlek method is specific mostly, but not entirely, to the preparatory phase, as a variety inflicted in the monotony of uniform training.

Interval training

The term interval training does not necessarily refer to a well-known method, but rather to all methods performed with a rest interval (figure 106).

1. THE REPETITION METHOD, of distances longer or shorter than the racing distance develops specific, or racing endurance. Longer repetitions place a strong de-

mand on the aerobic component of the racing endurance, since the speed of performance is very close to the racing speed. On the other hand, shorter repetitions solicit the anaerobic component since often the performer develops an O_2 debt. Obviously in the latter case the intensity is slightly higher than that of a race. An important asset of the repetition method is the development of willpower via the demand to perform many repetitions. The total volume of work may be 4–8 times that of the racing distance with a rest interval which might be between 5–10 minutes depending on the repetition distance and intensity.

2. MODEL TRAINING may be considered as a variation of repetition training since an athlete is exposed to repeating several training distances. However, the originality of this method lies in the fact that it resembles the specifics of the race, thus the name model training. Therefore, the first part of training is composed of several repetitions much shorter than the racing distance. In addition to the shorter distance one performs an intensity close to (slightly higher or lower) racing velocity. Under such conditions the energy is provided by the anaerobic metabolic system, as is the case in a race. The mid part of training has to use distances and intensities which serve to improve and perfect the aerobic endurance. In order to exactly model the race, the last part of training employs once again short distance repetitions, which resemble and develop the final kick capacity. Such repetitions are performed under a certain level of fatigue (as in the race) and heavily tax again the anaerobic endurance (which, considering its specifics may be called speed of endurance).

Factors like total volume of work, velocity, rest intervals, and the number of repetitions, have to be calculated according to the individual's potential and the characteristics of the sport. The heart rate method may be employed for the calculation of the rest interval. Considering its specificity, this method has to be employed during the precompetitive, and competitive phases.

3. INTERVAL TRAINING, a method which was in fashion in Europe in the 1960's and over-rated in North America even in the 1980's, is rightly reconsidered for its merits of the development of endurance. Most of the exaggerations as far as interval training is concerned came from the fact that repetitions of short durations were expected to improve everything, including aerobic endurance. And obviously this never was the case. In fact there is no one method which can do everything for everybody. Only a wise combination of all methods knitted together according to the needs of the athletes and the specifics of the sport, may be successful. Interval training, as it is best known (duration of stimuli between 30–90 seconds), inadequately develops the aerobic energy production system, as well as the capacity to maintain what development there is throughout the competitive phase.

Interval training refers to the method of repeating stimuli of various intensities with a previously planned rest interval, during which the athlete does not fully regenerate. The duration of the rest interval is basically calculated by the heart rate method. The portions of distance to be repeated could be performed either by time

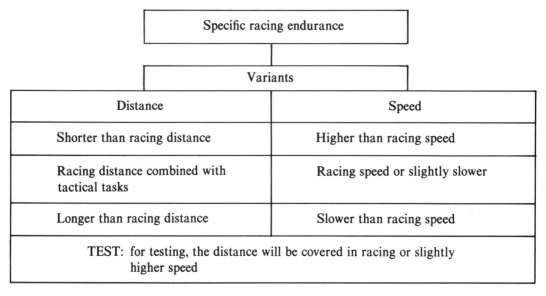

Figure 107.   Variants of specific racing endurance (modified from Pfeifer, 1981).

(i.e., 12 x 3 minutes) or precise distance (12 x 800 m). For a more efficient training effect, all three interval training methods should be combined.

1. The short distance interval training, between 15 seconds–2 minutes, which mostly develops anaerobic endurance.
2. The medium distance interval training, 2–8 minutes, which may develop both energy production systems, and
3. The long distance interval training, 8–15 minutes, with a main training effect of aerobic endurance improvement.

The main elements of progression are: intensity and duration of stimuli, the number of repetitions, rest interval, and activity during rest.

Specific racing endurance

The development of very specific endurance is realized by what Pfeifer (1982) calls "control, or racing method." As the term suggests the employment of such a method develops exclusively the endurance specific for each event/sport. The training dosage ought to be calculated in such a way that it corresponds specifically to physical, psychological and tactical characteristics of the selected sport (figure 107).

The development of endurance is a complex task, since in most sports there are combinations of both aerobic and anaerobic components. Consequently, in order to achieve a complex body adaptation several of the above methods and variants have to be used. But the physiological effect of a method does not have to be the only criteria of selecting a training method, there is also the psychological benefit of a method. Apparently, from a psychological point of view, training methods aiming at developing aerobic endurance (uniform and alternative) are superior to interval training (Pfeifer, 1982).

Training the Energy Systems: The Five Intensity Values

In all athletic programmes the intensity of training must be altered throughout a micro-cycle in order to enhance both the athletes' physiological adaptation to training, as well as the regeneration following a demanding training session. However, such alternation of intensities depends on the ergogenesis of the event and the characteristics of the training phase.

As far as the physiological profile of an endurance related event is concerned, in the first 15–20 seconds the energy demands are supplied by the phosphate system (ATP/CP), followed by the lactic acid (LA) system up to 1:30–2 minutes. If the event continues for a longer period of time, then energy demands are supplied by glycogen, which in the presence of O_2 is completely burned without producing lactic acid (fig. 10).

Therefore, since most sports use fuel produced by all the energy systems, training has to be more complex, exposing the athletes, especially during the last pan of the preparatory and the competitive phase, to all energy systems.

In order to assist coaches to conduct more scientific and better planned training, which has to consider the physiological profile and the energy requirements of a sport, five intensity values are proposed (figure 108). These intensities are listed from 1 to 5, in order of the magnitude of training demand: number 1 being the most, and 5 being the least taxing. For instance, the Lactic Acid Tolerance Training (LATT) is regarded as physiologically the most demanding, therefore it is considered as intensity number one (1). On the opposite end of the scale are the phosphase system training (number 4) and aerobic threshold training, (number 5) since the body can tolerate them much easier.

The heading of figure 108 explains the physiological characteristics of each value, which should be regarded as a training method. For instance, if the coach intends to use Lactic Acid Tolerance Training, he/she may employ one of the two durations suggested, with a set number of repetitions and a rest interval (RI) sufficient to re-move the lactic acid from the system. The coach will also consider the corresponding ratio of work to rcst interval, lactic acid concentration in milimoles (mmol) and the heart rate (HR). In order to reach such physiological characteristics the percentages of maximum intensity for the early and late preparatory phases are also suggested. The latter intensity also refers to the competitive phase. For a better understanding of the five intensities, each method is briefly explained below.

Lactic Acid Tolerance Training (LATT)

Athletes who can tolerate the pain of acidosis can perform better longer. There-fore the scope of LATT is to adapt to the acidic effect of LA, to buffer the LA

Intensity Symbol	Training for:	Duration of Reps.	# of Reps.	R.I.	Ratio Work/ R.I.	LA Conc. (m mol)	HR	% of Maximum Intensity	
								early	late
1	Lactic Acid Tolerance Training (LATT)	30" - 60" / 2" - 2.5"	2x2 - 4 / 4 - 6(8)	15' / >5'	1:2 - 1:3	12 - 18 Mx=20	Near Mx. or Mx.	>85	>95
2	Maximum Oxygen Consumption Training (MVO$_2$T)	3 - 5"	4 - 8(12)	2 - 3'	2:1	6 - 12	180	80 - 85	85 - 90
3	Anaerobic Threshold Training (AnTT)	1:30 - 7' / 8' - 1^h	3 - 5 / 6 - 2	5" / 5' - 45'	1:1 / 1:0.6 - 1:1.5	4 - 6	150 - 170	75 - 85	85 - 90
4	Phospate System Training (PST)	4 - 15"	10 - 30	1 - 3'	1:4 - 1:25	- - -	- - - -	- - - -	95
5	Aerobic Threshold Training (ATT)	10' - 2^h	6 - 1	1 - 2'	1:1 - 1:25	2 - 3	130 - 150	>60	>60

Figure 108. Suggested guidelines for training the << five intensities >> of the energy system (" represents seconds, minutes, and h hours).

effects, increase lactate removal from the working muscle, and to increase tolerance physiologically and psychologically to the hurt, pain and agony of training and competition. By adapting and learning to tolerate LA increases, the athlete can work more intensely and produce more LA which should not be inhibiting. Thus, towards the end of an event, more energy can be produced anaerobically. Maximum limits of LA tolerance can be reached in 4-50 seconds.

Recovery periods should be long enough to remove LA from the working muscle (15-30 minutes), otherwise the removal of LA will be prevented, acidosis being so severe that reduction in energy metabolism will cause a reduction in speed below the level necessary to increase the LA production. Thus the intended training effect would not be realized. Work periods of less than one minute require several repetitions (i.e. 4-8). Longer work periods (i.e. 2-3 minutes) are desirable, but only if the speed is sustained at a level high enough to cause excessive LA accumulation (12-16 mmol), thus producing high levels of aerobic power under conditions of extreme acidosis.

Psychologically, the purpose of LATI should be to push the athletes beyond the pain threshold. However, there should be caution, since overdoing the LATI' can lead to undesirable training states, critical levels of fatigue, and ultimately to overtraining. Therefore LAI'r should not exceed 1-2 workouts/week.

Maximum Oxygen Consumption Training (MVO₂T)

During training and competition both parts of the oxygen transport system, the central (heart) and peripheral (capillaries at the level of the working muscle), are heavily taxed to supply the required oxygen. Since the supply of O_2 at the working muscle level represents a limiting factor in performance and since athletes with large MVO_2 capacity have demonstrated better performances in endurance events, MVO_2T must be an important concern for both coach and athlete.

Increased MVO_2 results from an improved transportation of O_2 by the circulatory system, and increased extraction and utilization of O_2 by the muscular system. Therefore, a large portion of the training programme has to be dedicated to the development of MVO_2, which is best served by work periods of longer duration, 3–8 minutes or even longer, at 80–90% intensity (higher for shorter and lower for longer repetitions). The HR can be maximum or within ten bpm of maximum.

MVO_2 may also be improved in training through shorter work periods (30 seconds–2 minutes) provided that the rest interval is short as well (10 seconds–1 minute). Under such conditions, training effect results not from one or two repetitions (which may primarily solicit the anaerobic system) but rather through the accumulative effect of several repetitions (4–12) which will reach MVO_2.

Repeated work periods for MVO_2 as well as the other methods could be performed in straight sets (i.e., 12 x 3 minutes, with RI=1:30 minutes) as well as in sets (i.e., 3 x 4 minutes with RI = 1:30 minutes while RI between sets = 3 minutes). Since RI between sets is longer, this more extensive restoration time allows more work to be performed. Similarly, since intensive (but wise) work is often equated with improvement, coaches should test which method is more productive for their athletes.

Anaerobic Threshold Training (AnTT)

The AnTT refers to the intensity of an exercise at which level the rate of LA diffusion in the blood stream exceeds the rate of its removal. (AnTT = 4–6 mmol).

Short repeated work periods stimulate the anaerobic metabolism, but the level of LA produced in the muscles does not rise significantly above normal levels. The LA diffuses into the adjacent resting muscles thus lowering its concentration level; it is metabolized in the working muscle; and also it is removed from the blood by the heart, liver, and muscles at the rate it is accumulated.

Therefore training program designed to reach the AnTT have to produce LA at the rate beyond the ability of the above mechanisms to dispose of it. Such a program has to be around 60–90% of the maximum speed with a HR = 150–170 bpm. The duration of a work period can vary, but the work/RI ratio should be 1:1.

The AnTT is a trainable factor which can be expressed as a percentage of MVO_2. For well trained athletes the AnTT can be reached at 85–90% of MVO_2. (The intent of AnTT training is to elevate the threshold beyond 4 mmol, so that intensive work can be maintained without excessive accumulation of LA). During such training programs the subjective feeling of the athletes should be of mild distress and the speed just slightly faster than that of comfortable feeling.

Phosphate System Training (PST)

The intent of PST is to increase the ability of an athlete to be fast with less effort. PST should improve the propulsion off the starting blocks and in the early part of the event without using one s maximum speed. This is possible by applying short work periods of 4–15 seconds with a speed in excess of 95% of maximum.

Such a training program employs the phosphate energy system and the outcome of it is the increase of the quantity of ATP-CP stored in the muscle as well as increasing the activity of the enzymes that release energy through the ATP-CP reaction.

Long recovery intervals between work periods (work/RI ratio = 1:4–1:25) are necessary to ensure that the muscles CP supply is replaced completely. If the rest interval is shorter the restoration of CP will be incomplete and as a result anaerobic glycolysis rather than the phosphate reaction will become the major source of energy. This in turn will produce LA which will reduce speed and the desired training effect will not be realized. Therefore PST or sprint training should not cause muscle pain since this is a sign of anaerobic glycolysis.

Aerobic Threshold Training (ATT)

High aerobic capacity is decisive factor for all events of medium and long duration. Similarly it is also determinant for all sports where the O_2 supply represents a limiting factor. Utilization of ATT is beneficial for the vast majority of sports since it enhances quick recovery following training and competition; develops the functional efficiency of the cardiorespiratory and nervous systems; and enhances the economical functioning of the metabolic system. Finally it also increases the capacity to tolerate stress for long periods of time.

ATT is performed mostly through a high volume of work without interruption (uniform pace) interval training using repetitions longer than 5 minutes and the progressive elevation of intensity from a moderate to a medium fast speed within one training session.

The duration of an ATT session could be between 1–2.5 hours. The intended training effect may only be achieved where the LA concentration is between 2–3 mmol. With a HR of 130–150 bpm (sometimes even higher). Below these figures the training effect is questionable. During ATT the minute volume of blood is 30–40 litres while the O_2 intake approximates 4–5.5 litres/minute.

ATT is often the primary training method for the preparatory phase. During the competition phase ATT may be planned 1–2 times/week as a method of maintaining the aerobic capacity, and as a recovery session(s) so that intensity is reduced but the general fitness level is maintained.

Building the program

Now that the five intensities of training have been illustrated, the critical question is how to incorporate them within a training program. Traditionally a training program is designed by assigning certain physical, technical, or tactical objectives to certain days of a micro-cycle. Yet, the critical element in training is the training of the energy systems, which represents the foundation of good performance, in cooperation with the technical/tactical elements, based on knowledge of the physiological profile prevailing in a given event. Therefore when planning a micro-cycle, the coach should not write down the actual training content but rather the mathematical values of the intensities needed in the cycle, which will suggest the component(s) of the energy systems to be emphasized in that particular training session (figures 110–114). The distribution per micro-cycle of the five intensities depends on the phase of training, the athletes' needs, and whether or not a competition is planned at the end of the cycle. Therefore, as suggested by figures 110–114, when planning a micro-cycle the coach should first determine the five values in terms of percentages, and then distribute the values per days to meet the decided proportion.

LA Conc. (mmol)	Training for:	HR.	% of Max. Intensity	Training Effect	Training Benefits
20.0	Maximum anaerobic power	200			- high improvement in anaerobic end. - overemphasis may result in over- training
		200			
12.0	Lactic Acid Tolerance	200	85-90%		
8.0	MVO$_2$	190-200	80-90%		-considerable improvement in aerobic endurance - observe intensity for optimal benefit
		180			
		170			
	Anaerobic Threshold	160	(60)- 70-85%		
4.0		150			
		140			-improvement in aerobic endurance
		130	60%		
2.0	Aerobic Threshold	120	50%		
		110			-little improvement in aerobic endurance
		100			
1.1	Resting State	>80			

Figure 109. A summary of the effects of the five intensities on training the energy systems (made by Alan Roaf, 1988).

A major training concern for the distribution of intensity values in a micro-cycle is the athlete's physiological reaction to training and the level of fatigue generated by a given intensity as illustrated by the dynamics of overcompensation (estimated at the bottom of each example). An intensity from the top of the scale of intensities (figure 108), or intensity number 1, will constantly generate higher levels of fatigue which are illustrated by the magnitude of the depth of overcompensation curve. Therefore, such a training session (figure 111 on Monday PM) is followed by two sessions of intensity 5, which by being less demanding facilitates overcompensation. On the other hand, several training sessions aimed at improving adaptation to LATT may be planned in two consecutive days (figure 113 Thursday and Friday). Such an approach, which is often necessary in training, results in high levels of fatigue and overcompensation occurs only following the light training session planned on Saturday AM (intensity number 5) and the free weekend.

Combinations of various intensities in a training session often are a necessity. For instance, a combination between intensities 1 and 5, or 4 and 5 suggests that after working an anaerobic component (i.e. number 1 and 4), which are the most taxing and fatiguing ones, a less demanding intensity (i.e. number 5) can be planned. Such a combination will enhance the development or maintenance of aerobic endurance, and especially will facilitate the rate of recovery between training sessions.

Physiological adaptation to the profile of an event may result in other possible combinations as well. One such possibility could be a: 4 + 3 + 1. Such a combination in fact models a race in which the beginning (an aggressive start) relies on the energy produced by the phosphate system (4); the body of the race which uses the energy produced by the lactic and oxygen systems (3); and the finish where the ability to tolerate the increased levels of lactic acid (1) can make the difference between winning and losing.

The incorporation of a scientific basis in the methodology of planning is a necessity if the coach expects high efficiency from the time invested in planning the training. The application of the five intensities to the training plan incorporates the entire spectrum of the energy systems necessary in all endurance-dominant, or endurance-related sports: from the phosphate, to the lactic acid, and then the aerobic system.

In this method the coach plans mathematical values, the rationing and distribution of which in a given micro-cycle depends on the ergogenesis of the sport, the phase of training, and the athlete's needs.

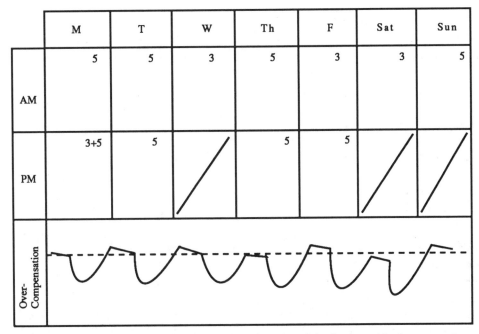

Figure 110. Early preparatory micro-cycle where the ration of the five intensities is suggested as: ATT = 75% and AnTT = 25%.

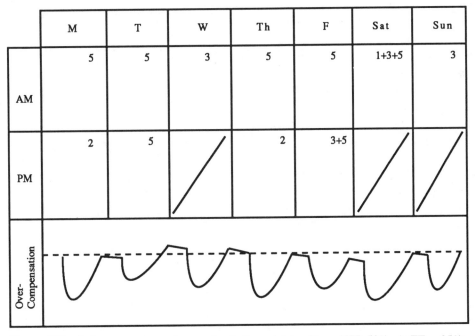

Figure 111. Late preparatory micro-cycle. Ration of intensities: ATT=50%; AnTT = 25%; $MVO_2T = 20\%$; LATT = 5 %.

	M	T	W	Th	F	Sat	Sun
AM	5	2	3	5	5	2	
PM	4+5	5			1	3		

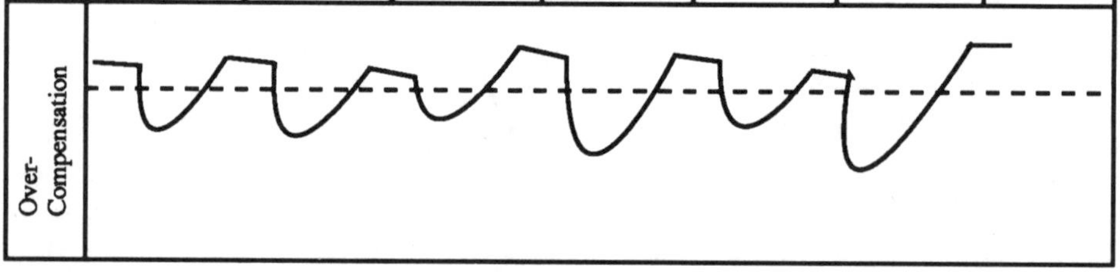

Figure 112. Pre-competitive micro-cycle. Ration of intensities: ATT = 40%; AnTT = 20%; MVO_2T = 20%; PSP = 10%; LATT = 10%.

	M	T	W	Th	F	Sat	Sun
AM	5	3	5	4+ 5	3	1+ 5	
PM	4+5	4+5+1			2	1		

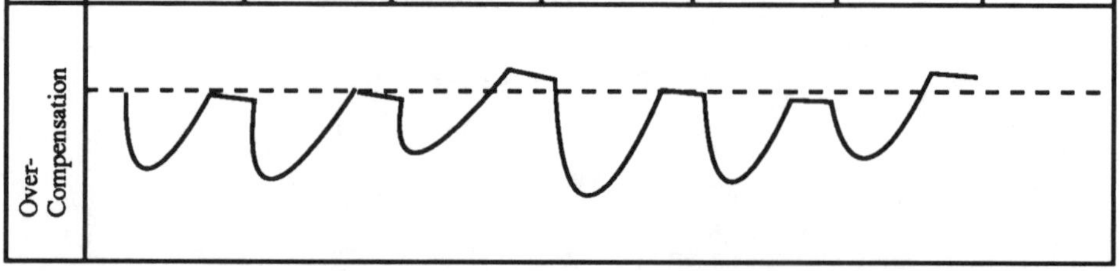

Figure 113. Competitive phase micro-cycle without competition on weekend. Ration of intensities: ATT = 20%; LATT = 20%; MVO_2T = 20%; PST - 20%; AnTT = 20%.

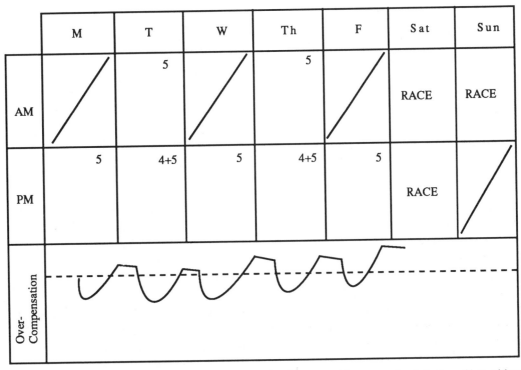

Figure 114. Competitive phase (unloading) micro-cycle with competition on weekend. Ration of intensities: ATT = 80%; PST = 20%.

In order to avoid the undesirable effects of overtraining, the sequence and frequency of the intensity symbols has to be considered with the concept of overcompensation strictly adhered to.

Under such circumstances planning becomes more scientific, has a logical sequence, and observes the important training requirement of alternating high with low intensity stimuli so that fatigue is constantly succeeded by regeneration.

SPEED TRAINING

One of the most important biomotor abilities required in sports is speed, or the capacity to travel or move very quickly. From a mechanical point of view speed is expressed through a ratio between space and time. The term speed incorporates three elements:

1. reaction time,
2. frequency of movement per time unit, and
3. speed of travel over a given distance.

The correlation between these three factors assists the assessment of the performance of an exercise requiring speed. Thus, in sprinting, the final outcome depends on the athlete's reaction at the start, the speed of travel throughout the body of the race (i.e., force of propulsion) and his/her stride frequency.

Speed is a determinant ability in many sports like sprinting events, boxing, fencing, team sports and others. For sports where it is not a determinant factor, the inclusion of speed activities in training enhances the attainment of high intensity training. Consequently, speed training represents an important concern for almost every sport.

Ozolin (1971) implies that there are two types of speed:

1. GENERAL speed, which is defined as the capacity to perform any kind of movement (motor reaction) in a rapid manner. Both general and specific physical preparation enhance general speed.

2. SPECIAL speed on the other hand, refers to the capacity to perform an exercise, or skill, at a given speed, which is usually very high. Special speed specific for each sport, is developed through specific methods explained briefly in this section. Whatever the type of speed sought, a positive transfer cannot be expected unless the structure of movement, both kinematic and dynamic, is similar to the skill pattern.

Maximum speed of a runner is not achieved instantly but rather after an acceleration of at least 30 m. The speedogram (graphical representation of one's speed over a given distance) shows that maximum speed is reached after the 40 m mark, or 5 seconds after the start (Zatzyorski, 1980) and can be maintained quite steadily for up to 80 m. From that point on it fluctuates due to CNS fatigue and the showing of inhibition (Harre, 1982). Further improvements are achieved only by improving power, speed endurance and power endurance.

Factors Affecting Speed

1. HEREDITY   As compared to strength and endurance training, which are more trainable (following an adequate training the athlete may achieve spectacular improvements without having of extraordinary talent), speed training requires more natural talent, and is determined by heredity. Hence, the mobility of the nervous processes, the quick alternation between excitation and inhibition, and the capacity to regulate the neuro-muscular co-ordination pattern (De Vries, 1980), may lead to a high motor frequency. In addition, the intensity and frequency of the nervous impulses represent determinant factors in achieving high speed.

The property of skeletal muscle represents a limiting factor in speed potential (Dintinman, 1971). This reflects the difference in make-up and proportion of slow twitch muscle fibers (red muscle), and fast twitch fibers (white muscle) which contains a lower quantity of reddish pigments, making the muscle fibers look rather pale. The white muscle fibers contract faster than their red counterparts, which is a great asset for a sprinter. Therefore, according to De Vries (1980) the ultimate maximum speed capacity is limited by the intrinsic speed of the muscle tissue, thus suggesting that heredity represents an important factor in performing quick movements.

2. REACTION TIME   Also an inherited feature, reaction time represents the time between when an individual is exposed to a stimulus and the first muscular reaction

or the movement performed by him/her. From a physiological standpoint reaction time has five components (Zatzyorski, 1980):

1. the appearance of a stimulus at the receptor level,
2. the propagation of the stimulus to the CNS,
3. the transmission of the stimulus through the nervous path and the production of the effector signal,
4. the transmission of the signal from the CNS to the muscle, and
5. the stimulation of the muscle to perform the mechanical work. The most time elapses during the third component.

Reaction time to both simple and complex or choice situations must be made in sports (Dintinman, 1971). Simple reaction is the predetermined, conscious response to a previously known signal performed unexpectedly (i.e., the gun in sprinting). Choice or complex reaction time, on the other hand, refers to the case where an individual is presented with several stimuli and has to choose between them. Obviously, the latter is the slower, and the time delay increases as a result of increasing the number of choices. Reaction time has to be distinguished from reflex time, which is an unconscious response to a stimulus (i.e., the tendon's reflex to an external contact). Similarly, another term of high importance in speed training is movement time, or the time that elapses between the start and finish of a movement. Reaction time is a determinant factor in most sports and may be improved with proper training. Zatzyorski (1980) suggests that the reaction time to a visual stimulus is shorter for trained (0.15–.20 seconds) as opposed to untrained individuals (0.25–0.35 seconds). The reaction time to sonar stimuli is slightly shorter: 0.17–0.27 seconds for untrained, and 0.05–0.07 for international class athletes.

3. ABILITY TO OVERCOME EXTERNAL RESISTANCE   In most sports, power, the force of a muscle contraction or the capacity of an athlete to display force, is one of the determinant factors in performing fast movements. During training and athletic competitions, external resistance to athletes' quick movements exist in the form of gravity, the apparatus, environment (water, snow, wind), and the opponents. In order to defeat such opposing forces the athlete has to improve his/her own power, so that by increasing the force of muscular contraction he/she is capable of increasing the acceleration of his/her skills.

Often a skill must be performed not only quick, but must also be repeated in the same manner for a long period of time. Therefore, in speed training the development of power has to be complemented with the development of muscular endurance which facilitates the display of quick but prolonged work.

4. TECHNIQUE   Speed, frequency of a movement, and reaction time are very often a function of technique. The acquisition of a rational, effective form facilitates the performance of a skill quickly by shortening levers, correctly positioning the center of gravity, and utilizing energy efficiently. In addition, an important role must also be given to the performance of a skill with ease and a high degree of co-ordination as a result of conscious and reflex relaxation of the antagonistic muscles.

5. CONCENTRATION AND WILLPOWER It seems that rapid movements are facilitated by a high degree of power. Consequently, the speed of a movement is determined not only by the mobility and the harmonious character of the nervous processes, but also by the frequency of the nervous impulses, by their precise manner, and by strong concentration. Willpower and strong concentration are important factors for the achievement of high speed. Therefore, the incorporation of special sessions to solicit the athlete's psychological qualities are imperative in speed training.

6. MUSCLE ELASTICITY Muscle elasticity and the ability to relax alternatively the agonistic with antagonistic muscles are important factors in the achievement of a high frequency of movement and correct technique. In addition, joint flexibility represents an important ingredient for performing movement with high amplitude (i.e., long strides) which in any sport requiring fast running is paramount. Consequently, the inclusion of daily flexibility training is imperative, especially for ankles and hips.

Methods Used to Develop Speed

Methodical characteristics

The following three methodological elements, are significant to speed training and will aid in understanding the subsequent material:

1. THE INTENSITY OF STIMULI employed in training, if any improvement is expected, should lie in the range between submaximum and supermaximum. However, a pre-condition to such intensity of training is a good technique. The acquisition of good skill has to be achieved by employing stimuli of intermediate, medium, and sometimes submaximum intensities. An optimal training effect results when training stimuli are optimal, which usually occurs when speed training is not preceded by any other training but the customary warm-up. Furthermore, speed training is more effective when it follows days of rest or low intensity training. Similarly, if such abilities are to be developed in the same training lesson, they have to be planned for the end of the lesson.

2. THE DURATION OF STIMULI like any other component of training has to be optimized. A minimum duration is considered to be the time required to accelerate to maximum speed. If the duration of stimuli is too short and maximum speed is not reached, the only outcome is the improvement of the phase of acceleration but not optimal speed. Both the minimum and maximum duration of stimuli cannot be categorically specified although for sprinters a suggested range is 5–20 seconds. A much longer duration would enhance anaerobic endurance. As in any other component of training, the duration of speed training stimuli is individual, and necessitates a knowledge of the athlete's abilities, especially his/her potential to maintain maximum speed. When, as a result of acquiring fatigue, maximum speed cannot be maintained, the exercise should stop.

3. THE VOLUME OF STIMULI Stimuli employed for speed training are among the most intensive to which the CNS and neuromuscular system is exposed. There-

fore, the optimal volume of stimuli, though individual differences exist, should be low. The volume of stimuli is a function of intensity and the phase of training. Stimuli employed to develop aerobic endurance, present mostly during the preparatory phase, may prevail for up to 90% of the total volume of training, which may range between 10–20 times the competition distance per training lesson. As for stimuli with maximum and supermaximum intensity, they may endure for two-thirds up to double the competition distance (Harre, 1982), with a total volume of work between 5–15 times that of the competition distance.

4. FREQUENCY OF STIMULI The total amount of energy expended during speed training is low as compared to endurance training. The energy expenditure per time unit, however, is much higher than in many other events or sports. This explains why fatigue shows quite quickly in a speed training lesson, which in turn suggests that maximum intensities may be repeated 5–6 times per lesson, 2–4 times per week during the competitive phase (Harre, 1982).

5. REST INTERVALS. Between any repetition of training stimuli, the athlete requires a rest interval which should ensure almost a complete restoration of his/her working capacity, otherwise high intensity work may be impossible to repeat. Therefore, the rest intervals ought to facilitate an optimal recovery, during which LA should be reduced, and O_2 debt restored almost entirely. Lactic acid, which plays a restrictive role in speed training, reaches a maximum level between 2–3 minutes following the termination of a stimulus. On the other hand, the interval should not be so long that the CNS's excitability level fades away (Harre, 1982). Consequently, considering individual characteristics, the rest interval between intensive stimuli may be around 4–6 minutes. If longer intervals are employed (say 12 minutes) a short warm up is recommended so that the CNS excitability level is elevated. Should the coach employ sets of short distance repetitions, then following each set a longer rest interval (6–10 minutes) is desirable.

During normal intervals (2–6 minutes) an active rest such as a light jog or walk is advisable while for intervals that exceed 6 minutes, a combination of passive and active rest is suggested.

Training methods to develop reaction time

1. THE DEVELOPMENT OF SIMPLE REACTION TIME may be achieved by employing the following methods (Zatzyorski, 1980):

a. REPEATED REACTION, which is based on the arousal of an individual following a stimulus, either at the instant of a signal (visual or sonar) or altering the conditions of performing a skill. Examples: repeated starts at varied time lapses between "get set" and the starting signal; changing the direction of travel at the signal of the coach, anticipate and react differently to a known skill or movement performed by an opponent, etc.

b. THE ANALYTIC method refers to performing parts of a skill or technical elements under relieved (easier) conditions, where the reaction to a signal or the speed of movement is facilitated. For instance, an athlete reacts faster to a starting signal if his/her hands are placed on a slightly elevated spot compared to his/her feet. Under such conditions, the athlete's body weight is not equally distributed; therefore he/she may react with the arms faster than under standard conditions.

c. THE SENSOMOTOR method (Gellerstein, 1980) refers to the liaison between reaction time and the ability to distinguish very small time lapses, or micro-intervals of tenths of a second. It is assumed that those who can perceive the time difference between various repetitions are equipped with a good reaction time. Such exercises ought to be performed in three phases:

Phase 1: at the signal of the coach, the athlete performs starts with maximum speed over a short distance (say 5 m). After each repetition the coach tells him/her the performance time.

Phase 2: as above, but the athlete has to estimate the performance time before the coach tells the exact time. In this manner, the athlete learns the perception of his/her reaction time and speed.

Phase 3: at this time the athlete has to perform starts in times previously decided. As a result, the athlete learns to direct his/her reaction time.

The improvement of reaction time depends very much on the athlete's concentration, and to where his/her attention is focused. If the concentration is directed toward the movement to be performed rather than on the starting signal, then the athletes reaction time is shorter. The reaction time is also shorter if for a few tenths of a second prior to the start the muscles are isometrically tense (i.e., press the feet against the starting blocks). And finally, reaction time depends also on the time lapse prior to the starting signal. Zatzyorski (1980) suggests that optimal time between the "get set" and the start itself is 1.5 seconds.

2. THE DEVELOPMENT OF COMPLEX (CHOICE) REACTION is achieved by the development of two abilities:

a. REACTION TO A MOVING OBJECT, which is typical for team sports and those involving two opponents. For instance, when a team mate passes the ball, the receiver has to: see the ball, perceive its direction and speed, select his/her plan of action and perform it. These four elements comprise the hidden reaction, which takes between 0.25–1.0 seconds (Zatzyorski, 1980). The longest period of time is required by the first element, especially if the object is unexpectedly received by a player. The sensory time, the time necessary to perform the other three elements is much shorter: 0.05 seconds. Consequently, during training the coach should stress mostly the first elements, the ability to visualize the moving object. Various exercises where the ball (or actions in boxing, fencing, etc.) is sent toward the player from unexpected positions, directions, or at unexpected speeds, enhances the reaction to moving objects. Also, the use of various games, or playing in smaller areas than standard also improves the reaction to a moving object.

b. SELECTIVE REACTION, or selection of the appropriate motor response from a set of possible responses to the actions performed by partners and/or opponents or even as a result of a quick alteration of the performing environment. For instance, a boxer takes a defence stance, and chooses the best reaction to respond to his/her opponents' actions. Similarity, a downhill skier selects the optimal posture according to the slope and snow. The development of selective reaction ought to be performed in a progressive manner. For instance, in boxing or wrestling, the athlete is first taught a standard reaction to a given technical element. As the athlete automizes the skill, he/her is taught a second variation of this standard reaction.

By now the athlete has to select which of the two variations is more efficient at a given time. At a later phase, new elements are added so that he/she will know all the defence and counter-offence skills appropriate for a given action, and must select the most appropriate and effective one under various conditions.

Zatzyorski (1980) implies that top class athletes react with the same speed for both simple and complex reactions. He suggests that each movement has two phases: 1. the isometric, or the phase when the muscle tone is high, equally distributed in the muscle, and ready to act. 2. the isotonic phase, when the actual movement, or reaction occurs. Often, top class athletes have such a good reaction that they react even before the opponents execute the second phase.

Training methods to develop speed

1. REPETITION is the basic method used in speed training. It refers to repeating a set distance several times at a given speed. Although the sought result is the improvement of speed, this method may also lead to the improvement of a skill or technical element, since only through repetition can a movement become a dynamic stereotype. The repetition method was born to compensate for the fact that maximum speed cannot be maintained for a long period of time. Since a single performance of the competitive distance does not result in performance improvements, the repetition method serves a paramount role. In order to achieve speed improvements, consistency of speed over a given distance, and superior training effects, several repetitions are necessary.

During repetition training the athlete's psyche, will, and conscience are of paramount importance. What should dominate the athlete is a will to surpass his/her maximum speed by overcoming the limiting factor(s). The need of being relaxed is of secondary importance, since relaxation is a normal training outcome. Ozolin (1971) claims that the athlete's thoughts, will, and concentration should be directed towards performing a repetition at maximum speed, since such psychological and mental preoccupation assists the athlete to reach superior speed and neuro-muscular co-ordination. Also, the athlete's main concentration ought to be directed at rapidly performing a dominant movement, which as a result will accelerate the performance of associated movements. For instance, while sprinting an athlete should concentrate on accelerating the arm movement, which, based on a co-ordination between them and the legs, will result in a faster leg movement. And finally, an athlete's concentration also has to be directed toward accomplishing a specific task, like covering a given distance in a given time. This method is applicable not only for speed but also for power training (i.e., reach with legs, or arms an object placed at a optimal height).

Repetition training with maximum speed under standard conditions (i.e., flat ground) could be performed in two ways:

a. the progressive method, where the speed is increased progressively until reaching one's maximum. This is advisable for beginning athletes or for sports where speed is developed through technical and tactical skills.

b. repetitions are performed with maximum speed throughout the training lesson. This method is usually restricted to advanced athletes and those whose techniques are very good.

Two variants of repetition training exist:

a. repetitions with maximum speed under relieved conditions. This method is applicable to various sports, and is performed by reducing the external resistance by: using lighter implements in athletics, shortening the oar's leverage in rowing, reducing the surface of the blade in rowing and the paddle in canoeing, etc. Similarly, external forces are used to achieve a superior speed: run, cycle, row, or paddle with the wind blowing from behind, or cycle behind a motorcycle.

b. repetitions with maximum speed under conditions of added resistance. By employing this method, speed development is achieved indirectly. Thus, the speed of performing an exercise is superior if prior to it, for a short period of time, the athlete does weight training (Florescu et al, 1969), or performs against a resistance (i.e., swim, skate, or run being held back by an anchored rubber cord; row or swim with a collar around the boat or swimming providing extra resistance; ski or skate wearing a heavy vest).

2. THE ALTERNATIVE method refers to a relatively rhythmical alternation of movements (repetitions) with high and low intensities. The addition and reduction of speed is performed progressively, while the phase of maximum speed is maintained steady. Such a method leads not only to increasing the speed but also to perform with ease and relaxation.

3. THE HANDICAP method allows athletes with different abilities to work together, provided that all have equal motivation. When a repetition is performed, each individual is placed in such a way (ahead or back depending on his/her speed potential) that all should reach the finish line, or the end of the acceleration phase, at the same time.

4. RELAYS AND GAMES. Considering their emotional feature both relays and games may be extensively used to improve speed, especially for beginners, or top athletes during the preparatory phase. One advantage is that this method will likely eliminate excessive strain, and provide enjoyment and fun.

The speed barrier

Following the application of standard methods, speed development reaches a certain ceiling, which Ozolin (1971) calls the "speed barrier". By employing the same training methods with a few variations and little excitement, the athlete reaches a level when everything is monotonous, and as a consequence, speed is no longer improved. In order to break the speed barrier new stimuli are required, new excitement has to break the monotony of training, and the employment of standard methods. Novelty in training represents stronger and more exciting stimuli which will result in corresponding physical and psychological alterations.

Among the most efficient methods to surpass the speed barrier are those performed under decreased conditions, where the external resistance is reduced. Thus, inclined running, or with the wind blown from behind gives the athlete a new sense of speed which will lead to further improvements. Under these new conditions the CNS, the neuro-muscular co-ordination, will readapt to the new requirements of performing an exercise. The multiple repetitions of new stimuli will create new and more rapid adaptations resulting in an elevation of the speed ceiling. Decreased load methods have been quite extensively used by Soviet sprinters. The inclined track (2–3°) seems to increase the athlete's speed by 17% over the descending portion and by 13% when the athlete entered the horizontal section (Obbarius, 1971).

However, the employment of decreased load methods should facilitate accelerations which could be reproduced under normal competitive conditions. Further, these methods must be restricted to advanced athletes whose skills are firmly automized, and who as a consequence can handle skillwise supra-rapid accelerations.

FLEXIBILITY TRAINING

The capacity to perform movement over a broad range is known as flexibility, or quite often mobility, and is of significant importance in training. It is a prerequisite to the performance of skills with high amplitude and increases the ease with which fast movements may be performed. The success of performing such movements depends on the joint amplitude, or range of motion, which has to be higher than that required by the movement. Thus, there is a need for a flexibility reserve, which has to be developed in order to be on the safe side.

An inadequate development of flexibility, or no flexibility reserve, may lead to various deficiencies, suggested by Pechtl (1982) as being:

1. learning, or the perfection of various movements is impaired;
2. the athlete is injury prone;
3. the development of strength, speed and co-ordination are adversely affected;
4. the qualitative performance of a movement is limited. (When an individual has a flexibility reserve his/her skills may be performed more rapidly, energetically, easily and expressively.)

Factors Affecting Flexibility

1. Flexibility is affected by the form, type, and structure of a joint. Ligaments and tendons also affect flexibility; the more elastic they are the higher the amplitude of a movement.

2. The muscles passing or being adjacent to a joint also affect flexibility. In any movement, the contraction of a muscle which acts actively (agonists) is paralleled by the relaxation or stretching of the antagonist muscles. The easier the antagonistic muscles yield, the less energy is spent to defeat their resistance. The capacity of a muscle fibre to stretch increases as a result of flexibility training. However, flexibility is often limited, regardless of the amount of training invested, if the antagonistic muscles are not relaxed, or if there is a lack of co-ordination between contraction (agonists) and relaxation (antagonists). Therefore, it is not surprising that individuals with poor co-ordination, or an inability to relax the antagonistic muscles, may have a low rate of flexibility development.

3. Age and sex affect flexibility to the extent that younger individuals and girls as opposed to boys, seem to be more flexible. Maximum flexibility appears to be reached at 15–16 years of age (Mitra and Mogos, 1980).

4. Both general body temperature and specific muscle temperature influence the amplitude of a movement. Wear (1963) found that flexibility increases by 20% following a local warm-up to 115° F (40° C), and decreases by 10–20% by cooling the muscle to 65° F (18° C). Similarly, the amplitude of a movement increases following a normal warm-up since progressive physical activity intensifies blood irrigation of a muscle, making its fibres more elastic. Consequently, performing stretching exercises prior to warming up (which seems to be an accepted theory by many North American athletes) is undesirable to say the least. As indicated by the sequence of exercises to be followed during warm-up (refer to chapter on training lesson) flexibility exercises follow after various types of easy jogging and calisthenics. By the time flexibility movements are performed, the muscle temperature has increased, thus facilitating the muscle fibres to stretch without causing eventual harm. Zatzyorski (1980) investigated the effects of no warm-up, warm-up via physical exertion for 20 minutes, and via hot bath at 40° C for 10 minutes, upon flexibility. The results were as expected. The highest degree of flexibility was achieved following normal warm up and was 21% greater than that resulting from the hot bath, and 89% higher than that resulting from no warm-up at all.

5. Flexibility also varies in accordance with the time of day. The highest amplitude of movement seems to be performed between 10:00 and 11:00, and 16:00 and 17:00, while the lowest likely occurs earlier in the morning (figure 115). The explanation seems to lie with the continuous biological changes (CNS and muscle tone) which occur during the day (Ozolin, 1971).

6. A lack of adequate muscle strength also inhibits the amplitude of various exercises (Pechtl, 1982), thus strength is an important component of flexibility, and should be properly regarded by the coach. However, there are coaches and athletes who hold the impression that strength gains limit flexibility, or that substantial gains in flexibility have a negative influence upon strength. Such theories are based on the fact that the increase in muscle size decreases the joints' flexibility. The capacity of a muscle to stretch, however, can not affect its ability to perform strength movements.

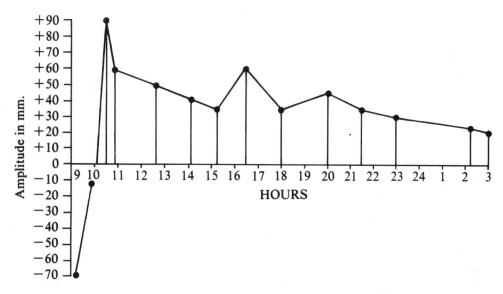

Figure 115.   The range of movement varies with the time of day (from Ozolin, 1971).

Strength and flexibility are compatible because the first depends on the cross section of the muscle while the latter depends on how far a muscle can be stretched. These are two different mechanisms and therefore not eliminating each other. Gymnasts who are both strong and very flexible are genuine proof of this concept. One must remember, though, that an incorrect methodology of developing strength or flexibility may lead to questionable results. Consequently, in order to avoid any surprise, strength training has to be concurrent with flexibility training.

7. Fatigue and emotional state affect flexibility performance very significantly. A positive emotional state has positive influence upon flexibility as compared to depressive feelings. Similarly, flexibility is also affected by fatigue (Mitra and Mogos, 1980) be it a general state of exhaustion, or fatigue accumulated towards the end of a training lesson.

Methods Used to Develop Flexibility

In order to develop flexibility, one of the following three groups of methods may be employed:

1. the active method, comprised of: a. static method; b. ballistic method
2. the passive, and
3. the combined method, or the proprioceptive neuro-muscular facilitation (PNF) (developed by Kabat in 1958).

Before briefly exploring each method, it is rather important to mention that there exists some contradiction regarding which method is more efficient. Many coaches and athletes prefer the static method for the fear that the ballistic one may lead to muscle pull. Although PNF has some limitations in its application, that is, it is applicable only to the hip and shoulder joints, this method is often preferred. However, several authors (Zatzyorski, 1980, Mitra and Mogos, 1980, Pechtl, 1982) viewed both the active and the passive methods as being equally effective. Similarly, comparative studies (Norman, 1973) between the three groups of methods concluded that there is no difference between their effectiveness.

1. THE ACTIVE method is a technique whereby maximum flexibility of a joint is achieved exclusively through an individual's muscular activation. This method refers to both the extent of which the agonistic muscles flex as well as the relaxation and yielding to such a force by the antagonistic muscles. When using the static method two segments of a limb are flexed to the utmost point of flexibility, holding this position for 6–12 seconds. The ballistic method is performed through active swings of one segment of a limb, which is mobile, against another limb which is held still.

2. THE PASSIVE method achieves maximum flexibility through the assistance of a partner, or by employing a weight. In the first case, a partner holds or presses a limb towards its maximum point of flexibility, without the subject's active involvement. This method is applicable for the following joints: ankle, hips, vertebral column, shoulders, and wrist. The use of weights (barbells, dumbbells) is recommended for the improvement of ankle, knee, and shoulder flexibility. It is not suggested for the hips or vertebral column since the weight may exceed one's pain tolerance, or may press two segments of a joint to bend beyond its limits thus resulting in eventual muscle pulls. In any case, the load of weight has to be low, carefully applied, and very progressively increased. Such training must always be done under close supervision.

3. THE COMBINED method (PNF) requires the limb to be actively flexed to the joint's limits, then execute a maximum isometric contraction against the resistance of a partner. The athlete then attempts to lift the limb voluntarily to a more acute angle which is beyond previous limits. Once again, the same routine is performed: the athlete performs a strong isometric contraction against the resistance provided by a partner. The isometric contraction may be performed for 46 seconds with as many repetitions as the athlete can physically tolerate and that is methodologically necessary.

The Methodology of Developing Flexibility

The area of the methodology of training refers to two types of flexibility: general and specific. General flexibility refers to the idea that each athlete has to have a good mobility of all bodily joints, irrespective of specific requirements of a sport or event. Such flexibility is a requirement in training, and it assists the athlete to undertake various training tasks and perform substantial unspecific exercises, or elements from related sports. On the other hand, specific flexibility implies the quality which is sport or joint specific (i.e., specific flexibility of a hurdler differs drastically from that of a butterfly swimmer).

Since the development of flexibility is more easily achieved at a younger age, it has to be part of the training program of each young athlete, irrespective of sport specialization. If a desired degree of flexibility is achieved, it does not mean that flexibility training should be neglected. On the contrary, from this point on, flexibility programs must have the objective of maintaining the achieved level.

Flexibility exercises have to be incorporated in the warm-up part of a training lesson. As already indicated, flexibility exercises have to be preceded by a general warm-up (jogging and calisthenics) of at least 10 minutes. The selection of exercises and their complexity and difficulty has to be related to the athlete's level of preparation and the specifics of the sport. Each selected exercise has to be performed in 3 6 sets of 1-15 repetitions (or up to a maximum of 8 - 120 repetitions per lesson), while during the rest interval relaxation exercises have to be considered (shake the group of muscles that have performed, or execute a light and short massage). Throughout performance the amplitude of an exercise has to be increased progressively and carefully. At first exercises are performed with an amplitude which does not challenge the athlete, increasing it then progressively up to one's limits. From this point on, each repetition should aim to reach this superior limit, and even to further it.

For the ballistic method there is a high variety of exercises: flexions, extensions, and swinging. As suggested by Bompa et al (1981) flexibility may be achieved by employing free exercises, medicine balls, stall bars, and benches. The use of medicine balls (i.e., flex the hips while holding the ball with arms extended) increases the leverage of a limb. As well, it accentuates the momentum, which results in a more effective development of flexibility.

For both the static and PNF methods the athlete tries to take the position of the joints so that the sought flexibility will be enhanced. Then the performer statically maintains the position for 6-12 seconds (6-10 sets) for a maximum total of 100-120 seconds per training lesson for the chosen joints. Such a time requirement may be built up in a progressive manner over a period of time (10-18 months). Throughout the performance of static flexibility the performer should attempt to relax the antagonistic muscles so that they will yield to the pull of the agonists, thus reaching a more acute angle between two limbs.

As far as the periodization of flexibility is concerned, most of it has to be achieved during the preparatory phase. The competitive phase will be regarded as a maintenance period, when the energy and strain placed upon muscle groups will be directed towards specific training. However, in either case, flexibility has to be part of an everyday training program and should be performed towards the end of the warm up. Best results were attained when flexibility was trained twice a day (Ozolin, 1971). Even athletes performing 4-6 training lessons per week still may develop flexibility during early morning training, thus ensuring an adequate flexibility.

CO-ORDINATION TRAINING

Co-ordination is a very complex biomotor ability, closely interrelated with speed, strength, endurance and flexibility. It is of determinant importance, not only for the acquisition and perfection of technique and tactics, but also for their application in unfamiliar circumstances such as the alteration of terrain, equipment and apparatus, light, climate and meteorologic conditions, and opponents. Co-ordination is also solicited in space orientation, when the athlete's body is in unfamiliar conditions (vaulting, various jumps, trampolining) as well as in circumstances when the athlete loses his/her balance (i.e., slippery conditions, landing, quick stops, contact sports).

The level of co-ordination is reflective of an ability to perform movements of various degrees of difficulty very quickly, with great precision and efficiency, and in accordance with specific training objectives. It is considered that an athlete with good co-ordination is capable not only of performing a skill perfectly, but also of rapidly solving a training task to which he/she is unexpectedly exposed.

The physiological basis of co-ordination lies on the co-ordination of the nervous processes of the CNS. A human's body is a unitary whole composed of various organs, systems and functions. The complexity of the organ's and system's functions are constantly regulated and co-ordinated by the CNS. One of the main CNS functions is the selection and execution of a fast and accurate response to a stimulus through the efferent (away from nervous centre) nervous path to certain effectors (Mittra and Mogos, 1980).

Athlete's movements, be they voluntary or reflex, simple or complex, are the result of muscular contractions, which may act to facilitate the movement (the agonists) or inhibit it (the antagonistic muscles). Movements of a more complex nature, which have not yet been automized, are limited by certain factors, especially an unco-ordinated excitation, which might affect the ratio of agonist and antagonist involvement, resulting in an uncontrolled and poorly co-ordinated movement. The regulation off the motor activity implies the differentiation of and reaction to a stimulus with high precision and quickness. As a result of many repetitions of a skill or technical element, the fundamental nervous processes of excitation and inhibition become properly co-ordinated, resulting in stable, well co-ordinated, efficient, and fine motor skills.

The Classification of Co-ordination and Its Degree of Complexity

1. GENERAL CO-ORDINATION governs the capacity to rationally perform various motor skills, irrespective of sport specialization. Every athlete following a multilateral development should acquire an adequate general co-ordination. Since multilateral development must commence with the initiation into a sport, by the time of specialization general co-ordination has to be well assimilated. Under such circumstances general co-ordination represents the basis from which specific co-ordination can be developed.

2. SPECIFIC CO-ORDINATION reflects the ability to perform various movements in the selected sport very quickly, but also with ease, flawlessness and precision. Thus, specific co-ordination is closely linked to the specificity of motor skills, and equips

the athlete with additional abilities in order to perform efficiently in training and competition. Specific co-ordination is achieved as a result of performing, throughout an athletic career, many repetitions of specialized skills and technical elements. Consequently, a gymnast may be extremely co-ordinated in his/her sport, but unco-ordinated in basketball.

Specific co-ordination also incorporates the development of co-ordination combined with other biomotor abilities, according to the characteristics of the selected sport. An athlete may be said to have co-ordinalion of speed like in slalom skiing, freestyle swimming, or hurdling, when he/she is able to perform a skill very fast subject to a specific rhythm and tempo. Co-ordination of speed is dependent upon three main factors(Mitra and Mogos,1980):

1. the time necessary to acquire a complex skill with the specific and required precision, and tempo (rate of speed or rhythm).

2. the time necessary to react to a signal or an opponent's actions. (Since such co-ordination is closely linked to reaction and movement time, their development or a high innate ability is essential to performance), and

3. the time necessary to adapt or adjust individual skills or movements to newly created situations or impeding actions. The degree of precision attained during such quick changes occurring throughout a competition (i.e., team sports, alpine skiing) and the time elapsing from the time of a signal or an opponent's action to an athlete's reaction are often determinant to the final outcome. A high degree of co-ordination of speed is required in order to rapidly and correctly respond to a challenge.

Sports requiring strength necessarily require a development of the co-ordination of strength as exhibited by the performance of wrestlers, weight lifters, hammer throwers and gymnasts. In such sports the precision, ease, and rapidity of a movement or skill requires high co-ordination, strength and power. A less co-ordinated athlete usually performs with exaggerated strain, rigidity, and wasted energy. And finally, co-ordination of endurance implies the ability to perform highly co-ordinated skills over extended periods of time, as in team sports, boxing, and judo. For this particular type of co-ordination, endurance is an essential component, since a lack of it elevates fatigue which, as a result, affects some of the CNS functions including co-ordination.

A skill, according to its pattern, performance over time, and orientation in space, has various degrees of complexity, Zatzyorski (1980) proposed the following criteria to qualify co-ordination:

1. degree of difficulty: a skill, or movement may be easy or difficult. Basically, cyclic skills are less complex, and thus easier to acquire, as opposed to acyclic ones.

Therefore, those learning an acyclic skill may claim to be exposed to more difficult tasks.

2. precision of performance: A movement may be performed with a high degree of precision when it matches the challenge of a motor task in time, angles and dynamics. Usually, a skill performed with high precision is biomechanically sound and physiologically efficient. In other words, it is very economical.

3. duration of acquisition: The complexity of a skill is also associated with the time required to acquire it. A well co-ordinated individual acquires a skill much faster than someone with inferior ability. Similarly, in sports characterized by a rapid alternation of rhythm, situations or performance requirements, as well as a high variety of skills (i.e., team sports, boxing, wrestling) the time span between opponent action and individual reaction to solve a technical or tactical problem, is determinant to the technical result. Under such circumstances the athlete is required to have a high degree of specific co-ordination and adaptability as well.

Factors Affecting Co-ordination

Prior to discussing methods which would lead to the development of co-ordination, it is rather important to outline factors which limit it, since their improvement will result in the improvement of co-ordination. Co-ordination may be limited by one or more of the following factors:

1. THINKING or athletic intelligence. An outstanding athlete does not impress only with amazing and superior skills or tremendous biomotor abilities, but also with his/her thoughts and ways of solving complex and unforeseen motor or tactical problems. This is not possible without a specialized thinking based on years of training and experience. In many sports skillfulness and cleverness are the result of precise, and quick-thinking. A determinant factor is the ability to analyze; to select multiple information collected by motor, visual, and sensory analyzers. Following a quick analysis (separation of the information received by the CNS into elements) the significant information is retained and synthesized to produce the optimal reply. Through a fine co-ordination of contraction and relaxation, the muscle chains are selected and ordered to perform according to the specific time and situation of performance. The quickness of implementing the selected action often may ensure the superiority of an athlete/team over others. On the other hand, the suppleness of thinking is the result of the balance between the fundamental nervous processes (excitation and inhibition) and the rapidity originating from the power of those processes.

2. FINESSE AND PRECISION of THE SENSORY ORGANS, especially the motor analyzers and kinesthetic sensors (the sensors of movements), as well as balance and the rhythm of muscular contraction also represent important factors (Mitra and Mogos, 1980). Through systematic training kinesthesia improves, resulting in an ability to perform more co-ordinated, precise, efficient and quick skills.

3. MOTOR EXPERIENCE, as reflected by a high variety of skills, constitutes a determinant factor in co-ordination ability, or the ability to learn quickly. Co-ordination is developed and perfected through a long process of learning varied skills and technical elements. Such a process, during which the athlete is continually exposed to new situations and environments, enriches motor experience, facilitating a fine coordination.

4. THE LEVEL OF DEVELOPMENT OF OTHER BIOMOTOR ABILITIES like speed, strength, endurance, and flexibility, impact upon co-ordination, since there is

Table 30. Methods used for the development of co-ordination (based on data from Hirtz, 1976, Pechtl, 1982)

No.	Method	Example of Exercises
1	Unusual starting position of an exercise	Various jumping exercises (long, or deep jumps) sideways or backwards.
2	Perform skills with the opposite limb, or in an unusual position	Throw the discuss, put the shot with the opposite arm. Kick the ball, or dribble with the opposite arm. Boxing in a reverse guard.
3	Alter the speed or tempo/rhythm of performing a movement	Increase progressively the tempo. Variations of tempo.
4	Restrict or limit the space of performing skills.	Decrease playing space in team sports
5	Change technical elements or skills	Employ long jumping techniques which are not familiar (i.e., hitch kick). Perform the most comfortable jumping technique over apparatus, or obstacles, with both the normal take off leg and the other one.
6	Increase the difficulty of exercises through supplementary movements	Various shuttle run and relays employing diversified apparatus, objects and tasks to be achieved
7	Combined known with newly formed skills	Parts or routines in gymnastics, figure skating. Play the game having the task of employing a newly learned skill.
8	Increase the opposition or resistance of a partner	Use varied tactical schemes against a team employing an additional player. Play or fight (wrestle) against various teams (partners during the same match).
9	Create unusual performance conditions	Variations of terrain (hilly) for running, or cross country skiing. Row or swim in wavy water. Perform skills with heavy vests. lay on various fields (asphalt, grass, synthetic, wood).
10	Perform related or unrelated sports	Various games or plays. Technical elements or skills of various sports.

such a close relationship among all of them. A poor ability in one area represents a limiting factor on the perfection of co-ordination.

Methods Used to Develop Co-ordination

As compared to other biomotor abilities, for the development of co-ordination there are not too many very specific methods. At the same time, co-ordination is a natural, inherited ability. For those individuals who are not gifted with good co-ordination and who acquire complex skills very slowly, it is rather erroneous to expect tremendous improvements as a result of applying some of the techniques suggested below (table 30).

A successful program of developing co-ordination should rely heavily on the acquisition of a high variety of skills. Consequently, all the young athletes involved in a sport specialization should be exposed to skills of other sports, which would ultimately improve co-ordination. Pechtl (1982) implies that all athletes should be continuously taught new skills from their specific or other sports, otherwise co-ordination and consequently learning capacity decreases. Throughout phases of improvement in co-ordination the coach should try to employ exercises with progressively increased complexity. The complexity and difficulty of a skill may be increased also by employing various conditions, apparatus, and sport equipment (table 30). Exercises for co-ordination should be included in the first part of the training lesson when an athlete is rested, thus having a higher concentration capacity. And finally, co-ordination is most successfully acquired at an early age, when the plasticity (ability to alter and adapt in conformity to the environment) of the nervous system is much higher than in adulthood (Pechtl, 1982).

CHAPTER THIRTEEN

Talent Identification

The process of identifying the most talented athletes to involve them in an organized training program has to be one of the most important concerns of contemporary sports. Everyone can learn to sing, dance, or paint, but very few individuals ever reach a high level of mastery. Therefore, in sports, as in the arts, it is important to discover the most talented individuals, to select them at an early age, to monitor them continuously, and to assist them to climb to the highest level of mastery.

In the past, and even today in most western countries, the involvement of a youngster in a sport is based mostly on tradition, ideals, desire to take part in a sport according to its popularity, parental pressure, a high school teacher's specialty, the proximity of sport facilities, etc. For East European training specialists, such methods are not satisfactory anymore since individuals who, for example, had a natural talent for distance running, often ended up as mediocre sprinters. Obviously, the outcome rarely led to high performance.

As far as elite athletes are concerned, a coach's work and time has to be invested in those individuals who possess superior natural abilities. Otherwise, the coach's talent, time and energy are wasted, or, at best, produce mediocrity. Therefore, the main objective of talent identification is to identify and select those athletes who have the greatest abilities for a chosen sport.

Talent identification is not one of the newest concepts in athletics, however, not much is formally done about it, especially in the Western World. In the late 1960's and early 1970's, most East European countries established specific methods for identifying potentially high class athletes. Some of the selection procedures used were discovered and directed by scientists who then advised the coach which youngsters had the required abilities for a sport. The results were more than dramatic. Quite a few medalists in the 1972, 1976, 1980, and 1984. Olympic Games, particularly from former East Germany, were scientifically selected. The same may be said for Bulgaria in 1976, almost 80 per cent of its medalists were the result of a thorough talent identification process.

In Romania in 1976, a group of scientists and rowing specialists selected young girls for rowing. The initial 100 girls were selected from 27,000 teenagers. By 1978, the groups had been reduced to 25, most of whom made the team for the Moscow Olympics. The result: 1 gold, 2 silver, and 2 bronze medals. Another group selected in the late 1970's produced five gold and one silver at the 1984 Olympic Games in Los Angeles, and 9 medals at the 1988 Seoul Olympic Games.

The talent identification process has to be a continuous preoccupation of training specialists and coaches in order to further its advances and to improve the psychobiological criteria with which to discover more talented individuals for high performance athletics.

The utilization of scientific criteria in the process of talent identification has several advantages:

1. It substantially reduces the time required to reach high performance by selecting individuals who are gifted in a given sport.
2. It eliminates a high volume of work, energy, and talent on the part of the coach. The coach's training effectiveness is enhanced by training primarily those athletes with superior abilities.
3. It increases the competitiveness and the number of athletes aiming at and reaching high performances levels. As a result, there will be a stronger and more homogeneous national team capable of better international performance.
4. It increases an athlete's self confidence since one's dynamics of performance are known to be more dramatic compared to other athletes of the same age who did not go through the selection process.
5. It indirectly facilitates the application of scientific training, since sports scientists who assist in talent identification can be motivated to continue to monitor the athletes' training.

TALENT IDENTIFICATION METHODS

In training, there are two basic methods of selection, natural and scientific.

1. NATURAL SELECTION is considered the normal approach, the natural way of developing an athlete in a sport. It assumes an athlete enrolls in a sport as a result of local influence (school tradition, parents' wishes, or peers). However, the performance evolution of athletes determined by natural selection depends, among other factors, on whether the individual, by coincidence, happens or doesn't happen to take part in a sport for which he/she is talented in. Therefore, it may often occur that an individual's performance evolution is very slow, mostly because the selection of the ideal sport was incorrect.
2. SCIENTIFIC SELECTION is the method by which a coach selects prospective youngsters who have proven that they possess natural abilities for a given sport Thus, compared to individuals identified through the natural method, the time required to reach high performance for those selected scientifically is much

shorter. For sports in which height and/or weight is a requirement for instance (e.g., basketball, volleyball, football, rowing, throwing events), scientific selection should be strongly considered. Similarly, the same may be said for other sports in which speed, reaction time, co-ordination and power are dominant (e.g., sprinting, judo, hockey, jumping events in athletics). With the assistance of sport scientists, such qualities can be detected. As a result of scientific testing, the most talented individuals are scientifically selected or directed to an appropriate sport.

CRITERIA USED FOR TALENT IDENTIFICATION

High performance athletics requires specific biological profiles of athletes with outstanding biomotor abilities and strong physiological traits. The science of training has made impressive steps forward in the past decades, which is one of the main reasons for constant improvements in athletic performance. Other dramatic improvements have also been made in quantity and quality of training.

However, if an individual involved in sports has a biological handicap, or lacks the necessary abilities for a given sport, then even an excessive amount of training cannot overcome the initial lack of natural ability in a particular sport. Therefore, scientific talent identification is vital to high performance athletics.

Those not selected for high performance athletics are not excluded. They can take part in recreational programs where they can fulfill their physical and social needs or even participate in competitions.

Optimal training requires optimal criteria for talent identification. The objectivity and reliability of selection criteria has been the preoccupation of several authors (Radut, 1967; Mazilu and Focseneanu, 1976; and Dragan, 1979, etc.). Not necessarily in the order of importance, some of the main criteria are:

1. HEALTH, an absolute necessity for everyone participating in training. Therefore, before being accepted into a club, each youngster must have a thorough medical examination. The physician should recommend, and the coach should select for training, only very healthy individuals.

During the examination, medical and testing specialists should also observe whether the candidates have physical or organic malfunctions and make recommendations accordingly. For dynamic sports (e.g., hockey, basketball, track and field, swimming, boxing) an individual with a malformation should not be selected, but for sports with static characteristics (e.g., shooting, archery, bowling) such a discrimination should be more liberal. Similarly, the physiological status of an individual, i.e., the ability to move arms, legs, etc., should also play a role in talent identification, since physiological disparities can play a restrictive role. Once again, the eventual discrimination between candidates has to be correlated with the physiological needs and specifics of a sport.

2. BIOMETRIC QUALITIES, or anthropometric measurements of an individual, are important asset for several sports and, therefore must be considered among the

main criteria for talent identification. Height and weight, or the length of limbs, often play a dominant role in certain   sports. However, during the early stage of talent identification, which for some sports is performed at the age 4–6 (e.g., gymnastics, figure skating, swimming), it is rather difficult to predict the dynamics of an individual's growth and development. Therefore, during the primary phase of talent identification, one has to look mostly for an harmonious physical development. This can be done by examining the leg joint, hip and shoulder widths and the ratio between the latter two.

At a later age (teens), hand plates (growth plates in the wrist region) and hand radiography (X-ray) techniques may be used to test whether growth is complete. If the tester concludes growth is complete, the coach may make decisions as to whether the height of a given athlete is optimal for a particular sport.

3. HEREDITY, a very complex biological phenomenon, often plays an important role in training. Children tend to inherit their parent's biological and psychological characteristics, although education, training, and social conditioning, inherited qualities may be slightly altered.

The view on the role of heredity in training is neither uniform nor unanimous. Radut (1967) regards heredity as having an important, but not absolute role in training, while Klissouras et al (1973) consider improvements in physiological capabilities will ultimately be limited by the athlete's genetic potential. The latter authors imply that systems and functions are genetically determined: the lactic acid system to the extent of 81.4 percent, heart rate, 85.9 and maximal VO_2, 93.4 percent.

Muscle Fiber Distribution

The proportion of red and while muscle fibers in humans seems to be genetically determined. Similarly, the metabolic function of these fibers also differs. The red, or slow-twitch fibers, have a higher myoglobin (acts as a store for oxygen which is carried by the blood to the working cell) and, therefore, are biochemically better equipped for aerobic (endurance) work.

On the other hand, the white or fast-twitch fibers have a high content of glycogen (carbohydrate), and are better for anaerobic or short and intensive types of exercises (Gollnick et al, 1973). The percent of muscle fibers cannot be altered but extensive, specific training may increase the capabilities of muscle fibers and change their bio-chemical structure.

Based on the above, an athlete who inherits a higher proportion of red fibers may have a higher probability of performing successfully in sports in which endurance is a requirement. Similarly, when the white fibers are dominant, the athlete is naturally equipped for sports in which intensity (speed and/or power) prevails.

Biopsy, the technique of extracting muscle tissue and then counting the proportion of two fibers, can be used to determine those groups of sports in which an individual is likely to perform most successfully. This knowledge can then be coupled with psychological and biometric characteristics and the candidate can be directed to sports for which he/she is best equipped.

4. SPORT FACILITIES AND CLIMATE play a restrictive role in the kind of sports for which athletes are selected. Therefore, regardless of an individual's qualities for a given sport (e.g., canoeing), if the natural conditions (water) or facilities do not exist, an athlete might better practice a sport for which he/she is not as talented.

5. THE AVAILABILITY OF SPECIALIST, or the level of knowledge of the coach in the area of talent identification and testing, also restricts the selection of candidates. The more numerous and sophisticated the scientific methods used for talent identification, the higher the probability of discovering superior talents for particular sports. Universities, which are well-equipped with testing facilities and scientific specialists, are grossly underutilized both for the scope of selection, and for the monitoring of athletes' training programs. A coach cannot cope with high athletic demands alone. The co-operation between qualified personnel, sport scientists and coaches is vital, if dramatic progress in training is attempted.

THE PHASES OF TALENT IDENTIFICATION

Comprehensive talent identification is not solved in one attempt, but is performed over a few years in three main phases:

1. THE PRIMARY PHASE OF TALENT IDENTIFICATION, in most cases, occurs during pre-puberty (3–10 years). It is dominated mostly by a physician's examination of a candidate's health and general physical development and is designed to detect any body malfunctions or eventual disease.

The biometric portion of this examination could focus on three main concepts:

(a) discovering physical deficiencies which may play a restrictive role in a candidate's sports endeavours;

(b) determining a candidate's level of physical development through simple means, such as the ratio between height and weight; and

(c) detecting eventual genetic dominants (e.g., height) so children may be directed toward those groups of sports in which they might specialize at a later age.

Considering the early age at which this primary phase is completed, it furnishes the examiner with only general information about a child. Definite decisions are premature since candidates' future dynamics of growth and development are still relatively unpredictable. However, for sports like swimming, gymnastics, and figure skating in which comprehensive training has already begun at a young age, the primary identification phase should be thoroughly performed.

2. THE SECONDARY PHASE OF TALENT IDENTIFICATION is performed during and after puberty, between the ages of 9–10 for gymnastics, figure skating and swimming, 10–15 for girls and 10–17 for boys for other sports. (Dragan, 1979). It represents the most important phase of selection. This phase is used with teenagers who have already experienced organized training.

Techniques used in secondary selection must assess the dynamics of the biometric and physiological parameters, since the body should already have reached a certain level of adaptation to the specifics and requirements of a given sport. Consequently, the health examination should be very detailed and aim at detecting obstacles to performance increase (e.g., rheumatism, hepatitis, acute renal disease).

The critical moment for a child in the puberty phase is when dramatic growth changes occur (i.e., when lower limbs grow visibly). Therefore, along with the examination of general physical development, specialized training on the athlete's growth and development has to be considered. Popovici (1979) implies that intensive, heavy load, strength training performed at a very early age limits growth (height) by hastening the closure of the fibrous cartilage of the bones (i.e., premature closure of long bones).

For some sports (e.g., throwing events, rowing, wrestling, and weightlifting), a wide shoulder width (bi-acromial diameter) is significant since strong shoulders are closely related to an individual's strength, or at least represent a good frame on which to develop strength.

As a guideline, Popovici (1979) suggests that at 15 years, girls should have a biacromial diameter of 38 cm and boys at 18 should have one of 46 cm. Popovici also claims both the length of the foot and the arch are important in some sports (i.e., a flat-footed individual is limited in jumping, tumbling, or running).

Similarly, joint looseness may also affect performance in sports in which strength is critical (e.g., wrestling, weightlifting). Consequently, anatomical and physiological malformations, or genetic inadequacies, should be considered important talent identification elements.

For athletes going through a training program based on natural selection, all of the above aspects affect an individual's performance evolution and, therefore, must be of continuous concern to a coach.

During the secondary phase of talent identification, sports psychologists start to play a more important role by performing comprehensive psychological testing. Each athlete's psychological profile has to be compiled to reveal whether he/she possesses the psychological traits required for a given sport. These tests will also help decide what future psychological emphasis might be necessary.

3. THE FINAL PHASE OF TALENT IDENTIFICATION primarily concerns national team candidates. It has to be very elaborate, reliable, and highly correlated with the specifics and requirements of a sport.

Among the main factors one must examine are: the athlete's health, his/her physiological adaptation to training and competing, his/her ability to cope with stress and most importantly, his/her potential for further performance improvements.

An objective assessment of the above is facilitated by periodic medical, psychological and training tests. Data from these tests have to be recorded and compared to illustrate their dynamics from the primary phase throughout an athletic career.

For each test, an optimal model should be established and each individual compared to that model. Only outstanding candidates should be considered for the national team.

GUIDELINES FOR TALENT IDENTIFICATION CRITERIA

The criteria for talent identification, including tests, standards, and the optimal model, have to be sport specific. In many sports, especially in those in which endurance or a high volume of work are crucial, the final selection has to be based not only on the athlete's working capacity, but also on the body's ability to recover between training sessions. Dragan (1979) identifies the following testing criteria:

1. Athletics (Track and Field):

   a. Sprinting:
      - reaction time (and the ability to repeat reactions continuously)
      - neuro-muscular excitability
      - co-ordination and good muscular relaxation capacity
      - ability to cope with stress
      - the height/trunk ratio, long legs

   b. Middle distance events:
      - anaerobic power and max. VO_2/kg of body weight
      - lactic acid concentration (the level of excess lactic acid in the blood following heavy exercise) and the O_2 deficit
      - the ability to cope with stress
      - high concentration span capacity and the ability to maintain it for a prolonged time

   c. Distance running/walking:
      - VO_2 max/kg of body weight
      - cardiac volume
      - high resistance to fatigue, perseverance, motivation

   d. Jumping events:
      - reaction time and explosive strength
      - tall athletes with long legs
      - high anaerobic power
      - ability to cope with stress

      - high concentration span and the ability to maintain it for a prolonged time

   e. Throwing events:
      - tall and muscular individuals
      - high anaerobic power
      - large bi-acromial diameter
      - reaction time
      - high concentration span and the ability to maintain it for a prolonged time

2. Alpine Skiing:
   - courage
   - reaction time
   - co-ordination
   - high anaerobic power

3. Basketball:
   - tall, long arms
   - high anaerobic power
   - high aerobic capacity
   - coordination
   - resistance to fatigue and stress
   - tactical intelligence, and cooperative spirit

4. Boxing:
   - great concentration span
   - courage
   - reaction time
   - co-ordination and tactical intelligence
   - high aerobic capacity
   - high anaerobic power

5. Cycling:
   —high aerobic capacity
   —cardiac volume (medium) and high
     V0$_2$ capacity
   —ability to cope with stress
   —perseverance

6. Cross-country skiing:
   —high aerobic capacity
   —tall individuals
   —perseverance, staunchness
   —resistance to fatigue and stress

7. Diving:
   —vestibular balance (inner ear)
   —courage
   —co-ordination
   —great concentration span
   —ability to cope with stress

8. Fencing:
   —reaction time
   —co-ordination
   —tactical intelligence
   —resistance to fatigue and stress
   —high anaerobic and aerobic capacity

9. Figure Skating:
   —co-ordination, aesthetic appeal
   —vestibular balance
   —harmonious physical development
   —high anaerobic and aerobic capacity

10. Gymnastics:
    —co-ordination, flexibility, power
    —vestibular balance
    —perseverance
    —capacity to cope with stress, emotional
      balance
    —high anaerobic power
    —short-medium height

11. Hockey/lacrosse:
    —tall, long arms, large bi-acromial
      diameter

    —tactical intelligence, courage,
      cooperative spirit
    —high aerobic and anaerobic
      capacity
    —strong, robust

12. Judo:
    —co-ordination
    —reaction time
    —tactical intelligence
    —long reach and large bi-acromial
      diameter

13. Kayak-canoeing:
    —large bi-acromial diameter,
      long arms
    —concentration span
    —high anaerobic and aerobic
      capacity
    —resistance to fatigue and stress

14. Rowing:
    —high anaerobic and aerobic
      capacity
    —co-ordination, concentration span
    —tall, long limbs, large biacromial
      diameter
    —resistance to fatigue and stress

15. Rugby:
    —tall, robust, large bi-acromial
      diameter
    —courage, staunchness
    —tactical intelligence, and coopera-
      tive spirit
    —high aerobic capacity
    —speed and power

16. Speedskating:
    a. short distance
    —reaction time, power
    —co-ordination
    —high anaerobic and aerobic
      capacity
    —tall, long legs

b. long distance
—high aerobic capacity
—VO$_2$ max/kg of body weight
—tall, long legs

17. Shooting:
—visual-motor co-ordination
—reaction time
—concentration span, resistance to fatigue
—emotional balance
etc.

18. Soccer:
—co-ordination, co-operative spirit
—resistance to fatigue and stress
—high anaerobic and aerobic capacity
—tactical intelligence

19. Swimming:
—low body density
—long arms and big feet, large bi-acromial diameter
—high anaerobic and aerobic capacity

20. Volleyball:
—tall, long arms, and large bi-acromial diameter
—high anaerobic and aerobic capacity
—resistance to fatigue and stress
—tactical intelligence, and cooperative spirit

21. Water Polo:
—tall, large bi-acromial diameter
—high anaerobic and aerobic capacity
—tactical intelligence and co-operative spirit
—resistance to fatigue and stress

22. Weightlifting:
—power
—large bi-acromial diameter
—co-ordination
—resistance to fatigue and stress

23. Wrestling:
—co-ordination, and reaction time
—high anaerobic and aerobic capacity
—tactical intelligence
—large bi-acromial diameter, long arms

THE MAIN FACTORS FOR TALENT IDENTIFICATION

In an attempt to discern the main factors for performance and talent identification, Kunst and Florescu (1971) identified:

1. motor capacity,
2. psychological capacity, and
3. biometric qualities (including body somatotype and anthropometric measurements).

Although these three represent the main factors for all sports, their emphasis differs with each sport. A more effective talent identification system for a sport should start with the characterization of the sport, its specifics, and then, based on this analysis, isolate the main factors for selection.

For sport characterization, each of the three factors has to be expressed as a percentage to reflect their relative influence on success. For example, good performance in high jumping depends on the following three factors, with the relative emphasis of each being expressed as a percentage:

Motor capacity 50%   Psychological Capacity 10%   Biometric 40%.

Furthermore, each factor must be subdivided into the three main elements which incorporate it, with their relative importance expressed as a percentage as well. Thus, the main three elements and their emphasis in training for the motor capacity of a high jumper are:

Strength 45%   Jumping Power 35%   Coordination 20%

Knowing the characteristics of the spon and the relative importance of them, it is then important to determine the main factors for talent identification and the emphasis to be placed on each element. When the three elements of each factor are expressed they must be very specific and stated in order of importance. Figure 116 illustrates the characteristics of wrestling, while figure 117 suggests the main factors for talent identification for wrestling.

By comparing the main factors for performance with those for talent identification (Figures 116, 117), the reader realizes sequence and emphasis differ. For the sequence of the performance factors, the motor capacity prevails, but this is not the case for talent identification. In the latter, psychological capacity is considered the most important.

In talent identification, for someone uninitiated to wrestling, it is more important to possess the main psychological traits and the desire to wrestle, since a beginner may hardly be expected to have developed the motor capacity. Furthermore, of the three dominant elements in motor capacity, co-ordination and speed (which is one of the two components of power), are more likely than endurance to have been inherited

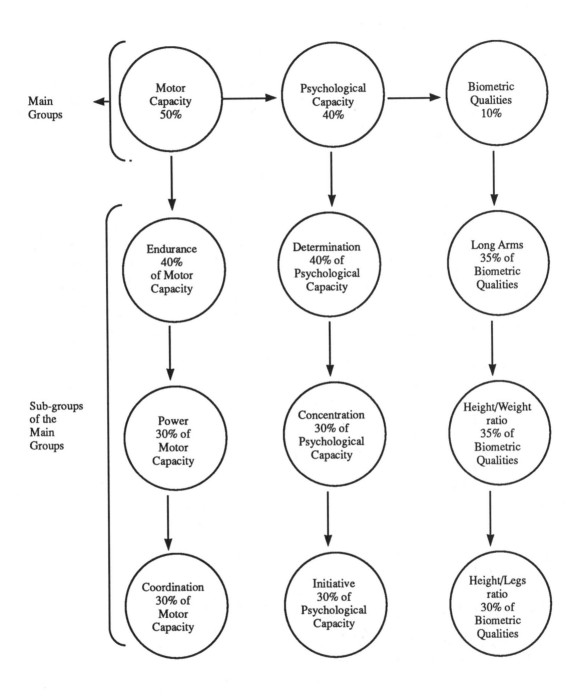

Figure 116. The main factors for performance in wrestling (from Kunst and Florescu, 1971).

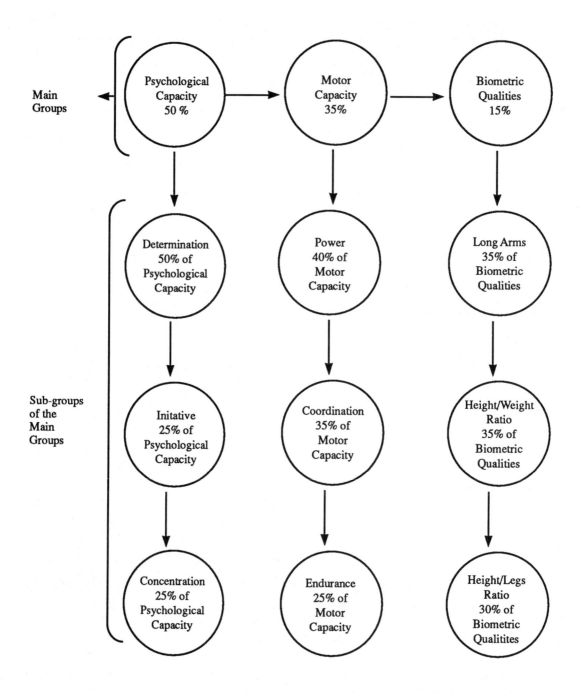

Figure 117. The main factors for the talent identification for wrestling. Note the differences from Figure 116 (from Kunst and Florescu, 1971).

Table 31. Biometric measurements for men's rowing (Radut, 1973).

Ranking	Test 1 Height, arms above head (cm)	Test 2 Arm Span (cm)	Test 3 Height of upper body (cm)	Test 4 Length of legs (cm)	Test 5 Shoulder width (cm)	Test 6 Reach from crouch position (cm)	Test 7 Specific amplitude (cm)	Test 8 Body Weight (kg)
I	249	201	73.5	121	53.5	48.5	169	96
II–III	246	199	70.8	120	52.1	45.5	165	93.5
IV–VI	244	197	68.9	119	51.7	45.0	164	92
VII-XII	242	195	65.7	117	49.9	44.4	161	87.2

as natural abilities. Through training, an athlete can make more dramatic gains in endurance than in co-ordination, or even power (the speed component).

Finally, the importance of biometric qualities has to be viewed relative to the specifics of the sport. While for some sports some qualities may be crucial, (e.g., height in basketball or the ratio between height and weight in rowing), for other sports the ratio between various parts of the body and a harmonious development are important, but not critical. (e.g., figure skating).

In each sport, there has to be an ideal, accepted model for both the main factors of performance and talent identification. During the latter stages of athlete development, with the assistance of sport scientists, a coach can test all the candidates and compare their qualities with the ideal model. Those who are closer to the model can be selected for the high performance group.

A more scientific model can also be developed, but in this case, the role of sport scientists is very important. An optimal biometric model based on athlete measurements taken at various Olympic Games and world championships has been developed for men's rowing by Radut (1973). Radut found certain biometric measurements correlate very highly with the athlete's final standing in top championships. Consequently, the abilities of candidates for elite rowing clubs were compared with the model (table 31 and figure 118), and those with the highest scores were selected.

The eight biometric tests considered the most relevant for rowing were:

1. standing, back against the wall, arms above the head. The score was considered the average of the two highest reaches performed with the tips of the longest fingers.
2. standing, back against the wall, arms extended laterally at shoulder height.

3. sitting, legs extended, back against the wall. Measure the distance from the floor to above the shoulder joint (the acromion).

4. seated, back against the wall, legs extended. Measure the distance from the wall to the flat of the foot.

5. shoulder width, measured as the distance between the two deltoid muscles.

6. standing on a measuring bench, take a crouch position (both heels on the bench) and reach as low as possible. Measure the lowest point reached.

7. specific amplitude: the length of the legs plus the additional length from the knee to the foot.

8. the body weight in kilograms.

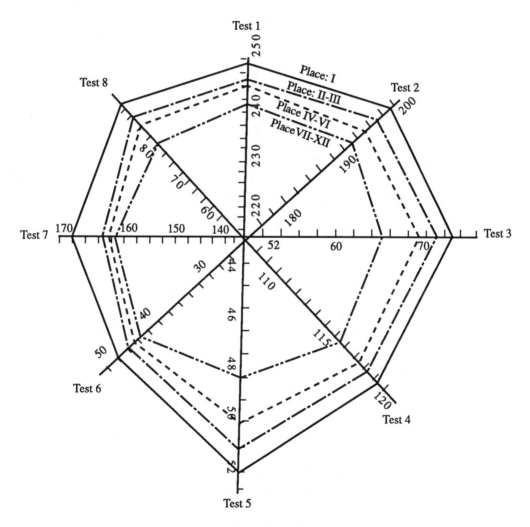

Figure 118. The model of biometric measurements for men's rowing (from Radut, 1973).

The scores of the above tests were plotted in an octagonal shape (Figure 118), and the scores of any candidate for an elite program may be compared with those ranking in the top 12 in the world. The closer to the outside edge of the octagon, the better.

Optimal models for selection may also be compiled for the physiological and bio-motor abilities. Examples of such models are presented in figure 119. The examples represent women's rowing and are based on data from world class athletes. Once again, a candidate's scores have to be compared with the optimal model, and only those whose scores produce, in this case, an octagonal shape, will be selected for elite class programs.

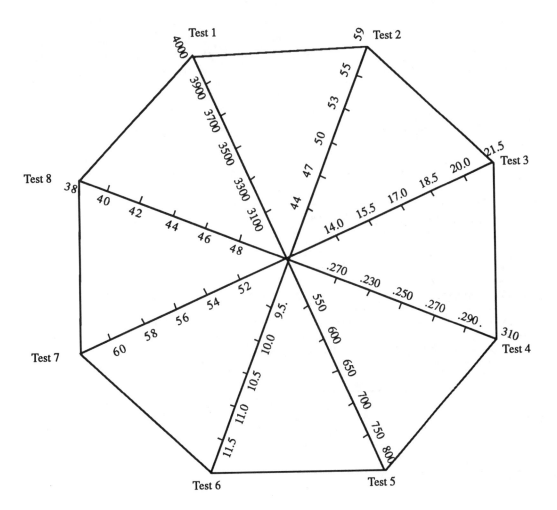

Figure 119. An optimal model of talent identification for women's rowing (from Szogy, 1976).

A close co-operation between coaches, training specialists, and sports scientists can produce such models for each sport. Obviously, the outcome of such co-operation will be a more scientific talent identification system for elite athletes. This should result in dramatic increases in performance.

While technological sophistication in testing and monitoring athletes' training progress seems to be a constant and essential feature of today's athletic world, talent identification must be considered an attribute of at least equal importance.

The human material—the talent with which the coach works—often makes the difference between international or provincial level performance. Talented kids are everywhere. One just has to develop the means to identify them and then expose them to well-planned and methodical training. Although the coach recognizes this necessity he cannot do it alone. It is the job of sport scientists to identify the dominant parameters, develop the model, and then apply it to identify talented individuals to be recruited for a sport. Only a combined effort can result in better talent identification criteria, superior training methods and sophisticated testing and training monitoring. The final outcome will be better results in international meets.

Athlete's name: _____ Club: _____ Date: _____

Height: _____ Weight: _____ Age: _____ Occupation: _____

Test #	TESTS	Symbol	Units	World Ranking			Candidate's scores
				I	II–III	IV–VI	
1	VO₂max	VO₂max	ml	4100	3900	3700	
2	VO₂max/kg	VO₂/kg	ml/kg	59	56	53	
3	VO₂max/heart rate	VO₂/HR	ml	21.5	20.0	18.5	
4	VO₂max/HR/kg	VO₂/HR/kg	ml/kg	.310	.290	.270	
5	Cardiac volume	CV	ml	800	750	700	
6	Cardiac volume/Body wt.	CV/kg	ml/kg	12.0	11.5	11.0	
7	Aerobic metabolic rate	Aerobic	%	62	62	62	
8	Anaerobic metabolic rate	Anaerobic	%	38	38	38	

REFERENCES

1. Agnevik, G.; Saltin, B. Moto Cross *Idrottfysiologi*, Rapport Nr. 3 Framtidern, 1967.
2. Alderman, R. B Psychological Behavior in Sport Philadelphia, W. B. Saunders Co. 1974.
3. Alexeev, M. A. About the physiological mechanisms of developing motor skills based on I. P. Pavlov's findings. Moskrow, *Teoria i praktika phyzicheskoi kulturi*, 12, 1950.
4. Asmussen, E. Deflective exercises. *Legemsovlser*, 2. 25–35, 1936.
5. Asmussen, E.; Boje, O. Body temperature and capacity of work. *Acta Physiol. Scand:* 10: 1–23, 1945.
6. Astrand, P. O.; Saltin, B.: Maximal Oxygen Uptake and Heart Rate in Various Types of Muscular Activity. *J. Appl. Physiol.,* 16, 1961.
7. Astrand, P. O.; Rodahl, K. Textbook of Work Physiology. New York, McGraw-Hill Book Co. 1970 and 1985.
8. Barnard, R.; Gardner, G.; Diaco N.; MacAlpern, R.; Hedman, R. Cardiovascular responses to sudden strenuous exercise, heart rate, blood pressure and ECG. *J. Appl. Physiol.* 34(6); 833–837, 1973.
9. Baroga, L. Tendinte contemporane in metodologia dezvoltarii fortei. (Contemporary trends in the methodology of strength development). *Educatia Fizica si Sport,* 6: 22–36, 1978.
10. Belinovich, V. V. Obuchenie v fisycheskom vospitanii. (The teaching process in physical education). Moskow, *Physkultura i Sport,* 1958.
11. Bensson, H.; Klipper, M. Z. The Relaxation Response. New York, William Morrow and Co. In. 1976.
12. Berger, R. A. Effects of varied weight training programs on strength. *Research Quarterly,* 33: 168, 1962.
13. Bergstrom, J., L. Hermansen, E. Hultman, and B. Saltin. Diet, muscle glycogen and physical performance. *Acta. Physio. Scand.* 71:140–150, 1967.
14. Bernstein, D. A.; Borkovec, T. D. Progressive relaxation training. Champaign, Ill. Research Press, 1973.
15. Bielz, M. Rating the effort in high performance rowing. Ph.D. Thesis, Institute of Physical Culture, Leipzig, 1976.
16. Bigland-Ritchie. B. EMG/Force Relations and Fatigue of Human Voluntary Contractions. *Exercise and Sport Sciences Reviews.* Editor, Doris Miller. The Franklin Institute Press. Volume 9, 75–117, 1981.
17. Bigland-Ritchie. B., R. Johansson, O. C. J. Lippold, and J. J. Woods. Contractile Speed and EMG Changes During Fatigue of Sustained Maximal Voluntary Contractions. *J. Neurophysiol.* 50(1): 313–324, 1983.
18. Bigland-Ritchie, B., Dawson, N., Johansson, R., and Lippold, Reflex Origin for the Slowing of Motorneuron Firing Rates in Fatigue of Human Voluntary Contractions. *Journal of Physiology,* 379: 451–459, 1986.
19. Binkhorst, R. A.; Hoofd, L.; Vissers, C. A. Temperature and free-velocity relationship of human muscle. *J. Appl. Physiol.* 41: 471–75, 1977.
20. Blohin, I.–G. 1965 In: Gandelsman and Smirnov: Fisyologischeskie osnovi metodiki sportivnoi trenirovki (The physiological foundations of training) Moskow, *Physkultura i Sport,* 1970.
21. Bompa, T. Antrenamentul in periooda pregatitoare (Training methods during the preparatory phase). Bucharest, *Caiet Pentre Sporturi Nautice* 3, 22–24, 1956.
22. Bompa, T. Antrenamentul in diferite perioade de pregatire (Training content in different stages of preparation). Timisoara, 1960.

23. Bompa, T. Analiza fiziologica a pistelor din campionatul mondial de canotaj, 1964. (A physiological analysis of the rowing races during the 1964 world Rowing championships). Timisoara, the XIth Research Conference, 1964.

24. Bompa, T. Criteria pregatirii a unui plan depatra ani (Criteria of setting up a four year plan). Bucharest, Cultura Fizica si Sport, 2, 11–19, 1968 (a).

25. Bompa, T. Individualizarea: un factor psihologic de antrenament. (Individualization: a psychological factor of training). International Symposium on Sports Psychology, Moskow, 1968.

26. Bompa, T. Unele aspecte ale refacerii psihologice dupa efortful de competitie. (Some aspects of the athletes psychological recovery following the strain of performance). Conference for research in sports psychology, Bucharest, 1969.

27. Bompa, T. Planul psihologic al atletilor in competitie. (Athlete's psychological plan for competition). Symposium of Psychology of Coaching, Brasov, 1970.

28. Bompa, T. The national rowing squad plan for the 1976 Olympic games. Montreal, CAAO. 1975.

29. Bompa, T. Theory and Methodology of training. Toronto, York University, 1976.

30. Bompa, T. The Model of the National Rowing Team plan for the 1980 O. G. St. Catharines, 1979.

31. Bompa, T.; Hebbelinck, M.; Van Gheluwe, B. A biomechanical analysis of the rowing stroke employing two different oar grips. The XXI World Congress in Sports Medicine, Brasilia, Brazil, 1978.

32. Bompa, T.; Bompa Tamana,; Zivic, T. Fitness and body development exercises. Dubuque, Iowa, Kendall/Hunt Publishing Co., 1981.

33. Brooks, G. A., and T. D. Farley. *Exercise Physiology*. MacMillan Publishing Company. New York, 1985.

34. Brooks, G. A., and T. Fahey. *Exercise Physiology: Human Bioenergetics and its Applications*. Macmillan Publishing Coompany, 1985.

35. Brouha, L. Training specificity of muscular work. *Rev. Canad. Biol.* 4: 144, 1945.

36. Bucher, C. A. Foundations of physical education. Saint Louis, The C. V. Mosby Co., 1972.

37. Bucur, I. C. Metode si mijloace utilizate pentru revenirea atletilor. (Techniques and methods employed for athlete's recovery). Timisoara, CNEFS, 1979.

38. Bucur, I. C.; Birjega, M Sinteza cursului de educatie fizica (synopsis of the theory of physical education). Timisoara, I. P. B. T. 1973.

39. Carlile, I. Effect of preliminary passive warming-up on swimming performance. *Res. Quant.* 27: 143–151, 1956.

40. Catina, V., Bompa, T., Antrenamentul stiintific al atletilor. (A scientific approach to athlete's training). Medical Research Symposium, Cluj, 1968.

41. Cercel, D. Posibilitatile de aplicare a antrenamentului modelat in handbal (Means of applying modeling in training handball). *Educatia Fizica si Sport,* 53, 13–18, 1974.

42. Chariev, R. M. A comparison of two variants of training structures under the conditions of weekly competitions. Moskow, *Scientific Research Collection,* 63–80, 1974.

43. Chudinov, V. I. Specific exercises for the development of the motor abilities. Moskow, *Teoria i praktika physicheskoi* kulturi, 11, 1960.

44. Conlee, R. K. Muscle glycogen and exercise endurance: a twenty year perspective. *Exercise and Sport Sciences Reviews,* 15:1–28, 1987.

45. Costill, D. L., Coyle, E. F., Fink, W. F., Lesmes, G. R, and Witzmann, F. A. Adaptations in skeletal muscle following strength training. *J. Appl. Physiol.* 46(1): 96–99, 1979.

46. Counsilman, J. Handling the stress and staleness problems of the hard training athletes. Toronto, International Symposium on the Art and Science of Coaching. Vol. I, 15–22, 1971.

47. Cratty, B. J. Movement behaviour and motor learning. Philadelphia, Lea and Febiger, 1967.

48. Cratty, B. J. Coaching decisions and research in sport psychology. *Research Quarterly,* 13, 1970.

49. Cratty, B. J. Psychology in Contemporary Sport. New Jersey: Prentice-Hall Inc., 1973.

50. Cratty, L. W., A comparison of learning of a fine motor skill to learning a similar gross motor task, based upon kinesthetic cues. *Res. Quart.* 33, 212–221, 1962.

51. Dal Monte, A. The functional values of sport. Firente, Sansoni, 1983.

52. Dal Monte, A.; Sardella, F.; Faccini, P.; Lupo, S. Metabolic requirements in boxing. I. S. A. S. Roma, 1985.

53. Deci, E. L. Effects of externally mediated rewards on intrinsic motiv. *Journal of Personality and Social Psychology,* 18: 105, 1971.
54. Demeter, A. Refacerca organismului in football. (Organism recovery following soccer training). *Football,* 312: 8–14, 1972.
55. Dempster, W. T. Analysis of two-hand pulls using free body diagrams. *Journal of Applied Physiology,* 13(3): 469–480, 1958.
56. De Lorme, T.; Watkins, A. Progressive resistance exercises. New York, Appleton-Century-Crofts, 1951.
57. de Vries, H. A. The looseness factor in speed and 0_2 consumption of an anaerobic 100 yard dash. *Res. Quart.* 34: 305–313, 1963.
58. de Vries, H. A. Physiology of Exercise for Physical Education and Athletics (Third Edition). Dubuque, Iowa, Wm. C. Brown Company Publishers, 1980.
59. Dintiman, G. B. Sprinting speed. Springfield, Ill. C. C. Thomas Publisher, 1971.
60. Dons, B.; Bollerup, K.; Bonde-Petersen, F.; Hancke, S., The effects of weight-lifting exercise related to muscle fiber composition and muscle cross-sectional area in humans. *Europ. J. Appl. Physiol.* 40:95–106, 1979.
61. Donskoy, D. cited by Trodoresau, L.; Florescu, C. in: Some directions regarding the perfection and masterness of technique and strategy. (Ghibu, E., ed.). Bucharet, Stadion, 1971.
62. Dragan, I. Refacenea organismuliu dupa antrenament (Organism recovery following training). Bucharest, Sport-Turism, 1978.
63. Dragan, I.; Stanescu, I. Refacerea organismului dupa antrenament: o necesitate. (Organism recovery following training, a requirement of contempory athletics). Bucharest, Stadion, 1971.
64. Dragan, I.; Constantinescu V.; Popovici, A.; Carmen, D. Aspecte biologice a formei sportive (Biological aspects of peaking). Bucharest, CNEFS, 1978.
65. Dyachikov, V. M. How the Russian high jumpers succeeded at Rome. *Legkaia Atlatika,* 12, 1960.
66. Dyachikov, V. M. The perfection of athlete's physical preparation. In: Ozolin, N. (ed.) Sovremenaia sistema sportivnoi trenirovki (Athlete's training system for competition) Moskow, Physkultma i Sport, 1964.
67. Edgerton, V. Morphology and histochemistry of the soleus muscle from normal and exercise rats. *American Journal of Anatomy,* 127: 81–88, 1970.
68. Edington, D. W.; Edgerton, V. R. The Biology of Physical Activity. Boston, Houghton Mifflin Co. 1976.
69. Eiselen, G. Gymnastic übungen (gymnastics exercises). Berling Verlag, 1845.
70. Elkins, U. C.; Leden, U. M.; Wakim, K. G. Objective recording of the strength of normal muscles *Archiv. Phys. Med.* 33, 639–647, 1957.
71. Epuran, M. Psihologia sportului contemporan. (Psychology and the contemporary athletics). Bucharest, Stadion, 1974.
72. Erdelyi, G. Gynecological survey of female athletes. *J. Sports Med.* 2: 174–179, 1962.
73. Espenschade. A. S. Motor development. In: W. R. Johnson (ed.) Science and Medicine of Exercise and Sports. New York, Harper and Row Publishers, 1960.
74. Fabiato, A., and F. Fabiato. The effect of pH on myofilaments and the sacroplasmic reticulum of skinned cells from cardiac and skeletal muscle. *J. Physiol. (London).* 276:233–255, 1978.
75. Faraday, G. In: Ozolin, N. G. Sovremennaia systema spartivnoi trenirovky (Athlete's training system for competition). Moskow, Phyzkultura i Sport, 1971.
76. Farfel, V. S. Physiologi v sportom (Sport's physiology). Moskow, Phyzkultura i Sport, 1960.
77. Fenz, W. D. "Coping mechanisms and performance under stress." *Medicine Sport,* 29: 96, 1976.
78. Fieldman, H. Effects of selected extensibility exercise on the flexibility of the hip joint. *Res. Quart.* 37(3): 326–329, 1966.
79. Florescu, C.; Dumitrescu, V.; Predescu, A. Metodologia desvoltari calitatilor fizice. (The methodology of developing physical qualities). Bucharest, CNEFS, 1969.
80. Fox, E. L. Sports physiology. Philadelphia, W. B. Saunders Co. 1979.
81. Fox, E. L.; Bowes, R. W.; Foss, M. L. The physiological basis of physical education and athletics. Dubuque, Iowa, Wm. C. Brown Publishers, 1989.

82. Fox, E. L.; Mathews, D. K., Interval training Philadelphia, W. B. Saunders, Co. 1974.

83. Friman, G. Effects of clinical bed rest for seven days of physical performance. Acta Med. Scan. 205 (5): 389–393, 1979.

84. Frost, R. B. Psychological concepts applied to physical education and coaching. Reading, Mass. Addison-Wesley Publishing Co. 1971.

85. Gallway, W. T. Inner Tennis, New York: Random House, 1976.

86. Gandelsman, A. B.; Smirnov, K. M. Physiologicheskie osnovi metodiki sportivnoi trenirovki. (The physiological foundations of training). Moskow, Phyzkultura i Sport, 1970.

87. Gellerstein, C. G. quoted by Zatzyorski. In Matveev L. P. and Novikov, A. D. Teoria i metodika physicheskogo vospitania (The theory and methodology of physical education). Moskow, Phyzkultura i Sport, 1979.

88. Ghibu, E. Mijloace si proceduri pentru pregatirea Jocurilor Olimpice din 1980 (Means and procedures regarding the preparation for the 1980 Olympic games). Bucharest, CNEFS, 1978.

89. Ghibu,; Smionescu, C.; Radut, C.; Hurmuzescu, A.; Navasart, N.; Florescue, C. Aspecte psihologice ale formei sportive. (Psychological aspects of peaking). Bucharest, CNEFS, 1978.

90. Ghircoiasu, M. Energia metabolismului (The energetic metabolism). Bucharest, Sport-Turism, 1979.

91. Gionet, N. Is volleyball an aerobic or an anaerobic sport? Volleyball Technical Journal, 5(Feb.) 31–35, 1986.

92. Gippernreiter, S. G. Weather, temperature, and organisms' reactions. Moskow, Phyzkultura i Sport, 1949.

93. Goldberg, A.; Etlinger, J.; Goldspink, D.; Jablecki, C. Mechanism of work-induced hypertrophy of skeletal muscle. *Med Sci Sports.* 7(3): 185–198, 1975.

94. Goldspink, G. The combined effects of exercise and reduced food intake on skeletal muscle fibers, *Jr. Cell-Comp. Physiol.* 63: 209–216, 1964.

95. Gollnick, P.; Armstrong, R.; Sembrowich, W.; Sepherd, R.; Saltin, B. Glycogen depletion pattern in human skeletal muscle fiber after heavy exercise. *J. Appl. Physiol.,* 34(5): 615–618, 1973.

96 Gollnick, P.; Armstrong, R.; Sanbert, C.; Sembrowich, W.; Sepherd, R.; Saltin, B. Glycogenm depletion patterns in human skeletal muscle fibers during prolonged work. Pfügers Arch., 334: 1–12, 1973.

97. Gollnick, P. D.; K. Piehl; C. W. Scubert IV; R. B. Armstrong; B. Saltin. Diet, exercise, and glycogen changes in human muscle fibers. *J. Appl. Physiol.* 33: 421–425, 1972.

98. Goncharov, N. I. cited by Zatsyorski, V. M. In: Athlete's physical abilities. Moskow, Physkultura i Sport, 1968.

99. Gordon, E. Anatomical and biochemical adaption of muscle to different exercises. *J. A. M. A.,* 201:755–758, 1967.

100. Grantin, K. Contributions regarding the systematization of physical exercises. *Theory and Practice of Physical Culture,* 9, 1940.

101. Gregory, L. W. Some observations on strength training and assessment. *J. Sports Med.* 21:130–137, 1981.

102. Guilford, J. P. A system of psychomotor abilities. *Am. J. Psych.* 71, 164–174, 1958.

103. Hahn, E. The transition phase and the psychological preparation. *Leichtathletik,* 28, 377–380, 1977.

104. Halliwell, W. R. Strategies for enhancing motivation in sport. In: Klavora: Coach, Athlete and the Sport Psychologist. Toronto: Twin Offset Ltd., 1979.

105. Harre, D. (Ed.) Trainingslehre. Berlin, Sportverlag, 1982.

106. Hennig, R. and T. Lomo. Gradation of force output in normal fast and slow muscles of the rat. *Acta. Physiol. Scand.* 130: 133–142, 1987.

107. Herberger, E. Rudern. Berlin, Sportverlag, 1977.

108. Hettinger, T., Isometric muscle training. Stuttgard, Georg Thieme Verlag, 1966.

109. Hettinger, T.; Müler E. Muskelleistung and Muskeltraining. *Arbeitsphysiologie,* 15: 111–126, 1953.

110. Hill, A. V. The maximum work and mechanical efficiency of human muscles and their most economical speed. *Journal of Physiology,* 56: 19–41, 1922.

111. Hirtz, P. The perfection of coordination; an essential factor in physical education. Körpererziehung, 26: 381–387, 1976.
112. Höger, H. The structure of long-term training programs. In: Harre, D. (ed). Trainingslehre. Berlin, Sportverlag, 1971.
113. Hollman, W. Der Arbeits and Trainingseinflus auf Kresilauf und Atmung. Darmstag, 1959.
114. Howald, H. Objectives measurements in rowing. Minden, *Rudersport*, 4, 1977.
115. Hultman, E. Physiological role of muscle glycogen in man, with special reference to exercise. *Cir. Res.* 20–21 (Suppl. 1):I99–I114, 1967.
116. Hultman, E., and K. Sahlin. Acid-base balance during exercise. *Am. College of Sport Med.* 8:41–128, 1980.
117. Hunsicker, P. A. Arm strength at selected degrees of elbow flexion. Wright air development center. Wright-Patterson Air Force Base-Ohio. 1955.
118. Ikai, M.; Yabe, K. Comparison of maximun muscle strength produced by voluntary and electric stimulation. Cited by: Schroeder, W. in: The correlation of force with the other motor abilities. *Theorie und Praxis der Körperkultur.* 12: 98–121, 1969.
119. Iliut, G.; Dumitrescu, C. Criterii medicale si psihice ale evaluarii si conducerii antrenamentului atletilor (Medical and psychological criteria of assessing and directing athlete's training). Bucharest, *Sportul de Performanta*, 53: 49–64, 1978.
120. Illin, S.V. 1959 quoted by Zatzyorsky, V. M. in: Athlete's physical abilities. Moskow, Phyzkultura i Sport, 1968.
121. Israel, S. Das Akute Entlastungssyndrom. *Theorie Und Praxis Der Körperkultur,* 12, 1963.
122. Israel, S. The acute syndrome of detraining. Berlin, GDR National Olympic Committee, 2: 30–35, 1972.
123. Ivanova and Weiss cited by Schroeder, W. in: The correlation between force and the other motor abilities. *Theorie und Praxis der Körperkultur,* 12: 98–110, 1969.
124. Jacobsen, E. Progressive Relaxation. Chicago, University of Chicago Press, 1938.
125. Jonath, W. Circuit-Training. Berlin, Limpert, 1961.
126. Kabat, H. Proproceptive facilitation in therapeutic exercises. In: M. S. Licht (Ed.) Therapeutic Exercises. Baltimore, Waverley Press, 1958.
127. Kaijser, L. Oxygen supply as a limiting factor in physical performance. In: Limiting Factors in Human Performance (ed J. Keul). Stuttgart: G. Theime, 1975.
128. Kalinin, V.; Ozolin, N. The dynamics of athletic shape. Moskow, *Legkaia Atlatika*, 10, 1973.
129. Karlsson, J. Muscle ATP, CP, and lactate in submaximal and maximal exercise. *Department of Physiologica; Gymnastick.* 382–391, 1971.
130. Karlsson, J., B. Saltin. Oxygen deficit and muscle metabolites in intermittent exercise. *Acta Physiol. Scand.* 82:115–122, 1971.
131. Karpovich, P. V.; Sinning, W. E. Physiology of Muscular Activity. Philadelphia, W. B. Saunders Co. 1971.
132. Karvonen, M.; Kentala, E., Mustala, O. The effects of training on heart rate. A longitudinal study. *Am. Med. Exp. Bio. Fen.* 35: 307–315, 1957.
133. Keul, J.; Doll, E.; Keppler, D. Muskelstoffwechsel, Munchen, Barth-Verlag, 1969.
134. Klavora, P. An attempt to derive inverted-u curves based on the relationship between anxiety and athletic performance. In: D. M. Landers. Psychology of Motor Behavior and Sport. Champaign, Ill: Human Kinetics, 1978.
135. Korcek, I. The assessment of quantitative and qualitative indices in team sport's training. Bratislava, *Trener,* 2, 6–9, 1974.
136. Korman, A. K. The Psychology of Motivation. Englewood Cliffs, N. J. Prentice-Hall Inc. 1974.
137. Korobov, A. V. In: Ozolin, N. G. Sovremenaia systema sportivnoi trenirovky (Athlete's training system for competition). Moskow, Phyzkultura i Sport, 1971.
138. Kots, I. M. Lecture Series, Concordia University, Montreal, Dec. 1977.
139. Krestovnikov, A. N. Sports Physiology, Moskow, Phyzkutlura i Sport, 1938.

140. Krestovnikov, A. N. The physiological basis of physical education. Moskow, Phyzkultura i Sport, 1951.
141. Krüger, A. Periodization, or to peak at the right time. *Track Techniques,* 54, 1720–1724, 1973.
142. Kruglanski, A. The effects of extrinsic incentive on some qualitative aspects of task performance. *Journal of Personality* 39 (December): 606–617, 1971.
143. Kusnetsov, V. V. Kraftvorbereitung. Theoretische Grundlagen Der Muskelkraftwiklung. Berlin, Sportverlag, 1975.
144. Lachman, S. J. A theory relating learning to electro-physiology of the brain. *Journal of Physiology,* 59, 275–281, 1965.
145. Lagrange, Cited by Zatsyoski, V. M. in: Athlete's physical abilities. Moskow, Physkultura i Sport, 1968.
146. Laizan, L.; Zub, E. The index of the athletic shape. Moskow, *Legkaia Atletika,* 6, 30–31, 1976.
147. Lauru, L. Physiological study of motion. *Advanced Management,* 22, 1957.
148. Lawther, J. D. Sport psychology. Englewood Cliffs, Prentice-Hall, 1972.
149. Lazarus, R. S. Patterns of Adjustment. New York, McGraw Hill Book Co., 1976.
150. Lehman, B. I. (1955) cited by Ozolin, N. G. in: Sovremennaia systema sportivnoi trenirovky (Athlete's training system for competition). Moskow, Fizkultura i Sport, 1971.
151. Leshaft, P. Children's Education, Moskow, SPB, 1910.
152. Letunov, S. P. (1950) cited in: Ozolin, N. G. Sovremenaia systema sportivnoi trenirovky (Athlete's training system for competition). Moskow, Fizkultura i Sport, 1971.
153. Logan, G. A.; McKinney, W. C. Kinesiology, Dubuque, Iowa, Wm. C. Brown Company Publishers, 1973.
154. Lowe, R., and McGrath, J. F. Stress, arousal and performance. In: Project Report: AF1161–67 Air Force Office of Strategic Research, 1971.
155. Ludu, V. Coordonarea si metodica desvoltarii ei. (Coordination, and its methodology of development). Bucharest, CNEFS, 1969.
156. Lukes, H. J. The effect of warm-up exercises on the amplitude of voluntary movement. Master's thesis, University of Wisconsin, 1954.
157. Luthe, W. Method, research and application in medicine. *American Journal of Psychotherapy.* 17: 174–195. 1963.
158. Luthe, W.; Shulz, J. H. Autogenic Therapy: Volume 1. New York: Grune & Stratton, 1969.
159. MacDougall, J. D., Limitations to anaerobic performance. Proceedings: Science and the Athlete. Hamilton, Coaching Association of Canada and McMaster University. 1974.
160. MacDougall, J. D.; Sale, D. G.; Elder, G.; Sutton, J. R. Ultrastructural properties of human skeletal muscle following heavy resistance training and immobilization. *Med. Sci. Sports.* 8(1): 72, 1976.
161. MacDougall, J. D.; Ward, G. R.; Sale, D. G.; Sutton, J. R. Biochemical adaptation of human skeletal muscle to heavy resistance training and immobilzation. *J. Appl. Physiol.* 43(4): 700–703, 1977.
162. MacDougall, J. D.; Sale, D. G.; Moroz, J. R.; Elder, G. C. B.; Sutton, J. R.; Howald, H. Mitchondrial volume density in human skeletal muscle following heavy resistance training. *Med. Sci. Sports.* 11(2): 164–166, 1979.
163. Mader, A.; Hollmann, W. The importance of the elite rowers metabolic capacity in training and competition. *Beiheft zu Leistungssport* 9: 9–59, 1977.
164. Mainwood, G. W., and J. M. Renaud. The effect of acid-base balance on fatigue of skeletal muscle. *Can. J. Physiol. and Pharmacol* 63:403–416, 1984.
165. Marasescu, N. Metode noi pentru antrenamentul de mare performanta (New methods in high performance training). *Education Fizica si Sport* 5: 34–39, 1980.
166. Margaria, R.; Ceretelli, P.; Aghemo, P.; Sassi, G.: Energy Cost of Running J. *Appli. Physiol.,* 18, 1963.
167. Marsden, C. D., J. C. Meadows, and P. A. Merton. Isolated single motor units in human muscle and their rate of discharge during maximal voluntary effort. *J. Physiol (Lond).* 217: 12P–13P, 1971.
168. Martens, R. Influence of participation motivation on success and satisfaction in team performance. *Res. Quart.* 41, 1970.

169. Martin, B. J.; Robinson, S.; Wiegman, D. L.; Anlick, L. H. Effects of warm-up on metabolic responses to strenuous exercise. *Med. Sci. Sports.* 7: 146–149, 1975.

170. Mathews, D. K.; Fox, E. L. The Physiological Basis of Physical Education and Athletics. Philadelphia, W. B. Saunders Co. 1971.

171. Mathews, D. K.; Fox, E. L. The Physiological Basis of Physical Education and Athletics. Philadelphia, W. B. Saunders Co. 1976.

172. Matveev, L. P. Periodization of sports training. Moskow, Fizkultura i Sport, 1965.

173. Matveev, L. P.; Kalinin, V. K.; Ozolin, N. N. Characteristics of athletic shape and methods of rationalizing the structure of the competitive phase. Moskow, *Scientific Research Collection,* 4–23, 1974.

174. Matveev, L. P.; Novikov, A. D. Teoria i medodika physicheskogo vospitania. (The theory and methodology of physical education). Moskow, Phyzkultura i Sport, 1980.

175. McClements, J. D.; Botterill, C. B. Goal-setting in shaping of future performance in athletics. In: Klavora. P. and Daniel, J. V. (eds) Coach, Athlete and the Sport Psychologist. Toronto, Twin Offset Limited, 1979.

176. Meichenbaum, D. Cognitive behaviour modification. New York, Plenum Press, 1977.

177. Meyers, C. R. Measurement in Physical Education. New York, The Ronald Press Co. 1974.

178. Mitra, G.; Mogos, A. Metodologia educatiei fizice scolare. (Methodology of high school physical education). Bucharest, Sport-Turism, 1980.

179. Molette, R. Power training. Brussels, Cross Promenade, 1963.

180. Morehouse, L. E.; Miller, A. T. Physiology of exercise. St. Louis, C. V. Mosby Co., 1971.

181. Morehouse, L. E.; Gross, L. Maximum Performance, New York: Simon & Shuster, 1977.

182. Morgan, R. E.; Adamson, G. T. Circuit Training. London, 1959.

183. Morpurgo, B. Cited by Mathews, K. M. and Fox, E. L. In: The Physiological Basis of Physical Education and Athletics. Philadelphia, W. B. Saunders Co. 1976.

184. Muido, L. The influence of body temperature on performance in swimming. *Acta Physiol. Scand.* 12: 102–109, 1948

185. Muresan, I. Ciclul saptaminal de antrenament. (The weekly training cycle). Bucharest, C. N. E. F. S. 1973

186. Naatanen, R. The inverted-U relationship between activation and performance. A critical review. *Activation and Performance,* 1970

187. Neilson, N. P.; Jensen, C. R. Measurement and statistics in Physical Education. Belmount, Wadsworth Publishing Co. Inc. 1972

188. Neugebauer, H. P. Planning and organization processes of training. In: Harre, D. (ed.). Trainingslehre. Berlin, Sportverlag, 1971.

189. Nideffer, R. M. The Inner Athlete: Mind Plus Muscle for Winning Thomas Y. Crowell Co., New York, 1976.

190. Nikiforov, I. B. About the structure of training in boxing. Moskow, *Scientific work,* 81–91, 1974.

191. Norman, S. R. The influence of flexibility on velocity of leg extension of the knee. Master's thesis, University of Illinois, 1973.

192. Novikov, A. D. Physical abilities. *Treoria i prakika physicheskoi Kulturi.* 1, 2–12, 1941.

193. Obbarius, D. I. cited by Ozolin, N. G. In: Sovremenaia systema sportivnoi trenirovky (Athlete's training system for competition). Moskow, Phyzkultura i Sport, 1971.

194. Orlick, T. D.; Mosher, R. "Extrinsic Awards and participant motivation is a sport related task. *International Journal of Sport Psychology,* 8, 1978.

195. Oxendine, J. B. Psychology of motor learning. New York: Appleton-Century-Crofts, 1968.

196. Ozolin, N. G. Sovremennaia systema sportivnoi trenirovky (Athlete's training system for competition). Moskow, Phyzkultura i Sport, 1971.

197. Paul, G. L. Physiological effects of relaxation training and hypnotic suggestion. *Journal of Abnormal Psychology,* 74: 425–437, 1969.

198. Pavlov, I. P. Conditioned reflexes. London, Oxford University Press, 1927.

199. Pavlov, I. Twenty years of experience in studying the nervous system activity. Moskow, U. S. S. R. Academy of Science, 1951.

200. Pechtl, V. The basis and methods of flexibility training. In: Harre, D. (ed.). Trainingslehre. Berlin, Sportverlag, 1982.
201. Pelletier, K. R. Mind as a Healer, Mind as Slayer. New York: Delta, 1977.
202. Pendergast, D. Physiological aspects of physical activity. Graduate Course: S. U. N. Y. A. Buffalo, N.Y. 1971.
203. Penman, K. Ultrastructural changes in human striated muscle using three methods of training. *Research Quarterly*, 40: 764–772, 1969.
204. Pfeifer, H. Methodological basis of endurance training. In: Harre, D. (ed.). Trainingslehre. Berlin, Sportverlag, 1982.
205. Phillips, W. Influence of fatiguing warm-up exercises on speed of movement and reaction latency. *Res. Quart.* 34: 370–378,1963.
206. Popescu, O. Coeficientul de oboseala in cursele de canotaj. (The fatigue coefficient of rowing races). Bucharest, U. C. F. S., 1957.
207. Popescu, O. Principii privind antrenamentul cu greutati. (Some principles regarding weight training programs). *Studii si Cercetari* 4: 20–16, 1958.
208. Popescu, O. Metode de recuperare in sporturile de apa. (Techniques of recovery employed in aquatic sports). *Educatia Fizica si Sport* 10: 48–52,1975.
209. Provins, K. A.; Salter, N. Maximum tonque exerted about the elbow joint. *J. Appl. Physiol.*, 7, 393–398, 1955.
210. Puni, A. T. Some theoretical aspects of athlete's volitional preparation. In: Epuran, M. (ed.) Psihologia sportului contemporan (The psychology of contemporary sports). Bucharest, Station, 1974.
211. Ralston, H. J.; Polissan, M. J.; Inman, V. J.; Close, J. R.; Feinstein, B. Dynamic feature of human isolated voluntary muscle in isometric and free contractions. *J. of Appl Physio.* 1: 526–533, 1949.
212. Razumovski, E. A. cited by Ozolin, N. G. in: Sovremenaia systema sportivnoi trenirovky (Athlete's training system for competition). Moskow, Phyzkultura i Sport, 1971.
213. Reindel, H.; Roskamm, H.; Gerschler, W. Interval training. Munich, Johan Ambrosius Barth, 1962
214. Riddle, K. S. A comparison of three methods for increasing flexibility of the trunk and hip joints. Doctoral dissertation, University of Oregon, 1956.
215. Ritter, I. Principles of training. In: Harre, D. (ed.). Trainingslehre. Berlin, Sportverlag, 1982.
216. Rosen, G. The Relaxation Book. Englewood Cliffs, N.J.: Prentice-Hall Inc., 1977.
217. Roskamm, H. H. Optimum Patterns of Exercise for Healthy Adults. *J. Can. Med. Ass.*, 22, 1967.
218. Rudik, P. A. The idiomotor representation and its importance in training. Warsaw, *Sport wyczynowy*, 8, 1967.
219. Ryan, D. Relationship between motor performance and arousal. *Research Quarterly*, 33: 279–287 1962.
220. Sahlin, K. Metabolic changes limiting muscular performance. *Biochemistry of Exercise*. Vol. 16. 1986.
221. Saltin, B.; Astrand, P. O.; Maximum Oxygen Uptake in Athletes. *J. Appl. Physiol.* 23, 1967.
222. Sauberlich, H. E.; Dowdy, R. P.; Skala, J. H. Laboratory tests for assessment of nutritional status. Cleveland, Ohio, CRC-Press, 1974.
223. Schacter, S. The interaction of cognitive and psychological determinants of emotional state. In: Spielberger, C.(ed). Anxiety and behaviour. New York, Academic Press, 1966.
224. Schmidt. Cited by Zatsyorski, V. In: Athele's physical abilities. Moskow, Physkultura i Sport, 1968.
225. Scholich, M. Kreistraining. Berlin, Verlag Bartels & Weritz K. G. 1974.
226. Schroeder, W. The correlation between force and the other motor abilities. *Theorie und Praxis der Körperkultur*, 12: 98–49, 1969.
227. Serban, M. Aspecte psihologice ale formei sportive (psychological aspects of peaking). *Educatia Fizica si Sport*, 6: 38–46, 1979.
228. Setchenov, I. M. On the question of the increase of the human muscle working capacity. Selected works. Moskow, 1935.
229. Siclovan, I. Teoria antrenamentului Sportiv (Theory of Training). Bucharest, Stadion, 1972.
230. Siclovan, I. Teoria antrenamentului Sportiv (Theory of training). Bucharest, Sport-Turism, 1977.
231. Siebert, W. W. The formation of skeletal muscle hyperthopy. *Z. Klin. Med.* 109: 350, 1929.

232. Simoneau, J. A.; Lortie, G.; Bouley, M. R. Marcotte, M.; Thibault, M. C.; Bouchard C. Human skeletal muscle fiber type alteration with high-intensity intermittent training. *European Journal of Applied Physiology,* 54: 250–253, 1985.

233. Singer, R. N. "Motivation in sport" *International Journal of Sport Psychology,* 8: 3–21, 1977.

234. Singer, R. N.; Lamb, D.; Loy, J. W.; Malina, R. M.; Kleinman, S. Physical Education: An Introductory Approach. New York, The MacMillian Co., 1972.

235. Smith, R. E, Sarason and Sarason. Psychology: The Frontiers of Behavior. New York, Harper & Row, 1978.

236. Sopov, K. Guidance of training the training process Moskow, *Sport Za rubezhon,* 9, 6–7, 1975.

237. Spielberger, C. D, Gorserch, P. L., Lustene, R. E., STAF Manual Palo Alto, Ca: Consulting Psychologists Press, 1970.

238. Talyshev, F. Recovery. *Legkaya Atletika,* 6: 25–29, 1977.

239. Teodorescu, L. Aspecte teoretice si metodice ale jocurilor sportive. (Theoretical and methodological aspects of team sports). Bucharest, Sport-Turism, 1975.

240. Teodorescu, L.; Florescu, C. Some directions regarding the perfection and masterness of technique and strategy. In: The content and methodology of training (Ghibu E. ed.). Bucharest, Stadion, 1971.

241. Tesch, P. Muscle fatigue in man. *Acta Physiologica Scandinavica Supplementum.* 480: 3–40, 1980.

242. Thorndike, E. L. Fundamentals of Learning. New York, New York Teachers College, 1935.

243. Timofeev, V. N. The mechanism of formation the motor skills. Moskow, Lectures, 1954.

244. Topalian, G. G. 1955. Cited by Ozolin, N. G. in: Sovremnaia systema sportivnoi trenirovky (Athlete's training system for competitions). Moskow, Phyzkultura i Sport, 1971.

245. Torngren, L. The Swedish gymnastics book. Esslingen, 1924.

246. Tutko, T.; Richards, J. W. Psychology of coaching. Boston, Allyn and Bacon Inc., 1971.

247. Uhov, V. Cited by Zatsyorski, V. M. In: Athlete's physical abilities. Moskow, Physkultura i Sport, 1968.

248. Uhtomski, A. Learning about the dominant, University of Leningrad, 1950.

249. Urmuzescu, A. Contributii pentru un model de forma sportiva pentru probele de rezistenta (Contributions for a model of athletic shape in endurance events). *Educatie Fizica si Sport,* 9, 38–38, 1977.

250. Van Huss, W. D.; Albrecht, L.; Nelson, R.; Hagerman, R. Effect of overload warm-up on the velocity and accuracy of throwing. *Res. Quant.* 33: 472–475, 1962.

251. Vanek, M. Sports psychology, its use and potential in coaching. Toronto, F. I. Productions, 1972.

252. Vanek, M.; Cratty, J. B. Psychology of the superior athlete. Toronto, MacMillan Co. 1970.

253. Voelz, C. Motivation in Coaching a Team Sport. Washington, D. C.: AAPHER Publications, 1976.

254. Wear, C. L. Relationships of flexibility measurements to length of body segments. *Res. Quant.* 34: 234–238, 1963.

255. Weber, E. Eine physiologische Methode, die Leistungsfähigkeit ermudeter menschlicher Muskeln zu erhöhen. *Arch. Physiol.* 385–420, 1914.

256. Webster, D. Soviet secret weapon. *International Olympic Lifters,* 2: 24–26, 1975.

257. Wickstrom, R. L.; Polk, C. E. Effect of the whirlpool on the strength-endurance of the quadriceps muscle in training male adolescents. *Am. J. of Phys. Med.* 40: 91–92,1961.

258. Yakovlev, N. N. Sports Biochemistry. Leipzig, DHFK, 1967.

259. Zalessky, M. Coaching, medico-biological, and psychological means of recovery. *Legkaya Atletika,* 7: 20–22, 1977.

260. Zatzyorski, V. M. Athlete's physical abilities. Moskow, Physkultura i Sport, 1968.

261. Zatzyorski, V. M. The development of endurance. In: Matveev, L. P. and Novikov, A. D. (eds.). Teoria i metodica physicheskoi vospitania (The theory and methodology of physical education). Moskow, Phyzkultura i Sport, 1980.

262. Annual training macrocyle. Moskow, *Legkaia Atletika,* 7, 27–30, 1974.

263. Dorland's Illustrated Medical Dictionary (25th Edition). Philadelphia, W. B. Saunders, Co. 1974.

264. Webster's Third International Dictionary. Toronto, Encyclopedia Britannica Inc. W. Benton Publishers, 1971.

APPENDIX 1

Simple Methods of Monitoring Training

In order to properly assess athletes' improvement and reaction to training, every coach should employ, as scientifically as possible, monitoring techniques. Some coaches/clubs have access (and financial means) to laboratories, where physiological, psychological and biomechanical testing can be administered in order to evaluate athletes' improvements, performance efficiency, technical effectiveness, and mental power. Others do not have such opportunities. Irrespective of testing opportunities, the proposed simple and practical monitoring charts are useful for each athlete since organized testing is performed just a few times per year. In between, if anything, training is monitored randomly.

Throughout a training program a coach must have some feedback to the load used in training. Such a feedback can be of physiological and psychological nature, and can be recorded daily on the following charts. The first two charts (heart rate and weight) allow the coach to monitor training from a physiological viewpoint, whereas the balance would reflect the psychological reaction.

Attached are two sets of charts. The first is used as an example whereas the blank ones can be photocopied by a coach and used for his/her own needs. As the reader can see in the top of the chart, there is a space to write the name of the athlete and the month of the year. Each chart is made for 31 days, or the maximum number of days a month has. The chart should be filled-up daily by each athlete and placed either in the locker room or be part of each athlete's training log.

It is essential that the coach look at the charts of each athlete before the training session, so that the training program may be changed according to the athlete's psychological state and level of fatigue. For instance, if the "heart rate" chart indicates a high level of fatigue or the chart for the "length of sleep" shows just 4 hours of restless sleep then the daily training program must be made easier, with no high intensity (which normally increases the level of fatigue).

How To Fill-up the Charts and What They Illustrate?

The heart rate chart is very useful for monitoring athlete's reaction to the previous day's training program.

Before an athlete is to use the chart he/she should know the *base heart rate* (BHR) which represents the heart rate taken in the morning before stepping out of bed. The heart rate taken over 10 seconds and multiplied by 6. Taking the blank chart a dot, representing the BHR, is placed in the lower 1/3 of the chart (as exemplified by the attached chart) and write in the space provided the value of the heart rate. Then he/she completes upward and downward all the spaces of the chart. As the athlete continues to take the BHR daily, he/she constantly places the dots on the chart, linking them together with a line to form a curve.

The BHR illustrates the athlete's physiological state, and reaction to training. Under normal conditions the curve does not have too many deflections. However, the dynamics of the curve could change according to the phase of training as well as to the state of the athlete's adaptation to the training program. Therefore, as an athlete adapts to training the BHR curve drops progressively. The better the adaptation the lower the curve. Certainly, the curve may often depend on the chosen sport. Usually athletes from endurance dominant sports have lower BHR levels.

The BHR also reacts to the intensity of training of the previous day. Where the BHR increases in one day by 6–8 beats per minute over the standard curve it could mean that the athlete did not tolerate well the training program, or he/she did not observe a normal athletic life-style. In such a case, the coach should find out from the athlete what is the actual reason. In either case, the planned training program has to be changed so that it does not add to an already high level of fatigue. When the curve decreased to its standard levels the normal program can resume.

The *body weight* chart (BW). If the BHR can be used to monitor training for short term then BW can be employed for long term. A well trained athlete, whose diet is correlated to the volume and the intensity of training, should have a steady BW.

However, BW can have some fluctuations especially during the transition phase, where some athletes gain some weight. During the preparatory phase, however, it quickly drops to the normal levels. If, on the other hand, the coach plans for a longer time a very challengeable training program, a volume and intensity of training beyond one's threshold of tolerance, it can result in a high level of fatigue. When fatigue is acute, it is often duplicated by a loss of appetite. As a result the athlete starts losing weight.

BW loss, however, does not occur abruptly, but on the contrary, it is a long term process. If the curve of BW drops constantly it can be a sign of a critical level of fatigue, and even possible overtraining. In such a case the athlete should be examined by a physician, the diet by a nutritionist, and the training load decreased until the athlete fully recovers.

The second chart, which monitors *psychological traits* and appetite, has a high correlation between them. Where an athlete experiences a high degree of fatigue, sleeping patterns are disturbed while appetite depreciates. These in turn are correlated with a tiredness sensation, and training and competitive willingness. All of them decreases as the level of fatigue, or overtraining are experienced.

The curves of the second chart represent a real-life situation of an athlete training to compete in the Olympic Games. By adequately changing the training program and improving the diet, which included supplements, the athlete recuperated and competed as expected in the games (fourth place).

The proposed simple and practical charts for monitoring training are very useful for the serious athlete. Many undesirable situations can be prevented by filling them up every day, and having the coach examine them prior to every training session. Spending a minute a day may help an athlete to avoid overtraining!

NAME _____   MONTH _____

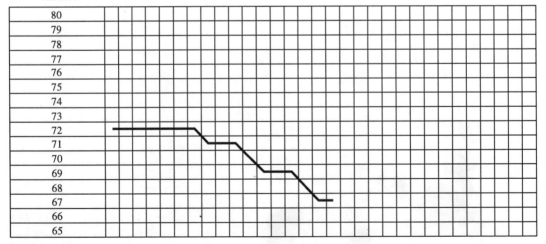

HEART RATE

| | 1 | 2 | 3 | 4 | 5 | 6 | 7 | 8 | 9 | 10 | 11 | 12 | 13 | 14 | 15 | 16 | 17 | 18 | 19 | 20 | 21 | 22 | 23 | 24 | 25 | 26 | 27 | 28 | 29 | 30 | 31 |

72
71
70
69
68
67
66
65
64
63
62
61
60
59
58
57
56
55
54
53
52
51
50
49
48
47
46
45
44
43

WEIGHT

80
79
78
77
76
75
74
73
72
71
70
69
68
67
66
65

NAME _____   MONTH _____

LENGTH OF SLEEP	1	2	3	4	5	6	7	8	9	10	11	12	13	14	15	16	17	18	19	20	21	22	23	24	25	26	27	28	29	30	31
12 + HOURS																															
11																															
10																															
9																															
8																															
7																															
6																															
5																															
4																															
NO SLEEP AT ALL																															

QUALITY OF SLEEP

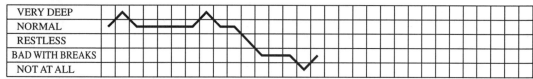

VERY DEEP																	
NORMAL																	
RESTLESS																	
BAD WITH BREAKS																	
NOT AT ALL																	

TIREDNESS SENSATION

VERY RESTED																	
NORMAL																	
TIRED																	
VERY TIRED																	
PAINFULL TIREDNESS																	

TRAINING WILLINGNESS

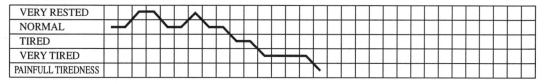

VERY GOOD																	
GOOD																	
POOR																	
UNWILLING																	
DID NOT TRAIN																	

APPETITE

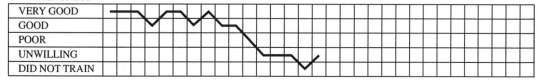

VERY GOOD																	
GOOD																	
POOR																	
EAT BECAUSE SHOULD																	
DID NOT EAT																	

COMPETITIVE WILLINGNESS

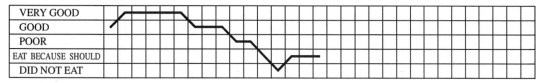

HIGH INDEED																	
AVERAGE																	
LOW																	
NOT AT ALL																	

NAME _____   MONTH _____

HEART RATE

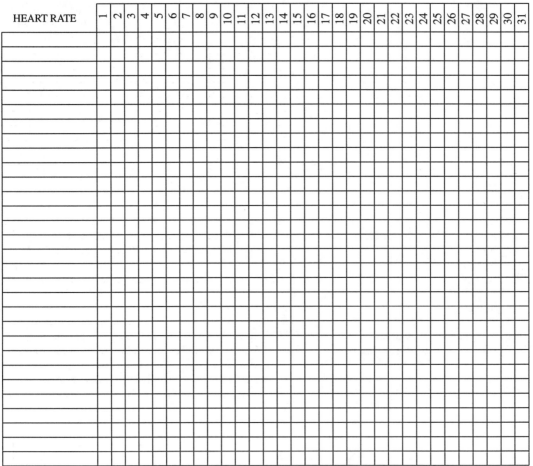

WEIGHT

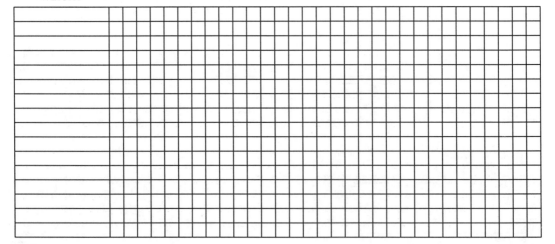

NAME _____   MONTH _____

LENGTH OF SLEEP	1	2	3	4	5	6	7	8	9	10	11	12	13	14	15	16	17	18	19	20	21	22	23	24	25	26	27	28	29	30	31
12 + HOURS																															
11																															
10																															
9																															
8																															
7																															
6																															
5																															
4																															
NO SLEEP AT ALL																															

QUALITY OF SLEEP																															
VERY DEEP																															
NORMAL																															
RESTLESS																															
BAD WITH BREAKS																															
NOT AT ALL																															

TIREDNESS SENSATION																															
VERY RESTED																															
NORMAL																															
TIRED																															
VERY TIRED																															
PAINFULL TIREDNESS																															

TRAINING WILLINGNESS																															
VERY GOOD																															
GOOD																															
POOR																															
UNWILLING																															
DID NOT TRAIN																															

APPETITE																															
VERY GOOD																															
GOOD																															
POOR																															
EAT BECAUSE SHOULD																															
DID NOT EAT																															

COMPETITIVE WILLINGNESS																															
HIGH INDEED																															
AVERAGE																															
LOW																															
NOT AT ALL																															

APPENDIX 2

Blank Charts for Annual Plans
Blank Chart For a Four-Year Plan

THE CHART OF THE ANNUAL PLAN

TYPE:

YEAR:

COACH:

ATHLETE'S NAME(S)					TRAINING OBJECTIVES			
		PERFORMANCE	TESTS/STANDARDS	PHYSICAL PREP.	TECHNICAL PREP.	TACTICAL PREP.	PSYCHOL. PREP.

DATES	MONTHS
	WEEKENDS
CALENDAR OF COMPETITIONS	DOMESTIC
	INTERNATIONAL
	LOCATION
PERIODI-ZATION	TRAINING PHASE
	STRENGTH
	ENDURANCE
	SPEED
	MACRO-CYCLES
	MICRO-CYCLES
PEAKING INDEX
TESTING DATES
MEDICAL CONTROL DATES
CAMP/SEMI-CAMP

Micro-cycles: 1 2 3 4 5 6 7 8 9 10 11 12 13 14 15 16 17 18 19 20 21 22 23 24 25 26 27 28 29 30 31 32 33 34 35 36 37 38 39 40 41 42 43 44 45 46 47 48 49 50 51 52

TRAINING FACTORS

VOLUME

INTENSITY

PEAKING

%100	1
90	2
80	3
70	4
60	5 PEAKING
50	■ PHYS. PREP.
40	▤ TECH. PREP.
30	▥ TACT. PREP.
20	▨ PSYCH. PREP.
10	

363

THE CHART OF THE ANNUAL PLAN

TYPE:

YEAR:

COACH:

ATHLETE'S NAME(S)

TRAINING OBJECTIVES

	PERFORMANCE	TESTS/STANDARDS	PHYSICAL PREP.	TECHNICAL PREP.	TACTICAL PREP.	PSYCHOL. PREP.

DATES — MONTHS, WEEKENDS

CALENDAR OF COMPETITIONS — DOMESTIC, INTERNATIONAL, LOCATION

PERIODI-ZATION — TRAINING PHASE, STRENGTH, ENDURANCE, SPEED, MACRO-CYCLES, MICRO-CYCLES

1 2 3 4 5 6 7 8 9 10 11 12 13 14 15 16 17 18 19 20 21 22 23 24 25 26 27 28 29 30 31 32 33 34 35 36 37 38 39 40 41 42 43 44 45 46 47 48 49 50 51 52

TRAINING FACTORS — COMPULSORY EXERCISES, OPTIONAL EXERCISES, SKILL ACQUISITION, ROUTINES, PEAKING INDEX, TESTING DATES, MEDICAL CONTROL DATES, CAMP/SEMI-CAMP

PEAKING 1 2 3 4 5

% 100 90 80 70 60 50 40 30 20 10

— VOLUME
--- INTENSITY
••• PEAKING

■ PHYS. PREP.
▥ TECH. PREP.
▤ TACT. PREP.
▨ PSYCH. PREP.

THE CHART OF THE ANNUAL PLAN

TYPE:

YEAR:

COACH:

DATES	MONTHS																																																			
	WEEKENDS																																																			
CALENDAR OF COMPETITIONS	DOMESTIC																																																			
	INTERNATIONAL																																																			
	LOCATION																																																			
PERIODIZATION	TRAINING PHASE																																																			
	STRENGTH																																																			
	ENDURANCE																																																			
	SPEED																																																			
	MACRO-CYCLES																																																			
	MICRO-CYCLES	1	2	3	4	5	6	7	8	9	10	11	12	13	14	15	16	17	18	19	20	21	22	23	24	25	26	27	28	29	30	31	32	33	34	35	36	37	38	39	40	41	42	43	44	45	46	47	48	49	50	51	52
PEAKING INDEX																																																				
TESTING DATES																																																				
MEDICAL CONTROL DATES																																																				
CAMP/SEMI-CAMP																																																				

TRAINING FACTORS

	%100	1
	90	2
	80	3
	70	4
	60	5
	50	PEAKING
	40	
	30	
	20	
	10	

——— VOLUME

– – – INTENSITY

• • • • PEAKING

◼ PHYS. PREP.

▦ TECH. PREP.

▥ TACT. PREP.

▨ PSYCH. PREP.

365

THE CHART OF THE ANNUAL PLAN

TYPE:

YEAR:

COACH:

DATES							
CALENDAR OF COMPETITIONS	MONTHS						
	WEEKENDS						
	DOMESTIC						
	INTERNATIONAL						
	LOCATION						
PERIODIZATION	TRAINING PHASE						
	STRENGTH						
	ENDURANCE						
	SPEED						
	MACRO-CYCLES						
	MICRO-CYCLES						

MICRO-CYCLES numbered: 1 2 3 4 5 6 7 8 9 10 11 12 13 14 15 16 17 18 19 20 21 22 23 24 25 26 27 28 29 30 31 32 33 34 35 36 37 38 39 40 41 42 43 44 45 46 47 48 49 50 51 52

COMPULSORY EXERCISES	
OPTIONAL EXERCISES	
SKILL ACQUISITION	
ROUTINES	
PEAKING INDEX	
TESTING DATES	
MEDICAL CONTROL DATES	
CAMP/SEMI-CAMP	

TRAINING FACTORS

	% 100	1
——— VOLUME	90	2
– – – INTENSITY	80	3
• • • PEAKING	70	4
▓ PHYS. PREP.	60	5
▦ TECH. PREP.	50	PEAKING
▥ TACT. PREP.	40	
▨ PSYCH. PREP.	30	
	20	
	10	

THE CHART OF THE ANNUAL PLAN

YEAR:

COACH:

DATES	MONTHS				
	WEEKENDS				
CALENDAR OF COMPETITIONS	DOMESTIC				
	INTERNATIONAL				
	LOCATION				
PERIODI-ZATION	TRAINING PHASE				
	STRENGTH				
	ENDURANCE				
	SPEED				
	MACRO-CYCLES				
	MICRO-CYCLES	1 2 3 4 5 6 7 8 9 10 11 12 13 14 15 16 17 18 19 20 21 22 23 24 25 26 27 28 29 30 31 32 33 34 35 36 37 38 39 40 41 42 43 44 45 46 47 48 49 50 51 52
PEAKING INDEX					
TESTING DATES					
MEDICAL CONTROL DATES					
CAMP/SEMI-CAMP					

TRAINING FACTORS

PEAKING - - - - -

VOLUME km/wk ——

SPEED % OF Mx. — -

PEAKING
1
2
3
4
5

367

THE CHART OF THE ANNUAL PLAN FOR TRIATHLON
YEAR:
COACH:

DATES	MONTHS		1	2	3	4	5	6	7	8	9	10	11	12	13	14	15	16	17	18	19	20	21	22	23	24	25	26	27	28	29	30	31	32	33	34	35	36	37	38	39	40	41	42	43	44	45	46	47	48	49	50	51	52
	WEEKENDS																																																						
CALENDAR OF COMPETITIONS	DOMESTIC																																																					
	INTERNATIONAL																																																					
	LOCATION																																																					
PERIODIZATION	TRAINING PHASE																																																					
	STRENGTH																																																					
	ENDURANCE																																																					
	SPEED																																																					
	MACRO-CYCLES																																																					
	MICRO-CYCLES		1	2	3	4	5	6	7	8	9	10	11	12	13	14	15	16	17	18	19	20	21	22	23	24	25	26	27	28	29	30	31	32	33	34	35	36	37	38	39	40	41	42	43	44	45	46	47	48	49	50	51	52
PEAKING INDEX																																																							
TESTING DATES																																																						
MEDICAL CONTROL DATES																																																						
CAMP/SEMI-CAMP																																																						

TRAINING FACTORS

PEAKING — — — — —

VOLUME km/wk ———

SPEED % OF MX. ———
100 90 80 70 60 50 40 30 20 10

PEAKING 1 2 3 4 5

TRAINING FACTORS

PEAKING — — — — —

VOLUME km/wk ———

SPEED % OF MX. ———
100 90 80 70 60 50 40 30 20 10

PEAKING 1 2 3 4 5

TRAINING FACTORS

PEAKING — — — — —

VOLUME km/wk ———

SPEED % OF MX. ———
100 90 80 70 60 50 40 30 20 10

PEAKING 1 2 3 4 5

OBJECTIVES

	19	19	19	19
PERFORMANCE				
PHYSICAL PREPARATION				
TECHNICAL PREPARATION				
TACTICAL PREPARATION				
PSYCHOLOGICAL PREPARATION				

TESTS AND STANDARDS

TRAINING FACTORS

% 100
90
80
70
60
50
40
30
20
10

—— VOLUME

—— INTENSITY

•••• PEAKING

☐ Physical Prep
☐ Technical Prep
☐ Tactical Prep
☐ Psychological Prep

369

GLOSSARY OF TERMS

Actin   A protein involved in muscular contraction.

Action Potential   The electrical activity developed in a muscle or nerve cell during activity or depolarization.

Active Transport   The movement of substances or materials against their concentration gradients by the expenditure of metabolic energy.

Acyclic   A skill made out of actions which are constantly changing, without being similar to others.

Adaptation   Persistent changes in structure of function particularity related to response to increments in training load.

Adenosine Diphosphate (ADP)   A complex chemical compound which, when combined with inorganic phosphate (P_i), forms ATP.

Adenosine Triphosphate (ATP)   A complex chemical compound formed with the energy release from food and stored in all cells, particularly muscles.

Adipose Tissue   Fat tissue.

Afferent Nerve   A neuron that conveys sensory impulses from a receptor to the central nervous system.

Agonistic Muscles   Muscles directly engaged in a muscular contraction and working in opposition to the action of other muscles.

All-Or-None Law   A stimulated muscle or nerve fibre contracts or propagates a nerve impulse either completly or not at all.

Alpha Motor Neuron   A type of efferent nerve that innervates extrafusal muscle fibres.

Alveoli (plural); Alveolus (singular)   Tiny terminal air sacs in the lungs where gaseous exchange with the blood in the pulmonary capillaries occurs.

Amortization phase   The amortization phase is the eccentric or yielding phase of an activity. Amortization occurs just prior to the active or push-off phase of an activity, and includes the time from ground to the reverse movement.

Anabolic   Protein building.

Anaerobic   In the absence of oxygen.

Anaerobic Glycolysis   The incomplete chemical breakdown of carbohydrate. The anaerobic reactions in this breakdown release energy for the manufacture of ATP as they produce lactic acid (anaerobic glycolysis is known as the lactic acid system).

Anaerobic Threshold   That intensity of workload or oxygen consumption in which anaerobic metabolism is accelerated.

Androgen   Any substance that possesses masculinizing properties.

Antagonistic Muscles   Muscles that have an opposite effect on movers, or agonist muscles, by opposing their contraction.

ATP-PC System   An anaerobic energy system in which ATP is manufactured when phosphocreatine (PC) is broken down.

Axon   A nerve fibre.

Back extensor   Muscle involved in straightening the back.

Ballistic   Dynamic muscular movements.

Barbell A bar to which varying weights are attached; usually held with both arms.

Biceps brachii Elbow flexor of upper arm.

Bilateral exercise Using both arms or legs at the same time to perform an exercise.

Biomotor (abilities) The capacity to perform a range of activities, such as strength, speed, and endurance. They are both genetically determined, and influenced by training.

Bodybuilding A sport in which muscle size, definition, and symmetry determine the winner.

Capillary A fine network of small vessels located between arteries and veins where exchanges between tissue and blood occur.

Carbohydrate Any group of chemical compounds, including sugars, starches, and cellulose, containing carbon, hydrogen, and oxygen only. One of the basic foodstuffs.

Cardiac Output The amount of blood pumped by the heart in one minute.

Cardiorespiratory Endurance The ability of the lungs and the heart to take in and transport adequate amounts of oxygen to the working muscles, allowing activities that involve large muscle masses (e.g., running, swimming, bicycling) to be performed over long periods of time.

Central Nervous System The spinal cord and brain.

Concentric Contraction The shortening of a muscle during contraction.

Conditioning Augmentation of the energy capacity of muscle through an exercise program. Conditioning is not primarily concerned with the skill of performance, as would be the case in training.

Cross-Bridges Extensions of myosin.

Cyclic A skill comprised of motions which are repeated continuously.

Density The mass per unit volume of an object.

Detraining Reversal of adaptation to exercise. Effects of detraining occur more rapidly than training gains, with significant reductions of work.

Dumbbell Small weight of fixed resistance; usually held with one arm.

Eccentric Contraction The muscle lengthens while contracting (developing tension).

Efferent Nerve A neuron that conveys motor impulses away from the central nervous system to an organ of response such as skeletal muscle.

Electrical Potential The capacity for producing electrical effects, such as an electric current, between two bodies (e.g., between the inside and outside of a cell).

Endomysium A connective tissue surrounding a muscle fibre or cell.

Endurance The capacity of performing work for an extended period of time.

Energy The capacity or ability to perform work.

Energy System One of three metabolic systems involving a series of chemical reactions resulting in the formation of waste products and the manufacture of ATP.

Enzyme A protein compound that speeds up a chemical reaction.

Epimysium A connective tissue surrounding the entire muscle.

Estrogen The female androgen.

Excitation A response to a stimulus.

Exercise-Recovery The performance of light exercise during recovery from exercise.

Extracellular Outside the cell.

Extrafusal Fibre a typical or normal muscle cell or fibre.

Fasciculus (singular); Fasciculi (plural) A group or bundle of skeletal muscle fibres held together by a connective tissue called the perimysium.

Fast-Twitch Fibre (FT) A muscle fibre characterized by fast contraction time, high anaerobic capacity, and low aerobic capacity, all making the fibre suited for high power output activities.

Fat   A compound containing glycerol and fatty acids. One of the basic foodstuffs.

Fatigue   A state of discomfort and decreased efficiency resulting from prolonged or excessive exertion.

Fatty Acid (Free Fatty Acid)   The usable form of triglycerides.

Flexibility   The range of motion about a joint (static flexibility); opposition or resistance of a joint to motion (dynamic flexibility).

Force Deficit   The inability of involving all the muscle fibers to perform an athletic action.

Free weights   Weights not part of an exercise machine (i.e., barbells and dumbbells).

Gamma Motor Neuron   A type of efferent nerve cell that innervates the ends of an intrafusal muscle fibre.

Glucose   Simple sugar.

Glycogen   The form in which glucose (sugar) is stored in the muscle and the liver.

Glycogenesis   The manufacture of glycogen from glucose.

Glycolysis   The incomplete chemical breakdown of glycogen. In aerobic glycolysis, the end product is pyruvic acid; in anaerobic glycolysis (lactic acid system), the end product is lactic acid.

Golgi Tendon Organ   A proprioceptor located within a muscular tendon.

Growth Hormone A hormone secreted by the anterior lobe of the pituitary gland that stimulates growth and development.

Hamstring   Muscle on the back of the thigh that flexes the knee and extends the hip.

Hemoglobin (Hb)   A complex molecule found in red blood cells which contains iron (heme) and protein (globin) and is capable of combining with oxygen.

Homeostasis   The maintenance of relatively stable internal physiological conditions.

Hormone   A discrete chemical substance secreted into the body fluids by an endocrine gland that has a specific effect on the activities of the other cells, tissues, and organs.

Hyperplasia   An increase in the number of cells in a tissue or organ.

Hypertrophy   An increase in the size of a cell or organ.

Innervate   To stimulate, to transmit a nervous energy to a muscle.

Intensity   It refers to the qualitative element of training such as speed , maximum strength and power. In strength training intensity is expressed in load of 1RM.

Intermittent Work   Exercises performed with alternate periods of relief, as opposed to continuous work.

Intermuscular Coordination The ability of coordinating many neuromuscular units to act simultaneously to perform a task.

Interneuron (Internuncial Neuron)   A nerve cell located between afferent (sensory) and efferent (motor) nerve cells, It acts as a "middleman" between incoming and outgoing impulses.

Interstitial   Pertaining to the area or space between cells.

Interval Training   A system of physical conditioning in which the body is subjected to short but regularly repeated periods of work stress interspersed with adequate periods of relief.

Intramuscular Coordination   The ability of coordinating many neuromuscular units to act simultaneously to perform a task.

Isokinetic Contraction   Contraction in which the tension developed by the muscle while shortening at constant speed is maximal over the full range of motion.

Isometric (Static) Contraction   Contraction in which tension is developed, but there is no change in the length of the muscle.

Isotonic   Pertaining to solutions having the same tension or osmotic pressure.

Isotonic Contraction   Contraction in which the muscle shortens with varying tension while lifting a constant load. Also referred to as a dynamic or concentric contraction.

Kilogram-Metres (kg-m)   A unit of work.

Lactic Acid (Lactate)   A fatiguing metabolite of the lactic acid system resulting from the incomplete breakdown of glucose (sugar).

Lactic Acid System (LA System)   An anaerobic energy system in which ATP is manufactured when glucose (sugar) is broken down to lactic acid. High intensity efforts requiring one to three minutes to perform draw energy (ATP) primarily from this system.

Machine   Resistance training equipment that dictates the direction of the exercise movement and the body position.

Macro-cycle   A phase of training of 2–6 weeks long.

Maturation   Progress toward adulthood.

Metabolism   The sum total of the chemical changes or reactions occurring in the body.

Metabolite   Any substance produced by a metabolic reaction.

Micro-cycle   It represents a phase of training of approximately one week.

Millimole   One thousandth of a mole.

Mitochondrion (singular); Mitochondria (plural)   A subcellular structure found in all aerobic cells in which electron transport system take place.

Mole   The gram-molecular weight or gram-formula weight of a substance.

Motoneuron (Motor Neuron)   A nerve cell, which when stimulated, effects muscular contractions. Most motoneurons innervate skeletal muscle.

Motor End-Plate   The neuromuscular or myoneural junction.

Motor Unit   An individual motor nerve and all the muscle fibres it innervates.

Multiple Motor Unit Summation   The varying of the number of motor units contracting within a muscle at any given time.

Muscle Bundle   A fasciculus.

Muscle Spindle   A proprioceptor surrounded by intrafusal muscle fibres.

Muscular Endurance   The ability of a muscle or a muscle group to perform repeated contractions for a longer period of time.

Muscle receptors   Are proprioceptors which monitor systems related specifically to skeletal muscles. These receptors include the Golgi tendon organ and muscle spindle, which send information to higher brain centres about muscle tension, static length, velocity of stretch, and pressure.

Myofibril   That part of a muscle fibre containing two protein filaments, myosin and actin.

Myoglobin   An oxygen-binding pigment similar to hemoglobin that gives the red muscle fibre its colour. It acts as an oxygen store and aids in the diffusion of oxygen.

Myosin   A protein involved in muscular contraction.

Nerve Cell   See **Neuron**.

Nerve Impulse   An electrical disturbance at the point of stimulation of a nerve that is self-propagated along the entire length of the axon.

Neuro-muscular   The nerve and muscular systems.

Neuron   A nerve cell consisting of a cell body (soma), with its nucleus and cytoplasm, dendrites and axons.

Oblique   Muscle on side of abdominal area.

Oxygen Debt   The amount of oxygen consumed during recovery from exercise, above that ordinarily consumed.

Oxygen System   An aerobic energy system in which ATP is manufactured when food (principally sugar and fat) is broken down. This system produces ATP most abundantly and is the prime energy source during long-lasting (endurance) activities.

Perimysium   A connective tissue surrounding a fasciculus or muscle bundle.

Periodization   It represents a process of structuring training into phases.

Periodization of strength   It structures the training program into phases in order to maximize one's capacity to meet the specifics of strength according to the needs of a sport event.

Phosphagen   A group of compounds; collectively refers to ATP and PC.

Phosphagen System   See ATP-PC system.

Phosphocreatine (PC)   A chemical compound stored in muscle, which when broken down aids in manufacturing ATP.

Plasma   The liquid portion of the blood.

Plateau   Period during training when no observable progress is made.

Plyometrics   Are drills or exercises aimed at linking sheer strength and scope of movement to produce an explosive-reactive type of movement. The term is often used to refer to jumping drills and depth jumping, but plyometrics can include any drills or exercise utilizing the stretch reflex to produce an explosive reaction.

Power   Performance of work expressed per unit of time.

Proprioceptor   Sensory organs found in muscles, joints, and tendons, which give information concerning movement and position of the body (kinesthesis).

Protein   A compound containing amino acids. One of the basic foodstuffs.

Psychotonic   A psychological technique of relaxation.

Range of motion   Movement allowed by the body's joints and body position in a particular exercise.

Receptor   A sense organ that receives stimuli.

Reflex   An automatic response induced by stimulation of a receptor.

Repetition   The number of work intervals within one set.

Repetition Maximum (RM)   The maximal load that a muscle group can lift in one attempt. Also called "one repetition maximum" (1RM).

Resistance training   The use of various methods or equipment to provide an external force to exercise against.

Rest   Resting during recovery from exercise.

Sarcolemma   The muscle cell membrane.

Sarcomere   The distance between two z lines; the smallest contractile unit of skeletal muscle.

Sarcoplasm   Muscle protoplasm.

Sarcoplasmic Reticulum   A network of tubules and vesicles surrounding the myofibril.

Sensory Fibre   See Afferent nerve.

Sensory Neuron   A nerve cell that conveys impulses from a receptor to the central nervous system. Examples of sensory neurons are those excited by sound, pain, light, and taste.

Set   The total number of repetitions performed before a rest interval is taken.

Slow-Twitch Fibre (ST)   A muscle fibre characterized by slow contraction time, low anaerobic capacity, and high aerobic capacity, all making the fibre suited for low power output activities.

Somatotype   The body type or physical classification of the human body.

Spatial Summation   An increase in responsiveness of a nerve resulting from the additive effect of numerous stimuli.

Specific Gravity   The ratio of the density of an object to the density of water.

Specific Heat The heat required to change the temperature of a unit mass of a substance by one degree.

Specificity of Training Principle underlying construction of a training program for a specific activity or skill.

Stabilizers Muscles that are stimulated to act to anchor, or stabilize the position of a bone.

Statis Contraction See Isometric contraction.

Spotter Individual responsible for the safety of a trainee who is performing a lift.

Stimulus (singular); Stimuli (plural) Any agent, act, or influence that modifies the activity of a receptor or irritable tissue.

Strength The force that a muscle or muscle group can exert against a resistance.

Stretch or myotatic reflex It refers to a reflex which responds to the rate of muscle stretch. This reflex has the fastest-known response to a stimulus (in this case the rate of muscle stretch). The myotatic/ stretch reflex elicits contraction of homonymous muscle and synergist muscles (those surrounding the stretched muscle which produce the same movement), and inhibition of the antagonist muscles.

Synapse The connection or junction of one neuron to another.

Synergist Muscle Muscle that actively provide an additive contribution to the agonist muscle during a muscle contraction.

Temporal Summation An increase in responsiveness of a nerve, resulting from the additive effect of frequently occurring stimuli.

Testosterone The male sex hormone secreted by the testicles; it possesses masculinizing properties.

Tetanus The maintenance of tension of a motor unit at a high level as long as the stimuli continue or until fatigue sets in.

Tonus Resiliency and resistance to stretch in a relaxed, resting muscle.

Training An exercise program to develop an athlete for a particular event. Increasing skill of performance and energy capacities are of equal consideration.

Training Frequency The number of times per week for the training workout.

Triglycerides The storage form of free fatty acids.

Troponin A protein involved in muscular contraction.

Twitch A brief period of contraction followed by relaxation in the response of a motor unit to a stimulus (nerve impulse).

Valsalva Maneuver Making an expiratory effort with the glottis closed.

Variation Process of changing exercise variable to provide a different training stimulus.

Vein A vessel carrying blood toward the heart.

Vitamin An organic material in the presence of which important chemical (metabolic) reactions occur.

Volume A quantitative element of training.

Watt A unit of power.

Wave Summation The varying of the frequency of contraction of individual motor units.

Weight lifting An Olympic competitive sport in which the highest total poundage in two lifts-snatch and clean and jerk-determine the winner.

Weight training A strength training program employing the resistance provided by weights, such as barbells and dumbbells.

Work Application of a force through a distance. For example, application of one pound through one foot equals one foot-pound of work.

Z Line A protein band that defines the distance of one sarcoma in the myofibril.

INDEX